D1607707

The Life and Work of General Andrew J. Goodpaster

American Warriors

Throughout the nation's history, numerous men and women of all ranks and branches of the U.S. military have served their country with honor and distinction. During times of war and peace, there are individuals whose exemplary achievements embody the highest standards of the U.S. armed forces. The aim of the American Warriors series is to examine the unique historical contributions of these individuals, whose legacies serve as enduring examples for soldiers and citizens alike. The series will promote a deeper and more comprehensive understanding of the U.S. armed forces.

Series editor: Roger Cirillo
An AUSA Book

The Life and Work of General Andrew J. Goodpaster

Best Practices in National Security Affairs

C. Richard Nelson

Published in partnership with
the Association of the U.S. Army,
the Atlantic Council of the United States and
the Eisenhower Legacy Council
ROWMAN & LITTLEFIELD
Lanham • Boulder • New York • London

Published by Rowman & Littlefield
A wholly owned subsidiary of The Rowman & Littlefield Publishing Group, Inc.
4501 Forbes Boulevard, Suite 200, Lanham, Maryland 20706
www.rowman.com

Unit A, Whitacre Mews, 26-34 Stannary Street, London SE11 4AB

British Library Cataloguing in Publication Information Available

Library of Congress Cataloging-in-Publication Data

Names: Nelson, C. Richard, author.
Title: The life and work of General Andrew J. Goodpaster : best practices in national security affairs / C. Richard Nelson. Other titles: Best practices in national security affairs
Description: Lanham, MD : Rowman & Littlefield Publishers, Inc., [2016] | Includes bibliographical references and index.
Identifiers: LCCN 2016035197 (print) | LCCN 2016037051 (ebook) | ISBN 9781442272286 (cloth : alk. paper) | ISBN 9781442272293 (electronic)
Subjects: LCSH: Goodpaster, Andrew J. (Andrew Jackson), 1915-2005. | Generals--United States--Biography. | United States. Army--Officers--Biography. | National security--United States--Decision making--History--20th century. | National security--United States--Decision making--Case studies. | Group problem solving--United States--Case studies. | United States--History, Military--20th century. | United States Military Academy--Biography. | North Atlantic Treaty Organization--Biography. | Cold War.
Classification: LCC E745.G66 N45 2016 (print) | LCC E745.G66 (ebook) | DDC 355.0092 [B] --dc23

Printed in the United States of America

"Take responsibility and get results."
—Andrew J. Goodpaster

Contents

Preface ix

Introduction: Why Goodpaster Matters xiii

I: Earning a Reputation **1**

1 Midwestern Roots (1915–1935) 5

2 Molding a Soldier (1935–1939) 15

3 Preparing for War (1939–1943) 33

4 Close Combat (1943–1944) 45

5 Strategic Planning (1944–1947) 69

6 First Generation Soldier-Scholars (1947–1950) 87

II: Conducting National Security Affairs **95**

7 Establishing NATO (1951–1954) 97

8 Eisenhower White House (1954–1961) 117

9 Commanding an Infantry Division (1961–1962) 167

10 The Joint Staff (1962–1967) 177

11 National War College (1967–1968) 201

12 Vietnam (1968–1969) 207

13 SACEUR NATO (1969–1974) 215

III: Collaborative Leadership **235**

14 Woodrow Wilson Center (1974–1977) 237

15 Superintendent, West Point (1977–1981) 243

16 Bringing Ideas to Power (1974–2005)   263

17 Connecting the Past and Future (1974–2005)   275

18 The Goodpaster Legacies: "What Would Andy Do?"   285

Acknowledgments   295

Selected Chronology of Andrew J. Goodpaster   297

Sources   301

Index   307

About the Author   323

Preface

There is no higher responsibility than that of the president and his advisors when making decisions about war. As Bob Woodward put it:

> The decision to go to war is one that defines a nation, both to the world and, perhaps more importantly, to itself. There is no more serious business for a national government, no more accurate measure of leadership. [1]

Few, if any, gained more firsthand experience in making such decisions during the Cold War than General Andrew J. Goodpaster (1915–2005). Goodpaster was a respected insider who participated at the highest levels of government in many of the most important decisions of the second half of the twentieth century. As President Eisenhower's staff secretary, he was the *de facto* originator of the National Security Council process and served as a mentor and role model to his successors down to the present day. In doing so, Goodpaster learned and taught best practices in national security affairs.

Goodpaster's life provides a valuable case study of the importance of experienced soldier-scholars with high integrity on national security teams. More importantly, his approach provides a model that has remained relevant over periods of great technological and geopolitical change. Goodpaster's example can teach us how best to think about complex national security problems that have no easy answers and the kind of collaborative leadership needed to get the job done.

General Goodpaster did not want this book to be written, at least initially in 1994 when the idea was posed by Ken Weisbrode. Goodpaster believed that biographies, particularly autobiographies, tended to be too self-serving. Yet, like General Marshall, one of his mentors who also had strong misgivings about biographies, Goodpaster wanted succeeding generations to share in what he had learned.

With this in mind, Goodpaster reluctantly agreed to a book, and I helped organize preliminary efforts at the Atlantic Council. We conducted interviews and compiled bibliographies of his work, but failed to produce a manuscript. Following these efforts, Goodpaster's colleagues at the Eisenhower Institute who served with him in the White House launched another effort to produce a book. These efforts resulted in Robert Jordan's biography, *An Unsung Soldier: The Life of Gen. Andrew J. Goodpaster.*

In supporting all of these efforts and working with Goodpaster for nearly ten years, I came to understand why political and military leaders of seven administrations consistently brought Goodpaster into the inner circles of decision making. Goodpaster learned well from some of the best mentors and from unparalleled high-level experiences. In sharing what he learned, Goodpaster was quick to attribute ideas and practices to Marshall, Eisenhower, and others. Many of these ideas go back much farther and Goodpaster, by his example, served as a bridge connecting important ideas and ideals across generations. Indeed, Goodpaster had much of value to pass on to future generations and well beyond the Army.

Toward this end, my purpose in developing this book was to share what Goodpaster learned about best practices in national security affairs. To do this, I examined what Goodpaster said, what he did, and what he wrote. I also consulted with other people who worked closely with him in many capacities.

Each new generation of national security officials believes they are facing challenges of unprecedented complexity and uncertainty. In retrospect, however, all challenges are similar to the extent that they need to be well thought through. Goodpaster acquired this habit and practiced it over decades wrestling with such problems.

Adjutant, West Point, 1939. Official photo. *Source*: **Courtesy of George C. Marshall Library**

Supreme Allied Commander, Europe, 1969. Official photo. *Source*: **Courtesy of George C. Marshall Library**

NOTE

1. Bob Woodward, *The Commanders*, (New York: Simon & Schuster, 1991) 34.

Introduction

Why Goodpaster Matters

Andrew Jackson Goodpaster led people, institutions, and ideas in a variety of highly demanding positions for seven decades, engaging the most powerful leaders and the most intelligent thinkers. He participated in many of the most challenging U.S. national security decisions in the second half of the twentieth century. In the process, he gained a reputation for carefully reasoned strategic thinking and exceptional integrity, both personal and intellectual.

Goodpaster's experience spanned the Great Depression, World War II, the Cold War, the Vietnam War and the post–Cold War transition, times of enormous geopolitical and technological change. Few, if any, gained as much experience at the highest levels. And in the process, he developed an insider's perspective of best practices in conducting national security affairs during seven administrations.

IN BRIEF

Goodpaster was chosen repeatedly to join the inner circle of national security authorities because of his mind, manner, and method. Goodpaster thought like a mathematician (his first love) and an Army engineer (his profession), with the benefits of a broad education and wealth of experience in international relations.[1] He was an intelligent, independent thinker, neither a "hawk" nor a "dove."

Goodpaster's manner was engaging; he was a natural leader. In addition to being tall, handsome, and friendly, he was exceptionally courageous, cool under pressure, and selfless. Goodpaster's emotional intelligence was "off the scale."[2] His integrity was beyond reproach.

His methods were collaborative—a style that reflected a strong capacity to engage effectively the necessary people to work in concert to achieve the best possible outcomes. In particular, Goodpaster's collaborative leadership exemplified exercising influence through reason.

Goodpaster's leadership skills consistently earned for him respect from those below, those above, and peers. This high regard led to positions of increasing responsibility and, when given added responsibilities, he proved dependable. He had exceptionally high standards and consistently did more than required.

For a soldier, there is no better measure of accomplishment than leadership in combat. Goodpaster was put to the test in World War II in one of the bloodiest campaigns of the war. During the battles for Monte Cassino, Italy, Goodpaster was twice wounded and earned the Distinguished Service Cross, the nation's second-highest award for valor.

After mastering leadership at the tactical level, Goodpaster learned strategic leadership from General George C. Marshall as one of a dozen strategic planners in Marshall's Washington command post. After the war, Goodpaster was encouraged to pursue graduate studies in international relations at Princeton, where he earned a PhD, becoming one of the Army's first soldier-scholars.[3]

Goodpaster soon had opportunities to apply what he had learned about strategic thinking when General Eisenhower was recalled to active duty to establish the initial NATO military headquarters in 1951. Goodpaster was selected for the advance party and given responsibility for establishing the intelligence, operations, training, and planning functions. Goodpaster drafted NATO General Order #1, establishing the new allied command.

Following Eisenhower's election as president, he asked Goodpaster to participate in the Solarium Project, a comprehensive effort to think through options for the Cold War strategy after Stalin's death. Eisenhower then brought Goodpaster into the White House as his staff secretary responsible for ensuring that the president was well informed on national security affairs on a daily basis during his remaining six years in office.

On learning of his central role serving President Eisenhower, President Kennedy asked Goodpaster to remain in the White House to help the new administration with the transition. Similarly, President Nixon called on Goodpaster to help design his national security system—a system that provided the model for several succeeding administrations. Subsequent presidents likewise called upon him for counsel.

When President Kennedy asked retired General Maxwell Taylor to become chairman of the Joint Chiefs of Staff after the Bay of Pigs debacle, Taylor selected Goodpaster to be his assistant. For the next five years, Goodpaster was at the right hand of the chairman of the Joint Chiefs of Staff, continuing to experience the challenges of leadership at the highest levels, often involving intractable problems with no good options. Subsequently Goodpaster became the deputy commander in Vietnam under General Creighton Abrams, following the Tet Offensive. Goodpaster also represented the Joint Chiefs at the Paris Peace Talks on Vietnam.

General Goodpaster's next challenge was to lead NATO forces during the Cold War as the Supreme Allied Commander, Europe (SACEUR) from 1969 until his first retirement in 1974. At that time, "détente" was threatening allied solidarity while trends in the military balance were unfavorable for NATO. Politically, it was the most trying period in the history of the alliance, as the allies coped with the fallout from the Vietnam War and a dangerous crisis in the Middle East that saw NATO raise its alert to the highest level since the Cuban missile crisis.

A different kind of leadership challenge drew Goodpaster out of retirement in 1977 when he was asked to lead West Point after a major cheating scandal. The institution was in a deep crisis, perhaps the worst in its nearly two-hundred-year history.

During his second retirement, Goodpaster continued to be active in national security affairs for another three decades. With his collaborative leadership, Goodpaster organized other influential thinkers into working groups to address key policy issues. He also served on presidential commissions and blue ribbon panels and represented the president on special missions. Through these and other efforts, Goodpaster brought power to ideas and ideas to power.

His intellectual honesty enabled him to transcend policy differences between administrations to a degree unusual in Washington. This made him particularly valuable in periods of transition involving changes in political leadership with new personalities and priorities, as well as changes in the security environment, such as the transition from World War II to the Cold War and then the post–Cold War world.

Over his remarkably active ninety-year life, Goodpaster led from positions of authority as well as in advisory roles. In the process, he inspired others. For his leadership, he earned the nation's second highest military award in World War II and the nation's highest civilian award, the Presidential Medal of Freedom, for "lifetime accomplishments that have changed the face and the soul of our country."[4]

TOO IMPORTANT TO IGNORE

The essence of leadership, according to Goodpaster, involved "taking responsibility and getting results." In particular, he was devoted to getting results in national security affairs. Overall, some of these challenges were handled well and some not so well, but all provided Goodpaster with a valuable understanding of best practices in national security affairs. These lessons remain relevant today in similarly complex and uncertain times. As Lieutenant General Brent Scowcroft, a colleague and former national security advisor, noted, General Goodpaster remains "too important to ignore."[5]

NOTES

1. The influence of math is indicated in Goodpaster's handwritten informal doodles that often were differential equations. For examples, see Goodpaster papers, box 11, folder 12, Marshall Library.

2. Jane M. O'Brien, president of St. Mary's College, interview with author, June 3, 2010.

3. While there were previously well-educated soldiers, Goodpaster was a test case by Colonel George "Abe" Lincoln for select officers to obtain a broad graduate education that went against the grain in Army personnel practices. Due in part to the success of the Goodpaster case, the practice became widely accepted by the Army.

4. Ronald Reagan, March 26, 1984, White House website, https://www.whitehouse.gov.

5. Brent Scowcroft, interview with author, June 10, 2010, Washington, DC.

I

Earning a Reputation

One way to understand why Goodpaster became involved in so many important national security events is to examine how he earned a widely held reputation that enabled him to be chosen frequently by numerous top military and political leaders. Goodpaster earned this respect by being tested in a wide variety of ways over decades rather than as a result of gaining fame in connection with a specific challenge.

One's reputation begins to be shaped early in the first few decades of life. Looking back over the ninety-year life span of Andrew Jackson Goodpaster, one can see how his early nurturing, the skills he developed, the choices he made, and the opportunities he seized consistently earned for him respect that would catapult him to the top.

But life is not lived looking back; it occurs only in the present with an eye on an uncertain future. Goodpaster did not know that he was destined to have his dream of being a math teacher dashed by the Great Depression. He did not know that the concerns expressed by his mother about troubling developments in her native Poland would lead him to the battlefields of Italy. His family had no significant military tradition, so he would not have dreamed of becoming a highly decorated four-star general and commanding the armies of sixteen NATO countries. He performed well in school and was the first in his family to go to college, but he could not imagine earning a PhD from Princeton. He had no idea that he would be mentored by some of the country's best soldiers and scholars. Furthermore, had he been given his first choices, in many cases, they would have taken him in entirely different directions.

As it turned out, Goodpaster's story is one of leadership in providing security in uncertain times . . . when it is needed most. To begin with, Goodpaster looked the part: tall, blond, handsome, with a rich baritone voice. He was easygoing, calm, patient, friendly, and well liked. He listened well and made a point of understanding the views of others. Goodpaster was intelligent and asked insightful questions. He was articulate, clear, and concise. He was courageous, exceptionally honest, and loyal. Most importantly, he was dependable. No matter how hard the task or how short the deadline, Goodpaster got the job done.

TIMES OF TECTONIC SHIFTS

Goodpaster's journey was shaped by momentous events beyond his or anyone's anticipation at the time. Cumulatively, a series of developments in the decades before and during Goodpaster's youth set in motion changes that would lead to the tremendous upheavals of the global Great Depression and World War II. World War I had triggered a slide toward authoritarianism that became apparent in Russia after the 1917 revolution overthrew a corrupt, unpopular Tsarist regime. The Bolsheviks seized power in the name of social justice for the working classes but imposed an oppressive totalitarian regime at enormous costs. Communism gained traction throughout Europe among populations disturbed by the wide gap between the few rich and many poor.[1]

Radical forces were also on the rise in Germany where the defeat in World War I, the Great Depression, and the burden of reparations undermined German confidence in their leaders. Under such conditions, the former German minister of justice noted: "The world is not ruled by reason, but by passion, and when a man is driven to despair he is ready to smash everything in the vague hope that a better world may arise out of the ruins."[2]

Such attitudes fueled the National Socialist movement, the Nazis, led by Adolph Hitler. By 1932, he was called

> the most successful orator that Germany has ever possessed. . . . He fans the flames of hatred just as unscrupulously as he arouses the most exaggerated hopes. . . . Hitler can lay hold on them in their innermost sensibilities when he raises his cry for unity, promises them the "respect" of the world as the fruit of unity.[3]

By 1933, virtually all of the leaders of the German Weimar Republic during the previous fourteen years were swept away by the Nazi tide. State and local governments served at the will of Berlin. Trade unions were seized, and religious organizations were co-opted for the most part. The universities were "cleansed" and the press "assimilated." Even the powerful German generals were gone. Goebbels dictated understanding of the past, interpretation of current events, and the vision of the future. Nazi use of fear and nationalism supplanted the liberal principles of the German Federal Republic.[4]

GROWING THREAT IN ASIA

For different reasons, Japan also was a growing threat, especially to China and Russia. By World War I, Japan was the dominant power in East Asia. Using an alliance with Britain as a pretext, Japan declared war on Germany in August 1914 and occupied German territories in China along with German islands in the Pacific. These acquisitions were upheld by the Versailles peace conference.[5]

As the Japanese Kwangtung Army stationed in Manchuria was gaining influence in Japan's ruling circle, Chinese anti-Japanese nationalism was growing. Chinese Communist forces, with strong financial and military aid from Moscow, agreed at least nominally to a united front with General Chiang Kai-shek's Kuomintang forces against the Japanese. The League of Nations condemned Japanese aggression, but proved powerless.

Japanese militarism was partly fueled by a lack of natural resources exacerbated by the Great Depression. Moderates in Japan's ruling cabinet were assassinated in 1932, and social unrest was checked by government repression. By the mid-1930s, industrial production began to grow again, spurred by demand for armaments. Power was increasingly concentrated in military hands with the collaboration of a few industrialists.

Of course, these developments in Asia and Europe were not preordained. Nobody knew where they would lead. There was no consensus among political leaders about what to do at home and abroad. For the most part, leaders were focused on domestic concerns, especially the devastating impact of the Great Depression. These challenges brought out the best and worst in people and spawned the "greatest generation," including Goodpaster.

NOTES

1. See for example, Harold Laski, "Lenin and Mussolini," *Foreign Affairs* (September 1923), excerpted January, February 2012, 7–10.
2. Erich Koch-Weser, "Radical Forces in Germany," *Foreign Affairs* (April 1931), excerpted January, February 2012, 18–21.
3. Paul Scheffer, "Hitler: Phenomenon and Portent," *Foreign Affairs* (April 1932), excerpted January, February 2012, 21–23.
4. Hamilton Fish Armstrong, "Hitler's Reich: The First Phase," *Foreign Affairs* (July 1933), excerpted January, February 2012, 24–26.
5. Fairbank, Reischauer, and Craig, *East Asia: The Modern Transformation*, 1965.

Chapter One

Midwestern Roots (1915–1935)

Goodpaster was a product of his midwestern roots and the Great Depression. He grew up on a small farm on the outskirts of St. Louis among people who had a strong work ethic. Family and religion were important, but the community was tolerant of ethnic and religious differences. Not wealthy, but with a lively intellect, Goodpaster blossomed in these surroundings.

Andrew Jackson Goodpaster was born in Granite City, Illinois, on February 12, 1915. Granite City is near the center of America, in the Mississippi River valley, across the mile-wide river from St. Louis. The "mighty Mississippi" dominated the scene. It linked north and south commerce in the agricultural heartland. Upriver was the farm implement center of the world, with John Deere, International Harvester, J. I. Case, and Farmall factories in the Quad Cities. Just downriver, the Missouri River flowed into the Mississippi and provided one of the main avenues to the West. A little farther south, the Ohio River joined the Mississippi, linking the East with the Midwest. Along these arteries were clustered grain storage elevators, meat packing plants, and the rest of the infrastructure supporting the once labor-intensive agricultural sector of the country.

Nearly everyone was tied to farming. Goodpaster's earliest memory, from about age two, was of friends and neighbors coming together to thresh wheat with "marvelous tractors pulling threshers." In their small farmhouse with five children and no running water, he recalled neighbor ladies bringing their favorite dishes to share with the men working the fields. The mood was "festival-like."[1]

Chapter 1

OLD WORLD TIES

Although he would later be known by friends and colleagues as "Andy," he was first known as "Jackie" or "Jack" to more easily distinguish him from his father, Andrew Jackson Goodpaster, Sr., who was also known as "Jack." Young Jack was actually the fourth in his family to bear that name going back to his great-grandfather.[2]

The Goodpaster family roots included members who farmed the mountains of eastern Kentucky (Bath County), Tennessee (Washington County), and Virginia (Rockingham County). In about 1830, the Goodpasters moved to Morgan County, Indiana, where Jackie's father, Andrew Jackson Goodpaster, Sr., was born on a farm.[3]

Jackie's great-grandmother, Scythia Carpenter, was from Bath County, Kentucky, where the family had moved before the American Revolution. The Carpenter family, with a change in the family name from *Zimmerman*, was of German descent, dating back to German settlers in colonial Virginia. The hardscrabble life and mountain music were dominant themes in the Goodpaster family.[4]

Jackie's mother, Teresa Mary Mrovka, on the other hand, was the eldest of thirteen children in a large Polish Catholic family. Her parents, Paul Mrovka and Marianna Pytlik, emigrated in the 1880s from a part of Poland that had been partitioned and was under Prussian rule. In Prussia, Paul worked as a railroad conductor and was jailed after making a comment about the kaiser: "If the Kaiser keeps doing what he's been doing, someone is going to kill him." At the time, there was strong resistance to German rule. After being released or escaping from jail, he decided to immigrate to the United States, arriving in 1882. He got a job as a coal miner in Northumberland County, Pennsylvania, becoming a U.S. citizen in 1888. In the early 1900s, he moved to Illinois where he continued coal mining until his death in 1920.[5]

These two family lines came together in East St. Louis, Illinois, where Goodpaster was a conductor of a streetcar line that connected Alton, Illinois, with St. Louis, Missouri. He also operated a small farm and previously worked on railroads, where he first became a conductor.

While operating a streetcar, Goodpaster was attracted to one of his regular passengers, Teresa Mrovka, who was on her way to work as a seamstress in St. Louis from her home in Collinsville, on the eastern outskirts of East St. Louis. She was pretty and smart. While she was Catholic and Polish, Goodpaster was Protestant and German, with two children living with him from a previous marriage that ended in divorce.[6]

They overcame their Protestant-Catholic, German-Polish differences and were married. Working out their religious differences was not easy because both had strong faith. Goodpaster was opposed to converting to Catholicism and would not agree to raise their children in the Catholic Church. Furthermore, Teresa, by marrying a divorced Protestant, was not tolerated by the Catholic faith, so she left the Catholic Church and became active with her husband and family in the local Disciples of Christ (mainline Protestant) Church. Importantly, the manner in which Jackie's parents resolved such fundamental differences was reflected in a family environment of religious tolerance.[7]

They settled on a small farm nearby in Granite City, on the north side of East St. Louis. There they had three children: Walter, Jack, and Isa May. Also in the home were James and Eleanor from the father's earlier marriage. There, Jack was very close to his mother. He described her as "close to being a saint in her devotion to other people . . . she was a model of . . .thoughtfulness, kindness." These traits would also come to characterize Jack.[8]

When Jack was seven years old, the family moved to Indiana, where they tried to make a living with full-time farming. They bought a farm near Monrovia, but could not make it work, so his father sought jobs in automobile plants in Michigan. At the same time, Jack's mother was not satisfied with the local schooling opportunities, so after about three years, the family moved back to Granite City. They rented out their farm in Indiana and Goodpaster Sr. got a job once again with the St. Louis-Alton electric railway.[9]

Recalling his father about sixty years later, Jack noted that he was regarded as very intelligent, "a problem-solver." For example, he solved the problem of streetcars, operating on single-track lines with bypasses, having no regular schedules. Riders never knew when the next train would arrive. Goodpaster developed an algorithm for the trains to operate in a dependable manner. Such early lessons about taking responsibility and being dependable took root in Jack and grew into defining characteristics.[10]

Growing up, Jack inherited his parents' quest for knowledge. He recalled: "On my mother's side, they were very intelligent. She and her sisters always stood right at the top of their class. And that matched well with my father, who did well in school, so well in high school, that he was kept on for a time to teach some of the incoming high school students."[11]

Religion and music played integral roles in the Goodpaster family. Even though his parents had somewhat of a mixed marriage—Protestant and Catholic—they shared similar values and respected each other's thinking. Jack remembered: "Both my father and my mother were religious people. He had a great interest in the Bible [and] read . . . to us. . . . And my mother was very meticulous in attending church."[12]

Music also was an important part of family life. Jack's mother, in particular, had an "interest in the finer things of life." She, along with other family members, had musical talent and a very keen interest. Jack's dad also enjoyed music, and he knew many of the ballads of Appalachia from his family's roots. As soon as they could afford it, they purchased a phonograph and accumulated a diverse collection of records. The family enjoyed singing, especially Jack. Later, he would be tempted to attend the Julliard School of Music, but decided instead to pursue mathematics.[13]

Both parents also valued education. Jack noted:

> I do recall, my mother encouraged us to do well in school, to "be serious about it." . . . She regarded education as a tremendous opportunity. She got that from her mother and father, who brought it from Europe. . . . In our town, Granite City, great emphasis was placed on the quality of education. We had excellent schools.[14]

Figure 1.1.   Goodpaster Enters McKendree College at Age 16. *Source*: **Courtesy of Goodpaster Family**

Jack excelled in school. He was promoted ahead of his class twice, graduating at age sixteen. In addition to his academic achievements, he was athletic, playing center on the Granite City High School football team. Goodpaster also demonstrated strong aptitude for singing and speaking. He played key roles in school plays for three years and was a member of the debate team. Just before graduation in 1931, he gave the Memorial Day speech. [15]

Math was Jack's main interest in school, an interest that would launch him on his career. As he recalled:

> I was particularly taken with mathematics . . . I admired very much a couple of my math instructors and it seemed to me that's something I would like to be. I went to McKendree College in Lebanon, Illinois, about 25 miles east of St. Louis, majoring in mathematics. [16]

However, his plans to become a math teacher were "derailed" by the Great Depression.

> I think the term "derailed" is exactly correct; there was sort of a process that we went through at that time. You would go to college for two years, get a teaching certificate, teach for a while, then complete your college, then get a higher level teaching job, do that for a while, then go on to university and get advanced degrees. And I felt that's the course that I was on until the Depression came and hit us very hard . . . the result was that we had no more money to use for . . . college. . . . So I had to drop out and look for a job. [17]

Jack's interest in math complemented his interest in engineering. In particular, he was inspired by the work of the Army Corps of Engineers on the Mississippi River. The Corps had built a series of locks and dams to facilitate tow boats and barges navigating rapids and to help control the threat of floods—not always successfully. Jack recalled the disastrous flood of 1927, in particular. Young Goodpaster also was impressed with the Eads Bridge across the Mississippi at St. Louis designed by Army engineers, including Robert E. Lee. [18]

His father, aware of Jack's interest in engineering, brought home a copy of a West Point yearbook from the class of 1925 that he borrowed from a friend whose son had graduated from the U.S. Military Academy. Thus, Jack soon learned that West Point was the main source of officers for the Army Corps of Engineers, making the academy an appealing prospect. [19]

GREAT DEPRESSION

The decade following the 1929 stock market crash saw unparalleled poverty in the United States and abroad. These were desperate times. More than ten million Americans had no income of any kind, and there was no safety net; five thousand banks failed, taking with them the savings and hopes of millions. Masses were homeless and hungry; hundreds of thousands drifted, searching for work and food. At a time when one in three Americans lived on a farm, the Depression was compounded by severe drought beginning in mid-1930, and thousands of tenants were forced off their land. [20]

The Goodpaster family was not spared: "I think my father's wages were cut by a third. And the times were very, very tight. And it was true throughout that whole area, being a manufacturing area, it was hit quite hard and everybody was struggling to just make it during that period."[21]

After two years of college, Goodpaster earned a limited elementary teaching certificate, but could find no job as a teacher. He did get a job as a laborer in East St. Louis at one of the several slaughter houses and meat packing plants, the Hunter Packing Company.[22] The work was hard and dangerous. The nauseating smells drifted downwind for miles.[23]

In these difficult times, Jack Goodpaster was elected president of the first union organized at the Hunter plant, Local 530, Amalgamated Meat Cutters and Butcher Workmen's Union. At age nineteen, he became the principal spokesman for workers seeking fair wages and safe working conditions. In the process, he developed empathy for workers that later translated into a sincere concern for soldiers, especially those at the lowest levels.[24]

Taking on the responsibility of a labor leader during the Depression no doubt made a strong impression on Goodpaster. He knew firsthand the plight of the workers, and he also knew how to make a persuasive argument from his experience as a debater in high school and college.

RADICAL POPULISTS

The impact of the Great Depression was global and hit Europe particularly hard, still torn by the losses and destruction of World War I. These conditions gave rise to authoritarian movements, particularly in Polish communities and Germany. Goodpaster recalled growing concern about developments in Europe:

> In 1933 and '34 . . . my attention in the main was drawn to some of the things that were going on in the world by the radio broadcasts of Huey Long and of Father Coughlin—and I recall my grandmother who had come from Poland. . . . I recall her comments that something . . . very dangerous [was] going on . . . radical and dangerous to the people of the world. I do not recall that she ever mentioned Hitler, but she did mention the idea of police states, authoritarian regimes, and the subjugation by people that she and my grandfather had really left Poland to avoid. And this radical language of Father Coughlin and Huey Long was very troubling to her.[25]

Goodpaster's recollection of his family being alarmed by radical populists, such as Father Charles Coughlin indicates another feature of these troubled times. Coughlin's radio broadcasts and newspaper reached thirty million people, a huge listening audience for that time. They denounced the concentration of wealth in the hands of a few and sharpened political divisions in the country. While initially supportive of the newly elected president, Franklin D. Roosevelt, and his "New Deal," Coughlin became a strong critic and vituperatively anti-Semitic, blaming the Depression on an international conspiracy of Jewish bankers.[26]

Goodpaster also recalled his father being inspired by the progressive senator Robert M. La Follette of Wisconsin. La Follette was a champion of minority and women's rights and against the increasing political power caused by the consolidation of wealth and power. La Follette also opposed U.S. involvement in World War I.[27]

Spurred by such commentators, public emotions were volatile in the United States during the Depression. Hungry workers were competing for fewer jobs at lower wages. Labor unrest reached a high as the number and scope of strikes surged in 1934.[28] Organizing workers were often labeled "reds," and were sometimes confronted violently by strikebreakers. Goodpaster recalled the deep impressions made in knowing what it means to be poor and see other people who are even poorer, who have to scrape for the bare essentials of food, shelter, and health care, while hoping to provide education for their children.[29]

The tragedy of the Great Depression persisted for more than a decade, inflicting enormous pain on nearly everyone. In these times of great turmoil, people and their governments searched for causes, blame, and alternatives. Efforts by political leaders failed to reduce unemployment and restore economic growth.

As the debates became increasingly polarized, Goodpaster was not pulled toward ideological or political extremes. If anything, one can detect early signs of skepticism of simple solutions to complex problems.[30]

A WAY OUT OF THE GREAT DEPRESSION

After working about thirteen months, Jack Goodpaster and many other laborers were laid off as the Hunter Meatpacking Company reduced its workforce in 1934 and went out of business shortly thereafter. The following month, December 1934, Goodpaster found work at a Standard Oil gas station. He also studied surveying when he was not working, keeping up his interest in engineering. The gas station soon also succumbed to the hard times and failed.[31]

During this time, he learned that competition for an appointment to West Point in 1935 had been reopened due to the death of the local congressman, which resulted in confusion about how the appointment should be handled. Representative Charles A. Karch, a Democrat, died in office on November 6,

1933. His seat remained vacant until March 4, 1934, when Edwin M. Schaefer, another Democrat, became the representative of the Illinois 22nd Congressional District. In the interim, appointments to the service academies for the class beginning in July 1935 had not been announced, and the office staff was faced with claims that an appointment to West Point had been promised to two individuals (not Goodpaster), so the matter was resolved through an open competitive exam.

About fifty took the exam, and Goodpaster scored very well. On November 4, 1934, his mother answered a knock on the door to find Melvin Price, Congressman Schaefer's secretary, informing her that "you have a future general in your family," her son having won the appointment for the following summer. In June 1935, he boarded a train for West Point.[32]

NOTES

1. Goodpaster, interviews by James McCall, Washington, DC, June–July, 2001, Atlantic Council series transcribed by U.S. Army Center of Military History, Ft. McNair, Washington, DC., hereafter "McCall interviews."

2. Andrew J. Goodpaster IV's father, AJG III, was named after his uncle, AJG II, who was one of the sons of AJG I, but not AJG III's father, so there is technically a break in the direct naming lineage (AJG III's father had a different name). Source: Sarah Nesnow, Goodpaster granddaughter and family archivist, e-mail message to author, July 7, 2012.

3. Goodpaster, McCall interviews.

4. Ibid.

5. Ibid.

6. Goodpaster, McCall interviews and Susan Goodpaster Sullivan, interview with author, August 10, 2010.

7. Sarah Nesnow, Goodpaster family archivist, and Susan Goodpaster Sullivan, in correspondence with author, February 26, 2014.

8. Goodpaster, McCall interviews.

9. Goodpaster, videotaped interview by James Billington, March 18, 2004, for Veterans History Project (American Folk Life Center, Library of Congress, AFC/2001/001/29916); hereafter "Billington interview."

10. Goodpaster, McCall interviews.

11. Ibid.

12. Ibid.

13. Sullivan, interview with author, July 15, 2012.

14. Goodpaster, McCall interviews.

15. Goodpaster, Billington interview.

16. Goodpaster, McCall interviews.

17. Ibid.

18. Ibid.

19. Ibid.

20. See Garraty, *The Great Depression*; Mitchell, *The Depression Decade*; Bernake, *Essays on the Great Depression*; Brokaw, *The Greatest Generation*, 6.

21. Goodpaster, Mandel interviews, July 31, 2001, Washington, DC, tape 1; McCall interviews; Goodpaster, Colonel William Johnson and Lieutenant Colonel James Ferguson, Army War College Oral History interview, Washington, DC, January 9, 1976; hereafter "Johnson and Ferguson interviews."

22. Ibid.

23. Goodpaster in Security Questionnaire, Atomic Energy Commission, Form 86, completed September 16, 1975, Goodpaster Papers, box 83, file 24, Marshall Library.

24. Billington interview. March 18, 2004.

25. Goodpaster, McCall interviews.

26. See Brinkley, *Voices of Protest*, especially 93–95.

27. Goodpaster, interviews by Johnson and Ferguson, January 9, 1976, Washington, DC.

28. See for example the AFL-CIO website historic chronologies.

29. Goodpaster, interviews by Johnson and Ferguson, January 9, 1976, Washington, DC.

30. In his accounts of the period in several oral histories, Goodpaster expressed no particular favoritism of conservative or liberal programs. If anything, he seemed to share his family's concern about extremists.

31. Security Investigation for Sensitive Position, Standard Form 86, U.S. Civil Service Commission, Goodpaster Papers, box 40, file 6, Marshall Library; Susan Goodpaster Sullivan, interview with author, July 15, 2012.

32. Goodpaster, video interviews by Ken Mandel, Washington, DC, July-August 2001, hereafter "Mandel interviews." Price was elected to the House in 1944 and served as chairman of the House Armed Services Committee, 1975–1985.

Chapter Two

Molding a Soldier (1935–1939)

WEST POINT: "JACK" BECOMES "ANDY"

West Point transforms people. With a unique socialization process, it infuses young men with the DNA of the Army. The extent to which these values and practices are imprinted indelibly varies, but to greater or lesser degrees, they are evident four years later.

Sometimes the process even changes the name by which they are known. The Army prefers to know troops simply by first name, middle initial, and last name. Drill rolls and class rosters reflected this convention and, to be consistent, West Point encouraged cadets to sign their names accordingly, such as "Andrew J. Goodpaster."

Goodpaster reported on July 1, 1935, along with 666 other young men, to join the class of 1939. More than 200 would fail to complete their first year, due largely to academic deficiencies (mainly math) and to resignations because of an inability to adapt to military discipline. Eventually 456 cadets would graduate, compared to 301 graduates in the preceding year, the class of 1938. Among the foreign cadets at the time were one from China, one from Siam (Thailand), two from Ecuador, and four from the U.S. Territory of the Philippine Islands.[1]

His was the first of the larger classes as rising fears of war in Europe and Asia led Congress to authorize an increase in the size of the Corps by about 600 cadets. By comparison, the Naval Academy was about twice the size. This expansion, the first since World War I, brought academy enrollment to a total of 1,964 cadets.[2]

Goodpaster had several advantages going for him when he entered West Point. At twenty, he was older and more mature than most of his classmates. He was tall for the times, six foot, two inches, and very intelligent. Further, he already had completed more than two years of college, majoring in math—the primary subject in the engineering curriculum at West Point.

He also had a few disadvantages. The chief one was that he was clueless about the Army. On day one he didn't know whom to salute or the myriad of customs and traditions of West Point. But Andy learned quickly by mistakes that upperclassmen were only too eager to point out.

Goodpaster was aware that the main purpose of West Point was leadership, to produce Army officers, not just college graduates. The initial orientation, called "Beast Barracks," began on July 1, 1935, and lasted about two months before the academic year commenced. Goodpaster learned discipline, the basic skills of a soldier, and, more importantly, the challenges of leadership. Goodpaster recalled his initial impressions:

> West Point had sent each of us some advanced material and there was, I think, no more than a sentence that said the initial training will be demanding. And that was an understatement . . . it was extremely demanding.[3]

Sometime during the first few weeks, the reality set in that West Point was about more than an engineering curriculum. On some level, Goodpaster and the others understood that by joining the Army, they were taking on the risk that they may have to sacrifice their lives; that commitment was expected of soldiers. But it took on a more personal meaning during bayonet and hand-to-hand combat training or at some other point when the reality dawned on each new cadet that he may be required to kill another person. That was a heavy responsibility, but unavoidable.

In molding a soldier, the process worked on both the outside and inside of the individual. The outward, physical attributes were the most immediately obvious; one needed to look like a soldier with an appropriate military bearing. That involved standing tall with shoulders back, chest out, and, especially for plebes, bracing in formations and during meals, by pulling their chins well back against their necks. There was a seemingly obsessive attention to details, like placing the tip of each thumb on the first joint of the first finger with the hand along the seam of the trousers when standing at attention during the daily formations.

Goodpaster learned daily lessons about the values of competition and cooperation. More than in most other colleges, much of life at West Point is experienced as part of a group, including marching in formations, especially during the first year. In Beast Barracks, he experienced the unforgettable emotional uplift of a platoon, dog tired after a long day of work, marching back to the barracks to the chant of a cadence that came to be known as "Jody Calls." These cadence calls shifted one's mind away from the fatigue of the body. As a result, each person felt stronger as part of the team.

Figure 2.1. Plebe Goodpaster, 1935. Official photo. *Source*: Courtesy of Goodpaster Family

After Beast Barracks, Goodpaster was assigned to A Company, composed of the tallest men in each class so that the heights in each company would be uniform during parades. He lived with this group of about one hundred men in the Central Area of barracks, usually three men to a small room where they slept, studied, and were constantly subject to inspection. Lifelong friendships were born under such tight, demanding conditions. Among these was his roommate, Thomas Jonathan Jackson Christian, the grandson of "Stonewall" Jackson, who was also known as "Jack."[4]

ETHICS

The inward, more subtle part of the transformation process dealt with building a strong moral character, essential to becoming an officer and gentleman. Indeed, conduct unbecoming an officer was a court-martial offense in the Army, so it was imperative to teach cadets what conduct was expected and what was not tolerated.

Honor was the cornerstone of the West Point experience and a long-standing ideal of the military profession. Honorable behavior was considered essential in building trust, which was fundamental to good leadership. And good leadership, in the Army's view, was based more on character than technical proficiency.[5]

The concept of honor can be both simple and complex, depending on the standards and circumstances. West Point provided each cadet with experience in what it takes to build a reputation for honorable behavior. Cadets were held accountable to each other on a daily basis. This learning process evolved but had always begun with the simple proposition that cadets will not lie, cheat, or steal. To underscore the importance of these norms, the consequences were severe: dismissal in most cases.

The honor code was fragile, dependent on each new cohort of cadets to adopt it, protect it, and live thereafter by the high standards it inspired. The objective was not to produce candidates for sainthood, but to begin to build reputations for honesty. Administered primarily by the upper class cadets, it foundered at times such as World War I when all of the upper classes were graduated early, leaving the system in inexperienced hands. During Goodpaster's time at West Point, the chairman of the Honor Committee sensed a "decline in the interest of the Corps in the system." The chairman attributed this in part to the recent substantial expansion in class size which implied lower standards and to the demands from the Tactical Department to use the honor code to enforce "more and more regulations." The chairman then recommended more instruction on honor, especially for plebes.[6]

Goodpaster came to play an important role in this process of ethical development. During his second class (junior) year, he was elected to the

Honor Committee by his cadet company and took on important responsibilities, including the education of other cadets from diverse social, economic, religious, and geographic backgrounds.

About sixty years later, Lieutenant General Edward Rowny recalled Goodpaster in this latter role:

> I met Cadet Andrew J. Goodpaster in the late summer of 1937. I was a plebe and he was a Second classman, or "Cow," as third-year West Pointers were known. . . . Goodpaster addressed our class on the significance and importance of Honor.
>
> Goodpaster was a cadet from central casting, more than six feet tall, handsome, and muscular. He had a stentorian voice and commanding presence. His impressive talk had a lasting impact on me, a talk I consider on par with the "Duty, Honor, Country" speech given by General MacArthur at West Point in 1962. With great conviction, sincerity and eloquence, Goodpaster told us that henceforth we would be men of honor, possessed of the highest standards of honesty and morality. We would be dealing with no material things but the lives of soldiers under our command; therefore, we would have to be men of the highest integrity and character. He said that cadets do not lie, cheat or steal or tolerate those who do. The notion that cadets must report honor violations of other classmates was a new and difficult concept to most of us. His words, like those of MacArthur, still ring in my ears and later automatically came up when I was tempted to do wrong. As much as Goodpaster helped me in later years, nothing served me better than his speech to us in 1937 on Honor. [7]

Among the responsibilities that may be placed on cadets at West Point, serving on the Honor Committee is among the heaviest. Whereas the majority of responsibilities are individual in nature, such as being responsible for grades and personal appearance, the Honor Committee was responsible for deciding the fate of anyone accused of violating the honor code. The decision was entrusted to the members of the committee, consisting of one representative elected from each of the twelve cadet companies.

Honor representatives chosen by the cadets in their second class (junior) year sat in on the Honor Committee meetings to learn about issues and procedures, but they did not vote until their final year. The senior honor representatives chose a chairman who, when advised of a possible honor violation, assigned another committee member to investigate the case and report back to the committee. If the investigation revealed a likely violation, then the individual accused appeared before the Honor Committee, where he was confronted with the evidence and given the opportunity to explain his case. The committee then voted; a unanimous vote was necessary to find a cadet guilty. If he was found guilty, then the cadet was immediately moved out of the barracks, a report was made to the commandant, and in most cases he was dismissed from the academy. [8]

Part of the ethical training also involved mandatory chapel attendance. Goodpaster found the Protestant services familiar and enjoyed singing in the choir for four years. Subsequently he would identify himself in terms of religion as "Army chapel Protestant."[9]

INTELLECTUAL GROWTH: CRITICAL THINKING

At West Point, Goodpaster also learned to think rigorously and communicate more effectively. Since 1802, West Point's curriculum had been designed around engineering with a strong foundation in mathematics. Math courses amounted to about one and one-half hours per day, six days per week, for two years. English was another major subject during the first two years to "stimulate a desire to read, appreciate the best in literature, write correctly [focus on expository writing] and talk effectively." The common curriculum also included physics, chemistry, electrical engineering, history, philosophy, economics, government and law, along with Spanish and French. Physical education classes included boxing, wrestling, fencing and horsemanship. Classes began at 7:55 a.m. and lasted until 3 p.m., five days each week, plus classes on Saturday morning, followed by a parade and inspection Saturday afternoon. Sports completed the rest of the weekday afternoons. After dinner, cadets were expected to study until Taps. That amounted to a very full schedule.[10]

Classes were small, about fifteen cadets per instructor. In most classes, each student had a requirement to participate actively. For example, in math, the class usually began with each student at the blackboard being given a drill problem to solve; their results were there for all to see. Many of the problems required using slide rules, so they became skilled at this method of computation early in their engineering studies. Further, they were graded daily in almost every class. At the end of each month, grades were posted, and cadets were reassigned to classes according to their standing in each subject. Under such pressure to keep up, cadets could not afford to postpone studies until the final exams and then cram.

Goodpaster excelled from the beginning. By the end of his first year, he ranked first in his class in English, third in math, and second in overall class standing—a position he would maintain until graduation. His intellectual growth reflected his aptitude for math and engineering, along with a keen interest in international affairs.[11]

SPORTS

Athletics was also an essential part of Goodpaster's West Point experience and leadership training. "Every man an athlete" was the norm and required each cadet to participate in either an intercollegiate or intramural sport each season. The emphasis on sports at West Point dates back at least to 1816 and recognized the similarities between athletic competition and war. Indeed, the origins of many sports lie in military training. As General Douglas MacArthur put it, "Upon the fields of friendly strife are sown the seeds that, upon other fields, on other days, will bear the fruits of victory."[12]

Goodpaster enjoyed football and played for three years in high school and two years at McKendree College.[13] He also tried out and made the Army football team. While not excelling, he was on the B-Squad for four years, where they mainly ran the offensive plays and defensive alignments of the opposing teams each week in scrimmages with the starting team for Army.[14]

Goodpaster also made the Army swim team during his first two years at West Point. Like football, swimming was physically and mentally demanding. Grueling workouts left the swimmers exhausted and made it difficult to stay alert in their studies. Furthermore, each swimmer hoped to achieve a personal best time every time they competed. It was an individual competition with oneself as well as the opponents.

LEADERSHIP

Although much has been written about leadership, there is no substitute for firsthand experience. During Beast Barracks, Goodpaster learned how it felt to obey orders, building empathy for those being led. He termed it learning by osmosis. "We learned more leadership skills than we realized."[15]

The best judges of leadership are often those being led. They know whom they respect and trust. For this reason, peer evaluation was an important part of the process of identifying leaders at West Point. By his junior year, Goodpaster was selected to be the sergeant major. Among other responsibilities, he prepared duty rosters, which helped him know most of his classmates by name. By his senior year, Goodpaster was rated among the top cadets of his class. In recognition of his demonstrated leadership skills, he was appointed the regimental adjutant, one of the four top leaders of the Corps. His room in the Central Area of barracks had a plaque inscribed with the names of other cadets who had previously held this position, including Robert E. Lee and George Patton. His roommate and close friend, Jack Christian, was another cadet captain.[16]

At the weekly parades, Goodpaster stood in front of the assembled Corps of Cadets and gave the initial commands in a clear, authoritative voice. In the same capacity, nearly every day he would stand on the "poop deck" above the cadets in Washington Hall during meals and announce the orders for the day.

Among his extracurricular activities, Goodpaster continued to enjoy sing-ing. He was a member of both the Cadet Chapel Choir and the Glee Club for four years. He also was active in the "Hundredth Night Show," celebrating only one hundred days remaining until graduation. He became most noted, however, for his performance of selections from *The Mikado*, Gilbert and Sullivan's famous comic operetta. Goodpaster had found it difficult to de-cline a request by the tactical officer in charge of the cadet orchestra. For years thereafter, he was known for his rendition of "Willow, Tit-Willow" otherwise known as "On a Tree by a River."[17]

Goodpaster also made time to frequently tutor other cadets struggling in classes. In some cases, such as that of Mike Davison, Goodpaster's tutoring saved cadets from failure that would have eclipsed brilliant careers. Davison eventually reached the rank of four-star general. Such efforts combined to make Goodpaster very highly regarded. As described by his classmates in his senior yearbook, "for four years we've been able to say 'Ask Andy, he knows.'"[18]

DOSSY

In terms of important decisions, few things rank as high as choosing a spouse. In this regard, Andy and Dossy chose well. It all began during Christ-mas of his plebe year when the fourth class men were required to remain at West Point while the other classes went on leave. Without most upper class men around to harass them, and relieved from daily academic pressures, the plebes relaxed, enjoyed movies, and attended dances, referred to as "hops." The more formal dances included hop cards[19] that could be used by the cadet escorting a date to designate who else would have the pleasure of dancing with his date for a particular dance number. Trevor DuPuy, an upper class-man who went on to become a noted military historian, was one of a few upper classmen remaining at West Point over the holidays and invited Good-paster to sign up for one of the dances with his date, a Miss Dorothy Ander-son. She was an attractive, very popular young woman and the daughter of Lieutenant Colonel Jonathan Waverly Anderson, the superintendent's execu-tive officer. Known as "Dossy," she was born in the Philippines and came from a third-generation Army family.[20]

Goodpaster's courting, however, was curtailed until the next summer:

> On July 11, 1936, [a date] she has forgotten, but I've never forgotten, I was able to escort her to one of the hops. One of my colleagues . . . was doing the same, so there was a bit of competition. But there were hops every night . . . so we both had an opportunity. We both had a little bit of a disciplinary problem, but mine was over before his was. And so, I began to "drag" [date] her, as the saying went, take her to the hops during the remainder of that summer and by

the time summer was over . . . we were . . . pretty well attached. . . . [But in] the spring of 1937 [her father] was assigned as a student at the Naval War College at Newport. And she traveled back and forth by train between Newport and West Point, so that we could see each other as that year progressed.[21]

Dossy preferred the name "Andy" for Goodpaster and decided to use that name. That also helped distinguish him from his roommate in conversations. So the transformation from "Jack" to "Andy" was completed.[22]

AN INTERNATIONAL VIEW

Goodpaster did not see Dossy for three months during the summer of 1937 while he was one of six cadets selected, along with Naval Academy midshipmen, for a cruise to Europe on a battleship, the *USS New York* (BB-34), accompanied by the battleship *USS Arkansas*. This gave Goodpaster a firsthand look at the deteriorating situation in Europe. After crossing the Atlantic and navigating the Skagerrak and Kattegat Straits around Denmark's Jutland Peninsula, the battleship moored at Kiel, the main German naval base. There, Goodpaster was given three weeks shore liberty to travel throughout Germany. He first went to Hamburg, where he was met by the U.S. Army attaché and his assistant. He was told, "Young man, look around you; this is a country that is going to war." Goodpaster recalled:

> During those three weeks, we saw uniforms everywhere and we saw what looked like a . . . militarizing society. That made a very profound impression on us because we knew that Hitler was calling for revenge and was calling for a correction or a change in the terms of . . . the Versailles treaty. Back at West Point . . . Professor Beukema, . . . a classmate of Eisenhower's and Bradley's, who was the head of our history department . . . in his lectures expressed his view, that it would not be long until war would break out again in Europe. And in all likelihood, before it was over, the United States would be drawn into it. So we had that sense that the world was headed toward war and . . . we would be drawn into it.[23]

After visiting Germany, Goodpaster sailed on the battleship to Lisbon and was briefed on the Spanish Civil War. Again, he got a close look at how war had changed. He noted that, unlike World War I, which had taken a devastating toll on the soldiers on both sides, the Spanish Civil War, with Germany and the Soviet Union supporting the opposing sides, was taking a tremendous toll on the civilian population. The deliberate killing and mistreatment of civilians in Spain opened Goodpaster's mind to the possibility that this could be a more common feature of warfare in the future.[24]

Following this trip, Goodpaster returned to West Point and resumed dating Dossy. To keep the relationship alive, she had to commute regularly, initially from Newport, Rhode Island, then from Washington, DC, after her father's transfer.

FIRST MENTOR: GEORGE "ABE" LINCOLN

Goodpaster was inspired by the Army officers teaching at West Point. They were intelligent and set very high standards. "We had some very impressive instructors, leaders. The man who was the head of infantry instruction was a major named Omar Bradley, they were a very fine lot."[25]

Among his instructors, he became closest to Captain George A. Lincoln in the Department of Economics, Government and History. Lincoln had graduated fourth in his class in 1929 and completed three years of study at Oxford as a Rhodes Scholar. Like Goodpaster, Lincoln was from the Midwest, a farm in Michigan. He was first in his high school class and attended Fairmont College in Wichita, Kansas, before winning an appointment to West Point.[26]

Goodpaster's strong academic performance and previous experience on the debate teams in high school and at McKendree College led Lincoln to invite him to join a small group of cadets for discussions on world affairs at his home. While entertaining the group in an informal setting, Lincoln would pose challenging questions and share his insights. In recalling these discussions, one of the participants, Edward Rowny, recalled Lincoln as "a truly global thinker [who] steeped us in the theories of geo-politicians."[27]

Lincoln also encouraged Goodpaster to join the debate team. Goodpaster became captain of the team that won a national championship. That experience enabled him to hone important skills that served him well throughout his career. Goodpaster was adept at thoroughly understanding all sides of arguments and listening closely to what others had to say. He was not argumentative, but could debate persuasively a line of reasoning. In particular, he developed a high level of intellectual dexterity in dealing with complex issues. Competitive debate also enabled him to distinguish between the emotional aspects of arguments and to focus more carefully on rational reasoning.[28]

Lincoln also introduced Goodpaster to methodical strategic thinking. Lincoln thought it was useful to expose his students to alternative analytic approaches. The dominant Army paradigm for planning, decision making, and issuing orders, at the time and for decades thereafter, was the "Operations Order," also called the "Five Paragraph Field Order." This format guided thinking for military operations at every level, from the lowest tactical unit to strategic thinking at the highest level. It involved initially framing the problem in terms of the "Situation," including both "enemy" and "friendly" forces. Significant attention was devoted to preparing an appropriate estimate of the situation before determining the best course of action to achieve the desired mission. As Goodpaster was to learn later, comprehensive situational awareness was a critical component of strategic thinking.

The second paragraph addressed the "Mission," usually a concise statement of who, what, where, when, and most importantly, why? The third paragraph, "Execution," communicated the commander's intent, the concept of operations, and the specific tasks assigned to each subordinate unit. The fourth paragraph dealt with "Administration and Logistics" and the requirements to support and sustain the operation. This, at the strategic level, helped illuminate the anticipated cost of the endeavor. Finally, the fifth paragraph was devoted to "Command and Signal" that included how to manage the operation.

While this approach pervaded Army thinking at the time, Lincoln favored the framework used by the Navy, termed "sound military decisions (SMD)."[29] This approach, first published by the Naval War College in 1936, provided another way of applying professional judgment to the conduct of war.[30]

SMD described a process for thinking through problems carefully while avoiding overreliance on doctrine, principles, and rules. Such sound military decisions were based on experience, education, and training. The latter two were, in turn, based on the study of successes and failures in war. To do otherwise, SMD cautioned, was to stake future security on the "possible availability of some military genius in time of need."

The process involved (1) the selection of the correct objectives, the ends toward which its action is to be directed under varying circumstances; (2) planning the detailed operations required; (3) transmitting intent so clearly as to ensure implementation of well-coordinated action; and (4) the effective supervision of such action.

The essence of SMD was thinking in terms of the relationship between causes and effects with emphasis on selection of the correct military objectives and the actions required for their attainment. In this approach, the objectives must be suitable, feasible, and achievable at reasonable cost. Suitability included consideration of the likely effects on future actions, especially the overall purpose. Feasibility included comparing friendly and enemy resources available, estimating the degree of difficulty given the obstacles, and reaching a determination that there is a reasonable chance of success. Achievability rested on determination of whether the likely gains would be worth the costs and understanding the likely consequences. This was an ongoing, dynamic process because of the constantly changing situation.

According to SMD thinking, the fundamental objective of the armed forces was to overcome the enemy's will to resist. This was mainly a function of isolating, occupying, or otherwise controlling the *territory* of the enemy. The most important single factor contributing to success was unity of effort, putting together a combined effort in a harmonious whole.

SMD also highlighted important personal attributes for military leaders, including a "creative imagination and the ability to think and to reason logically, fortified by practical experience and by knowledge of the science of war." Personal leadership attributes also were emphasized in the text, including modesty, patience, and toleration for the opinions of others.

Finally, the text noted that the mark of mental maturity is the ability to distinguish between preconceived ideas and fundamental knowledge. Intellectual honesty, unimpaired by the influence of tradition, prejudice, or emotion, was critical for sound military thinking.

Whereas the Army's Five Paragraph Field Order provided a concise, logical framework for thinking about military operations, SMD elaborated more on the process, including its dynamic nature. SMD also cautioned against becoming overly reliant on doctrine.

With his example, Lincoln proved to be an inspirational mentor for Goodpaster and other cadets. This would not be the last time their paths would cross. "He worked tirelessly in a self-effacing manner to train us and guide us throughout our careers," recalled Lieutenant General Edward L. Rowny clearly some seventy-five years later.[31]

Goodpaster's other studies at West Point exposed him to different ways of thinking. The heavy emphasis on math and engineering promoted his understanding of systematic problem solving. His study of history and law fostered his understanding of human responses to social challenges. This education was framed in the context of national service—duty, honor, country.

NEUTRALITY ACT

During this time frame, United States foreign policy was polarized between those favoring isolationism and those favoring aid to threatened, friendly countries. The political balance in Congress favored the isolationists during the 1930s. A series of Neutrality Acts was passed in response to growing concerns about the conflicts in Europe and Asia. In part, they reflected suspicions that bankers and arms manufacturers had conspired to spark World War I and draw in the United States. The legislation generally prohibited the United States from aiding any of the belligerents, particularly with arms or war materiel. The neutrality issue also became a topic for Goodpaster in intercollegiate debates.

The issue was also a topic for a group of the most influential scholars and business leaders outside of government making up the Council on Foreign Relations. The council addressed the Neutrality Act at a three-day conference in New York City in February 1939 and invited seniors from sixteen universities to attend. Goodpaster was selected to represent West Point. His participation was described by the council's secretary of study groups as the most outstanding.

> He thinks clearly and can express his ideas simply and directly. . . . At the closing dinner, he was selected as one of three spokesmen to deliver a 15 minute description of what he considered to be the most effective foreign policy for the United States. . . . It brought a salvo of applause from the Council members present. . . . An impressive feature of the three days was the sincere respect which Goodpaster earned from the college men and Council members alike. [32]

In presenting justification for changing the Neutrality Act, Goodpaster argued the need to allow the president more discretion in dealing with the constantly changing international environment. He cited Supreme Court cases upholding the powers of the president in foreign affairs and noted that, despite the best intentions of the act,

> We need not delude ourselves; we cannot prevent wars. As Rousseau says, 'Men have prevented little wars only to kindle greater ones.' An inherent conflict exists on the continent of Europe, and occasionally, in the future as in the past, it will break into war. . . . There is strong contention that the Neutrality Act is designed to prevent our getting into that same war. . . . We cannot [formulate a simple formula for peace] . . . *so we won't have to think. But we do have to think*" (italics added). [33]

This admonition to think objectively and to avoid simple responses when dealing with complex problems became a common Goodpaster theme for the next sixty-five years. Furthermore, at this critical juncture in U.S. foreign policy, Goodpaster emerged as an articulate internationalist to a group of the most influential leaders in government and business. This would not be the last time.

THE PRODUCT: A CRITICAL THINKING LEADER

As Goodpaster reflected nearly sixty years later:

> When we went into West Point, it was with a four year commitment to serve after graduation. We didn't think too much about that, but as time went on, the whole atmosphere was that this was a calling, that this was one of the great fields of service. . . . "Duty, Honor, Country" began to take hold of us . . . a feeling that to serve your country in the military was one of the worthiest things that we could do. So gradually . . . as I look back . . . they were training us for a lifetime of service and that appealed to us. We saw the officers there;

they were fine people. We knew of the service that those officers had given. We knew of the young graduates who had taken commands in the Civil War and carried out their responsibilities. So this was challenging and worthy in our opinion. And my classmates and I were just drawn completely into it. So that by the time I graduated, my aim was to continue to serve in the Army as a lifetime commitment.[34]

In what he called his life-shaping experience, he thoroughly internalized the values of duty, honor, country.[35] The *Howitzer* yearbook for 1939 capture much of the life and times of cadets in that day. In addition to pictures of students, faculty, sports, and inside humor, the theme was serious; they know they were going to war. The class of 1939 was the first of the large classes. They called themselves "fledglings, untried in the larger game for which we have been preparing." They hoped to be "worthy" of the West Point tradition and leave behind a Corps "better than they found it."[36]

GRADUATION 1939

By graduation, the world was closer to war. In Europe, diplomacy failed to halt aggression. The League of Nations proved powerless. The Spanish Civil War was a brutal test bed for political ideologies, military technology, and diplomacy. Following the military coup in 1936, Nazi Germany and Italy supported General Francisco Franco's forces, while the Soviet Union supported Republican forces. A relatively small number of American volunteers, such as the Abraham Lincoln Brigade, also fought on the Republican side, although the U.S. government remained neutral. With Franco's victory in 1939, the United States worked to ensure benevolent neutrality on the part of Spain that would deny the Axis powers valuable resources and strategically important locations.

In East Asia, the Japanese military high command was no longer content with an integrated economic system in Japan, Korea, and Manchuria and became increasingly obsessed with dominating China. By the end of 1938, Japanese forces captured much of north and central China, including Shanghai, Nanking, and Canton, effectively controlling the coast and isolating China except for overland routes from the Soviet Union and Southeast Asia. The brutality of Japanese forces in these operations, particularly during the "rape of Nanking," inflamed strong anti-Japanese sentiment that would persist for decades.

On June 12, 1939, President Roosevelt presented diplomas to Andrew J. Goodpaster and 455 other members of the class of 1939. The occasion brought to mind Roosevelt's earlier remarks: "To some generations much is given. Of other generations much is expected. This generation of Americans has a rendezvous with destiny."[37]

Andy and Dossy became engaged in the spring of 1939 and were married on August 28, during his three-month graduation leave. They proved to be a wonderful match for each other. For the next sixty-five years, they shared similar values and raised two daughters.

Following his longtime desire to become an engineer and in the tradition of those finishing in the top of their class, he was commissioned a second lieutenant in the Corps of Engineers. Like most of his classmates, Goodpaster desired an overseas assignment because they provided the most demanding and realistic training, being closer to the action. In 1939, the overseas choices were the defense of three overseas U.S. territories: the Philippines, the Panama Canal Zone, and the Territory of Hawaii.

For both Andy and Dossy, the Philippines assignment was their first choice. With more than seven thousand islands and a history of rebellion, it consistently presented real engineering and security challenges. In 1935, it was granted self-governing status as a commonwealth of the United States, and General MacArthur became the military advisor to the commonwealth government.

But Goodpaster did not get his first choice. The position with the 14th Engineers in the Philippines was not available as the incumbent extended his tour for a third year. When the position opened the following summer, the top graduate in the class of 1940 chose it, only to be killed at Bataan during the Japanese invasion.[38]

Instead, Goodpaster got his second choice, Panama, where the Army Corps of Engineers had overcome a wide range of challenges in constructing the Panama Canal between 1904 and 1914. Like the Suez Canal, control of the Panama Canal would be critical in wartime. Without it, the ability to transfer troops, ships, equipment, and supplies between the Atlantic and Pacific would be much more costly and time-consuming.

Goodpaster joined the Army at a time of extraordinary change and challenge. It was still very much the "old Army," as he put it, in contrast to what it would be in only a few years. When he came to West Point in 1935, "We very early were put on a horse because the cavalry was still very important." They also received instruction and training on tanks and aircraft, but the debate on appropriate roles for these kinds of forces was still not settled.[39]

Three days after the Goodpaster wedding in August 1939, Germany invaded Poland. The Polish cavalry was no match for the German armor *blitzkrieg*. The German attack was followed closely by the Soviet invasion of Poland from the east. The fall of Poland also touched Goodpaster on a personal level. The fate of his grandmother's relatives in Poland was unknown.

Figure 2.2.   2nd Lieutenant Goodpaster, 1939. Official photo. *Source*: Courtesy of National Archives and Records Administration (NARA)

Figure 2.3.   Andy and Dossy Wedding, 1939. *Source*: **Courtesy of Goodpaster Family**

NOTES

1. *Official Register of the Officers and Cadets*, U.S. Military Academy, 1935, 1936, 1937, 1938, 1939 and *Report of the Superintendent*, 1936, 1939.

2. Betros, *Carved from Granite: West Point Since 1902*, 75–76.

3. Goodpaster, McCall interviews, tape 2.

4. Sarah Nesnow, e-mail message to author, July 27, 2012.

5. Sorley, in *Honor Bright*, provides an overview of the role and evolution of the West Point Honor Code.

6. Ibid., 160, 52–53.

7. Edward J. Rowny, undated correspondence with Ken Weisbrode, about 1997. At the time Rowny entered West Point, he had already completed four years at MIT; not the typical eighteen-year-old plebe.

8. Roy J. O'Connor, former Honor Committee chairman, interview with author, May 2, 2012, Arlington, VA.

9. The 1939 *Howitzer* [West Point Yearbook], 170, and Goodpaster family correspondence with author, February 26, 2014.

10. *Report of the Superintendent*, 1936, 1937, 1938, 1939.

11. *Official Register of the Officers and Cadets, U.S. Military Academy*, 1936.

12. MacArthur, *Reminiscences*, 82. A similar quote has been attributed, probably incorrectly, to the first Duke of Wellington, that the battle of Waterloo was won on the fields of Eton.

13. Goodpaster, McCall interviews.

14. The 1939 *Howitzer*, 170, 404, 389.

15. Goodpaster, McCall interviews.

16. Goodpaster, Johnson and Ferguson interviews, January 9, 1976.

17. Goodpaster, McCall interviews.
18. Goodpaster, Johnson and Ferguson interviews, January 9, 1976; 1939 *Howitzer*, 339.
19. Dance cards were small, about three by four inches, decorative cards designed by the Cadet Hop Committee for each season. They had a pencil attached by an ornamental cord and the cards opened to a page with about twelve lines to record with whom the lady would dance during the evening. Cadets often agreed to exchange dances with dates and filled out the cards accordingly before the dance. The cards also served as mementos.
20. Dossy's father was a 1911 graduate of the Naval Academy, but chose the Army Field Artillery for his service. Goodpaster, McCall interviews.
21. Ibid.
22. Nesnow, correspondence with author, May 12, 2010.
23. Goodpaster, McCall interviews.
24. Ibid, 23–24.
25. Ibid.
26. Edwin A. Deagle, Jr. "Book Plan: General George A. Lincoln, Architect of American National Security," (unpublished) October 2010.
27. Edward Rowny, interview with author, May 3, 2013, Washington, DC.
28. Andrew J. Goodpaster Cadet Service Record and files, West Point Library. Rowny, interview with author, May 3, 2013.
29. Rowny interview with author, April 6, 2011.
30. *Sound Military Decisions,* U.S. Naval War College, 1936 (1942 edition).
31. Rowny, interview with author, May 3, 2013.
32. Edgar P. Dean in a letter to Lt. Col. Beukema, February 25, 1939, Goodpaster files, West Point Library. In his letter, Dean stressed that he is very "measured" in his use of "superlatives," and his letter is not meant as "flattery but as simple statement of fact."
33. Goodpaster, undated notes, "Suggested Changes for the Neutrality Act," Goodpaster file, West Point Library.
34. Goodpaster, McCall interviews.
35. Goodpaster, Billington interview, March 18, 2004.
36. 1939 *Howitzer*, 339.
37. Roosevelt in June 27, 1936, speech to the Democratic National Convention, Philadelphia. *Official Register of Officers and Cadets, 1935, 1939; Report of the Superintendent, 1935.* Stanley D. Dzuiban graduated first in the class.
38. Goodpaster, McCall interviews.
39. Goodpaster, McCall interviews.

Chapter Three

Preparing for War (1939–1943)

11TH ENGINEERS IN PANAMA (1939–1942)

Second Lieutenant Goodpaster and his new wife embarked from Brooklyn on a troop ship, the *Hunter Liggett*, along with other soldiers bound for Panama. En route, while the ship stopped at San Juan, Puerto Rico, Lieutenant Goodpaster had duty as the officer of the day, responsible for maintaining order and discipline. This time, however, he felt he failed somewhat at the task. The troops were not allowed to go ashore or have liquor on board, but they were well prepared to circumvent these restrictions. Several soldiers used long cords, attaching dollar bills to the end and lowering them from portholes to small boats below where the money was exchanged for bottles of rum tied to the cords and returned to the ship. The activity was not easily observed and plenty of rum was smuggled aboard. Apparently, no one had ever been successful in frustrating such efforts.[1] As a result, Goodpaster learned to never underestimate the ingenuity and resourcefulness of the GIs.

A few days later, the ship passed through the Panama Canal, and the Goodpasters disembarked at Balboa on the Pacific side. The Goodpasters were met by hosts from the 11th Engineers and taken to their quarters nearby at Corazal. He was assigned briefly as the assistant S-3, operations officer, then to A Company, the most junior of the three officers in the company. Initially, he was detailed with Sergeant Burke for six weeks to train about fifty recruits who had just joined the battalion. Goodpaster learned much about training soldiers to be engineers from Sergeant Burke, who lived up to the reputation of noncommissioned officers (NCOs) as being the indispensable "backbone of the Army."[2]

Engineer officers, who prided themselves on their ability to plan and build complex projects under difficult conditions, shared a quiz among themselves on the best way to build a flagpole. Some suggested first constructing an "A-frame"; others called for first sinking pilings on either side of the main pole, for example. But the correct answer was to simply give the order, "Sergeant, build the flagpole."[3]

As the world situation deteriorated, the Army decided to bolster defenses in the Canal Zone by sending two additional infantry regiments and aircraft. The task of building facilities for the new units fell to the 11th Engineers, led by a "very tough, very able" veteran of World War I, Lieutenant Colonel Frech. Time was urgent; the regiment was tasked to build barracks for the 5th Infantry Regiment within three weeks. The engineers were augmented with infantry and artillerymen so that one or two engineers supervised each of the other squads in construction. By the time the 5th Infantry arrived, the barracks, mess halls, latrines, and other facilities were completed.[4]

At one point during the construction, Lieutenant Colonel Frech told Goodpaster and the other officers to adapt standard Army designs to conditions in Panama. Jobs that normally would take over a year to complete were accomplished in several weeks of working feverishly. In one case, Goodpaster was responsible for building a theater and determined that the plans were inappropriate. The floor was too steep, so he changed the plans. Frech asked Goodpaster if he was building exactly according to design. Lieutenant Goodpaster replied that he was generally following the design, but he had made some changes. The colonel had recently been chastised by the inspector general for not following plans and told Goodpaster to return to the original design, which he did. But a few weeks later, Frech noted that the floor in the new auditorium was indeed too steep and asked Goodpaster why he had constructed it in such a manner. Goodpaster replied that he had been told to follow the design. Frech said "Well, the design doesn't make any sense. You've got to change it." Goodpaster responded, "Well sir, you told us to build it according to the design." Somewhat embarrassed, but maintaining his stern demeanor, nose-to-nose, Lieutenant Colonel Frech said, "Goodpaster, hereafter you just do what I tell you and never mind what I told you." That lesson in the vagaries of command made a lasting impression on Goodpaster.[5]

On October 1, 1940, Goodpaster was promoted to first lieutenant, but with pay remaining at the second lieutenant grade under new congressional authority granted to the services for expanding their ranks while limiting the costs. His commander continued to be impressed with his leadership abilities and engineering skills so, in the fall of 1941, he was chosen to command E Company, consisting of about one hundred engineers, a job that called for a captain.

On Sunday, December 7, 1941, Goodpaster was playing golf with Dossy at Fort Clayton when an engineer classmate who lived nearby called him over to listen to radio news that the "Japs are bombing Pearl Harbor." Initially Goodpaster thought it was a type of the Orson Welles "War of the Worlds" episode that had gripped the country in 1938, but after listening more closely, he realized that it was true. The troops were immediately put on alert. The main threat was sabotage of the canal. Intelligence reporting indicated spy networks were active in Panama. Rumors also were rife of Japanese aircraft carriers advancing toward the canal.[6]

By day's end, A Company was ordered to build a cantonment for the Japanese who lived in the area and were being rounded up. Initially they planned to house 250 Japanese people, but after Germany declared war on the United States, that estimate soon tripled to 750, including Germans and central Europeans from German-occupied countries. These internees were not U.S. citizens, unlike internees in California.

Within two days, they were building tent frames, mess halls, latrines, and guard towers to confine 1,800 internees. Thirty-six hours later they had a functioning four-acre cantonment and began to receive internees, who were put to work on the project. Some central Europeans who were engaged in helping to build the tent cities later had to be relieved of hammers and hatchets when they turned them against the German internees.[7]

Construction of additional facilities, including sites for the newly developed radar and airfields, continued for the next several months. The personnel of the 11th Engineers were then divided up to form the cadre for new engineer units as the Army embarked on a massive expansion. Morale was "very high" given the urgency of the situation. On February 24, 1942, Goodpaster was promoted to captain and continued commanding an engineer company. During this time frame, a local Army library was being closed and he was able to get a few books, including what turned out to be one of his prized possessions, a copy of Colonel George Marshall's *Infantry in Battle.*[8] He knew that the infantry was the core of the Army and that engineers, as well as other troops, had a secondary mission to fight as infantry should the need arise. Marshall, in the introduction, emphasized the differences between combat and peacetime training so that in combat a leader's "mental processes would not be paralyzed when he finds himself in situations where nothing is as he was taught to expect." Goodpaster's understanding of infantry tactics and leadership in combat would serve him well.[9]

Soon attention turned to sending the families of soldiers back to the United States. Dossy stayed as long as she could, but in March 1942, she finally left on a ship, the *Evangeline*, which was scheduled to go to New Orleans, but was rerouted because of German submarine reports. Dossy traveled with her friend, Mary McCaffrey; both young wives were pregnant. The *Evangeline* and two other ships were escorted by a destroyer to Tampa. From there, Dossy joined her parents in Fort Ord, California, where her father, Major General Anderson, was posted.[10] Meanwhile, in August 1942,

Goodpaster was sent to Camp Claiborne, Louisiana, to join a new engineer regiment.

Dossy went into labor on September 6, at a time that coincided with a practice air-raid alert for the Fort Ord area, making for a challenging drive to the Peninsula Community Hospital where she gave birth to Susan. Three weeks later, Dossy, her baby daughter, and her mother boarded a train for Louisiana to join Goodpaster. Their luggage was lost en route, so when they arrived in Alexandria, Louisiana, they had only their hand-carried luggage, posing an added challenge for a new mom. Dossy learned that her friend, Mary McCaffrey, had given birth to a son, Barry, on November 17. Barry McCaffrey, with Andrew Goodpaster as his godfather, went on to become a four-star general.[11]

As an Army brat,[12] Dossy was aware that families moved often. By the end of the war, the Goodpaster family had lived in fourteen different places. After their brief visit with Goodpaster in Louisiana, Dossy and Susan moved to Fort Sam Houston, Texas, to stay with Dossy's mother for a short time. In that time frame, her father, Major General Anderson, had left Fort Ord in command of the 3rd Infantry Division, which later made the initial landings at Casablanca. With most of the Army destined for overseas deployment, Army families sought homes near other friends and family members during the war. Dossy and Susan moved to Denver, Colorado, to be near the Erlenkotter family with whom they had become close friends in Panama; Susy Erlenkotter was young Susan's godmother.[13]

By this time, German forces had occupied most of Europe and were advancing on Moscow. In the Far East, Japanese forces scored impressive victories at Pearl Harbor, in the Philippines, Wake Island, Guam, Singapore, Malaya, and Hong Kong. By mid-1942, Japanese forces had eliminated most Western strongholds in the South Pacific and Southeast Asia. The military situation was bleak for the Allies.

390TH ENGINEERS (1942–1943)

Goodpaster was promoted to major on October 29, 1942, and assigned as executive officer of the newly formed 390th Engineer General Services Regiment under Colonel Winslow at Camp Claiborne, Louisiana. It was a heavy construction regiment with all-black troops except for the officers. Plans called for half of the officers to be black, but none were available.[14]

The new soldiers were farmers from the South. Major Goodpaster expected them to be strong and physically fit, but instead found them in very poor health in most cases. Dental problems were rampant, and dentists extracted more teeth in a short time than Goodpaster believed ever possible. With better food and health care, the troops became fit and learned how to operate heavy equipment including bulldozers, build bridges, and clear mine-fields. [15]

The regiment was not coming together as a functional unit, however. The black troops were very responsive to their officers, but tensions developed between the new troops and the black NCOs who had prior service but came from the North, mainly Philadelphia and New York. Initially the southern troops refused to take orders from the northern NCOs, because they were "just as black." These tensions, however, were reduced considerably with help from two senior black NCOs in their late fifties or early sixties who had served in the 9th Cavalry. With Goodpaster, these two sergeants met with the southern troops and talked about how the Army operates as a team in which every person must do his part to ensure success. [16]

Racial tensions with the local community, however, remained a problem. The troops wanted to carry personal weapons with them for protection when on pass to Alexandria, Louisiana, but Goodpaster did not allow it. Instead, he had them accompanied by military police.

Goodpaster focused training and leadership on building a cohesive team around the unit missions, and the unit made considerable progress. The 390th Engineers passed their overseas test but, before the unit deployed, Goodpaster received orders to attend the Command and General Staff College at Fort Leavenworth, Kansas.

The usual nine-month course was shortened in wartime to nine weeks and was designed to prepare officers for command at higher, regiment and division, levels. Whereas most prior training had focused on the skills of the various branches of the Army, Leavenworth emphasized combining the various branch specialties (infantry, armor, artillery, communications, logistics, and engineers) into coherent organizations, usually at the division level (about 15,000 to 20,000 troops). The likelihood that the students would soon be leading troops in combat focused their attention. [17]

Goodpaster was particularly impressed with one of the 700 students in the class who seemed to know more about logistics than the other 699 combined. The student was also from the Women's Army Corps, a WAC, whom Goodpaster would meet again later in the war. [18]

By the time the class ended, the tide of war had begun to shift in the Allies favor. In North Africa, the British captured Tunis, and the Americans seized Bizerte, resulting in the surrender of 275,000 German and Italian troops. The Germans also had recently suffered a crushing defeat by the Red Army at Stalingrad, with 150,000 soldiers killed and 107,000 captured.

With these successes, General Marshall pushed for an early cross-Channel invasion. The British, however, maintained that the military balance was not yet favorable, preferring instead to launch an invasion of Italy. The differences were ironed out in May 1943 at the Trident Conference in Washington. A compromise was reached in which the target date for a cross-

Channel invasion was moved up to May 1944, while the invasion of Italy would go ahead in the meantime.[19]

48TH ENGINEERS (1943–1944)

After graduating from the Command & General Staff College in April 1943, Goodpaster was assigned as commanding officer of the 48th Engineer Combat Battalion and was soon promoted to lieutenant colonel. This was his dream assignment—combat engineers prepared the way for the infantry and armor units, often in front of the attacking or defending units, clearing mine fields, bridging rivers, and building roads. Combat engineers especially had to be prepared to fight as infantry. Company- and battalion-level commands were considered the most satisfying assignments because of the opportunities to know the troops personally.

The new battalion was formed by splitting the 48th Engineer Regiment, providing a veteran cadre for the 48th and 235th Engineer Combat Battalions and the 1108th Engineer Group Headquarters.[20] The 48th was on training maneuvers in Louisiana when Goodpaster took charge the day after the battalion had completed a grueling twenty-five-mile hike. The battalion comprised a Headquarters Company and three line companies: A/Able, B/Baker, and C/Charlie. The soldiers came from forty-two of the forty-eight states and were very concerned about what type of commander would lead them into combat.[21]

Goodpaster took command shortly after the battalion had failed its overseas training test. He found a pervasive "we-they" attitude among the officers, NCOs, and troops that spurred mutual antagonism and worked at cross-purposes. He dealt with this by engaging his officers, sergeants, and men in discussions about their concerns and what they each had to do to accomplish their mission. Eventually the unit reached a "magic moment" when there was understanding, acceptance, and commitment to the mission that enabled the battalion to work well together to pass deployment tests. Once again, he was successful in transforming a dysfunctional unit into a team capable of accomplishing assigned missions.[22]

It did not take long for Goodpaster to make strong, favorable impressions on the 48th Engineers. They were satisfied that their new commander was competent. According to the men:

> He was a soldier's idea of what an officer should be. He knew tactics and he knew men. There was something about him that could inspire men to go out of their way to complete his orders. He had confidence in his men; and although he adhered rigidly to rank, he spoke to the men as if he were one of them. There were many times when he would call an officer aside and let him know what he was doing wrong in no uncertain words. . . . The men had worried

about what type of commander they would have to take with them into the field when their time came. But now they were satisfied. [23]

Everybody learned by doing—including by making mistakes. The field maneuvers included live-fire tactical exercises, combat in cities, engineer skills, and additional rifle marksmanship training. On one exercise, Lieutenant Colonel Goodpaster was captured by the opposing forces while conducting a reconnaissance in front of friendly forces. [24] But, overall, they passed their tests and were told by Colonel Anderson, the 1108th Engineer Group commander, that they would soon be transferred overseas. [25]

RACE RELATIONS AGAIN

Following maneuvers, the battalion returned to Camp Gruber, Oklahoma, for final training prior to deployment. During this time, Goodpaster was tasked to serve on a general court-martial of five black soldiers from another unit accused of murder. The local sheriff and lawyers came to the trial, arguing that, following a disorder in Leesville, the sheriff noted black soldiers running away and shot at them, killing one of the soldiers. Because they were allegedly participating in the disorder, they were all charged with being accomplices in murder. Goodpaster asked the president of the court-martial—an officer with twenty years more seniority—to review previous testimony. After his review, Goodpaster pointed out that the soldiers came into town much later than the original disturbance and thus could not have been participants. The soldiers were declared not guilty. [26]

Goodpaster was well prepared for this responsibility. He was first in his class in military law at West Point and, while in Panama, had been detailed to give a refresher course on military law to a group of about fifty officers. This experience, combined with his work with the 390th Engineers, was a "revelation" to Goodpaster about race relations in the South. [27]

GOOD-BYES AND EMBARKATION

Saying good-bye to loved ones when headed off to war was painful for all. Nobody knew if they would ever see each other again. On August 10, 1943, the battalion boarded a train at Braggs, Oklahoma. For security reasons, the troops did not know their destination. However, once they sensed whether the train was generally headed east or west, they would know whether they were destined to fight in the European/North African Theater or in the Pacific. The train headed north through Canada because of the congested rail lines in the United States, but eventually they determined that they were headed east. [28]

On August 12, they arrived at Camp Miles Standish, about thirty-five miles southeast of Boston. Here they underwent another in a long series of equipment checks. The 48th was initially slated to go to the United Kingdom (UK) as part of the build-up for the invasion of Europe and turned in all of their equipment, expecting to draw new equipment in the UK. But the orders were changed because operations in North Africa were not going well. So the 48th drew their own equipment back from depot and prepared for deployment elsewhere. [29]

The battalion, however, was understrength. To perform their missions, they were authorized 32 officers and 632 enlisted men; however, they were lacking about 100 troops. Third Army Headquarters levied a requirement on other engineer units to provide the men needed. Naturally, the men sent were not the best. Some had only been promoted to the required grade a day earlier, lacking the experience and qualifications commensurate with the grade. Others had medical problems that precluded them from field duty, making them nearly useless. Only about twenty were fit. When Goodpaster complained, he was threatened by a visit from the Third Army Inspector General. Goodpaster called the bluff and the Third Army staff backed down, sending him the troops he needed. [30]

As they prepared to depart, every piece of equipment had to be marked and measured along with the personnel to make sure the loading plans could accommodate the actual troops and their equipment. Shortages in equipment and personnel were filled. On August 20, the battalion boarded a sealed troop train for New York harbor. There they embarked on the *U.S.S. Edmund B. Alexander* and sailed the following day. [31]

ALLIED STRATEGIC DEBATE

Meanwhile, at the highest echelons, the next round of the strategic debate was being played out at the August 1943 Quadrant Conference in Quebec. After twelve days of bitter debate, the planned course of the war at this point was resolved in favor of Churchill's strong preference to open the Mediterranean to Allied shipping from Suez to Gibraltar by capturing Sicily, then invading Italy to tie down German forces and prevent them from defending more heavily against a cross-Channel invasion. Such a campaign could knock Italy out of the war quickly and threaten German oil supplies in the Balkans. Stalin also argued for opening another major front as soon as possible. General Marshall, on the other hand, believed strongly that the cross-Channel invasion was the most direct route to Berlin and should receive the top priority, and a major campaign in the Mediterranean would divert resources from the top priority. Admiral King and others in the U.S. Navy argued for a higher priority for ships and landing craft in the Pacific Theater.[32]

The Allies confirmed that the cross-Channel invasion, Operation OVER-LORD, was the top priority in the European Theater, with the Mediterranean Theater a second priority. Nevertheless, the Sicily-Italy operations would be launched first because the build-up of troops and supplies in Britain would not be sufficient to launch a successful invasion for several more months.

Underlying the strategic debate were the different circumstances of Britain and the United States. By this time, the British had already thrown nearly everything they had into the war; few reserves were left. The United States, however, was still mobilizing, and American leadership believed they could overmatch anything Germany and Japan could field.

LIFE ON A TROOP SHIP

Once underway, the troop ship joined others and formed a convoy, with destroyer escorts flashing signals as they moved slowly away from the coast. By this point, the 48th Engineers had coalesced as a team. As they recalled, "The men knew their officers and noncoms. . . . They had confidence in one another."[33]

Although the weather was excellent, and there were relatively few cases of seasickness, the crowded conditions made the voyage challenging, especially for eating and sleeping. Chow was served in shifts, with long lines stretching through compartments, up and down ladders throughout the ship. The troops were given red and black buttons that determined which shift would eat first on alternating days. As they neared the mess compartment, they were told to put their buttons in their right hand, their mess gear in their left and "hurry, hurry, hurry." But inevitably, when the ship rolled and men crowded together, wearing their Mae West life preservers constantly, at the same time passing through narrow hatches with trays of food, someone would lose balance, food would spill, and the decks became more slippery. No matter with which shift they ate, the food always seemed cold, and some men came down with dysentery.[34]

Sleeping presented another problem. There were not enough bunks, so the troops were organized into two shifts that alternated between noon and midnight. The bunks were stacked inches apart from the deck to the ceiling, making it difficult to turn over. It was hot, so the upper bunks near the ventilators were the most sought after. At night there was complete blackout because of the German submarine threat, especially just off the east coast of the United States. These U-boats had taken an enormous toll. Troops were constantly reminded "Blackout is now in effect; all lighting of cigarettes on the open deck is prohibited. Any infringement of these rules will jeopardize the lives of all hands on board."[35]

The worst thing for the troops, however, was the spare time to think. After physical exercise, guard duty, and card games, the men had plenty of time to ruminate about what they were facing. There was no turning back. They were on their way to war, a war they had read about and seen in the movies. Sometimes they felt proud to be part of such a noble effort. Sometimes they were anxious to be tested in combat. But they mainly hoped they would be up to the task and come home safely. And, as the days wore on, the novelty and initial excitement wore off. The ship seemed to be getting smaller and smaller.[36]

Finally, after two weeks at sea, they saw land. The troops recognized Gibraltar from the familiar logo of the Prudential Life Insurance Company. They were spellbound as they approached the stark white cliffs with the faint brown coastline of Spain in the distance on their left and Spanish Morocco on their right. As they passed through the strait and entered the Mediterranean, they knew they were probably headed for North Africa.

The next morning, the ship dropped anchor in a harbor that had a "strange, oriental appearance." In the late afternoon, they came alongside a long quay, disembarked, and finally set foot on land in North Africa, on September 5, 1943. They had landed at Mers El Kebir and, while waiting in the early evening to be picked up by trucks, one of the soldiers attempted to light a cigarette; he was warned that they were now in the war zone, and the place was bombed often.[37]

The battalion was trucked during the night through Oran to a staging area nearby. The next morning, Lieutenant Colonel Goodpaster gave everyone in the unit a fresh start by rescinding all punishments accumulated for previous misconduct while stateside.[38]

In the meantime, secret negotiations between the Allies and Italians resulted in the arrest of Mussolini in Rome, and on September 8, 1943, Italy surrendered. The Germans had anticipated such a move and disarmed the Italian troops. The following day, after Allied troops had gained control of Sicily, the U.S. Fifth Army under General Mark Clark, landed at Salerno, beginning a long and bloody campaign to gain control of Italy.

At that time, Field Marshal Albert Kesselring commanded all German forces in the Mediterranean Theater, including Italy and North Africa. He staged a daring rescue of Mussolini from prison on September 12 and organized the defense of Italy with General Heinrich von Vietinghoff in command.

On September 11, 1943, the 48th Engineers moved to near a French Foreign Legion training area at St. Denis du Sig. Here the training intensified, both during the day and especially at night. The emphasis was building "Bailey Bridges" developed by the British. The battalion practiced constructing bridges in total darkness, working as quietly as possible. If noises were heard by the training cadre, they would send up a flare and detonate charges of explosive TNT.[39]

Another priority was mine clearing. Again, they trained extensively at night to avoid observation by the enemy and drawing artillery fire. They were introduced to a new explosive, composition C, that could be molded into shapes that made for more effective demolitions. The battalion practiced clearing minefields while under fire from .30 and .50 caliber machine guns. They also laid minefields and suffered their first casualty when Sergeant McGinnis of Able Company was wounded while assisting with booby-trap instruction. This accident resulted in the troops handling demolitions much more carefully.[40]

Figure 3.1. North Africa

NOTES

1. Goodpaster, Mandel interviews.
2. Goodpaster, McCall interviews.
3. Ibid.
4. Ibid.
5. Goodpaster, McCall interviews and Mandel interviews, tape 4.
6. Goodpaster, Billington interview, March 18, 2004.
7. Goodpaster, McCall interviews.
8. Ibid.
9. Gooodpaster, Mandel interviews, August 1, 2001, tape 5; George C. Marshall *Infantry in Battle*, 1934 edition, ix.
10. Gooodpaster, Mandel interviews, August 1, 2001, tape 5. Another favorite Goodpaster reference was the *Battle of Booby's Bluff*, 1928, providing an Engineers' perspective of a series of six solutions to the same attack problem, each designed to teach lessons learned from errors made in the previous solution.
11. Susan Goodpaster Sullivan, e-mail message to author, July 30, 2012.
12. Slang for *daughter* or *son* of an Army member.
13. Susan Goodpaster Sullivan, phone interview with the author, June 27, 2010; correspondence July 30, 2012.
14. Goodpaster, McCall interviews.

15. Ibid.

16. Ibid.

17. Ibid.

18. Goodpaster, Johnson and Ferguson interview, January 9, 1976.

19. Pogue, *Marshall: Organizer of Victory,* 1943–1945, 193, 194, 198, 204, 206.

20. Technically termed "Engineer Combat Battalions" but more commonly called "combat engineer battalions."

21. William Smukler, technical sergeant and editor, *We the 48th*, 10.

22. Andrew Goodpaster in James M. Johnson, unpublished paper "Oral History of the Superintendency of General A. J. Goodpaster," Department of History, U.S. Military Academy, undated (interviews March 7 and 10, 1988), 66–67, Goodpaster Collection, West Point Library, hereafter "Johnson interviews."

23. Smukler, *We the 48th*, 13.

24. Goodpaster, McCall interviews; Smukler, *We the 48th*, 14.

25. Smukler, *We the 48th*, 15.

26. Ibid., 52–53.

27. Ibid.

28. Smukler, *We the 48th*, 15.

29. Goodpaster, McCall interviews; Smukler, *We the 48th,* 15, 16.

30. Ibid.

31. Ibid.

32. Pogue, *Marshall,* 241–51, 260.

33. Smukler, *We the 48th*, 16.

34. Ibid.

35. Ibid., 18.

36. Ibid.

37. Ibid., 19.

38. Ibid.

39. Ibid., 21.

40. Ibid., 22.

Chapter Four

Close Combat (1943–1944)

INTRODUCTION TO ITALY

After a month of intensive training, the 48th boarded the *Durbin Castle*, a British passenger ship that was pressed into service, and crossed the Mediterranean. On the morning of the third day, they were treated to a "picture postcard" view of the Isle of Capri, Mount Vesuvius, and Naples Bay. They were ferried ashore in small barges to piers at Bagnoli, just north of Naples, which had recently been taken by Allied troops. Most of the battalion assembled and moved to a small college campus, Constance Collegio de Ciano, which had previously been used by German troops as an ammunition dump. An extensive network of tunnels had been dug into the mountainside where the ammunition was stored and remained in huge quantities, perhaps booby trapped. The college buildings were camouflaged, and huge landscape murals were painted on the walls, reaching four stories high and blending in to the surroundings. Goodpaster had the battalion establish a perimeter defense to prevent any German infiltration efforts to blow up the ammunition. All night long, as the troops tried to sleep, they heard their sentries yell, "Halt, who goes there?"[1]

The battalion was assigned initially to VI Corps, Fifth Army. Among first impressions was the extent of the destruction to the town where they assembled. The bombing had destroyed nearly everything; the railroad station was a "tangled mass of steel." The rail marshaling yard was beyond repair; there were mounds of rubble everywhere.[2]

While awaiting the arrival of the remaining troops with the battalion's vehicles and heavy equipment, on October 16, 1943, the 48th was moved to Avellino by a truck company. Again, they were shocked by the devastating effects of the recent fighting and bombing. Only a few walls were left standing. Two days later, they moved to Caserta in the dump trucks of another Engineer company.[3]

Late evening on October 22, 1943, as Goodpaster met the remaining men and equipment of the 48th arriving in Naples harbor aboard the Liberty ship *Townsend Harris,* they came under attack by German aircraft. Units along the coast were alerted, including the main elements of the engineer battalion. As searchlights probed the sky, antiaircraft fire erupted throughout the area, and explosions drove home to the troops the importance of adequate foxholes.[4]

The following day, the first platoon of C Company was strafed by two German fighter aircraft. Several soldiers and civilians were killed, but none from Company C. Bombing and strafing attacks became frequent, almost every night. Finally, the battalion's vehicles and equipment arrived. At Caserta, the unit loaded up with landmines for defensive positions and moved to Alvignano, close to the front lines.[5]

Just as they were arriving, rains began that lasted for months. Everyone and everything was soaked. The rain alternated between intense downpours and fine drizzles that formed a haze in the valleys. What little help the raincoats and ponchos provided in repelling the rain was offset by their also retaining the moisture from sweat while laboring in such conditions.

The rains turned the roads into quagmires that required constant attention by engineers to keep them open. Potholes developed quickly and were filled by engineers, only to be reopened by endless convoys of passing trucks. For the troops, spare socks never dried completely and, after weeks and months, trench foot became a common problem.[6]

In early November 1943, Goodpaster tasked Charlie Company to provide a platoon in support of the 120th Engineers to clear mines for the 179th Infantry Regiment. During their first morning, the platoon was bombed three times and came under frequent machine-gun and rifle fire. The platoon then helped build a road culvert so that tanks could be brought forward. Noise from the engineer picks was heard by the enemy and soon the platoon was under direct fire from German 88mm guns. Incoming 88 rounds, unlike artillery and mortar fire, were especially fearsome because they arrived at their target without warning.[7]

Goodpaster next tasked Charlie Company to clear mines for the 4th Ranger Battalion along newly captured roads near Venafro and help secure the only bridge across the Volturno River. While clearing mines from the riverbed, Charlie Company also removed bodies of soldiers killed in securing the crossing.

Casualties among the 48th Engineers became more frequent. At Venafro, four men were killed, and three others lost legs to mines. Goodpaster assigned Able and Baker Companies to join Charlie Company along the slowly advancing front lines. Progress was only achieved at a high cost. By November 27, the battalion was engaged in the battle for Colli, the main Fifth Army objective. These efforts included constructing a 130-foot Bailey bridge across the Volturno while supporting the 34th Infantry Division. The bridge was also instrumental in enabling the Free French Forces to bring heavy equipment and launch successful attacks on the eastern flanks of the German lines. The rains continued through November, the rivers rose, and pontoon bridges were washed out frequently. [8]

Figure 4.1. Front Lines in Italy.

On December 1, 1943, the 48th Engineers were detached from VI Corps and assigned to II Corps to support the effort to breach the main German defensive Gustav Line by seizing Monte Cassino. At that time, the main effort was to take the town of Mignano in the valley and the surrounding heights, especially Mount Camino. After the attackers expended an enormous amount of artillery fire to dislodge the Germans and finally secured the high ground, Mount Camino became known as the "million-dollar hill." [9]

BUILDING HIGHWAY 48

After Mignano was finally taken, on December 15, Goodpaster received orders for the 48th to convert a railroad between Mignano and Cassino into a road for tanks within six days, a distance of six miles, four of which were in German hands. This was an enormous task. It involved transforming a narrow, destroyed and mined railroad bed into a wide highway, capable of supporting heavy vehicular traffic moving simultaneously in both directions. The Germans had made every effort to prevent the railroad bed from being used by the Allies. This included using a special railroad car outfitted with a hook that was dragged behind to dig up the ties and rails. Every bridge and culvert was blown, and all approaches were heavily mined. Railroad embankments had been turned into defensive positions covered with machine guns, patrolled by German soldiers at night and German Messerschmitt 109 aircraft during the day. [10]

As work got underway, Able Company was issued newly developed gasoline-powered chain saws to help remove the many trees that were blown by the Germans, creating obstacles along the road. But the initial experience with this new technology was problematic. Soon after the saws were started, the Germans heard the noise and began firing on the engineers. The work was completed without the chain saws. [11]

Lieutenant Colonel Goodpaster initially checked maps and aerial photographs to determine the magnitude of the job and how to organize the battalion's resources for the tasks. In addition to clearing the mines and restoring the roadbed, the main challenge would be in bridging the several rivers and streams. Goodpaster picked two officers to oversee construction at alternating sites, assigning Charlie Company the lead with Captain Van Campen, the commander, as the battalion engineer for the mission. Van Campen thrived on jobs that would shatter the nerves of most men. As a result, Charlie Company earned a reputation among the infantry, tankers, and artillery troops that led to their being requested for tough jobs. [12]

The following day Goodpaster reconnoitered the railroad beyond the forward infantry positions and reported that the railway was under observed enemy artillery, mortar, and automatic weapons fire. The initial tasks would involve a high-level Bailey bridge of approximately 110 feet in length and another medium-level Bailey bridge of about 100 feet. He also personally located and marked a minefield. [13]

Work began immediately on the first bridge site, which had been cratered, leaving a 345-foot gap 48 feet above a stream, less than 600 yards from the infantry outposts. The site was under German observation from high ground on both sides and to the front. Bulldozers were required to prepare the site for British tanks and trucks that would soon be sent forward. Two bulldozers from Baker Company worked through the night to prepare the site under nearly constant artillery and mortar fire. The operators were exposed, but protected by a machine-gun squad deployed around the site. At one point, a German patrol came within sight of the squad, but withdrew after an illumination shell lit up the area, exposing them. By 3:30 a.m., the site was prepared, the bulldozers pulled back, and other engineers came forward to build the bridge, completing the task the following evening. [14]

Lieutenant Colonel Goodpaster and Lieutenant Bud Showalter conducted another reconnaissance beyond the infantry outposts, reaching the base of Mount Lungo, one of the major German strongpoints guarding the Cassino Valley. They stopped only when they were pinned down by machine-gun fire and crawled out while rounds hit the ground and trees around them. [15]

The battalion numbered each major obstacle they encountered along the rail bed. By December 18, Charlie Company was working on Obstacle 8, where a major bridge had been destroyed and mines emplaced along the approaches. First the minesweepers moved forward with fixed bayonets on their rifles in heavy rain, then came the demolition teams to clear the roadbed of fallen trees and twisted rails. Next came the bulldozers to fill in the shell holes and bomb craters and grade the embankments for the bridge crossing. The site was under observation by Germans who called in artillery fire when anyone approached the site.

C Company, however, pressed forward. On December 19, they had the site prepared and moved the bridging forward. That morning they were shelled four times; one barrage of thirty 105mm rounds landed nearby, with the closest hitting within twenty-five yards. Because of the rain and thick mud, some of the rounds penetrated the ground before they exploded, lessening their impact. But others hit rock formations, fragmenting rock and shrapnel, compounding the effects. Goodpaster noted that the German artillery seemed to be coming from Mount Lungo, so the battalion contacted the 71st Artillery Brigade to conduct counter-battery fire. The engineers worked through the night and completed a 110-foot bridge by 6 a.m. the next morning after twenty-four hours of work. [16]

Obstacle 9 was a former three-span, 275-foot bridge that had been destroyed, with only the piers left partially standing. Goodpaster assigned the task of bridging this obstacle to Able Company, which decided to construct a lower bridge in a defile that would involve a shorter span and afford more protection from enemy fire. However, it also involved considerable work to cut down the approaches, abutments, and piers. Fourteen hundred pounds of explosives were used to prepare the site. While the bulldozers were grading the steep approaches, other engineers were sent to cut down large trees to be used in the revetments. They had to cross an open field to get to the nearest woods, but soon the Germans realized what they were doing and began shelling them and the bridge site. One round hit within twenty feet of a culvert where some of the men were eating and where infantrymen were

Figure 4.2.   Bridge on Highway 48. Official photo. *Source*: **Courtesy of Good-paster Family**

sheltered while evacuating wounded soldiers on stretchers. An infantry medic was killed and several others wounded.[17]

When the work was nearly completed, a direct hit on the bridge destroyed some of the stringers and part of the bracing, took out one transom, and killed

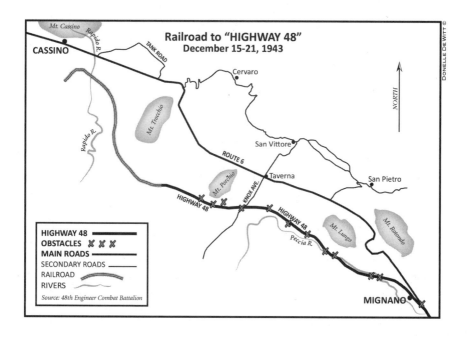

Figure 4.3. Highway 48.

one of the engineer sergeants. After repairs were made, one of the bulldozers became stuck in the mud while grading the steep approaches to the bridge. A T-2 tank retriever and another D-7 bulldozer were required to extract the bulldozer. This attracted more German artillery fire and one round landed close to the T-2, wounding the crew. The engineers rescued the crew and drove the T-2 to safety. In the meantime, the D-7 came under fire, and Sergeant Moore took charge, jumped on the exposed driver's seat, and was wounded but drove the bulldozer out of the area. He earned a Silver Star for his bravery under fire.[18]

By the time they had overcome Obstacle 9, the route became known as "Highway 48" for the 48th Engineers. One night, as Charlie Company was sent forward to work on the next obstacle, Goodpaster received a flash[19] message that the Germans were launching a counterattack on Highway 48 that night. Initial efforts to contact C Company failed, so the battalion operations officer went forward to locate and warn the company.[20]

He reached second platoon and had them stop and take up defensive positions. Lieutenant Reardon, the platoon leader, moved forward to contact third platoon and lead the rest of the company back to the battalion perimeter while the other two platoons were moving forward quietly, single file with men ten paces apart. Reardon thought he saw third platoon in the dark, but before he tried to make contact, he realized that they were Germans when he heard a command given softly in German. Fortunately, he was not observed. After the Germans moved on, he was able to connect with the other platoons and led the company to the battalion defensive perimeter. [21]

At noon on December 21, 1943, Lieutenant Colonel Goodpaster had his adjutant notify higher headquarters that "the road was officially open for all classes of vehicles." In six days, they had overcome a series of formidable obstacles, including several fast-flowing mountain streams. More than a dozen major bridges and culverts were constructed, including spans up to 350 feet and rising 85 feet above the water level. Fifth Army acknowledged the contribution of the 48th Engineers during this operation with an official commendation. [22]

For the next three months, the 48th was responsible for maintaining and improving the road. Heavy military traffic, rain, snow, and nearly continuous shellfire resulted in frequent craters, potholes, washouts, and other problems needing repair to maintain this critical lifeline. Coordinating priorities for use of the road was a challenge. The key was getting the right equipment and supplies to the front when needed as the road was jammed with tanks, men, truckloads of units moving forward, units being relieved, and the constant flow of medical evacuations. [23]

On Christmas Day, Lieutenant Colonel Goodpaster added his personal commendation to the team that had worked so well together. He noted that the six days that ended at noon December 21 were

> as hard an engineer test as any we will ever encounter. The job was done in time. It was done because every man threw all his strength, determination, and courage into the task, because every officer put all of his skill, leadership, and valor into it, and because the Battalion drove through to success as a hard-working, courageous team . . . these are the times that try men's souls. [24]

Christmas Day also brought a storm that reached almost hurricane strength. The rain turned to snow in the afternoon, and the cold became intense. Allied artillery fire focused on nearby Mount Porchia in preparation for an attack. Goodpaster gave Charlie Company a secret mission for which Lieutenant Reardon sought volunteers. They moved out at 5 a.m. with the task of establishing a forward observation post on Mount Lungo that would be used by General Mark Clark to observe the attack. [25]

Mount Porchia, along with Mount Trocchio, dominated the approach to Cassino. Although not a high mountain, Porchia dominated the Cassino Valley between Route 6 and Highway 48. The slopes were steep and rocky. The summit was elongated, running the entire length of the mountain, offering a clear view of the valley and approaches back to Mignano, five miles away. The German bunkers were well concealed and had excellent fields of fire across the steep, reddish-brown shale slopes. It was an imposing, strategic fortress arrayed across the entire valley.[26]

On January 4, 1944, Goodpaster was alerted of the impending Allied attack to gain control of Mount Porchia. The mission of the 48th was to open the way for tanks to move up Highway 48 and establish firing positions off the road near Mount Porchia to support an infantry attack by Task Force Allen. The engineers would then prepare defenses for these forward positions that were within hand-grenade range of German positions. Lieutenant Colonel Goodpaster, Captain Van Campen and Sergeant Attleson conducted a reconnaissance during the night of January 4. As they moved forward in a half-track, they soon found that the Germans were able to quickly monitor and locate any radio transmissions, bringing artillery to bear quickly. Then they came under rifle fire, with one round hitting Attleson's helmet. Once they scouted the positions, they returned, and Baker Company was dispatched to clear Obstacle 13.[27]

As the tanks and artillery of the First Armored Division were moving forward on Highway 48, a heavy Allied artillery barrage was launched against German positions on Mount Porchia. Then, Task Force Allen launched the attack with the 6th Armored Infantry Regiment in the lead. Goodpaster assigned each of his companies to support an armored infantry company. They took heavy casualties crossing open fields at the outset and as a result did not have sufficient forces to capture more than the lower elevations. By morning, the Allies, including the engineers, were pulled back. The attack had failed with heavy losses. At 5 a.m. on January 5, Goodpaster ordered all three companies to withdraw to the vicinity of the battalion command post and prepare defensive positions in anticipation of a German counterattack.[28]

FIGHTING AS INFANTRY

Goodpaster was proud of the way the battalion performed in combat, but now they would be tested in a new way, fighting as infantry. Losses in the infantry had been so heavy that Goodpaster was tasked to constitute the Task Force Allen reserve. This was a last resort because it meant that they would no longer be available to keep Highway 48 open. Without engineer assistance, the tanks, tank destroyers, and other heavy vehicles would hit mines or otherwise get bogged down, blocking the road to other traffic. At the base of Mount Porchia, the 48th established contact with units on the flanks from the 6th Armored Infantry and the 91st Recon, then dug in. It was another cold, windy, miserable, tense night, but the anticipated German attack never came.[29]

On the morning of January 6, the battalion was relieved and ordered back to resume work on Highway 48, including reconnoitering additional forward obstacles. By early afternoon, however, they were ordered to be prepared to move out as infantry within thirty minutes' notice. Able Company was just returning from its infantry deployment when they were alerted that they would be going back, this time attached to 3rd Battalion, 6th Armored Infantry. Goodpaster attached Charlie Company to the 1st Battalion and ordered Baker Company to clear Obstacle 13.[30]

That night, Goodpaster chose Lieutenant Orville Munson to command Able Company after Captain Lester became sick. With that choice, Goodpaster proved to be a good judge of character. A platoon leader without experience at the company level, Munson was tasked to lead an attack against positions that had repeatedly defied experienced infantry commanders. Munson took charge, moved out in the lead as the point man, and sent out flank guards to prevent the column from being ambushed. They passed through several streams and some farmyards before reaching the base of Mount Porchia. Many of the trees had tripwires stretched between them, neck high. As they were crossing a stream, one of the flank guards was caught on one of the wires as he was running to rejoin the main column. Once Able Company was across, Lieutenant Munson went forward to scout the way while First Sergeant Buckley waited with the company.[31]

After a short wait, Buckley began moving the company forward and was crossing an open field when shelling began, killing Sergeant Jacobs. They linked up with Lieutenant Munson just before they crossed Knox Avenue, a road that ran along the base of the mountain. Munson ordered the men to fix bayonets, and they moved along a narrow path. As they were making their way through a minefield, a mine exploded, wounding the first sergeant and three others. Sergeant Le Feverer's leg was nearly blown off and was amputated at the site. At about 8 p.m., Lieutenant Munson notified Goodpaster that the American infantry lines were not forward of the road as expected. Instead, he had encountered a German soldier on the road and shot him.[32]

That night, Goodpaster was ordered to attack Mount Porchia at 11 p.m. He put Able Company on the left flank, to strike diagonally toward the right side of the mountain. Once they heard fire, they were to attract as much attention as possible and move to make contact with friendly forces on the right—Charlie Company reinforced with a few infantry.[33]

Goodpaster watched through the night as the attack unfolded. He focused on the possibility that he would need to commit his reserves. He was not aware of the details of individual actions until later, but some of these details are worth noting.

The attack jumped off with Lieutenant Munson charging ahead, ordering his men to "run at full speed for the mountain." But when he looked back, nobody was following, so he returned and again ordered them to follow.

Again, no one came forward. As he was about to go back again, every man rushed forward simultaneously, shouting at the top of their lungs, overcoming their fright. [34]

They were nearing the top of the mountain when the Germans opened fire with machine guns and rifles, halting the charge. As A Company took cover in the darkness, Munson realized the platoons had become separated. In some cases, machine-gun crews found themselves with the ammunition and tripod in one platoon and the gun in another. One platoon drew friendly fire from another. The fighting was at close quarters and confusing. At one point, a German called out in good English, "I want to speak to your officer." An American infantry lieutenant stepped out of cover and moved forward to meet the German. As they came closer, the German shot the lieutenant and ducked behind cover before the men of Able Company could react. [35]

Meanwhile, Baker Company continued to work on clearing Obstacle 13 as the temperature dropped to near zero at midnight. B Company could hear the fighting nearby on Mount Porchia when they were notified that they were the reserve for the attack. There was only a handful of infantry surviving at that point. After Goodpaster argued unsuccessfully to allow B Company to finish its work and lead the British tanks forward to support the attack, B Company was ordered to take up positions on the left flank, near the base of the mountain, while fighting continued on their right. During this time, the German artillery zeroed in on Goodpaster's forward command post. Luckily nobody was injured before they evacuated. [36]

By dawn, Goodpaster saw Baker Company moving up the mountain, and German shelling becoming more intense. Suddenly, as the forward elements engaged in a firefight with dug-in troops, they realized it was Able Company. Sergeant Googoo was sent out to scout the position of a German machine gun that had pinned down A Company. He could not locate the gun, but reached the crest of the mountain and realized how this position dominated the lower slopes. Other scouts soon also reached the top, when friendly artillery began shelling the summit, wounding Sergeant Schreiner. [37]

Lieutenant Buckley took his platoon of B Company beyond the crest and established defensive positions on the reverse slope to avoid friendly and enemy artillery fire—the latter still focused on the forward slope. Captain Mardin, commanding B Company, organized the rest of the company defenses while he attempted to coordinate artillery fire and make contact with Able Company. [38]

Charlie Company was less fortunate. As they attacked on the right flank, they immediately came under withering fire. Sergeant Specker volunteered to attack a machine-gun nest and snipers that pinned down his platoon. He took a thirty-pound machine gun and, as he was moving forward, was hit several times. He nevertheless crawled to a position where he was able to return fire and destroy the machine-gun nest. As the firing abated, his squad moved forward in the darkness, assuming he had continued to press on. They did not discover his bullet-riddled body until late the next day. Sergeant Joe Specker earned the Medal of Honor posthumously for his valor, above and beyond the call of duty.[39]

Lieutenant Reardon, with first platoon of Charlie Company, moved up on the right, reaching the crest with three other men, and engaged Germans in a series of individual fights frequently punctuated with grenades from both sides. With several wounded and nearly out of ammunition, Reardon realized the odds were increasingly unfavorable and at about 3 a.m. pulled the men back down the mountain.[40]

Lieutenant Thames led second platoon of C Company on the right flank of the attack. As they advanced, they encountered a German machine gun firing from the entrance to a cave that gave a distinctive, hollow echo sound to the bullets. As they reached the top, a German soldier fired point-blank at Sergeant Plowman and missed while Lieutenant Thames returned fire, killing the German. Just beyond the crest, a German soldier was leading a counterattack, but was killed by second platoon soldiers before the attack could reach the summit. Firing was coming from all over the crest, with much of the fighting at ranges of fifteen yards or less. The Germans threw about twenty-five grenades. Sergeant Santjer was hit twice, got off a good shot, and saw the German soldier fall, but faced another German before he could raise his rifle, so he dove at the German with his bayonet. He then dodged among the rocks and accounted for two more kills before a German with a burp gun stepped out from the rocks and caught Santjer with a blast of automatic fire at point-blank range. Sergeant Santjer, killed instantly, was awarded the Distinguished Service Cross posthumously.[41]

By this time, the moonlight that had offered limited visibility completely disappeared. Lieutenant Thames whispered to Sergeant Treloar to check the right flank. After waiting a long twenty minutes without word from Treloar and suffering additional casualties, Thames ordered his men to withdraw to the infantry positions below them. As they withdrew, German soldiers kept up pressure, pursuing them with grenades and rifle fire, yelling "American swine." The remainder of C Company tried to cover the withdrawal of the few survivors with mortar and gunfire. Goodpaster saw tracers from both sides outlining the fighting. Eventually the survivors, including Sergeant Treloar, managed to slip through the German positions and reach the original positions near the base where German probes and counterattacks were halted, but the incoming mortar fire continued.[42]

Lieutenant Katzbeck, with a small party from third platoon of C Company, also reached the crest during the attack, just in time to meet and halt a German counterattack. He was unable to contact anyone else and assumed that the fighting to his left was Able and Baker Companies. As his isolated position became increasingly untenable during the night, he brought his men back. As he went to check in at the infantry command post, a shell landed nearby, killing nine infantrymen.[43]

As dawn came, Goodpaster saw bodies all over the face of the mountain. The taste of defeat was bitter. The Germans had thwarted another attempt to capture Mount Porchia. Casualties were high, with only a few men from the 6th Infantry remaining. When the next attack was launched, these men joined the 48th Engineers.[44]

SECOND ATTACK ON MT. PORCHIA

With devastating casualties and intolerable weather, the thought crossed the mind of Goodpaster and virtually every other soldier on the battlefield, "If I survive, . . . " But they also understood that they had no choice but to soldier on.

After Able Company dug in, Lieutenant Munson took a group of men to get more ammunition, especially grenades, to deal with the German machine guns. He also wanted to scout the possibility of infiltrating near the railway on the left to get to the rear of the German machine guns rather than attacking them again from the front. He warned his men to be quiet and to not answer any calls from the mountain. During the night Germans had yelled in English in efforts to get Americans to disclose their positions. They had gone on only a short while when they were hailed in English. Munson replied loudly, "Back to camp," but continued to move forward.[45]

As the detachment was crossing a small knoll, a grenade exploded at the front of the column, wounding Lieutenant Munson. He pretended to be dead as a German patrol kicked him a few times, took his submachine gun and ran back down the knoll. After a short while, Munson got up, grabbed a carbine and tried to rejoin his company. Instead, he ran into two surprised Germans who surrendered as Munson threatened them with his carbine. He finally made it with his prisoners back to an aid station where he was treated and evacuated further to the rear.[46]

Meanwhile, another Able Company detachment was trying to find Munson when they ran into machine-gun fire, followed closely by rifle fire on both flanks. The Americans hit the ground and began returning fire. Sergeant Stern, near the center of the column, stood up and called for both Able Company and the Germans to cease firing. He spoke German and told the Germans that they were surrounded. He ordered them to "Come out. We will not shoot you. If you stay where you are, American troops in your rear will surround you in a few minutes." After a short scuffle in the bushes, six German soldiers carrying their machine guns came out. Able Company recovered their wounded, placed a guard around the prisoners, and made their way back to Knox Road, where they met an infantry colonel who directed them to take up positions on the forward slope of the mountain.[47]

About 10 a.m., Charlie Company organized two patrols of volunteers to clear snipers from the mountain. Lieutenant Reardon led one group on the right, and Lieutenant Thames led another on the left. Reardon made it about a third of the way up before being pinned down by machine-gun fire. Reardon's patrol returned fire, diverting attention so Reardon could escape. Meanwhile, Lieutenant Thames spotted another machine gun about three hundred yards away, took careful aim, and fired, killing the gunner. His patrol flushed two more snipers before drawing attention from Germans at the crest.[48]

Both patrols then returned, and Goodpaster consolidated defenses at the base of the mountain. Shortly thereafter, Goodpaster was notified that his three companies would be reinforced by infantry machine-gun units and he was to launch a new attack on Mount Porchia at 4 p.m. Given the experience the previous night, Goodpaster anticipated another tough fight with German soldiers who were determined to hold the mountain.[49]

With infantry machine guns providing covering fire from below, Goodpaster had three companies attack simultaneously. Resistance was surprisingly light. A few German snipers tried to halt the advance, but were eliminated. The going got tougher near the top, but the attack continued to press forward. Some of the German soldiers surrendered. Lieutenant Reardon, on the right flank, led Charlie Company over the same ground where he had fought the previous night and reached the summit. He called down to Lieutenant Thames to bring his platoon up because that part of the crest seemed clear. Charlie Company hurried to the top, established outposts, and set up defensive positions.[50]

As Able and Baker Companies worked their way up the mountain, they were slowed by fire from a German 88. During the firing, American tankers below spotted a puff of smoke coming from a house to the left of the mountain. The tankers moved into position and fired on the house, silencing the gun and flushing out the German crew. The men of Able and Baker Companies encountered scattered rifle and mortar fire, but reached the ridge and established positions on the reverse slope. In notifying higher headquarters that the mission had been accomplished, Goodpaster was immensely proud of his men.[51]

GOODPASTER'S LUCK RUNS OUT

Goodpaster seemed to lead a charmed life in the view of his men. His various battalion command posts had been hit several times by mortar and artillery fire without resulting in his injury. Similarly, while on his frequent reconnaissance missions, he came under rifle and machine-gun fire, and he crossed unmarked minefields.

His luck ran out, however, following the second attack on Mount Porchia. Goodpaster was meeting with two other battalion commanders to coordinate their defenses just after seizing the high ground when they came under mortar fire. One of the armored infantry commanders had his helmet off while using his radio and suffered a severe head wound. It seemed unlikely that he would live. Goodpaster was wounded in the shoulder and upper arm by a shell fragment, but rendered first aid to the infantry officer and arranged for his evacuation. Goodpaster then searched for and found the next in command of the infantry battalion and, with him, organized the defenses. It was several hours before he finally made his way back for treatment. The engineers helped the armored infantry quickly organize the defensive positions with wire, foxholes and mines. For his leadership and gallantry in action during the battle, Goodpaster earned the Silver Star.[52]

The anticipated counterattack did not occur that night, although the outposts were harassed by rifle fire and mortar rounds that interrupted an otherwise quiet night. Nevertheless, the men were exhausted, wet, hungry, and numbed by the cold. They were thirsty and out of water. They resorted to drinking water from shell holes and mule tracks. Trench foot was also painful and widespread.[53]

The next morning, infantry troops brought ammunition and some K rations. Later in the afternoon the infantry made another climb to deliver fresh water and more K rations. The cold persisted, and as daylight faded, an infantry column crossed the valley, moved up the mountain, and finally relieved the engineers.[54]

As the companies reached their bivouac areas, it became apparent that they had suffered severe casualties. Some of the missing men eventually turned up. Some had been in positions with the infantry and did not get word of the relief, some had been away on medical or resupply details, and many were hospitalized. After consolidating, the 48th Engineers moved to Ceprani for forty-eight hours of much deserved rest, recuperation, and replacement of personnel and equipment. About one hundred men had been lost.[55]

For their extraordinary efforts on Mount Porchia between January 4 and January 8, 1944, the 48th Engineers earned the Presidential Unit Citation. Their collective effort was judged to be on the level for which an individual would receive the nation's second highest award for valor. The unit award is signified by a small, gold-framed, blue ribbon worn on the right breast of all 48th Engineer soldiers, commemorating this heroic battle.[56]

Soon the 48th was back to keeping Highway 48 open and extending the road up the Cassino Valley. Able Company was again tackling Obstacle 13. The road had deteriorated badly. Initial efforts to dig out the riverbanks and construct a culvert failed as the river soon washed out the embankments.

Two culverts were finally installed, but only after extensive efforts by the engineers working continuously in cold water. [57]

On January 12, Goodpaster tasked Baker Company to construct a tank bypass on Highway 6 to the right of Mount Porchia. The area was close to German positions and easily observed from nearby high ground, so the work would need to be done mostly at night. The ground was soggy, so to support tanks and heavy trucks, the engineers laid bundles of saplings crosswise and filled gravel over the top, making "corduroy" roads. They got off to a good start until about 11 p.m. when the moon rose, lighting the entire valley. Within about ten minutes, German artillery began shelling their position with increasing accuracy. Baker Company began taking casualties and pulled back from the site. Visibility was reduced the following night when they resumed work, but the shelling again interrupted their work. Finally, on the third night, they were able to complete the bypass in time for the tanks to cross to their attack positions. [58]

After withdrawing from Mount Porchia, German troops from the elite Hermann Goering Division manned defensive positions on Mount Trocchio, the last major line before Cassino. As Allied forces pressed forward slowly, the 48th Engineers prepared the way. Obstacles 13 through 17 were overcome as the railroad was transformed into Highway 48. Mines and artillery fire were constant problems, but the cold weather was also taking a heavy toll of casualties. Highly regarded First Sergeant Buckley of Able Company and his driver were killed when their jeep got caught in an artillery barrage. Shrapnel pierced his neck and he died at the aid station. The troops took up a collection and sent four hundred dollars to his wife and unborn baby. [59]

Despite the Allies having general air superiority, whenever there was a break in the weather, it seemed to be accompanied by more Luftwaffe strikes. Groups of up to twelve Messerschmitt fighters would sweep down the valleys, strafing the target-rich roads, command posts, and staging areas. The main air defense capability of the 48th was half-tracks mounted with .50 caliber machine guns. [60]

Eventually Mount Trocchio was taken, and the Germans fell back to their main defensive line, the last and most formidable part of the Gustav Line. This is where Field Marshal Kesselring chose to make his final stand before Rome. [61]

THE GUSTAV LINE

The Gustav Line consisted of a series of interlocking defenses across Italy from Gaeta to Ortona. It was an impressive piece of military engineering, among the most formidable defensive systems encountered by the British and Americans during the entire Second World War. Much of the line overlooked rivers with steep banks, in particular the Garligiano and the Rapido. Elsewhere, the line was characterized by either coastal marshland or high mountaintops. The Germans accentuated the natural defensive advantages by planting minefields and removing buildings and trees to create fields of fire. Natural caves were extended and defensive positions reinforced with railway girders, and concrete. Dugouts were created, linked by underground passages. Rather than a single line, the defenses were multilayered, with positions planned from which to launch instant counterattacks. [62]

At the center of the line stood the famous monastery of Monte Cassino, established in AD 529 by Saint Benedict. In addition to being the home of the world-renowned Benedictine Order and an irreplaceable library with priceless manuscripts and works of art, it was one of the finest defensive positions in Europe. It was built on five hundred meters of solid rock, dominating the valley. [63]

In November 1943, Hitler took a personal interest in the Gustav Line, ordering that it be upgraded to fortress strength. A system of antipersonnel mines interlocked with barbed wire entanglements was set up to cover the flatlands in front of the hills to a depth of up to four hundred yards beyond the river banks. A dam on the Rapido was blown to divert the river. The entire plain in front of Monte Cassino, already soggy from winter rain, became a quagmire. The Germans had time to survey every possible route of attack and to take countermeasures. Everywhere there were nasty surprises for the Allies—any attractive cover was mined or booby trapped. In addition, elite German troops were under do-or-die orders from their *Fuehrer*. [64]

The superiority of Allied air, tanks, and artillery was largely nullified by geography and winter weather. Defenses could be breached only by hand-to-hand fighting. In many cases, the only approaches were narrow, mountainside paths limiting troops to single file.

The Rapido River was about forty feet wide, a natural tank obstacle, situated between the Allied lines on the forward slopes of Mount Trocchio and the German defenses on the higher ground. Both sides probed each other's positions, but neither side could break through for more than a short time. Small patrols would frequently infiltrate behind the lines on both sides, but the campaign had reached a stalemate. [65]

If the Allies could get tanks across the Rapido, they would gain a major advantage, and the main task fell to the 48th Engineers. The river was only a few feet deep after the dam had been blown, but had stone revetments on either side to keep the river in its channel during times of high water. Tanks could ford the river, but were not able to negotiate the walls on either side.

Goodpaster tasked Lieutenant Munson to scout for possible fording sites near Route 6. During an early attempt to cross the river, Munson came under fire from a German machine gun and dove into the water, half swimming and half floating downstream until a bend in the river took him closer to the

American side. The next night, Munson had dynamite placed within two hundred yards of a crossing site to blast an exit in the riverbank. The following night, he brought a squad from Able Company to place charges, but as they approached the site, a flare burst overhead, and they were engaged by German machine guns on the opposite side. They tried again the next night, but when they entered the water, they were again halted by German fire. Finally, on the third night, Munson arranged for an infantry patrol to cross ahead and secure the far side, while the engineers set dynamite charges in the revetments on both sides. They moved back a safe distance, twisted the detonator and blew the walls into the river. Almost instantly, the Germans responded with everything available, from mortars to 240 mm guns. [66]

The commander of the 753rd Tank Battalion arrived soon thereafter and decided it was too dangerous to move tanks into such a narrow channel already under accurate German fire. A few nights later, the Texas National Guard 36th Infantry Division established a bridgehead but soon lost it to a German counterattack, with heavy casualties. Tanks, attempting to cross the river, quickly came under withering fire. The incoming artillery fire also blew away part of the riverbank, resulting in a much steeper bank on the German side, transforming the site into a tank trap. The four battalions on the beachhead were destroyed, suffering more than 2,100 soldiers killed, wounded, or captured. [67]

On January 23, 1944, General Clark ordered his three corps commanders to breach the Gustav Line as soon as possible and link up with the forces now contained on the Anzio beachhead. With II Corps in the center unable to cross the Rapido River with sufficient strength to gain entrance to the Liri Valley, Clark envisioned flanking attacks by X Corps in the west and the French Expeditionary Corps to the northeast. But X Corps was met with strong German counterattacks and was unable to move much beyond a small bridgehead across the Garigliano River. General Juin shifted his French forces southward and successfully attacked Monte Belvedere, about five miles north of Cassino. But his forces were now exposed, so pressure increased on II Corps to cross the Rapido, protect the French flank, and gain an opening to the Liri Valley. [68]

Major General Geoffrey Keyes, commanding II Corps, directed Major General Charles Ryder, commander of the 34th Infantry Division, to cross the Rapido and launch a two-pronged attack with one thrust along the river bank into the town of Cassino and the other directed across the mountains where the Monte Cassino Abbey was located and leading to the Liri Valley, a distance of about four miles. The 36th Division, which had largely been expended in earlier efforts to cross the Rapido, was directed to feint a renewed effort to cross the river. General Keyes gave Ryder all available corps engineers, including the 1108th Engineer Group. [69]

At the time, Lieutenant Colonel Goodpaster was acting commander of the 1108th Engineer Group while the commander was temporarily out of action. At the same time, Goodpaster remained in command of the 48th Engineers. His first tasking was critical to the Allied efforts to seize Cassino. After three failed attempts to cross the Rapido River with corduroy bridges, Major General Ryder told Goodpaster to find a way to get tanks across the river. Ryder knew Goodpaster well from West Point, where Ryder had served as commandant of cadets while Goodpaster was a cadet.[70]

By the morning of January 29, Goodpaster developed a plan to use the streambed as a road for about 1,500 yards to bring the tanks out, well positioned for an attack on the high ground northeast of Cassino. It was risky. The plan required tanks to enter the stream about 3,000 yards north of Cassino where the Germans had blown a bridge. The rubble from the demolition dammed the river, flooding the fields on both sides, making them nearly impassable to tanks and flooding the access road with a foot or more of water. The tanks would then have to follow the streambed for nearly a mile on a route that was largely exposed and probably heavily mined.[71]

To make sure the plan was feasible, Goodpaster personally conducted a nighttime reconnaissance of the route and directed a small group of engineers to prepare the entry site and remove antitank mines. While they were working, he completed his reconnaissance and on the way back ran into the lead tank, already making its way along the streambed. It was still dark when Goodpaster turned around and led the tank on foot the remainder of the way as artillery and sniper fire picked up the movement. As the lead tank moved forward, it set off antipersonnel mines just behind Goodpaster, sounding like "popcorn."[72]

The 756th Tank Battalion made the first successful tank crossing of the Rapido and, with the infantry, launched a successful attack resulting in a major penetration of the Gustav Line. For his heroic and determined efforts to get this critical job done, Lieutenant Colonel Goodpaster earned the Distinguished Service Cross, the nation's second highest award for valor.[73]

A few days later, on the evening of February 2, 1944, Goodpaster was meeting at dusk with battalion commanders of Combat Command A of the 1st Armored Division to plan an attack south of Cassino when he was badly wounded by German 88 mm gun fire. Shrapnel pierced his right shoulder. He was evacuated, and Major McCarthy took command of the 48th Engineers. While Goodpaster was being treated at the field hospital, doctors found that fragments had penetrated through his arm and lodged in his elbow. If the shrapnel had penetrated another one-eighth inch, his arm would probably have needed amputation.[74]

Major surgery and rehabilitation were required, so Goodpaster was shipped back to a hospital in North Africa and then to the United States, to

Fitzsimmons Army Hospital near Denver so that he could be treated near his family. [75]

48TH ENGINEERS OPEN THE WAY

The battle to take Cassino dragged on for months, characterized mainly by fighting hand to hand over small but critical pieces of terrain and individual buildings in the village.

While Goodpaster was being evacuated, II Corps planned another major attack to breach the Gustav Line at Cassino, this time with massive bombing that would not spare the Monte Cassino Abbey. The mission of the 48th Engineers was to provide another crossing over the Rapido River at Route 6 and to open the route through Cassino for the passage of tanks of Combat Command Baker of the 1st Armored Division. The 2nd New Zealand Division was to lead the attack on Cassino from the north, the 4th Indian Division was to seize the high ground to the east, and the British 78th Division was to conduct a demonstration to tie down German reinforcements from St. Angelo. [76]

The Allied buildup for the attack was massive, particularly with artillery. On March 14, the 48th Engineer Headquarters, along with other headquarters throughout the valley, received sealed orders that "Dickens is on tonight," confirming the attack would be launched. Early the next morning, the first thing the engineers heard was the drone of approaching aircraft. The rumble grew louder and louder until the whole valley rocked with vibration. High above the mountains, groups of thirty-six B-25 medium bombers in squadrons appeared from the south with tiny pursuit planes leaving vapor trails high above them.

Thousands of troops on the ground watched anxiously as five hundred bombers converged on the white monastery on the mountaintop. German antiaircraft batteries opened fire, their fire marked by puffs in the sky that climbed higher until a bomber took a hit. Nevertheless, the planes droned on relentlessly. The medium bombers were followed by B-17 Flying Fortresses, four-engine heavy bombers.

Suddenly the bombs were no longer falling on Cassino, they began to fall all over the valley, which was full of troops and equipment moved up for the attack. A squad from Baker Company, 48th Engineers was maintaining an aerial beacon near Venafro when the bombs began landing within 150 yards.

At 2 p.m. every Allied artillery piece in the valley opened fire, along with 8-inch naval guns, French 75s, and Italian railroad guns. Following a long barrage, the attack jumped off. The massive bombardment reduced the Monte Cassino monastery to rubble. The bombing also produced massive craters that provided additional obstacles for tanks, as well as new defensive positions for the Germans. Even when not occupied by German troops, the craters were quickly sown with anti-personnel mines that took heavy tolls on the attackers, who sought cover in the craters only to find them mined.

The attack bogged down and then settled back into a stalemate for two more months. Cassino eventually fell after the German forces were withdrawn on May 17, but only after enormous losses to both sides.

The 48th pressed on, living up to the motto "Open the Way" on its unit crest. It played key roles in the linkup with Allied forces trapped in the Anzio beachhead. It participated in the invasion of southern France, Operation AN-VIL/DRAGOON, landing on "Red Beach," the only landing opposed by German troops. It fought through France and Germany, including the liberation of the concentration camp at Dachau. While the brutality of war had forever changed the men, they found a new level of horror at Dachau, an experience they termed unbelievable. Finally, they led the 101st Airborne Division in seizing Berchtesgaden, Hitler's mountain redoubt. Among the awards earned by the men of the 48th were the Medal of Honor, four Distinguished Service Crosses and 36 Silver Stars. More than 125 were wounded and earned Purple Hearts; several like Goodpaster, were wounded multiple times.[77]

Goodpaster's combat experience taught him a lot about leadership and courage. He learned the importance of setting very high expectations for his troops. They were capable of far more than they ever thought possible when led by caring, confident commanders. Building Highway 48 under direct German fire in six days seemed impossible, probably even to Goodpaster. Yet, trusting each other to do their individual best, the team effort succeeded. In battle, Goodpaster led by example, never asking his men to do anything he wasn't willing to do. From that time on, Goodpaster's courage was never doubted. He would not be intimidated.

In chronicling such efforts, Ernie Pyle became a famous war correspondent. His dispatches from the perspective of the "dogface" soldier reached two hundred newspapers and more than four hundred weeklies in the United States. He covered the fourteen weeks of fighting between Naples and Cassino, with half of that time required to gain only the last seven miles at a cost of sixteen thousand casualties. Pyle detailed troops living in "almost inconceivable misery." He noted that the soldiers looked as though they had aged ten years, they were "exhausted in mind and in soul as well as physically." Pyle earned the Pulitzer Prize in 1944 for his reporting. In 1945, Pyle was killed in combat with the 77th Infantry Division in the Pacific.[78]

NOTES

1. Ibid., 25.
2. Ibid.

3. Ibid., 27.
4. Ibid.
5. Ibid., 28.
6. Ibid.
7. Ibid., 29.
8. Smukler, *We the 48th*, 31, 32; Billington interview.
9. Smukler, *We the 48th*, 34.
10. Ibid., 36.
11. Ibid., 36–37.
12. Ibid.
13. Ibid.
14. Ibid., 37–39.
15. Ibid., 39.
16. Ibid., 43–44.
17. Ibid., 45.
18. Ibid.
19. "Flash" messages are the most urgent priority, used only when contact with the enemy is imminent.
20. Smukler, *We the 48th*, 40.
21. Ibid.
22. Ibid., 46–48.
23. Ibid.
24. Ibid., 52.
25. Ibid., 53.
26. Ibid., 53, 66.
27. Ibid., 59–60.
28. Goodpaster, McCall interviews; Smukler, *We the 48th*, 59–62.
29. Smukler, *We the 48th*, 64–65.
30. Ibid., 66.
31. Ibid., 67.
32. Ibid., 69–70.
33. Ibid.
34. Ibid., 70.
35. Ibid., 71.
36. Ibid., 74.
37. Ibid.
38. Ibid., 75.
39. Ibid., 75, 294.
40. Ibid., 75.
41. Ibid., 76, 294.
42. Ibid., 76–78.
43. Ibid., 78.
44. Ibid.
45. Ibid.
46. Ibid., 79.
47. Ibid.
48. Ibid.
49. Ibid.
50. Ibid., 80.
51. Ibid.
52. Goodpaster, McCall interviews, 61–63; Smukler, *We the 48th*, 81; Major General Geoffrey Keyes, General Order 9, HQ II Corps, 23 January 1944, Goodpaster Papers, Marshall Library.
53. Ibid., 81.
54. Ibid.
55. Ibid., 81–82.

56. Ibid.

57. Ibid., 85–86.

58. Ibid., 86–87.

59. Ibid., 103–5.

60. Ibid., 95.

61. Goodpaster, McCall interviews, 58–59; Smukler, *We the 48th*, 87. Blumenson, *The United States Army in World War II*, 375.

62. Parker, *Monte Cassino*.

63. Ibid.

64. Ibid.; Smith, *The Battles for Cassino*, 10.

65. Smukler, *We the 48th*, 87–88.

66. Ibid., 88–90.

67. Ibid. Also, Parker, *Monte Cassino*, 61; Smith, *The Battles for Cassino*.

68. Blumenson, *The United States Army in World War II*, 366–67.

69. Ibid., 366–72.

70. *Official Register of Cadets and Officers, USMA 1938*. Goodpaster, McCall interviews.

71. Goodpaster, McCall interviews.

72. Ibid.

73. Goodpaster, McCall interviews; Mandel interviews, August 1, 2001, tape 7; and Smukler, *We the 48th*, 95, 96. Goodpaster was initially awarded a second Silver Star, later upgraded to a Distinguished Service Cross. Lt. Gen. Lee, General Order 28, HQ Mediterranean Theater of Operations, 29 January 1946.

74. Smukler, *We the 48th*, 90. Goodpaster, Veterans History Project video interview, March 18, 2004.

75. Goodpaster, McCall interviews.

76. Smukler, *We the 48th*, 108–10.

77. Ibid., 294, 265, 311.

78. Ernie Pyle, cited in Parker, *Monte Cassino*, 38, 39.

Chapter Five

Strategic Planning (1944–1947)

FITZSIMMONS ARMY HOSPITAL

In April 1944, Lieutenant Colonel Goodpaster was transferred from a hospital in North Africa to Fitzsimmons Army Hospital near Denver, where he would be located near his family. Dossy had rented a house, with Susan Erlenkotter, of another Army family from Panama. Several weeks earlier, Dossy had received an ominous Western Union telegram delivered by a very somber man. When she opened it she learned that her husband had been wounded. About a week later she got a V-mail letter from her husband telling her that he was recovering well. Then she got another telegram, followed by another V-mail letter. This time, Goodpaster had printed the letter with his left hand, so Dossy sensed the second wound must have been more serious.[1]

At Fitzsimmons Army Hospital, Goodpaster faced the challenge of either regaining the use of his arm or being discharged from active duty. After surgery and resetting the broken bones, the cast was removed, and Goodpaster found he had a range of motion of only about twenty degrees. Goodpaster was given anesthesia while nurses manipulated his arm, but progress was painfully slow.[2]

After about six months in hospitals, the doctor in charge of his ward at the hospital asked him what he would need to carry on his next assignment, given the limitations of his arm. Goodpaster replied somewhat sarcastically that it would seem to require only carrying a briefcase because he had been informed he was to be assigned to the Current Operations Group of the War Department's Operations and Plans Division (OPD). In that case, the doctor responded, "I'll discharge you. If you're here one more day, you will be retired medically."[3]

The OPD position, however, was filled just before Goodpaster was released from the hospital. Eager to return to troop duty, Goodpaster contacted Army Ground Forces and learned that he would be assigned to command an Engineer Group that was preparing to deploy to Europe.[4]

Not long after the Allied landings at Normandy on June 6, Goodpaster was released from Fitzsimmons on July 25, 1944. He received orders from the Army Adjutant General to appear before a Retirement Board, but Goodpaster disregarded them because he assumed they were superseded by the verbal orders from Army Ground Forces, who told him to check in with them by phone while en route to his Engineer command at Camp Rucker, Alabama; Ground Forces had to make one final check. On the way to Alabama, the Goodpaster family stopped to visit with their relatives in East St. Louis, where Goodpaster called Ground Forces. He was surprised to learn that his orders had been changed back to OPD.[5]

The change was because Colonel Lincoln, his mentor at West Point, overheard the conversation in which Army Ground Forces wanted to confirm that Current Operations, OPD, had released Goodpaster. Lincoln intervened and said that if Current Operations did not take Goodpaster, he wanted him in OPD's Strategy and Policy Group as one of Marshall's strategic planners.

Following his teaching assignment at West Point, Lincoln had been sent to London in 1942 as logistics advisor to the newly formed British-U.S. Combined Chiefs of Staff. Lincoln's work there was impressive, and he was called back in 1943 to join a small group of strategic planners working for General Marshall in the Strategy and Policy Group (SPG) of the War Department's Plans Division (WPD). Lincoln joined WPD while it was being restructured into the Operations and Plans Division that became known as General Marshall's "command post" for the global war.[6]

THE PENTAGON

Goodpaster reported to the Pentagon in August 1944 to become one of twelve strategic planners for General George C. Marshall. Goodpaster implored Lincoln to keep him for only a few months so he could take command of the Engineer Group in Europe, but to no avail. What was initially a big disappointment for Goodpaster turned out to be an invaluable opportunity. By this time, Marshall was the preeminent strategist among American military leaders.

In November 1944, shortly after Goodpaster's arrival, Lincoln was promoted to brigadier general, making him the youngest general on the General Staff. He also moved up from deputy to chief of the Strategy and Policy Group (SPG), replacing Brigadier General Albert C. Wedemeyer. As the head of SPG, Lincoln also became the Army's strategic planner, representing

General Marshall in the development of strategic plans and policies. According to one of the strategic planners, then-Colonel Edward Rowny, "General Marshall had absolute confidence in Abe's [Lincoln's] knowledge and judgment."[7]

In settling in at his new assignment, the Goodpasters found a house to rent on Granada Street in North Arlington, near a bus route that served the new Pentagon. During the preceding year, the War Department, along with the Navy Department, moved from the overcrowded Munitions and Main Navy buildings on the National Mall into the Pentagon, the world's largest office building.[8]

At work, Goodpaster found himself in good company. All of the planners were selected by Lincoln, put through a trial period, and approved personally by General Marshall. Nearly half, like Lincoln, were Rhodes Scholars. The group included several who would become prominent, including Dean Rusk, Charles "Tick" Bonesteel, and Edward Rowny. Not surprisingly, Lincoln also recruited Stanley Dzuiban, Goodpaster's friend and the top graduate in the West Point class of 1939. Many of the planners were also engineer officers.[9]

Throughout the War Department, there was a sense of urgency. In OPD, staff worked twelve to fourteen or more hours each day, seven days a week. Responses to messages from the field had to be completed within twenty-four hours. Paperwork that had been nearly overwhelming in the peacetime Army was reduced to a minimum.[10]

MARSHALL AS A MENTOR

By age twenty-nine, Goodpaster had mastered tactics by leading a battalion in offensive and defensive operations in combat. Now he had the opportunity to learn strategic thinking from a master, General George C. Marshall, whom Churchill would credit as the true organizer of victory in World War II. By that point, General Marshall had been the Army Chief of Staff for four years and was President Roosevelt's most trusted military advisor.[11]

General Marshall exuded self-discipline, knowledge, honesty, and frankness. He was articulate, with an amazing grasp of details. He had an obsession with brevity and clarity. Marshall understood well the pressures on busy leaders, especially the president, so he demanded that issues be presented as clearly and concisely as possible. He used special small stationery in corresponding with President Roosevelt so that memos could not exceed a half page. Goodpaster often recalled Marshall insisting that "if you can't put the gist of the issue on one page, you haven't thought it through."[12]

Marshall's military bearing gave him a commanding presence. He was the epitome of a selfless public official. He would tell the truth even if it would hurt his case, so he became especially well regarded in Congress. Marshall was exceptionally modest; he avoided publicity, as well as personal awards and honorary degrees, accepting them only when to do otherwise would reflect poorly on the United States. And, most importantly, he was trustworthy.[13]

General Marshall was also quick, tough, tireless, and decisive. He accepted responsibility, not blaming others when decisions turned out badly. Marshall also had an innate feel for what could reasonably be asked of the American people.[14]

Marshall clearly valued independent thought. As the Army expanded exponentially from a few hundred thousand to eight million troops, General Marshall could no longer rely on his personal knowledge of officers in making selections for high-level command and staff positions, so he had to determine which criteria were most important for promoting officers to the rank of general. Marshall engaged Goodpaster in this ongoing effort. After researching the problem, Goodpaster concluded that the capacity for independent thought was the key attribute for higher leadership positions. Similarly, Marshall had used the term "flexibility of mind" earlier in describing what he expected in military leaders, along with "military skill, physical stamina and strength of character."[15]

General Marshall's success was due in large part to his ability to think critically through complex problems, a capacity that he also demanded of his staff. He understood that most of the important problems facing the nation at war were complex, with no clear solutions. To help him make the difficult decisions and provide recommendations to the president, he relied on intelligent staff officers with good analytic skills who could reason through problems and provide insightful recommendations. As Goodpaster often noted, Marshall implored them to think it through. Marshall did not want a staff officer providing only a balanced assessment and a set of options for the chief to decide; he wanted staff officers to recommend the best course. With this approach, the staff officer also shared responsibility by having an important stake in the outcome of his recommendations.[16]

Marshall chose his commanders and staff carefully. He kept track of those officers whom he judged best qualified to serve in positions of high responsibility. For his staff, he wanted people with good ideas. As he put it:

> I don't like to keep any man on the job so long that his ideas and forethoughts go no further than mine. . . . When I find an officer isn't fresh, he doesn't add much to my fund of knowledge and worst of all, doesn't contribute to the ideas and enterprising push that are so essential to winning the war . . . [they should be replaced].[17]

Given the enormous scope of his job, General Marshall had to delegate authority. In doing so, he empowered subordinates by giving them his full support and not micromanaging them. Nevertheless, he also wanted to be fully informed, so his staff had to know the positions of the theater commanders and the other services. When faced with a difficult issue, Marshall would ask his staff frequently, "What does Eisenhower (or MacArthur) think about this?"[18]

Marshall did not dictate answers to problems. Instead, he put subordinate commanders or his staff to work on a problem. Once this produced a recommended option, it would then be discussed and critiqued in an objective manner based on the merits of the issue. Of course, General Marshall had the final word.[19]

General Marshall also organized his staff so that the functions of policies and resulting plans were separated from operations. Especially in wartime, the short-term demands of operations can easily overwhelm longer-term strategic thinking. By separating these responsibilities, Marshall was able to maintain a focus on the endgame of winning the war and especially the subsequent peace, another key lesson Goodpaster took to heart.

THE AMERICAN WAY OF WAR

Over the next three years, Goodpaster learned the different ways in which Marshall and the other leading Allied political and military leaders thought about war. No doubt the extent and persistence of these differences surprised Goodpaster, at least initially. When one is on the battlefield as a small part of large international formations, one assumes, or at least hopes, that those at the top leading the effort have agreed on a brilliant grand strategy. This, however, did not seem to be the case. Disagreement among the Allies and between them and the American military services was a regular feature of the strategic debate.

Between World War I and World War II, American Army leaders studied war and, for the most, part concluded that victory resulted mainly from defeating the enemy's armed forces and not from occupying territory.[20] They were also aware of the impact of technology on the ways in which wars were fought. Air power was increasingly important, and sea power was vital in controlling the oceans, especially the lifelines for Britain and Japan.

A major influence on the thinking of both Marshall and Eisenhower, and thus Goodpaster, was Major General Fox Conner—a leading Army strategic thinker during the 1920s and 1930s. During World War I, Conner served as General Pershing's operations officer (G-3) for the American Expeditionary Force. Lieutenant Colonel George C. Marshall worked under Conner, who regarded Marshall as an ideal soldier and a military genius. Conner developed a similarly high regard for Eisenhower after meeting him at the Infantry Tank School in 1919 and later arranged for Eisenhower to join him for three years in Panama serving with the 20th Infantry Brigade. More importantly, Conner tutored Eisenhower in military history, strategy, and international affairs. Conner had Eisenhower read from his extensive book collection, then engaged him with probing questions that honed Eisenhower's critical-thinking skills.[21]

Early on, Conner saw the likelihood of another war with Germany and the imperative of fighting in a coalition under a unified command. Conner also stressed that the need to mobilize a large, conscripted army within a democratic political context that included an ever-present political opposition would necessitate terminating a war as soon as possible. Democracies, he thought, have great difficulty sustaining political will when faced with high casualties. His teachings have been summarized as:

- Never fight unless you have to;
- Never fight alone; and
- Never fight for long.[22]

For Goodpaster, these lessons and the related fundamental debates over prosecuting the war were part of his daily operating environment. Experience, more than textbooks, framed his subsequent views on these critical subjects.

At this point, Goodpaster's supervisor, Brigadier General Lincoln, as the Army planner, represented the Army on all important joint and combined matters. In such a role, Lincoln and his small staff had to know General Marshall's thoughts and intentions on all of the key issues. This relationship put Goodpaster in regular contact with General Marshall and Secretary of War Henry Stimson.[23]

DEALING WITH DIFFICULT ALLIES: THE BALKANS CASE

One of Goodpaster's first tasks in the Strategy and Policy Group exposed him to a central problem of coalition warfare: how to deal with difficult Allies. From the earliest days of the war, there were fundamental differences about strategy between the Americans and British.

This problem came up again after Rome finally fell in June 1944. In September, Goodpaster was tasked to evaluate and prepare a response to a British proposal for light operations involving three landings along the Adriatic coast of Yugoslavia. Churchill was keen on the idea of launching operations in the Balkans to cut off a major source of oil for Germany and gain control of the area before the Soviets could do so. Marshall and the other

American Joint Chiefs opposed the idea because it would detract from the main effort, the cross-Channel invasion. [24]

Goodpaster, in his analysis, noted that Allied invasions in Italy, with similar terrain, had been very difficult to support and sustain. More importantly, with steep banks along the coast and other terrain advantages favoring the enemy, progress would likely be very slow. Similar operations in Sicily and Italy, once undertaken, had to be supported with huge commitments of resources; they were not light operations. Furthermore, they would likely drain resources from the cross-Channel invasion.

Goodpaster's draft response made a strong case in opposition to the British proposal and was consistent with the views of the other U.S. services, but Lincoln found Goodpaster's style "florid" and inappropriate. Lincoln advised Goodpaster that General Marshall did not want to "mock" Mr. Churchill. Goodpaster revised the paper accordingly and, in the process, learned how to craft more diplomatic responses. [25]

COORDINATING STRATEGIC PLANNING

As noted, General Marshall thought beyond the immediate challenges of winning the war to the longer-term problem of winning the peace. He and other leaders were painfully aware of how the seeds of World War II had been sown by the failure to conclude World War I with a sustainable peace. Thus, early in the war, Marshall began planning for the postwar challenges. In 1941, he established the Army's School of Military Government in Charlottesville, Virginia, and in 1943, the Civil Affairs Division within the War Department to prepare for the military government of occupied enemy territories. [26]

Marshall also had his staff plan for the ending of the war and its immediate aftermath. Much of the task fell to the SPG planners. As a result, Goodpaster became engaged in planning for postwar Europe, and General Lincoln tasked Goodpaster to outline a plan for the redeployment of U.S. forces from Europe to the Pacific for the final operations against Japan. Goodpaster worked with the troop control staff to develop the planning guidance for the transfer of forces that was approved by the Joint Chiefs of Staff (JCS). [27]

In the process of developing the planning guidance, Goodpaster noted that there were no plans for the sudden collapse or surrender of Japan, unlike the planning for the fall of Germany. For example, Plan RANKIN addressed actions to be undertaken in the event of such developments in Germany. [28]

Goodpaster suggested that Lincoln raise the issue with Marshall, and, if such planning had not been undertaken, then Marshall should propose to MacArthur that such a plan be prepared. After checking, Goodpaster was correct; there were no plans for the sudden collapse of Japan. In fact, MacArthur had initiated planning for the invasion and occupation of Japan, but limited the planning to only a small group in his headquarters. MacArthur was concerned that word would leak out that postwar planning was underway, and that would undermine combat operations because troops might be less willing to sacrifice if they thought the war was about to end.[29]

Marshall directed Goodpaster and a small group of planners to leave immediately for the Philippines, ostensibly to resolve some issues on base locations for units redeployed from Europe. Goodpaster was also tasked to coordinate with MacArthur's staff planning for the sudden collapse or surrender of Japan. The group left within twenty-four hours, but not before each person was given a series of seven vaccinations.[30]

Goodpaster found that MacArthur's staff had developed a plan, "BLACKLIST," that essentially converted the troop list for the invasion into an occupation force with much-reduced logistical requirements, assuming a cessation in hostilities. The plan also called for establishing a military government under MacArthur's headquarters.[31]

MacArthur, however, had not yet approved the plan, so it was still in draft form, and his staff would not provide a copy for Goodpaster to take back to Washington. Goodpaster, however, took very detailed notes. When Goodpaster returned to Washington after two weeks, Lincoln was with General Marshall and President Truman in Potsdam, just outside of Berlin, for a conference with the British and Soviet leaders to work out the postwar details following Germany's unconditional surrender on May 8, 1945. Goodpaster cabled Lincoln a summary of the planning for Japan, along with his critique of the main shortcomings of the planning.[32]

Just as the conference was beginning, President Truman, along with Marshall and Lincoln, was informed of the successful test of the atomic bomb on July 16 in New Mexico. Lincoln was already aware of plans to use the bomb soon and realized that this could lead to the sudden collapse of Japan, so he instructed Goodpaster to develop a viable occupation plan, based on his understanding of BLACKLIST, but with appropriate changes.[33]

The Potsdam Conference ran from July 17 to August 2 and dealt with the occupation of Germany, the reversion of German occupied territories such as Poland, war reparations for the Soviet Union, Nazi war criminals, and other issues. On July 21, Truman discussed the atomic bomb with Churchill, who concurred in its use against Japan. To keep the façade of Allied unity, on July 25, Truman also advised Stalin of the development of the new weapon of unusual destructive force. Stalin did not appear particularly interested, probably because he was already well informed on the atomic bomb by his intelligence service. On July 26, the leaders issued the Potsdam Declaration, an ultimatum broadcast to Japan, threatening total destruction if Japan did not agree to unconditional surrender immediately.

Previously, Colonel Bonesteel in SPG was working on ways to facilitate Japanese surrender. Allied policy called for the unconditional surrender of both Germany and Japan. However, Bonesteel argued that retaining the position of Emperor Hirohito could be useful in gaining compliance of the population during occupation. Although this position met with strong opposition initially, eventually it was accepted in the final plans.[34]

In the meantime, planning for the invasion was well underway at MacArthur's headquarters and OPD. Goodpaster and the other planners looked at alternatives, including invading Formosa, but concluded that such an operation would be too costly and not decisive. Similarly, Goodpaster and the SPG staff considered invading Japan through Hokkaido, but the terrain was very difficult, especially in winter. They also analyzed Navy proposals to conduct operations in the Yellow Sea to establish a complete blockade of Japan. The Joint Chiefs and President Truman agreed and approved plans and preparations to invade Okinawa, Kyushu, and Honshu.[35]

These plans called for two operations under the overall plan, called Operation DOWNFALL. The first, Operation OLYMPIC, involved 14 divisions landing on Kyushu, supported by the largest naval armada ever assembled, including 42 aircraft carriers, 24 battleships, and 400 destroyers and destroyer escorts. The OLYMPIC invasion was scheduled for November 1, 1945.[36]

The second invasion, Operation CORONET, called for an additional 25 divisions (the Normandy invasion involved 12 divisions in the initial landing) and was targeted on the Honshu beaches southwest of Tokyo. Most of these troops would be redeployed from Europe, according to Goodpaster's planning guidance.

The Japanese anticipated invasion plans very well. Very few beaches were suitable for large-scale landings, and most of these were found on Kyushu and Honshu, where Japanese defense plans focused. Japan redeployed four divisions from Manchuria and formed 45 new divisions between February and May 1945. More than 2 million troops were prepared to defend the Japanese home islands along with a civilian militia of about 28 million. The Imperial Japanese Navy staff estimated that up to 20 million Japanese would die as a result of an invasion.[37]

The U.S. Joint War Plans Coordinating Committee (JWPCC) in June 1945 estimated that U.S. casualties in an invasion of Japan would run between 130,000 and 220,000, with 25,000 to 46,000 killed. Secretary of War Stimson wanted an independent estimate and asked Quincy Wright and William Shockley to lead the analysis. They concluded that total Allied casualties would probably be in the range of 1.7 million to 4 million, with between 400,000 and 800,000 killed. They estimated Japanese casualties would probably be between 5 million and 10 million. Goodpaster recalled estimates that Japan would suffer about ten times the number of Allied losses.[38]

In August, Goodpaster was appointed to the JWPCC. Based on his familiarity with BLACKLIST, Goodpaster was assigned to the White Team during the final preparations of the plan for the occupation of Japan. The plan called for the Soviet occupation of the northern islands, including the northern part of Honshu, with the United States occupying the remainder of Honshu, the British occupying Kyushu, and the Chinese Shikoku. The plan was forwarded quickly to the State, War, Navy Coordinating Committee and also sent to the theater commander for comment before final approval by the Joint Chiefs. MacArthur objected strongly to the division of Japan.[39]

On August 6, 1945, a bomber from the 509th Composite Group, organized and trained under General Leslie Groves's Manhattan Project, dropped a "Little Boy" atomic bomb on Hiroshima. On August 9, another bomber delivered a different type of atomic bomb, a "Fat Man," on Nagasaki. Japan surrendered unconditionally on August 15.[40]

During his assignment to the JWPCC after the war, Goodpaster was also involved in developing the first war plans that incorporated the use of nuclear weapons. The challenge for planners was to develop the strategic concept for initial operations in the event of war with the Soviet Union, assuming hostilities might occur at any time in the next three years with not more than three months advance notice. Estimates credited the Soviets with the capability to overrun most, if not all, of Western Europe in a short time. Soviet ground forces could reach a total of 8.5 million troops.[41]

The JWPCC response was the PINCHER series of war plans that focused on the strategic advantages in atomic weapons and strategic airpower to destroy Soviet war-making capabilities. The delivery of atomic weapons by bombers required an extensive network of bases from which to launch, recover, and support these plans. Goodpaster's previous work on the postwar military force posture and base requirements helped in developing PINCHER plans.[42]

POSTWAR MILITARY FORCE POSTURE

In the final months of the war, Goodpaster was also involved in studies of postwar requirements for the Army worldwide, including the size, composition, and disposition of forces. These studies had to estimate how many and what types of forces, supporting logistics and base infrastructure were needed for the occupation period and beyond. By this time, it was clear that the Soviet Union was likely to be part of the problem, even though it was still an important ally. As part of this analysis, judgments were made about the importance of colonial territories, including those of the United States in the Philippines, where there was growing domestic opposition to reestablishment of colonial control.[43]

Part of this strategic thinking about postwar military requirements also had to include forces to be made available for the United Nations. Although it was not officially formed until October 24, 1945, planning for the UN was already well advanced. Much consideration was being given to eliminating weaknesses of the League of Nations and building upon the 1942 Atlantic Charter. Given the total military forces already existing at the time, the requirements for a UN force were enormous, even for the postwar period. Prudent planners were calling for one hundred or more divisions, fifty or more aircraft carriers and battleships, and commensurate numbers of bombers and fighters.[44]

In the midst of this rapidly changing environment, on April 12, 1945, President Roosevelt died suddenly, and the mantle of leadership fell on the shoulders of Harry Truman. A few weeks later, in early May, President Truman was visited by Philippine president Sergio Osmeña, who wanted to reaffirm the U.S. promise made in 1934 to grant independence to the Philippines on July 4, 1946. Although he was not opposed to Philippine independence, Truman also knew that the use of military bases there would continue to be important for the United States, so he told Secretary of War Stimson to come up with a solution by the next day.[45]

Stimson called in Lincoln, who brought Goodpaster because of his work on the postwar force posture and basing requirements, as well as another SPG planner, Phil Greasley, who was familiar with Air Corps requirements. The issue was familiar to Stimson, who had served as governor general of the Philippines. At the meeting, Stimson told them he wanted a short statement supporting Philippine independence for both presidents to sign. Stimson also added that General Marshall disagreed and favored a detailed list of base requirements. Stimson closed by instructing them to go talk to General Marshall, whose office was next door.[46]

General Marshall was expecting them and said, "I know what Mr. Stimson told you, but I have to tell you that unless we have this in specific detail, it's liable to prove worthless." Like Stimson, Marshall was familiar with the Philippines, having made his initial reputation there as a captain during the Philippine insurrection in the early 1900s, when his commanding general said, "I would be happy to serve under this officer in any grade."

At that point, Mr. Stimson came through the door between their two offices. This door was never closed because of his and Marshall's close working and personal relationship; they had great respect for each other. Stimson reviewed their two positions, emphasizing that he would not present a long list of things for the presidents to sign. Marshall reiterated that a general statement of principles would not suffice. Then General Marshall concluded the meeting with a kind of frosty twinkle in his eye, saying to the staffers, "Well, I think we've given you all the help we can, it's time for you to go to work."[47]

Lincoln, Goodpaster, and Greasley worked all night and produced three papers: one a short statement along the lines Stimson suggested, one a detailed statement of the type favored by Marshall, and a third combination with a short statement accompanied by a detailed appendix. Stimson and Marshall agreed on the third version. Although Marshall wanted the two presidents to sign both the statement and the appendix, Stimson overruled him. That morning, Truman and Osmeña signed the agreement reaffirming Philippine independence and allowing continued U.S. access to bases.[48]

VJ DAY, AUGUST 15, 1945

Goodpaster did not know about the atomic bomb until after it had been dropped on Hiroshima on August 6. The war ended on August 15, 1945, but the tremendous joy that Goodpaster felt was short-lived because the immediate aftermath posed a series of new and urgent problems. Demobilization of an Army that had grown to eight million became a problem, with constant congressional pressure. At the same time, the need for occupation forces to provide security and aid in Europe and Japan was enormous. People were starving, homes were destroyed, economies were in shambles, and much of the basic infrastructure had been destroyed. Security was fragile or nonexistent in many cases. Law and order were absent as individuals and groups fought to determine who would rule. Governments in Germany, Japan, and elsewhere were not functioning well.

In short order, the strategic environment changed dramatically. Nuclear weapons had apparently changed the nature of war. Other advances in military technologies, including jet aircraft, missiles, and radar, were progressing rapidly, but with high investment costs. While fascism in Germany and Italy, along with militarism in Japan, were defeated and thoroughly discredited, communism was on the march and found fertile ground in several of the devastated economies in Europe, such as Greece and Italy, along with the overseas colonies of Britain, France, and the Netherlands.

As this strategic environment became more complex, the unity of effort that resulted from the focus on defeating the Axis forces was lost. As a result, the challenge of determining priorities and allocating resources became more difficult. Wartime cooperation that helped balance Army-Navy relations was replaced by the more usual inter-service rivalry and competition over roles, missions, and declining budgets.

LIEUTENANT COLONEL GOODPASTER MEETS GENERAL EISENHOWER

Soon after General Marshall's retirement on November 18, 1945, President Truman asked him to lead a mission to China to broker a settlement between the Nationalists, led by Generalissimo Chiang Kai-shek, and the Communists, led by Mao Tse-tung.

On November 19, 1945 General Eisenhower became the chief of staff of the Army. Eisenhower immediately came under pressure to reduce the size of the Army rapidly. He was surprised by the political influence that groups could bring to bear to demobilize the Army in ways that would damage its effectiveness for a long time.[49]

In early 1946, Lieutenant Colonel Goodpaster met General Eisenhower for the first time. The occasion was the awarding of the Distinguished Service Cross (DSC) to Goodpaster for his role in the crossing of the Rapido River in the battle of Monte Cassino. Eisenhower's policy was to award a DSC or Medal of Honor personally whenever possible. Accordingly, Goodpaster, Dossy, and daughter Susan met in Eisenhower's Pentagon office where Pete Carroll, Eisenhower's assistant, read the citation.

Goodpaster was struck with Eisenhower's magnetic quality. Eisenhower was very impressive; he lived up to his reputation, in Goodpaster's eyes. These first impressions were reinforced by additional meetings over the next two years.

ADVANCED STUDY GROUP AND THE DREAM SESSIONS

Lieutenant Colonel Goodpaster met again with General Eisenhower the following year in conjunction with establishing an advanced study group. The idea grew out of Eisenhower's concern that the War Department was not devoting sufficient effort to anticipating future problems, especially those related to nuclear weapons. Dr. James Conant, president of Harvard University, in a lecture at the National War College in late 1946, suggested that the armed forces would benefit from a study of strategic problems likely to arise at the dawn of the atomic age.[50]

Conant had been retained by President Truman to continue to study the implications of atomic weapons. His lecture, entitled "The Atomic Age," would frame much of Goodpaster's strategic thinking over the next several decades.[51]

Conant noted that in addition to planning to support efforts by Bernard Baruch and others working toward international control of atomic weapons, serious planning should begin at once to deal with the threat of a surprise, devastating attack on cities and industries, the likes of which had never been contemplated seriously. Given such a threat, Conant suggested that planning focus on four interrelated issues: information about timelines for Russia's developing such capabilities, dispersion of U.S. assets, retaliation that might prevent such an attack, and survival.

Conant also raised the issue of whether the United States should face such a threat alone or as part of a limited international scheme. He noted that the latter arrangement had several problems: (1) a loss of freedom of action, (2) atomic weapons possibly falling into the wrong hands, (3) difficult command and control arrangements, (4) a system of two alliances that might make war inevitable, (5) loss of secrecy.

The advantages of an international scheme, however, were greater in Conant's thinking. An alliance provided a much greater and more dispersed targeting challenge for Russia, thus substantially increasing requirements for a successful attack. An alliance also provided globally dispersed opportunities to launch retaliatory strikes, making it impossible for Russia to destroy in a first strike. Conant cautioned that if such an alliance were formed, the door should always be held open for Russia to join in ways to reduce the chances of war.

Eisenhower was sympathetic to Conant's idea and tasked Major General Lauris Norstad, director of the Plans and Operations Division that succeeded OPD, to form a study group. Norstad, at Lincoln's suggestion, tapped Lieutenant Colonel Goodpaster and Lieutenant Colonel Don Zimmerman to organize the group. On January 22, 1947, the Advanced Study Group (ASG) was formed with Goodpaster in charge. Eisenhower's guidance was that they "evolve concepts of national security in light of advancements of the atomic age." The group was officially chartered on May 1 and authorized to consult with anyone and not be subject to tasking by other elements of the Army. [52]

In April 1947, Eisenhower met with the Advanced Study Group and told them that they had full autonomy in choosing subjects, methods, and approaches. They were to avoid subjects with which he was already engaged and should not deal with current affairs or training. He encouraged them to bring concepts to him any time. He wanted them to become highly regarded experts on future war to the extent that they would be invited to speak at universities. They were to study economics, international relations, and history and communicate regularly with scholars at the top universities. This meeting gave Goodpaster his first exposure to Eisenhower's style and thinking; he was impressed.

By this point, Goodpaster had already been in touch with leading strategic thinkers, such as Harold Sprout and Edward Earle at Princeton, Bernard Brodie at Yale, Grayson Kirk at Columbia, and James Conant at Harvard. Nearly all offered to help and consult with the ASG and arrange for their introduction to other scholars. [53]

Part of the ASG efforts became known as "Dream Sessions" led by General Lauris Norstad. They involved Goodpaster and other members of the Strategy and Policy Group of OPD plus invited guests. They met in the OPD Conference Room in the Pentagon each Wednesday afternoon. The meetings would often last until midnight.[54]

The purpose of the sessions was to think about twenty-five years into the future. Each person submitted a topic for discussion, and Norstad would select one for scheduling. If your topic was not selected, you had to give a short talk on why it was important and should be addressed in subsequent sessions.

Depending on the topic, guests were invited to attend. These included many who later became famous, such as Herman Kahn (early RAND strategic thinker, author of *On Thermonuclear War*); Captain Hyman Rickover (father of the nuclear-power Navy); and Captain Rayburn (originator of the idea of placing ballistic missiles on submarines). Other topics included ablative coating on reentry vehicles that eventually led to ballistic missiles and manned space flight; and the possibility of landing a man on the moon. The group often discussed long-term efforts to contain the Soviet Union, especially Kennan's ideas of containment.

MARSHALL PLAN

While assigned to the Advanced Study Group, Goodpaster also joined Lincoln on a special study group of the State, War, Navy Coordinating Committee (SWNCC) to consider what could be done to assist the slow recovery of war-torn nations, tasked by Marshall soon after he was sworn in as Secretary of State on January 21, 1947.

Goodpaster joined Charles Bohlen and George Kennan from the State Department in the study. Lincoln and Goodpaster initially favored a global approach to the recovery problem, but Kennan and Bohlen argued for dealing with Europe first because the problems were probably more manageable there and especially if European leaders played a major role in the program because they were thought to be in a much better position to understand the needs and priorities.[55]

The Special Study Group completed work on the program for European recovery, outlined in a speech by Secretary Marshall on June 5, 1947, at Harvard's graduation exercise. The program became known as the Marshall Plan and quickly gained broad support at home and abroad. Given Marshall's continued popularity in Congress, it eventually received critical financial support.

NEXT ASSIGNMENT

Goodpaster was highly regarded in OPD. For three years, his officer efficiency reports, prepared by Brigadier General Lincoln, were outstanding. Lincoln noted, for example, that Goodpaster was "extremely intelligent, thoughtful . . . experienced and capable in strategic and logistical planning of a joint and combined nature." He "has extraordinary ability to analyze quickly the most intricate and controversial problems and develop workable, simple and acceptable solutions. He is particularly experienced at working out joint matters . . . and in dealing with the State Department requiring the integration of political and military thought." Major General Norstad endorsed the reports, adding that "based on almost daily contact over a period of more than a year, he is the most outstanding officer I have known in his age and rank group." While working on the Joint Advanced Study Committee, Goodpaster was rated by a Navy captain, who noted that Goodpaster was "a sharp and decisive thinker . . . [and] also quite tolerant of views other than his own, particularly those of personnel of the other services." [56]

As Goodpaster was nearing completion of his three-year tour in the Pentagon, he began thinking about his next assignment. At this stage in the career of an engineer officer, graduate school was among the possibilities. Similar ideas occurred to General Lincoln, but with the view of a broader education than engineering. Lincoln wanted his cadre of bright young SPG officers, now with unique experience in strategic planning, to round out their education with the study of economics, government, and international affairs at the best universities. Lincoln wanted to create a group of soldier-scholars with the education and experience to deal effectively with the most intelligent and powerful people in the world. [57]

As a result of his work with the Advanced Study Group, Goodpaster was already familiar with senior scholars at Princeton, Yale, and Columbia. Lincoln forwarded some of Goodpaster's correspondence with these scholars to General Norstad, seeking his endorsement to send Goodpaster, Rowny, and Dzuiban to these schools for graduate schooling. Norstad gave a strong endorsement to the proposal, noting that this would provide valuable benefits to the War Department in the future by preparing such officers to serve at the highest levels. [58]

The director of Army personnel, Major General Paul, disapproved the request, implying that such efforts seemed to be self-serving. Norstad did not accept Paul's decision as final, and raised the issue with General Eisenhower, the chief of staff, noting that Goodpaster was one of the most outstanding officers in his grade in the Army and suggesting that he be earmarked for further development. Eisenhower concurred with Norstad, and Goodpaster was put on orders to Princeton University. Soon thereafter, Rowny was sent to Yale, and Dzuiban to Columbia. They became the first generation of soldier-scholars and charter members of the Lincoln Brigade. [59]

In this time frame, Brigadier General Lincoln turned down a promotion to major general and took a reduction in rank to colonel in order to return to West Point and head the Department of Social Sciences.

NOTES

1. Susan Goodpaster Sullivan, interview with author, June 27, 2010. Goodpaster, Mandel interviews, August 1, 2001, tape 7.

2. Ibid.

3. Susan Goodpaster Sullivan, correspondence with author, July 30, 2012.

4. Goodpaster, Billington interview.

5. Goodpaster, Johnson and Ferguson interview, January 9, 1976.

6. Deagle, "Book Plan." General George A. Lincoln, Architect of American National Security," (unpublished) October 2010.

7. Deagle, "Book Plan," chapters 7, 13; Rowny, interview with author, May 3, 2013.

8. Susan Goodpaster Sullivan, interview with author, March 2010.

9. Goodpaster, Mandel interviews.

10. Goodpaster, Johnson and Ferguson interview, January 29, 1976.

11. Perry, *Partners in Command*, 20, 29; Pogue, *George C. Marshall: Organizer of Victory 1943–1945*, 525.

12. Goodpaster, Mandel interviews, January 15, 2002, tapes 7 and 8. Also see Larry Bland, notes on George C. Marshall's behavior and values, *The Papers of George C. Marshall*.

13. Stoler, *George C. Marshall*, 77, 86, 111.

14. Ibid., 103–4; Goodpaster, Mandel interviews, January 15, 2002, tape 8.

15. Goodpaster, conversations with the author, 1995. Creel interview of Marshall, October 14, 1942, in Bland, *The Papers of George Catlett Marshall, Vol. 4,* 172, 173n4.

16. Goodpaster, Mandel interviews, January 15, 2002, tapes 8 and 9; Perry, *Partners in Command*, 19.

17. Pogue, *George C. Marshall: Organizer of Victory 1943–1945*, 525; Pogue, *George C. Marshall, Ordeal and Hope*, 324.

18. Goodpaster, Mandel interviews, January 15, 2002, tape 8.

19. Goodpaster, Mandel interviews, January 15, 2002, tapes 8 and 9.

20. Ibid.

21. D'Este, *Eisenhower*, 160–69. Goodpaster, McCall interviews.

22. Ibid.

23. Mandell interviews. Stimson, at age seventy-three, was called upon by President Roosevelt to become the secretary of war just days before the Pearl Harbor attack. He was a prominent Republican who was a veteran of World War I and who had previously served as secretary of war, secretary of state and governor of the Philippines.

24. See Bland, *George Catlett Marshall Papers, Vol. 4*, 85–88, 189–92.

25. Goodpaster, Mandel interviews, January 15, 2002, tape 9.

26. Pogue, *George C. Marshall: Organizer of Victory*, 455.

27. Goodpaster, Mandel interviews, January 15, 2002, tape 9. Also see Stephen Ambrose, "The Bomb: It Was Death or More Death," *New York Times*, August 5, 1995, 19, on Goodpaster's role.

28. Plan RANKIN addressed three cases of sudden changes in the German position. See Pogue, *U.S. Army in World War II, European Theater of Operations, The Supreme Command*, 106.

29. Goodpaster, Mandel interviews, February 11, 2002, tape 9.

30. Ibid.

31. Ibid.

32. See Bland, *George Catlett Marshall Papers, Vol. 5*, 244. Indeed, the "sudden collapse" scenario had just played out in Europe. On April 25, Mussolini had been captured and killed by partisans in northern Italy, Hitler committed suicide on April 30 as the battle of Berlin raged, German forces in Italy surrendered on May 1, German forces in Berlin surrendered to the Soviets on May 2, and German forces agreed to an unconditional surrender at General Eisenhower's headquarters early in the morning of May 7, with the cessation of operations and official surrender in Berlin on May 8, 1945.

33. Goodpaster, Mandel interviews, February 11, 2002, tape 9. Also Bland, *George Catlett Marshall Papers, Vol. 5*, 244, 246–47.

34. Ibid.

35. Goodpaster, Mandel interviews, January 15, 2002, tape 9.

36. Pogue, *U.S. Army in WWII, Strategic Planning for Coalition Warfare*, 480–89, 535–38; *U.S. Army in WWII, Global Logistics and Strategy, 1943–1945*, 577–88. Also see Skates, *The Invasion of Japan*, 160.

37. Skates, *The Invasion of Japan*, 102; Frank, *DOWNFALL: The End of the Imperial Japanese Empire*, 1999, 176, 203, 211.

38. Goodpaster, Mandel interviews, January 15, 2002, tape 8; Frank, *DOWNFALL*, 135–37, 140–41. 340.

39. Goodpaster, Mandel interviews, January 15, 2002, tape 9.

40. The "Little Boy" was a gun-type of fission device using Uranium-235; the "Fat Boy" was an implosion-type device using Plutonium 239, similar to the device first tested on July 16, 1945.

41. Schnable, *History of the JCS 1945–1947*, 74; Cline, *Washington Command Post*, 350–51; PINCHER series war plans, Record Group 165, ABC 381, USSR (3/2/46), Sec. 1-B, National Archives.

42. Ibid.

43. See, for example, February 13, 1947, Goodpaster memo of briefing Eisenhower on mobilization requirements in event of war with the Soviet Union,Record Group 165, ABC file, box 60, Sec. 6-C, National Archives.

44. Eric Grove, "UN Armed Forces and the Military Staff Committee," *International Security* 17, no. 4 (1993).

45. Goodpaster, Mandel interviews, January 15, 2002, tape 8; also Billington interview.

46. Ibid.

47. Ibid.

48. Ibid.

49. Goodpaster, Mandel interviews, January 15, 2002, tape 9.

50. James B. Conant, "The Atomic Age," lecture at the National War College, September 16, 1946, NDU Library Special Collections.

51. Ibid.

52. Memorandum no. 10-15-1, War Department, Washington, DC, 1 May 1947, Subject: Advanced Study Group, Plans and Operations Division, War Department General Staff, Goodpaster Papers, box 11, file 8, Marshall Library; also Goodpaster, Mandel interviews, January 15, 2002, tape 9.

53. Notes on Conference with General Eisenhower April 25, 1947, FF 4/10, War Department, Official Memorandums, April 7, 1947–August 7, 1947, Goodpaster Papers, 230, NDU Library.

54. Rowny, interview by the author, Washington, DC. Rowny was a member of the group.

55. Goodpaster, Mandel interviews, January 15, 2002, tapes 8 and 9.

56. Lincoln in Army Officer Efficiency Reports on Goodpaster, December 31, 1945 and June 30, 1947, Goodpaster Papers, box 54, files 1–18, Marshall Library.

57. Ibid., tape 10.

58. Ibid.

59. Ibid.

Chapter Six

First Generation Soldier-Scholars (1947–1950)

The next three years at Princeton provided Goodpaster with opportunities to study and learn from some of the best minds in academia. During the war, many of the most noted American scholars and scientists worked closely with the military establishment as part of the national war effort. Top faculty members at Princeton, Harvard, Yale, and other universities were involved, and many continued afterward to take an interest in national security affairs. When Goodpaster arrived at Princeton, he was no stranger to several faculty members.

MOVING TO PRINCETON

Rental properties were scarce and expensive in Princeton, so the Goodpasters decided to take a risk and buy a house. Of course, this also put them in debt, but the mortgage payments seemed manageable, and they were hopeful that they would build equity in their investment. Goodpaster, ever the engineer, loved to build things so he added a screened-in porch on the back of the house. In the process, he found that most of the walls of the basic house were not plumb, a result of "shoddy postwar construction."[1]

The small but comfortable Goodpaster house in Princeton provided a welcome environment for visits from other family members. For six-year-old Susan, it was great to have all four grandparents visit. She recalled sitting on the lap of her great-grandfather, Colonel George H. Morgan, while he told stories of the Indian Wars in which he earned the Medal of Honor.[2]

On Thanksgiving Day, November 25, 1948, Anne, the second Goodpaster daughter, was born. Although Dossy missed the family turkey dinner, she was thankful that this time her husband was home, and her Aunt Edith came to help with the cooking, housekeeping, and children.[3]

GRADUATE EDUCATION AND ACADEMIC MENTORS

The conflicting views about graduate-level education between the Engineer Branch and General Lincoln resulted in a fortuitous compromise that enabled Goodpaster to study for a master's degree in both engineering and international relations. He took a double load of classes and completed the requirements for both master's degrees in two years.

Civil engineering was Goodpaster's passion, dating back to his childhood fascination with bridges and dams along the Mississippi River and his strong aptitude for math. West Point's engineering curriculum also prepared him well for graduate studies.

At Princeton, Goodpaster's civil engineering studies focused on materials, particularly soils. The Department of Civil Engineering admitted relatively few students for graduate studies in order to maintain a low student-faculty ratio. He studied the physics and chemistry of minerals and materials, measuring and modeling the stability of soils and other materials, theoretical thermodynamics and fluid flow, as well as practical engineering problems.

Goodpaster's study of international relations at Princeton was guided by Professor Harold Sprout and Dr. Edward Mead Earle, both of whom knew Goodpaster from their time advising senior defense officials during the war. Professor Sprout, a distinguished scholar at Princeton since 1931, was a leader in the paradigm shift in the study of international relations from idealism to realism. Sprout, with his wife Margaret, continuously broadened thinking about international relations to include important linkages between the many complex factors and several academic disciplines that influence human decisions in the realm of international politics.[4]

Harold Sprout's focus was particularly appealing to Goodpaster. In their landmark 1945 textbook, *Foundations of National Power,* written during the closing days of World War II and published just after the atomic bombs had been dropped on Japan, Harold and Margaret Sprout summarized the primary challenge of the times:

> The Second World War has profoundly altered the relations of the United States with other nations. Venerable foreign policies—such as neutrality towards European wars and avoidance of military alliances with foreign powers—require fresh appraisal. . . . We may court disaster more terrible than those which have befallen Germany and Japan if, as in 1919, we turn our backs on the Old World and try to go about business as if the war had never occurred.

This is so in part because of the revolutionary character of developments in science and technology. . . .

If the probable price of war is devastation for everyone, victors and vanquished alike, the supreme importance of avoiding that catastrophe is self-evident. The consequences of perpetual limited war are more difficult to estimate . . .but a growing body of responsible citizens believes that economic welfare and human freedom cannot prosper in a garrison state perpetually menaced and mobilized for war. . . .

The paramount task of American statecraft, as we see it, is to devise and carry out a strategy that will protect our country and our people from military aggression, without destroying in the process the material prosperity and moral values and principles which give dignity to the individual. We know of no magic formula that will solve this problem . . . no panaceas. . . .

No single person, no single field of knowledge, can provide adequate answers.[5]

Goodpaster's other mentor was Dr. Edward Mead Earle, editor of the landmark 1943 book *The Makers of Modern Strategy*. Earle was a specialist in military affairs at the Institute for Advanced Study, where he organized and led the Princeton Military Studies Group that included Goodpaster. This group studied broad issues of security and strategy. For fifteen years, Earle's seminars produced ideas, scholars, and practitioners who shaped discourse and policy in Washington during World War II and the early Cold War years.[6]

Previously, during World War II, Dr. Earle had helped William Donovan organize the research and analysis division of the Office of Strategic Services, the forerunner of CIA. He also advised the commander of the Army Air Forces in planning the strategic bombing campaign against Germany. For such work, Earle received the U.S. Presidential Medal of Merit and the French Legion of Honor.[7]

The Institute for Advanced Study was independent from Princeton, although students and faculty of the two institutions frequently collaborated. The institute was founded in 1930 to encourage fundamental research on the way we understand the world. Prominent scholars at the institute have included Albert Einstein, Robert Oppenheimer, John von Neumann, and George Kennan.

During his studies, Goodpaster particularly enjoyed a series of seminars organized by Dr. Earle on the dynamics of Soviet policy, focusing on those issues that shaped policies. Guest speakers included the British historian and former diplomat Edward Hallett (E. H.) Carr, who wrote the fourteen-volume *History of Soviet Russia*. As a young diplomat, Carr also attended the 1919 Paris Peace Conference and helped draft the League of Nations section of the Treaty of Versailles. Arnold Toynbee, another noted British historian and institute faculty member, also addressed the seminar.

One of Dr. Earle's seminars that Goodpaster recalled as being particularly relevant to his future work was devoted to modern France. Only a year later, he found himself dealing with modern France and thinking about the comments of a young professor from Yale who noted during the seminar that the beginning of understanding the French was in seeing how they related to each other. It is with diffuse interpersonal hostility. Goodpaster often thought of that hostility when trying to navigate the *Place de l'Etoile* traffic circle in Paris, where twelve streets converge, and a timid driver stands little chance. [8]

After Goodpaster's first two years allotted by the Army for graduate study, Professor Sprout proposed to the Army that Goodpaster stay for a third year to complete his dissertation for a PhD in international relations. Once again, Engineer Branch disapproved the extension. Personnel policy provided for only two years of study because, during the time the Army officer was in school, he was unavailable to fill other positions, especially hardship tours overseas without families. Somebody else would have to fill the position to which Goodpaster would have been assigned.

But, once again, Engineer Branch lost the argument. Brigadier General Lincoln interceded with Lieutenant General Alfred Gruenther, who was then the G-3, Chief of Army Operations. He took the issue to the Army Chief of Staff, General Eisenhower, who overruled the Engineers and agreed that Goodpaster should continue to pursue studies at Princeton. [9]

Goodpaster's main requirement in his third year, then, was to complete a dissertation. He chose "National Technology and International Politics" as his topic. This subject was not surprising, given his recent experiences as a strategic planner during the war and postwar planning efforts to achieve a sustainable peace. Technology, especially the advent of nuclear weapons, played key roles in addressing both challenges. As Goodpaster noted in his introduction, analysts must take into account the pervasive influence of technology regardless of their field of interest. [10]

In his dissertation, Goodpaster noted that technology can be both

> a powerful servant and a subtle, yet ruthless, master . . . it has both favorable and unfavorable phases . . . it destroys in one place and builds in another . . . it yields abundance while it imposes stringent demands for raw materials. On the domestic scene, while it raises problems, it provides means which a capable government can devote to solving them. On the international scene, the problems raised are confronted by no agency, as yet, capable of applying the fruits of technology to their resolution. [11]

At the dawn of the Atomic Age and the founding of the United Nations, Goodpaster was interested in how technology influenced international politics. His four hundred-page dissertation explored the dynamic relationships between technology, national power and international relations. He noted that politics, economics, sociology, and military affairs were influenced by technology in dramatic but uneven ways that also altered national objectives and calculations of the global balance of power. Goodpaster noted the enormous resistance to change in developing new mechanisms to deal with the stresses created by technological advances.

Technology was viewed by most scholars at the time mainly in the context of the industrial revolution. Their focus was primarily on industrial production and improvements in manufacturing processes, although Princeton and the Institute for Advanced Study were also in the forefront of computer development. Concurrently, scholarship on international politics was concerned with the impact of the Great Depression, the two world wars and the failures of the League of Nations, several arms-limitations agreements, and diplomacy to resolve international disputes.

Professor Sprout, Goodpaster's dissertation advisor, was one of the leading scholars viewing international politics from a national-power perspective. Power, in turn, was viewed in terms of a broad set of components that contributed to a nation's influence, including industrial production, energy, transportation, communications, population, natural resources, military forces, and social and political structure, as well as technology and geographic factors. By 1950, the rise in American power was clear in both the many studies Goodpaster cited and the voluminous data presented in his dissertation. A cursory look at the typical measures of aggregate power of the United States and its allies compared to Germany, Italy, and Japan suggested that the outcome of the war was never in doubt. Goodpaster's personal experience, however, made him cautious of such conclusions. The decisions of political and military leaders were critical in determining how power was wielded.

In his dissertation, Goodpaster argued that technology contributed to enormous increases in the destructiveness of war. He was skeptical, however, about the prospects for reducing the threats posed by the technology of warfare. By making conflict more violent at all levels, technology also contributed to insecurity. As a result, security, particularly in the Cold War environment, was becoming more costly and more difficult to maintain. Nuclear weapons made traditional notions of defense outmoded; instead, strategic planning shifted toward deterrence. At the same time, the nuclear arms race posed challenging problems for traditional diplomacy and the United Nations. In this complex environment, political leaders ultimately had to decide how to deal with the consequences of technological changes nationally and internationally. And, given the dynamic, fungible nature of technological change, leaders should not be complacent about current arrangements of power and stability. [12]

While students usually try to narrow a complex research subject into a more manageable scope, Goodpaster demonstrated his analytic preference to frame problems at their highest level of generality and search for important linkages. His research provided a valuable lesson in how to think broadly about complex problems. Subsequently, he put this approach to good use in viewing problems in their fullest context.

Goodpaster completed and successfully defended his dissertation in the spring of 1950 and was awarded a doctorate. Goodpaster also forged several lifelong bonds with professors and students that were mutually beneficial. This network of academic associates was available to contribute independent thinking. One example that shows that the Princeton community held Goodpaster in high regard was the awarding of the James Madison Medal to him by the Association of Princeton Graduate Alumni in 1976. The medal recognized his distinguished career as a soldier, statesman, and scholar. [13]

LIEUTENANT COLONEL GOODPASTER, PHD, RETURNS TO THE PENTAGON

After completing his studies at Princeton, Goodpaster returned to the Advanced Study Group, which had recently been moved from the Army Staff to the Joint Staff where it became the Joint Advanced Study Committee. By broadening its membership, General Eisenhower sought to expand opportunities for new ways of thinking and bold initiatives. General Omar Bradley, after becoming the Army chief of staff, agreed and paved the way for transfer to the Joint Staff. [14]

In his new assignment, Goodpaster became involved in a study of the capabilities and limitations of nuclear weapons. The study, entitled "Nuclear Weapons from Pit to Target," examined each stage in the process of developing a weapon to delivering it. For example, it examined the likely availability of uranium, which at that time came from the unique pitchblende of the Shinkolobwe mine in Africa. The study group traveled to Los Alamos to observe a nuclear weapons test. In another study, the group examined a range of potential uses of nuclear weapons beyond delivery by aircraft. The Army and Navy were interested in analyzing the possible application of nuclear weapons to land warfare and war at sea. [15]

After learning about atomic weapons, Goodpaster became concerned that they were still treated mainly as research and development, "special weapons," and had not been incorporated into the main military systems that included planning, training, logistics, command and control, and the myriad of other systems necessary for efficient military operations. He envisioned a study of systems of systems to understand how best to incorporate atomic weapons, rather than rely on an uncoordinated, "trial and error" approach. [16]

Goodpaster briefed many of the Army's leaders about the work of the Joint Advanced Study Committee, including Lieutenant General Ridgway in October 1950. Ridgway expressed a strong personal interest in the committee and told Goodpaster to feel free to come and see him at any time to discuss any problem. In particular, Ridgway expressed an interest in carefully defining future national and military objectives. These "great unknowns," Ridgway noted, would determine the usefulness of our military plans and preparations.[17]

The Chinese intervention in the Korean War highlighted Goodpaster's concerns about the lack of attention to nuclear weapons. Goodpaster noted in a discussion with General Gruenther that "we are seriously negligent in not developing the capability to deliver a bomb on very short notice, even though the actual decision would require comprehensive analysis of the military, diplomatic and psychological factors." Goodpaster noted the lack of data on military effects of atomic weapons, but when pressed, he thought that the massed Chinese Army formations would probably be found to present viable targets.[18]

In thinking through some of the issues that related to the Korean War in addition to the possible use of nuclear weapons, Goodpaster noted that an "Asiatic Security Collaboration Program" would be useful in coordinating the efforts of several countries in Asia to better provide for their security with support from the United States and other countries.[19]

Lt. Colonel Goodpaster had been in this assignment for only about six months when he received a call from Colonel Robert Wood, a friend and former West Point instructor, now chief of the OPD strategy section, asking for help. Goodpaster was happy to oblige and inquired about what he could do to help. Wood said, "You can be on a plane with General Gruenther going to Brussels tomorrow at noon." Goodpaster asked, "What am I going to do there?" Wood replied "Well, General Eisenhower's about to take command and set up a collective security force in Europe, and we'd like you to go with an Air Force officer, and join General Gruenther [Eisenhower's chief of staff, who led the advance party]."[20]

NOTES

1. Susan Goodpaster Sullivan, interview with author, June 27, 2010.
2. Ibid.. Colonel Morgan was the son of a Civil War general, a graduate of West Point in 1880, and a veteran of the Indian Wars and World War I. He earned the Medal of Honor for bravery during a battle with Apaches in 1882. He was wounded, and a bullet remained imbedded near his heart for more than sixty years.
3. Ibid.
4. Rosenau et al., *The Analysis of International Politics,* 1–11.
5. Sprout and Sprout, *Foundations of National Power,* v–x.
6. For a description of Earle's contributions to the field of security studies, see David Ekbladh "Present at the Creation: Edward Mead Earle and the Depression-Era Origins of Security Studies," *International Security* 36, no. 3 (Winter 2011/2012): 107–41.
7. Ibid., 133.
8. Goodpaster, Mandel interviews, January 15, 2002, tape 10.
9. Ibid.

10. Goodpaster, "National Technology and International Politics," unpublished doctoral dissertation, Department of Politics, Princeton University, May 1950, 1–9.

11. Ibid.

12. Ibid., especially 279, 291, 296, 357–77.

13. Jordan, *An Unsung Soldier,* 20.

14. Undated "Information Sheet on the Joint Advanced Study Committee, Office of the Joint Chiefs of Staff," Goodpaster papers, box 11, file 18, Marshall Library. Also Goodpaster, Johnson and Ferguson interview, February 25, 1976.

15. Goodpaster, Mandel interviews, January 15, 2002, tape 9.

16. Goodpaster letter to Porter, November 7, 1950, Goodpaster Papers, box 11, file 8, Marshall Library.

17. Goodpaster memo, October 17, 1950, Goodpaster Papers, box 11, file 8, Marshall Library.

18. Goodpaster memo for record, December 12, 1950, Goodpaster Papers, box 11, file 8, Marshall Library.

19. Goodpaster notes, November 30, 1950, Goodpaster Papers, box 11, file 8, Marshall Library.

20. Goodpaster, Mandel interviews, January 15, 2002, tape 10.

II

Conducting National Security Affairs

PULLED TOWARD POLICY

For the next twenty-five years, Goodpaster would be pulled into the inner circles of international security decision making despite his wishes to return to troop duty. These positions offered opportunities to see firsthand how political and military leaders at the highest levels viewed the world. He also saw how they made decisions that yielded enormous consequences; some worked out well, while others were disastrous. As a result, Goodpaster increasingly came to understand the ideas and ideals that constituted best practices for national security affairs.

This period would also provide Goodpaster with his most influential mentor, Dwight D. Eisenhower. Goodpaster helped Eisenhower establish NATO's military headquarters. Appropriately, Goodpaster would follow Eisenhower as the Supreme Allied Commander two decades later. In the meantime, Goodpaster learned more about the ideas and ideals that contributed to the success of many of the great figures of the "Greatest Generation," including talented foreign leaders.

This time frame saw the end of the Korean War and the incremental steps that escalated into the Vietnam War. Goodpaster was again in the inner circles during this escalation.

Chapter Seven

Establishing NATO (1951–1954)

Faced with a growing threat of communist expansion, the foreign ministers, secretaries of state, and ambassadors from twelve Western countries met in Washington on April 4, 1949, to sign the North Atlantic Treaty. The U.S. Senate ratified it on July 21, 1949, but not without strong domestic opposition from former President Hoover and a group of Republican senators led by Robert A. Taft, who was also making his fourth bid for president. In addition to voting against the formation of NATO, Taft called for the withdrawal of American troops from Europe.[1]

The security environment, however, was deteriorating as the Soviet Union successfully tested a nuclear weapon on August 29, 1949, much sooner than anticipated, and communist forces gained control of China in October 1949. Only a few months later, North Korea invaded South Korea on June 25, 1950.

The Korean War caught the United States poorly prepared. President Truman quickly organized the first UN-backed collective security response to aggression, with seventeen nations providing troops under General MacArthur. Truman also appointed General Marshall as secretary of defense in September 1950 to manage mobilization of the armed forces. During fiscal year 1951, the U.S. armed forces expanded from 1,460,000 to 3,250,000 troops in what Marshall termed partial rectification of the "mistakes of the postwar demobilization." Full rectification to provide the strong military posture needed to prevent another world war was addressed in the Universal Military Training and Service Act of 1951 that augmented the Selective Service draft with universal military training and an eight-year service obligation for men under the age of twenty-six.[2]

The Korean War also exposed NATO as little more than a "paper guarantee." Under Article 5 of the treaty, the members agreed that an attack on one was an attack on all. Had there been such an agreement in the 1930s, it probably would have helped overcome the slow, disorganized European responses to German aggression. Nevertheless, even with such an understanding in 1950, the new organization was hollow in terms of military forces. Those that were already deployed were remnants of occupation forces, not well configured for defending Western Europe.

Despite a sense of urgency to establish the NATO alliance, it took more than a year to work out some of the details, including who should lead the organization. On October 19, 1950, President Truman wrote a letter to General Eisenhower, who was then president of Columbia University, and noted in a postscript, "First time you are in [Washington], I wish you'd come in and see me. If I send for you, we'll start speculators to work." Nine days later, Eisenhower visited Truman and the president told him that he was the unanimous choice of all the NATO countries to be the supreme commander. Eisenhower agreed to accept the challenge. His appointment was announced on December 19, 1950.[3]

THE ADVANCE PARTY

With only a one-day advance notice, in early January 1951, Goodpaster boarded a plane for Brussels in his new role as special assistant to General Alfred Gruenther, chief of staff to General Eisenhower, charged with establishing NATO's new military headquarters, the Supreme Headquarters, Allied Powers Europe (SHAPE). Goodpaster was sent initially to Brussels, the location of the Western European Union's Commanders-in-Chief Committee, headed by Field Marshal Bernard Montgomery. Many of the functions of that committee and staff would be incorporated into the new NATO military headquarters.[4]

As soon as they arrived in Brussels, Lieutenant Colonel Goodpaster and Lieutenant Colonel Robert Worden were told by General Gruenther to "get on a train, get down to Paris and set up the headquarters." They arrived in Paris after midnight and found an American headquarters in the Astoria Hotel, where they secured their briefcases full of classified papers. A few hours later, but still in the early morning, they set about to assemble American staff officers from Germany and the Mediterranean.[5]

The next day, Goodpaster and Worden met General Gruenther when he arrived at Orly Airport. Gruenther asked them, "What have you accomplished?" They laughed, but Gruenther was serious and insisted, "All right, now what have you accomplished?" So, with an added sense of urgency, they developed an initial plan for forming the headquarters, beginning with an advance-planning group, followed by an international planning group. By the end of January, the International Planning Group was formed and operating.

Goodpaster was becoming accustomed to working under intense pressures of time and enormous expectations of nearly impossible achievements.

EISENHOWER TAKES COMMAND

On January 6, 1951, President Truman, Secretary of State Dean Acheson and Secretary of Defense George Marshall gathered at Washington National Airport to send General Eisenhower off to take command of NATO forces. Eisenhower boarded the president's plane, the *Columbine*, for an eighteen-day tour of NATO. After a seventeen-gun salute, the military band played *'Til We Meet Again* as the plane departed.[6]

The plane touched down at Orly airport at 9 a.m. on Sunday and was met by a throng of photographers, journalists, and officials and several of General Eisenhower's wartime comrades. When he emerged through the door of the *Columbine*, General Eisenhower was greeted by considerable applause, but the crowd was even more enthusiastic with applause when Mrs. Eisenhower came to the door. The fact that he brought his wife, Mamie, was a show of confidence, and confidence among Europeans had been very badly shaken following the North Korean invasion of South Korea. Eisenhower's presence boosted hope in this new collective force led by a victorious and popular American commander.[7]

This enthusiastic greeting was not shared uniformly, however. A few weeks earlier, following the official announcement that General Eisenhower had been named to lead NATO forces, communist parties throughout Europe organized anti-NATO propaganda campaigns that included editorials, posters, and protest rallies. A Paris newspaper, with nearly half-a-million readers, bore a headline "General, Stay at Home." Denmark's *Land & Volk* featured cartoons ridiculing Eisenhower, and the French Communist Party issued a communiqué calling for workers to protest the installation of General Eisenhower in Paris. A crowd of four thousand demonstrators gathered at the Place de l'Etoile in Paris to protest Eisenhower's arrival.

Opposition to NATO was significant even in the United States, where Senator Taft declared that President Truman had no right to send additional U.S. troops to Korea or Europe without congressional consent. Senator Kenneth Wherry introduced legislation requiring congressional approval before committing more forces to NATO. The importance of placing any military undertaking in its complex geopolitical environment made a lasting impression on Goodpaster.[8]

On Monday morning, General Eisenhower began his tour of NATO capitals accompanied by Colonel Biddle, Lieutenant Colonel Oldfield, a public relations officer, and Major Vernon Walters, a talented linguist. Eisenhower's first meeting was with French premier René Pleven. Eisenhower wanted to assess the political will to support NATO in each country and report back to Congress.

After the tour, Goodpaster joined General Eisenhower and General Gruenther on their return to Washington to brief President Truman and Congress. During the trip, Goodpaster prepared materials to use with Congress and edited their planned testimony. The latter task was challenging for Goodpaster because Eisenhower and Gruenther preferred strong effect over good syntax. Nevertheless, the message General Eisenhower delivered to a joint session of Congress was compelling. In his talk, he noted

> We must accept, as we must always accept, the disadvantage militarily, internationally, that goes with peaceful intent and defensive purposes only. Any aggressor picks a day in which he intends to strike and builds everything to that point. We have to devise a scheme that we can support—over the next 20 years, 30 years, whatever time may be necessary—as long as the announced threat of aggression remains in the world and that means we must be ready at all times, one of the important times being today. [9]

The lesson for Goodpaster was that, in every endeavor, to first and foremost focus on the purpose. After the presentation, Senator Wherry acknowledged that General Eisenhower was very convincing, a dynamic speaker. Eisenhower followed that with a stimulating quarter-hour television address to the nation. General Gruenther and Colonel Goodpaster returned to Paris, while General Eisenhower and Mamie remained in the United States for several weeks while their quarters and the new headquarters near Paris were being readied.

GENERAL ORDER NUMBER 1

During the initial phase of establishing the new NATO military headquarters, Goodpaster and Worden worked very closely with General Gruenther to structure Northern Area Command in Oslo, Norway; Central Area Command in Fontainebleau, France; and Southern Area Command in Naples, Italy. Each one involved seemingly infinite complications. The team grew quickly into an advance-planning group of about two dozen Americans, then expanded to form the International Planning Group. At this point, General Gruenther and General Eisenhower brought in more senior officers to take over from Goodpaster and head the major staff divisions, including training, plans and operations, intelligence, logistics, and communications.

About three months from the time that Goodpaster was first sent to Paris, the headquarters was activated on April 2, 1951, with the promulgation of General Order Number 1 by which SHAPE assumed operational control of those Allied forces dedicated to the defense of Western Europe. The command was ready earlier, but the decision was made to not launch SHAPE on April 1, All Fools Day, because of the undesirable connotation of that date, especially in Europe. Fifty years later, while going to a meeting in the Pentagon with the author, Goodpaster pointed to a small, framed document on the wall in the E-Ring, labeled "General Order No. 1," and commented, "I wrote that."

General Eisenhower gave very clear instructions through Gruenther to model SHAPE along the lines of his headquarters in Britain during the war. The headquarters was to be truly international, completely integrated, and draw on senior officers who had WWII experience in similar organizations. In addition there were to be national military representatives with small detachments from each country to provide information and national perspectives.[10]

General Eisenhower envisioned SHAPE as more of a policy-making organization than an operational command headquarters, so he reduced the staff from a planned level of 600 to 250. Eisenhower also persuaded Field Marshal Bernard Montgomery[11] to become his deputy. Despite their differences and testy relationship during World War II, they respected each other. Early on, while in this position, Montgomery asked Eisenhower to teach him how to be a deputy commander because he had never served in that capacity. Montgomery learned quickly and they established a very good working relationship. As the deputy commander, Montgomery was responsible mainly for training and readiness.[12]

In addition to Montgomery, other senior officers selected for the initial SHAPE staff were Air Vice Marshal Edmund Hudleston as the Deputy Chief of Staff for Plans and Operations, General Francis Festing as Assistant Chief of Staff for Organization and Training, and General Terence Airey as Assistant Chief of Staff for Intelligence. Each had a distinguished background with relevant experience on Allied combined staffs in World War II. This experience enabled the headquarters to become operational within a very short period of time.

Goodpaster had several opportunities to work with Field Marshal Montgomery. On one occasion, while Montgomery was preparing to present a series of speeches on command doctrine, he discussed with Goodpaster the differences between the British and American approaches. Montgomery described the British approach, in which the commander would give his broad intentions to his chief of staff, who would then work with the subordinate command chiefs of staff to develop plans. Goodpaster agreed with Montgomery that the American approach was different, with the commander issuing broad mission orders directly to the subordinate commanders, who prepared their plans with appropriate mission statements. Montgomery questioned this approach, asking, "How would you know if their work was satisfactory? . . .You can't be sure that it's carried out as intended." Goodpaster responded, "Well, Field Marshal, suppose during World War II General Eisenhower had issued his mission-type order to you and to General Bradley, then sent his chief of staff down to talk to your chief of staff about the development of your order. What would you have done?" Montgomery said, "I would have seen him off."[13]

In other work, Goodpaster became aware of NATO vulnerabilities. Security, for example, was a problem, he noted, in part because communications with the northern commander in Oslo, Norway, went through East Germany and were assumed to be monitored. Much later, he would realize that many of these early problems were never fully rectified.

Out of necessity, Goodpaster learned the importance of integrating the independent national efforts with NATO. To help facilitate this, he was in charge of establishing linkages with other organizations, including the various American commands in Europe and the Mediterranean and with the elements of the American Military Defense Assistance Program (MDAP) that provided weapons, munitions, and other support to the European nations for rebuilding their forces.

Another of Goodpaster's responsibilities involved establishing the basis for planning for General Eisenhower. At that time, there was great attention being given in the United States to a presumed but unspecified date of maximum danger. That idea was, in part, the basis for preparation of National Security Council Report 68 (NSC-68) commissioned by President Truman in January 1950. NSC-68 outlined a strategy of containment and gained wide support following the North Korean invasion of South Korea.[14]

Eisenhower made clear to Goodpaster that he did not accept the idea of any particular date of maximum danger. However, he believed that a weak and uncoordinated Western Europe was very dangerous. So he focused on strengthening and arming the Allies, but not working toward some assumed date of maximum danger.

Part of the planning was, of course, based on intelligence. At that time, what would become a famous intelligence estimate that credited the Soviets with 175 divisions was published. As Goodpaster and the staff explored the intelligence more deeply, they found that some of the divisions were in a very high state of readiness, some could be called to readiness within thirty to sixty days, and others were little more than warehouses full of equipment. Thus, actual Soviet military capabilities were far less than implied by the gross figures.[15]

Nevertheless, the psychological implications of the military balance concerned General Eisenhower. He worried that Allies would feel hopelessly overwhelmed and "bow to counsels of defeat." These counsels maintained that NATO could never realistically match the Warsaw Pact because the gap between NATO forces and the Warsaw Pact forces was simply too great. The problem of defeatism was for Eisenhower "a make or break issue." Eisenhower was determined it would be a "make" operation. And Goodpaster immediately grasped the fundamental importance of the psychological dimension of military power.[16]

At the time when SHAPE was activated in 1951, planners estimated initial requirements that included ninety divisions. However, NATO forces consisted mainly of two American divisions and one British division in Germany. French forces were heavily committed to Indochina, and Germany had yet to rearm. Norway, Canada, Denmark, and Portugal also provided small contingents. In stark contrast, Soviet forces included seventy-five divisions and a similar number of satellite-nation forces at various stages of readiness.[17]

Despite this unfavorable military balance, Eisenhower did not believe Soviet forces would attack because of the U.S. advantage in nuclear weapons and the recent memory of the huge losses suffered by the Soviet Union during World War II. Nevertheless, upon assuming command, Eisenhower began a sustained effort to encourage the leaders of the other NATO countries to provide the forces necessary to defend Europe. Eisenhower viewed the threat of disunity within the alliance as comparable in significance to the Soviet threat and thus placed a high priority on building consensus among the Allies—another lesson that Goodpaster would carry.[18]

In the meantime, with troops in demand for the Korean War, the U.S. Joint Chiefs of Staff attempted to gain more control over U.S. forces in Europe at the expense of the SACEUR, but Eisenhower relied on Goodpaster to ensure that they did not succeed. In agreeing to take over the NATO command, Eisenhower had obtained a letter from President Truman indicating that, as the Supreme Allied Commander, Europe, Eisenhower would command U.S. forces to the extent he deemed necessary for the accomplishment of his mission. When the Pentagon continued to press the issue, Goodpaster advised them that they should pursue the matter through the North Atlantic Council and NATO's Military Committee. Apparently stymied, the Pentagon then shifted their efforts to gain control of forces only in the conduct of U.S. affairs. The power struggle continued, with Goodpaster working very closely with Eisenhower to retain SACEUR authority.[19]

THE THREE WISE MEN AND "GREENPASTURES"

To help build the political will to contribute the military forces required, will that was lacking in most member countries, Eisenhower relied a great deal on the "Three Wise Men." Officially termed the Executive Committee of the Temporary Council Committee (TCC), the three included Jean Monnet from France, the driving force behind forming a European Community; W. Averell Harriman from the United States, former ambassador to the Soviet Union and Britain; and Hugh Gaitskell from Britain, a former cabinet member and leader in the Labour Party. Gaitskell was replaced on the committee by Edwin Plowden when the Labour Party lost power to the Conservatives in the 1951 British election.

The TCC was established by the North Atlantic Council (NAC) at its meeting in Ottawa in September 1950 after efforts by the NAC and the Deputies Council to agree on a defense concept and a force structure bogged down over disagreements about forward defense and German rearmament. As a result, the NAC decided to form a small, higher level group of prominent persons representing the "big three," the United States, Britain, and France. They charged the Wise Men with reconciling NATO military requirements with the political-economic capabilities of the member countries.

General Eisenhower appointed Lieutenant Colonel Goodpaster and a British colonel as his liaison to the Three Wise Men. After their first meeting, Monnet pulled Harriman and Gordon aside and said, "You know that English officer is really a dull fellow, but I like Greenpastures. I like that Greenpastures, that's the man. We must arrange to have Greenpastures as our liaison man."[20]

Eisenhower agreed, and in this capacity Goodpaster met with the SACEUR once or twice a week. During their frequent meetings about the many issues raised by the Three Wise Men, Eisenhower was keenly interested in what could be done to assist efforts to bolster NATO capabilities and would ask Goodpaster "What can be done? How can we deal with a particular problem?" or "What kind of response would be appropriate?" Goodpaster would contribute ideas and often take his suggestion, with Eisenhower's approval, back to the Three Wise Men. During these engagements with Eisenhower, it became apparent to Goodpaster that they thought alike.[21]

By late 1951, the TCC, in conjunction with SHAPE, had produced a set of force goals that were adopted by NATO members at the Lisbon Summit in February 1952. The TCC also recommended that NATO move its civilian headquarters to Paris to be closer to SHAPE and the Organisation for European Economic Co-operation (OEEC) that had emerged from the Marshall Plan. Other key TCC recommendations were to appoint a distinguished person as NATO's secretary general and to establish a permanent council of ambassadors instead of meeting in continuous session.[22]

Also near the end of 1951, Goodpaster and a small team worked with General Eisenhower to prepare the First Annual Report of the Supreme Allied Commander, Europe. In this report, Eisenhower coined a phrase that characterized his efforts as developing an "expanding spiral of strength and confidence." Part of the expanding strength was reflected in the willingness of Western European members of NATO to increase defense spending from about $4.7 billion in fiscal year 1950 to $8.3 billion in fiscal year 1952. In addition, the United States added four divisions to NATO in 1951 and boosted military assistance by $4 billion, mainly for the North Atlantic area.[23]

During this first year at SHAPE, General Eisenhower developed a high opinion of Goodpaster. For example, he remarked at a dinner party with Averell Harriman, David Bruce, Harold Stassen and C. Z. Sulzberger that he had two of the most brilliant officers he had ever run into on his staff. One of them was Lieutenant Colonel Andrew J. Goodpaster, the other Lieutenant Colonel Pete Carroll. Eisenhower added that, if he were the president of General Motors, he would hire the two of them and pay them a very high salary, even though they didn't know a damned thing about the business, because in no time they would prove invaluable.[24]

Goodpaster grew closer to both Gruenther and Eisenhower, personally as well as professionally, in this time frame. General Gruenther would, on occasion, have dinners at his quarters with the Eisenhowers, to which Goodpaster and Dossy were also invited. The group would often wind up the evening singing army songs, something that Eisenhower particularly enjoyed.[25]

EISENHOWER RESIGNS TO RUN FOR PRESIDENT

In addition to helping Eisenhower and Gruenther prepare congressional testimony, Goodpaster often met with visiting congressional delegations. He soon noticed that these delegations had a strong Republican cast and that they would meet privately with Eisenhower for long periods. What Goodpaster may not have known was that General Eisenhower was being pressed by Republican leaders to run for president. Following his defeat by Truman in 1948, Governor Thomas E. Dewey had urged Eisenhower to announce his candidacy. General Lucius Clay, a friend, played on Eisenhower's disdain for isolationists in trying to convince Eisenhower to run.[26]

Following his initial trip to the NATO countries and his report to Congress, General Eisenhower met privately with Senator Taft and offered to repudiate any efforts to place his name in nomination for president if Taft would support American participation in NATO. Taft refused, arguing that NATO was more likely to provoke the Soviet Union than deter it. Taft saw NATO as costly and involving the United States unnecessarily in the old quarrels of Europe.[27]

Republicans continued to press him to run, but Eisenhower demurred. Although he was concerned about the leadership of the country, he felt a strong sense of duty to get NATO launched. Nevertheless, when his name was put in nomination for the New Hampshire primary in January 1952, he did not repudiate the call. Furthermore, he reminded his friend, General Clay, that according to Army Regulation 600-10.18a: "Members of the Regular Army, while on active duty, may accept nomination for public office, pro-

Figure 7.1. Eisenhower & Goodpaster at SHAPE, 1952. Official photo. *Source*: Courtesy of Goodpaster Family

vided such nomination is rendered without direct *or indirect* activity or solicitation on their part" (Eisenhower's emphasis). [28]

In the spring of 1952, Eisenhower reluctantly decided to accept the challenge after it appeared that Robert Taft was the clear frontrunner, and General MacArthur, recently relieved of his command for insubordination, was named as the keynote speaker for the upcoming Republican convention. Taft was an isolationist and MacArthur was, in Eisenhower's view, even more dangerous. Furthermore, Truman had announced that he would not seek reelection.[29]

At his request, General Eisenhower was relieved as the Supreme Allied Commander, Europe on June 1, 1952. Goodpaster assumed that General Eisenhower concluded that NATO was off to a reasonably good start and would be in good hands with General Matthew Ridgway as the new commander, along with Gruenther, Montgomery, and other capable officers now on board. Eisenhower felt that a stronger sense of duty called him back home.

With only a month before the Republican Party convention in Chicago, Eisenhower supporters managed to upset Robert Taft, the heavy favorite, for the nomination. In November, Eisenhower defeated Adlai Stevenson in a landslide election.

In the meantime, Goodpaster was promoted to colonel after serving for more than nine years as a lieutenant colonel. Almost a year later, in August 1953, General Ridgway's tour as SACEUR was curtailed when he was appointed chief of staff of the Army. Ridgway was succeeded as SACEUR by General Alfred Gruenther.

PRECISE COLLECTIVE THINKING: THE SOLARIUM PROJECT

Colonel Goodpaster was called back to Washington in June 1953 by President Eisenhower to participate in a national security strategy study organized by the White House. Joseph Stalin's death on March 5, 1953, provided President Eisenhower with an opportunity to rethink fundamentally U.S. relations with the Soviet Union now under different leadership. The national security policy of containment Eisenhower inherited from President Truman had been criticized by John Foster Dulles, Eisenhower's new secretary of state, who had argued for a "roll-back" strategy in the foreign policy plank of the Republican Party during the election campaign. Eisenhower was faced with what he believed was an overly simplistic choice between accepting communist expansion or risking a major war. Furthermore, Eisenhower believed that the current Korean War–level of security effort was not sustainable economically by the United States for the long term.[30]

Before deciding on a new policy, Eisenhower wanted a thorough evaluation of specific options. He organized a comprehensive study with detailed analyses of the implications of alternative strategies involving some of the best strategic thinkers. Meeting in the Solarium room of the White House to structure the study in May 1953 were the President; Robert Cutler, his National Security Advisor; John Foster Dulles, the Secretary of State; and C. D.

Jackson, Special Assistant to the President. The study, subsequently known as the "Solarium Project," was organized into three teams, each making the best case for adopting their assigned strategy. All three strategies were designed to contribute to the collapse of communist regimes. The strategies involved (1) containing communist expansion along the lines of the current policy outlined in NSC 153 (A: Containment Team); (2) explicitly defining U.S. security interests in terms of a line around the Sino-Soviet bloc periphery that, if crossed by communist forces, would threaten general war (B: Line-Drawing Team); and (3) "rolling back" efforts, short of war, to regain territories lost to communist expansion and produce a "climate of victory encouraging to the free world" (C: Roll-Back Team).[31]

Instructions to each task force required them to address about twenty key questions including: What general results were expected over what time frame? What specific actions should be undertaken by the United States to implement the policy? What current actions should be abandoned? What would be the estimated costs? What features should be made public, and what should be kept secret? What would be the likely effects on relations with others? Would the actions be consistent with U.S. commitments and the UN Charter? What would be the likely reactions of the Soviet Union and China? What would be the impact on public opinion in the United States and abroad? And what congressional actions would be required? The teams were also asked to consider the strategies once the Soviet Union had developed a sufficient nuclear stockpile to inflict substantial damage on the United States.[32]

The study group had twenty-one participants, seven on each team, with Goodpaster and several others selected personally by the president. Eisenhower later confided that he chose Goodpaster for the Roll-Back Team because he wanted someone with common sense that he could trust to insist on well-reasoned thinking. Furthermore, given Goodpaster's debate skills, he could be relied upon to present cogent arguments even if he disagreed with the basic premise.[33]

The Containment Team was headed by George Kennan, who originated the idea of containment with his 1946 long telegram from Moscow describing a brutal Soviet Union bent on expansion through intimidation and subversion that had to be contained. His views were made public in a *Foreign Affairs* article, "The Sources of Soviet Conduct," published under the pseudonym "Mr. X." In this article, Kennan argued that the "main element of any U.S. policy toward the Soviet Union must be a long-term, patient but firm and vigilant containment of Russian expansionist tendencies." Kennan was also the former director of the State Department's Policy Planning staff and author of the 1948 paper on U.S. objectives toward the Soviet Union that led to NSC policy document 20/4.[34]

Task Force B, the Line-in-the-Sand Team, was led by Major General James McCormack and Task Force C, the Roll-Back Team, was headed by Vice Admiral R.L. Connolly and included Lieutenant General Lyman Lemnitzer, Colonel Harold K. Johnson, and Colonel Goodpaster.[35]

The teams were given complete access to government information, including intelligence and analyses of the costs of various force postures and initiatives considered. They worked in complete secrecy at Fort McNair from 8 a.m. to midnight for five weeks from June 10 through July 15.

Goodpaster noted that, during their deliberations, "as we got into specific planning and evaluation and moved beyond rhetoric . . . thinking became more precise and a great deal more modest."[36] The costs, risks, and likely benefits of all three strategies became more apparent when they were exposed to this kind of detailed, precise thinking. As a result, Line-Drawing and Roll-Back became less attractive than Containment. Nevertheless, some aspects of the strategies propounded by Teams B and C did have merit, such as psychological operations and covert action that featured more prominently in the Team C approach. Massive Retaliation, featured more in Team B, became more problematic with recognition that the U.S. nuclear weapons monopoly would not last, thus negotiations to reduce and control these arms would make sense. Similarly, attempting to defend nearly everywhere against regional threats would drain U.S. resources.[37]

On July 16, 1953, the teams presented their best arguments to the president, the NSC cabinet principals, the JCS, the CIA director, assistant secretaries, and other key planning officials, a gathering of about sixty, including the study group. The Task Force C written report totaled about three hundred pages and argued that time was working against the United States. Ground had been lost to communist expansion for a decade, and the present situation would not provide an acceptable basis for a Cold War settlement. Furthermore, Soviet nuclear capabilities would soon neutralize the current U.S. strategic advantage. These trends and developments necessitated seizing the initiative, operating aggressively against the Soviet bloc by waging a political offensive combined with military operations short of war. While not advocating going it alone, the Task Force argued that we must be ready to proceed unilaterally. Traditional concepts of peace and war were no longer applicable. Mere containment was a sterile policy and would not suffice to achieve our true objectives.[38]

Goodpaster presented the Task Force C evaluation of the requirements for implementation of the Roll-Back policy. Goodpaster noted that present security organization and procedures were not sufficient to implement the strategy successfully because such a policy would require an aggressive interventionist manner with concepts and techniques that were foreign to Americans. Seizing such an initiative also would require unprecedented speed, coordination, and policy direction at the highest levels. Furthermore, the strategy required continuity of programs that the United States rarely, if ever, achieved. Goodpaster noted that it might take ten years to build a covert apparatus. In the meantime, the possibility of new technologies that could change the military balance would likely result in changes in priorities and fluctuations in program budgets. The proposed strategy also required a high degree of program security. One lapse in covert operations could destroy years of work. Finally, Task Force C estimated the cost of the strategy would require security expenditures to increase from the current Korean War–level of about 14.6 percent of the gross national product, to about 15.5 percent, resulting in a deficit of about $10 billion to $12 billion each year.[39]

President Eisenhower, after hearing the presentations, talked for about forty-five minutes without notes and summarized the arguments in a way that Kennan later described as "demonstrating his intellectual ascendancy over every man in the room." To that Goodpaster added, "George, that includes you." Kennan agreed, noting, "That's right, because Eisenhower knew the military side of it, which I did not."[40]

Eisenhower chose the hybrid policy of Containment Plus for the Cold War that was a sustainable balance of political, economic, and military power for long-term competition with the Soviet Union. He transformed the Truman administration's containment policy into a more robust deterrence, including covert support for dissidents and keeping the hope of liberty alive in central and Eastern Europe, while rejecting military action to roll back Soviet forces. According to Goodpaster, the kind of precise thinking exemplified by the Solarium Project moved the policy well beyond political rhetoric.[41]

The Solarium project served at least three purposes. First, it provided a comprehensive examination of alternative strategies early in the Eisenhower administration and at a time of transition in Soviet leadership. Second, it educated all the principals involved in implementing the strategy. They heard well-formulated arguments and heard directly the President's decision for the way forward. Finally, Solarium buried the notion of Roll-Back.[42]

In reflecting on the project several years later, Goodpaster noted that the presentations did not tell Eisenhower anything he did not already know. That judgment, while accurate, also suggests that perhaps Eisenhower organized the effort to either uncover some new ideas or to subject concepts such as Roll-Back to rigorous analysis that he thought would end up discrediting the approach, which in this case it did. In any event, the exercise did expose Goodpaster to Eisenhower's tendency to play Devil's advocate by proposing ideas with which he intuitively disagreed to see how they were debated.

Robert Bowie, the director of policy planning in the State Department, was tasked with translating the president's decision into policy guidance. He used the Solarium study, combined with the Joint Chiefs of Staff (JCS) "New Look" report that detailed a military strategy and force structure, the Oppenheimer report on nuclear weapons, the Edwards report on the estimated consequences of a Soviet nuclear attack, and various National Intelligence Estimates. The result was National Security Council (NSC) document 162/2, which was approved on October 30, 1953. NSC 162/2 served as the U.S. policy framework for the duration of the Cold War. At its core, the policy required maintaining a sufficient nuclear retaliatory capability and a viable economy. Eisenhower and Goodpaster would keep these priorities in mind. [43]

President Eisenhower, in choosing a Cold War policy, was mindful that it needed to be not only *desirable* in terms of policy objectives, but also *feasible* in terms of costs. He wanted to avoid the dramatic reductions in defense programs that typically followed the end of wars only to be followed by very costly crash programs to rebuild capabilities when faced with a new crisis. In 1953, Eisenhower was under pressure from Senator Taft and others to drastically cut defense spending after the Korean War. At the same time, the JCS were arguing for much more spending to meet the growing Soviet threat. Eisenhower's new strategy was lower in cost than what the JCS wanted, but higher than what Taft wanted. It was sufficient to meet the threat in Eisenhower's view, while not damaging the economy—another important lesson in strategy that Goodpaster grasped. [44]

MARSHALL'S NOBEL PEACE PRIZE

In 1953, General Marshall received the Nobel Peace Prize for his role in helping rebuild Europe after World War II. En route to receive the award, he was not feeling well and hoped to use the time onboard the ship crossing the Atlantic to rest and prepare his speech. But the five-day crossing was rough and he remained ill, so General Gruenther made his quarters near Paris available to General Marshall for further rest. Gruenther also instructed Colonel Goodpaster and Colonel Roy Lampson, the SHAPE historian, to help General Marshall prepare his remarks for the Nobel award ceremonies. [45]

Marshall was still in bed, looking quite ill, when Goodpaster and Lampson met with him several times. Marshall said that he wanted to stress the importance of history in his remarks, so Goodpaster and Lampson helped him draft his speech. After the ceremonies, General Marshall sent a letter to Goodpaster thanking him for his help with the Nobel lecture. In General Marshall's characteristic avoidance of rank, titles, and other customary salutations, it was addressed "Dear Goodpaster" and noted, "I doubt very seriously that I would have been able to complete the paper without your fine help." [46]

NUCLEAR WEAPONS MOVE FROM FISSION TO FUSION

During the last year of his assignment at SHAPE, General Gruenther established a small group to study the integration of nuclear weapons into NATO's defensive operations. The idea had been discussed in very general terms, but many member nations, the British in particular, wanted to develop specific concepts for how they would be used. The basic issue was whether nuclear weapons would be employed on a limited basis or would become the primary basis of defense planning. The latter case would signal a shift, with nuclear weapons becoming the dominant mode of combat.[47]

This "New Approach Group" included Goodpaster, an American Air Force officer, a British Army officer, a French Air Force officer, a French Naval officer, and a young Italian Air Force major. Much of the necessary classified information about nuclear weapons was "NOFORN," meaning that it was restricted from being shared with otherwise cleared foreign nationals. The group eventually worked out procedures to deal with the problem that included using templates for the blast, heat, and radiation effects of various nuclear weapons. Their planning was also aided by bringing in officers from the U.S. Strategic Air Command (SAC) who had U.S. nuclear weapons planning responsibilities.

As their planning proceeded, the design of nuclear weapons changed with the development of the hydrogen bomb in 1951 and successful tests in November 1952. The yields were much greater than the atomic bomb, increasing from about the equivalent of twenty thousand tons of high explosive TNT to about 20 million tons of TNT. Furthermore, the fusion design, coupled with a fission trigger, was much more efficient in terms of using nuclear fuel and the resulting yields were scalable, so the same thermonuclear design could be used to produce weapons of a wide range of yields.

Accordingly, the new target planning templates used by the New Approach Group could cover ten times the area of first generation atomic weapons. After their initial study was complete, Goodpaster and the team briefed the NATO subordinate commands, the national military headquarters, and the ministries of defense of the member nations. In the United States, the briefings included President Eisenhower, who was well informed on nuclear weapons from his time as Army chief of staff. At this point, Eisenhower, like Goodpaster and other planners, thought of the transition from fission to fusion devices as simply resulting in a much more powerful weapon, in a typical progression of military technology.[48]

BACK TO THE CORPS OF ENGINEERS—BRIEFLY

In early 1954, at about the time Colonel Goodpaster was scheduled to leave SHAPE, he got word that General Ridgway, the chief of staff of the Army, wanted him to come into the Pentagon to be assistant secretary of the General Staff. Goodpaster, however, was not anxious for the job, preferring to return to an Engineer command. Goodpaster talked to General Gruenther about the matter and asked him if he should be so bold as to write a letter to General Ridgway requesting that he not be considered to serve on the Army staff. Gruenther said, "Sure, you go ahead, but I think you're phoning from jail, but go ahead and write your letter." Goodpaster wrote to General Ridgway, noting that it had been nine years since he had any troop command or Engineer duty and thought it better that he should go to that type of assignment. Surprisingly, General Ridgway sent a cable to Goodpaster, with a copy to General Gruenther, saying that he fully agreed. General Gruenther added, in a short note to Goodpaster, "You are a very good letter writer."[49]

Returning to Washington in July 1954, Goodpaster went to the chief of Engineers office, where they welcomed him back and told him that he would be assigned to San Francisco as the district engineer. It was a confirmed assignment for two full years. With orders in hand, Andy, Dossy, Susan, and Anne moved to San Francisco where he was briefed on his responsibilities for Corps of Engineers military and civilian projects in the district that extended from Salt Lake City to Wake Island, including Hawaii.

In October 1954, when Goodpaster returned from visiting Engineer projects in the district, Dossy told him that there had been a call from Washington from the Secretary of the Army General Staff. When Goodpaster returned the call, he was told that the Chief of Staff, General Ridgway, would like to see him on Monday morning if possible. Goodpaster asked how long he would likely be in Washington. He was told, no more than forty-eight hours.[50]

Colonel Goodpaster flew back to Washington and went directly to the chief of staff's office, where he was met by Brigadier General Tony Biddle, whom he knew well from their recent tours at SHAPE. Biddle said, "I've got bad news for you," then reported that Pete Carroll, their colleague at SHAPE who was then assigned to the White House, had just died. Biddle added that the president has asked for Goodpaster to take over Carroll's White House job. Furthermore, Biddle commented, "General Ridgway doesn't want to discuss the issue with you. This is a done deal."[51]

Soon after returning to San Francisco, Goodpaster arranged for the household goods to be picked up for the move to Washington. They had arrived from Paris only a few days earlier. His confirmed two-year tour as an engineer lasted just two months, a brief but happy tour.[52]

NOTES

1. Smith, *Eisenhower in War and Peace*, 491.
2. George C. Marshall, *DOD Semiannual Report of the Secretary of Defense, January 1–June 30, 1951*, 2–7; 13–15.
3. Oldfield, "In the Beginning . . . There Was a Treaty," *Army*, April 1969, 54.
4. Goodpaster, Mandel interviews, tape 10. At that time, the Western European Union included Britain, France, Belgium, the Netherlands, and Luxembourg.
5. Ibid.
6. Oldfield, "In the Beginning," 52–59.
7. Goodpaster, Mandell interviews, tape 11. Oldfield, "In the Beginning," 56.
8. Oldfield, "In the Beginning," 55.
9. Ibid., 59.
10. Goodpaster, Mandel interviews, tapes 10 and 11.
11. Although perhaps more appropriately titled 1st Viscount Montgomery of Alamein, he was generally referred to as "Field Marshal" within the headquarters at the time.
12. Goodpaster, Mandel interviews, tapes 10 and 11.
13. Ibid., tape 11.
14. Ibid.
15. Ibid.
16. Ibid.
17. Smith, *Eisenhower in War and Peace*, 498; Goodpaster, Johnson and Ferguson interview, January 9, 1976.
18. Smith, *Eisenhower in War and Peace*, 498–99.
19. Goodpaster, Mandel interviews, tape 11.
20. Gordon, McKinsie interview, Washington, DC, July 22, 1975, in Truman Library oral history collection.
21. Goodpaster, Mandell interviews, tape 11; Goodpaster-drafted letter, Eisenhower to Harriman, December 14, 1951, Papers of Dwight David Eisenhower (hereafter "PDDE"), XII, 788–89.
22. Gordon, McKinsie interview.
23. *DOD Semiannual Report of the Secretary of Defense, January 1–June 30, 1951*, 61–65.
24. Sulzberger, *A Long Row of Candles*, 708–9; also see Eisenhower letter to his son, January 11, 1952, describing Goodpaster, Carroll and Starbird as "really brilliant," PDDE, XII, 872–73.
25. Goodpaster, Mandel interviews, tape 13.
26. Smith, *Eisenhower in War and Peace*, 502–14. General Clay had previously headed the Allied occupation forces in Germany.
27. Eisenhower, *At Ease*, 372; Smith, *Eisenhower in War and Peace*, 495–96.
28. Cited in Smith, *Eisenhower in War and Peace*, 508.
29. Smith, *Eisenhower in War and Peace*, 513–14.
30. Bowie and Immerman, *Waging Peace*, 45, 67, 96.
31. "Project Solarium Outline" June 1, 1953, White House, National Security Council Staff Papers, Disaster File, box 39 (Project Solarium), Eisenhower Library. Also see *Foreign Relations of the United States, 1952–1954, Vol. II, National Security Affairs, Part 1*, 326–443; 349–54. Hereafter *FRUS*.
32. Ibid.; Bowie and Immerman, *Waging Peace*, 125.
33. Goodpaster, Mandell interviews, January 15, 2002.
34. Handwritten note on Solarium Project, approved by president May 9, 1953, White House, National Security Council Staff Papers, Disaster File, box 39 (Project Solarium), Eisenhower Library. Kennan/Mr. X, "The Sources of Soviet Conduct," *Foreign Affairs* 25, no. 4 (July 1947): 575–76. Mitrovich, *Undermining the Kremlin*, 137.
35. Team C chairman, Adm. Richard Lansing Conolly, a veteran of World War I, where he earned a Navy Cross and World War II, where he commanded a squadron of destroyers, was president of the Naval War College. G. Frederick Reinhard was a veteran diplomat who had served in Moscow and on Eisenhower's SHAPE staff in World War II. Lt. Gen. Lemnitzer

served on Eisenhower's World War II staff and helped negotiate the surrender of Italian and German forces in World War II. Leslie Snowden Brady was a senior USIA official in Moscow. Kilbourne Johnson earned a Distinguished Service Cross in World War II. Colonel Harold K. Johnson survived the Bataan death march, the sinking of a Japanese transport moving prisoners of war to Japan, and internment in Japan and Korea.

36. Goodpaster in Pickett, op cit., 22.

37. "Summary of Points Made in Discussion Following Presentation by Task Forces," July 16, 1953, White House, National Security Council Staff Papers, Disaster File, box 39 (Project Solarium), Eisenhower Library.

38. Task Force C Report, July 16, 1953, White House, National Security Council Staff Papers, Disaster File, box 39 (Project Solarium), Eisenhower Library.

39. The complete set of Solarium Task Force reports is in OSS, NSC Series, Subject subseries, box 9 (Solarium), Eisenhower Library.

40. Goodpaster, Mandel interviews, tape 11.

41. Kennan, Goodpaster, and Bowie in Pickett, op. cit.

42. Bowie in Pickett, op. cit., 30–32.

43. *FRUS, 1952–1954*, 2: 565. NSC 162/2 Report to the NSC, October 30, 1953, White House, National Security Council Staff Papers, Disaster File, box 11 (NSC 162/2), Eisenhower Library.

44. Goodpaster, op. cit., 38.

45. Goodpaster, Mandel interviews, January 15, 2002, tape 8.

46. Marshall to Goodpaster, Goodpaster Papers, Research Guide by Aaron Haberman, xi, Marshall Library.

47. Goodpaster, Mandel interviews, January 15, 2002, tape 10.

48. Goodpaster, Mandel interviews, tape 10.

49. Goodpaster, Mandel interviews, January 16, 2002.

50. Ibid.

51. Ibid.

52. Ibid.

Chapter Eight

Eisenhower White House (1954–1961)

STAFF SECRETARY AND DEFENSE LIAISON

Eisenhower created the position of staff secretary out of frustration early in his administration. Initially, White House paperwork was not handled as efficiently as Eisenhower wanted, and he became frustrated when papers were lost or delayed. He said that he was not going to be his own sergeant major and wanted a more responsible system established. After about ten days, he had not seen much improvement, so he contacted Paul T. "Pete" Carroll, who was a student at the National War College and had served with Goodpaster on Eisenhower's staff at SHAPE. He told Pete, "We need a secretary of the staff and Carroll, you're it, starting from this moment."[1]

Eisenhower chose the title "Staff Secretary and Defense Liaison Officer" for the new position. He wanted this person to establish a close, substantive liaison with all of the government on national security affairs, especially with the State Department, Defense Department, CIA, and Atomic Energy Commission (AEC). The president wanted to keep day-to-day operations and activities out of the White House as much as possible, yet he needed to keep well informed.

The job was enormously stressful. Pete Carroll suffered a heart attack in early October and died. President Eisenhower called on Goodpaster for his replacement. On October 10, 1954, Goodpaster moved into his office just outside the Oval Office and the office of Ann Whitman, the president's personal secretary. He and his staff of five were nominally under White House chief of staff Sherman Adams, but in practice, Goodpaster worked directly for the president on a daily basis. Goodpaster's job was to assure that the president was well informed on all important national security issues and foreign intelligence. All national security–related White House documents, except for personal correspondence, went through Goodpaster. He briefed the president daily on national security developments. Goodpaster attended Cabinet and National Security Council (NSC) meetings, working closely with Secretary of Defense Charles Wilson and Secretary of State John Foster Dulles, National Security Advisor Robert Cutler and Sherman Adams. [2]

Despite his title and position on organization charts, Goodpaster was far more than a secretary. In addition to channeling all the intelligence, diplomatic, and military papers to the president, Goodpaster was responsible for ensuring that bad news or opposing views were not withheld. Similarly, in arranging meetings for the president, Goodpaster ensured that key participants were not barred from discussions. Most importantly, Goodpaster followed up to ensure that the president's decisions were carried out as intended. In most cases, he was in the room when decisions on key security issues were made. They developed such a close working relationship that Goodpaster was referred to as the president's *alter ego* and the only man from whom Eisenhower kept no secrets. Goodpaster wrote the authoritative record of the national security affairs of the Eisenhower administration for the next six years in his frequent memoranda of record of high-level meetings. These memos provided a common understanding of what transpired during discussions and any presidential decisions. They also assisted Goodpaster in following up on the implementation of the president's desires. [3]

Eisenhower frequently reminded Goodpaster of the importance of institutionally separating policy making from operations. The more immediate, active, and compelling nature of operations usually consumed the attention of staff members and resulted in the strong tendency of operations to "eat up policy." Instead, Eisenhower relied on the NSC to develop policy and ensure that it was integrated into long-term planning. Goodpaster was positioned at the intersection of policy, plans, and operations to ensure that they were well coordinated within the government and consistent with the president's intentions. [4]

Goodpaster, however, was not the president's national security advisor. That newly created position, assistant to the president for national security affairs, was first occupied by Robert C. "Bobby" Cutler, a quiet, discrete attorney who had served in World War I as an infantry officer and served on Stimson's War Department staff during World War II. Cutler was recommended to Eisenhower for the job by General Marshall. Cutler served in this position during 1953–1955 and again in 1957–1958. Eisenhower relied on Cutler for long-range planning orchestrated by the NSC, while Goodpaster focused more on day-to-day national security issues. [5]

Each morning, Goodpaster provided the CIA's daily briefing to the president, along with a summary of the State Department overnight messages and Defense Department activities. This briefing frequently raised questions from the president and triggered tasks for Goodpaster to follow up on with the responsible departments. In addition, Goodpaster would arrange ad hoc meetings for the president on issues of special interest that were not otherwise addressed. Furthermore, Goodpaster accompanied the president on most of his foreign trips.[6]

Following the morning briefing, Goodpaster would bring in a stack of papers for the president. As they paged through them, Eisenhower would inquire about the background of the problem or proposal, the nature and timing of any actions requested, and how it fit into the larger picture. The president posed questions about nearly every paper, and his mind worked very fast. This put Goodpaster under considerable pressure. As he put it, often he could feel "a little bit of moisture running down my back as I worked through [the review that] would normally be a half-hour, forty five minutes or sometimes more."[7]

Goodpaster also took careful notes at the Thursday morning meetings of the National Security Council. The president met regularly with the vice president, secretary of state, secretary of defense, secretary of the treasury, chairman of the Joint Chiefs of Staff, and director of Central Intelligence. The NSC met 366 times during the Eisenhower administration, with the president chairing 329 of the meetings. Goodpaster also attended Cabinet and other high-level meetings.[8]

While the relationship with Eisenhower grew closer, Goodpaster nevertheless avoided attending social functions at the White House. He much preferred spending his leisure time with Dossy, his family, and his Army friends.[9]

BATTLES WITHIN THE PENTAGON

The problem of inter-service rivalry was not resolved by the National Security Act of 1947, which integrated the military services within the Defense Department. One of Goodpaster's early ad hoc tasks came on December 1, 1954, when he was called by Secretary of Defense Wilson, who said he was having great trouble developing an integrated budget for the Defense Department. Wilson, former head of General Motors, wanted to bring the Chiefs over to meet with the president so they could get firsthand guidance. When Goodpaster raised the issue with the president, Eisenhower related his experience when President Truman asked him to come down from Columbia University and chair a meeting with the Joint Chiefs to prepare the first consolidated Defense Department budget. While intimately familiar with the challenge of developing a defense budget, Eisenhower was not sympathetic with Wilson's problem; he commented: "Hell, that's what I've got the Secretary of Defense over there for."[10]

Nevertheless, Goodpaster persisted because Wilson continued to be unable to get the service chiefs to agree on the defense budget. Eisenhower relented, and Goodpaster set up a meeting with the president, the secretary of defense and the Joint Chiefs of Staff in the White House. Eisenhower took charge immediately and said, "Let me tell you what I think are the principal needs in terms of shaping and maintaining our military forces." He started with the need for a strategic bombing capability; he then noted the need for collective forces in Europe, followed by the need for control of the seas, and finally, the need to insure the introduction of appropriate technologies. The president also emphasized that a sound economy was a fundamental element of national security. Eisenhower talked for about a half hour without a note. Then he sent the chiefs away to prepare a budget that was responsive to those needs.[11]

Goodpaster was once again impressed with Eisenhower's comprehensive grasp of the big picture and how all the pieces fit together, including the economy. Furthermore, like the Solarium Project experience, Eisenhower could articulate clearly a complex, integrated concept.

Shortly thereafter, Goodpaster got another call from Secretary Wilson asking if he could have the president put in writing what he had told the chiefs. Goodpaster had taken notes during the meeting so he agreed to raise the issue with the president. The president agreed to let Goodpaster draft a letter, which Goodpaster "doctored a little bit in terms of the need for engaging in lesser conflicts." Goodpaster pointed out his addition to the president, whereupon Eisenhower took his pencil and marked through the addition, then rewrote word for word what he had said. Then the president said, "Well, see if this meets Wilson's needs."

After receiving the letter, Wilson called Goodpaster again and asked if the letter could be made "just a little bit stronger." Goodpaster said he would try and drafted a letter. When Goodpaster showed the draft to the president, Eisenhower said, "The rest of this is fine, but this is not quite right." He then lined out with his pencil and wrote again, word for word, what he had said previously. At that point, he looked up at Goodpaster and said, "Now, Andy, this can either be done your way or my way, and I guarantee you that ultimately it's going to be done my way." Goodpaster replied, "Yes, sir, Mr. President. I think I understand." Goodpaster sent the letter to Wilson and recounted the story many times to subordinates over the next fifty years when they overedited his drafts.[12]

Goodpaster learned from this experience that the fundamental problem was institutional, not conceptual. Everyone understood what the president wanted, but they were unwilling to subordinate their individual bureaucracies to achieve the results intended.

This early episode also introduced Goodpaster to Eisenhower's skepticism regarding the need for increased defense spending. For the next six years, they would work hard to resist constant demands for increased spending. Eisenhower was familiar with the insatiable service appetites for more forces and new weapons driven more by technology than by strategy. The episode also highlighted Eisenhower's concern to avoid any predispositions to become involved in "lesser conflicts," foreshadowing the Vietnam War.

A related issue that captured Goodpaster's attention was Eisenhower's antipathy toward inter-service rivalry. Later, in 1957 with a new secretary of defense, Neil McElroy, onboard, the president launched an effort to reorganize the Defense Department that became the most spectacular legislative battle of the year. Goodpaster noted that Eisenhower and McElroy agreed that the core of the problem was the concentration of power in the services, especially in the service secretaries, the service military chiefs, and their respective staffs. The president noted that the armed forces had 130 liaison officers assigned to congressional work, with a similar cadre involved in public relations. The result was a fragmented, divisive effort. In his 1958 State of the Union address, President Eisenhower declared that he wanted to curtail these dysfunctional and wasteful practices. [13]

The president argued that any future war must be fought with all the services combined into a unified, concentrated effort. And, he argued, the peacetime organization of the Defense Department should be structured accordingly. Eisenhower elaborated on the problem, noting that the current system was too complicated to work in times of war, when minutes are as precious as months had been in the past. "Separate ground, sea and air warfare is gone forever, but our system, codified in law, has not kept pace with the changes." [14]

In February 1956, the Joint Chiefs asked Goodpaster to recapitulate for them the president's concept of their role. In his response, Goodpaster noted that Eisenhower envisioned that the JCS would work as a corporate body, not as advocates for their services. Eisenhower also advised the Joint Chiefs to not carry their internal fights to the public. The JCS should provide the key interface between the military and the country—a point of union with the public and its government. The Chiefs should provide their collective professional judgment on what is best for the country, the best means of preserving the peace. [15]

In pressing for reform, however, the president met with strong, immediate resistance to change, especially from influential members of Congress and from military service associations. Opponents charged that Eisenhower was trying to create a Prussian General Staff that would threaten liberty. In rebuttal, Eisenhower outlined his main proposals, including establishing unified commands for operational forces with a chain of command running from the president, through the secretary of defense and Joint Chiefs, to the unified commands, rather than through the services. He also proposed strengthening the chairman of the Joint Chiefs of Staff and making the secretary of defense responsible for all research and development.[16]

Eisenhower knew he was in for a heated debate, but he welcomed that. He understood that only through open, free, and thorough debate would any plan gain the necessary support of the majority of experienced military leaders. He also recognized his strengths and went around Congress with appeals directly to the American public. He wrote letters to influential Americans; a business friend sent twenty thousand copies of one of Eisenhower's letters to his friends. Soon members of Congress were deluged with letters of support for reorganizing the Defense Department.[17]

On August 6, 1958, President Eisenhower signed the Defense Reorganization Act into law. It was a compromise that contained some objectionable provisions, but it was an important step in the right direction. It gave the president, through the secretary of defense, the power to establish and control "unified or specified combatant commands for . . . military missions." The act curtailed the operational control of the services over deployed forces. It also established the position of director of defense research and engineering. Goodpaster knew that Eisenhower had won an important battle, but the war was not over.[18]

The struggle continued mainly over the Defense Department budget. Eisenhower believed strongly that a sound economy was a fundamental requirement of United States security and worked to contain the appetites of the services for more funds. The president was constantly fighting charges that increasing Soviet capabilities had shifted the military balance, demanding ever-larger U.S. expenditures, including for more military assistance to allies. At one point Goodpaster noted with his close advisors that Eisenhower even questioned whether it might be better to have some countries as neutrals rather than allies.[19]

The high priority Eisenhower accorded to the economy made a strong impression on Goodpaster. In 1961, near the end of the second term of the administration, Goodpaster noted that Eisenhower emphasized that "the thing that troubles him most in the whole security picture (with one exception) is financial in nature—the danger of excessive, unnecessary spending." The exception was nuclear war.[20]

THE PRESIDENT'S FOOTBALL (1954)

After a net evaluation of the likely damage that the Soviet Union could inflict on the United States with a nuclear attack, Gordon Gray, head of the Office of Defense Mobilization, spoke to Goodpaster about the need for developing a very thorough plan for presidential actions in the event of a nuclear attack. They both met with Eisenhower, who approved their suggestion. As of that time, President Eisenhower had reserved for himself the decision to use nuclear weapons. However, additional authorities and guidance were lacking for other actions by government agencies that might be needed in the event of a nuclear attack.[21]

Goodpaster and Gray developed and coordinated a comprehensive set of documents for the president to use to implement actions to deal with the likely consequences of a nuclear attack or other national emergency, including the delegation of authority to use nuclear weapons should the president be unavailable. These documents were put in a briefcase and carried by a presidential aide, often Goodpaster himself. The briefcase became known as the "football." Many of these original documents, with the initials "D.E." in the lower corner, were carried for use by several subsequent presidents. Goodpaster also noted Eisenhower's concern that military commanders understand the "letter and spirit" of his intentions regarding the use of nuclear weapons. To facilitate this, Goodpaster helped arrange annual meetings for the president exclusively with the responsible military commanders so they would learn firsthand about his concerns for "utmost discretion and understanding."[22]

BOMBER GAP (1954)

Another of Goodpaster's ad hoc tasks was to look into the bomber-gap issue following the publication of a National Intelligence Estimate (NIE)[23] concluding that Soviet bomber production would soon result in a bomber force larger than that of the United States. Eisenhower read the NIE and said, "I'm just not convinced. I'd like to know what's behind this judgment."

Goodpaster met with the CIA analysts who drafted the estimate and found that the key judgments, as in the previous year's version of this NIE, were based on estimated production capabilities, not actual inventories of aircraft produced. In fact, these capabilities were never reached; instead, the Soviets were shifting investment priorities to long-range missiles and space launch vehicles. When Goodpaster briefed the president on his findings, Eisenhower said, "That's all I need to know."[24]

Nevertheless, for the next two years, Eisenhower was under pressure from Congress, the Air Force and the defense industry to increase spending on bombers. The myth of a bomber gap was not laid to rest until after U-2 overflights of the Soviet Union confirmed many fewer bombers had been produced than estimated earlier. For example, by 1959, Goodpaster recorded at an NSC meeting, that Soviet long-range bomber production had been low and noted the first test of an intercontinental ballistic missile.[25]

NUCLEAR WEAPONS AND ARMS CONTROL

By 1954, Eisenhower, in discussions with Goodpaster and his close advisers, made it clear that nuclear weapons had changed the way general war would be conducted. In these private conversations, Eisenhower noted that it would have been impossible for him to invade the European continent the way he did in World War II if the Germans had nuclear weapons. In the atomic age, it would be virtually impossible to move large formations of land forces to Europe or Asia. Instead, we must rely on long-range aircraft and missiles to carry the attack to the enemy. Similarly, atomic attacks on the United States would create havoc and the need for ready reserve forces to restore order and rebuild production.[26]

For these reasons, in Eisenhower's view, the United States needed to move from a World War II and Korean War strategy and force posture to one that took into more account the impact of nuclear weapons. The resulting new national security strategy and force posture met with substantial resistance in the Pentagon and Congress and also required careful coordination with NATO allies. In November 1954, Goodpaster became involved in a series of strategy meetings on what was called the "New Look." Goodpaster noted that the president wanted to assure allies, in the face of some skepticism on the part of French military leaders, that nuclear weapons would be available in the hands of U.S. forces. Furthermore, the United States would make some accommodations in military assistance programs for developing forces for more integrated actions, without promising additional levels of funding.[27]

When the secretary of defense noted that the new nuclear strategy might enable the United States to bring home the two American divisions sent to bolster NATO, Goodpaster noted the president's disagreement. Nuclear forces were not a substitute for conventional forces. Eisenhower maintained that U.S. forces should not be reduced until European forces were stronger. Interestingly, the president added that spending $2 billion per year on military assistance to allied forces was a good investment in the long run because it would enable eventual reductions in U.S. forces required to bolster alliance forces.[28]

While aware of Eisenhower's desire to reduce the chances of nuclear war, Goodpaster also found that the president was serious about developing operational U.S. nuclear capabilities. For example, in December 1954, Eisenhower directed that custody of the weapons be transferred from the Atomic Energy Commission to the Department of Defense and arrangements be made for overseas deployments. This helped address the lack of operational nuclear capabilities that Goodpaster had noted earlier in his work with the Advanced Study Group. Goodpaster was now charged with following up the president's decision with the State and Defense Departments. As part of these efforts,

Eisenhower wanted to insure that spending was contained. Thus, he had Goodpaster get a statement from the AEC director that the new nuclear weapons programs proposed by the JCS would not require any additional facilities for producing weapons-grade nuclear material.[29]

In this time frame, Goodpaster also detected an evolution in Eisenhower's thinking about nuclear weapons. Previously, at NATO headquarters, Eisenhower thought of the transition from atomic to hydrogen bombs, or more accurately from fission to fusion devices, as simply resulting in much more powerful weapons, in the typical progression of military technology. However, in his White House discussions with Goodpaster, Eisenhower was increasingly of the view that fusion weapons truly changed the nature of warfare. In Eisenhower's mind, they made war "insanity . . . mutual suicide rather than a means of conducting any other kind of rational military action." Increasingly Eisenhower's thinking focused on preventing the use of these "terribly destructive devices."[30]

One of Eisenhower's early initiatives was his "Atoms for Peace" proposal presented to the United Nations General Assembly on December 8, 1953. He noted both the hopes for improving the human condition through atomic power and research and the need for collective efforts to reduce the dangers of catastrophic nuclear war. This was the first time that a national leader had posed the dilemma of these two aspects of nuclear power. In his speech, Eisenhower noted:

> My country wants to be constructive, not destructive. It wants agreement, not wars among nations . . . the United States pledges before you—and therefore before the world—its determination to help solve the fearful atomic dilemma—to devote its entire heart and mind to find the way by which the miraculous inventiveness of man shall not be dedicated to his death, but consecrated to his life.[31]

More specifically, Eisenhower boldly called for arms control talks to reduce and eventually eliminate nuclear weapons. He also called for the establishment of the International Atomic Energy Agency (IAEA) to promote and regulate the peaceful uses of atomic energy. Established in 1957, the IAEA also implemented safeguards to verify that nuclear energy was not used for military purposes and established standards for nuclear safety.[32]

In particular, Eisenhower was interested in arms-control negotiations with the Soviets. He tasked Goodpaster to follow closely the work of Harold Stassen, whom Eisenhower had appointed as his disarmament advisor. Stassen represented the United States on the five-nation UN disarmament subcommittee, but little progress was made on the multinational front.[33]

Goodpaster recommended that Stassen's proposed initiatives be incorporated into a broader framework and sequence of concrete actions to promote peace than the ambiguous treaty of amity and friendship proposed by the

Soviets. These actions should begin with aerial inspections. Goodpaster also suggested adding the atoms-for-peace initiative and calling for reciprocal inspections to build confidence and a code of conduct to reduce tensions in hot spots, especially in the Middle East and Asia. Eisenhower agreed with Goodpaster and decided that the United States could not undertake arms-control restrictions without assured provisions for aerial inspections. [34]

Goodpaster, in a 1958 memo, captured the evolution in thinking about nuclear weapons and national security policy. Dulles had advanced the idea of "Massive Retaliation" in December 1950 in response to former president Hoover's support for "Fortress America." While the deterrent value of Massive Retaliation was useful and avoided the need to have U.S. forces deployed everywhere threatened by the Soviet Union, U.S. allies were beginning to doubt the U.S. use of nuclear weapons that would lead to mutual suicide. As small wars posed an increasing problem, graduated deterrent capabilities were needed with a spectrum of nuclear weapons down to very low yields, along with improved conventional weapons, coupled with an invulnerable strategic retaliatory capability. Even with such a spectrum of capabilities, Goodpaster noted that deliberations concluded that graduated deterrence might succeed in stabilizing limited aggression in perhaps not more than 50 percent of the cases. [35]

OPEN SKIES AND THE GENEVA SUMMIT (1955)

Another Eisenhower initiative to improve the prospects for arms control was launched at the 1955 Big Four Summit meeting with the leaders of Britain, France, and the Soviet Union in Geneva. Before the meeting, the State Department favored a meeting at the heads-of-state level that was limited to setting an agenda that would then be pursued by the foreign ministers and the U.S. secretary of state. That, however, was not what President Eisenhower had in mind; he wanted a more substantive summit, and Goodpaster had to ensure that the bureaucracy supported the president's wishes.

Also at that time, Nelson Rockefeller was leading a presidential initiative on the war of ideas in an important campaign of the Cold War. This initiative involved developing ways to spread American ideas of freedom, democracy and human rights publicly and internationally. Part of this initiative also involved Rockefeller's organizing a study group that prepared a proposal for "Open Skies" allowing for overflight of each other's territory to better monitor military activity. [36]

The president, according to Goodpaster, thought that more transparency and better communication with the Soviets would serve U.S. purposes better than mutual recriminations. Furthermore, this was consistent with the priority of aerial inspections in arms control efforts. The president understood the limitations of Open Skies, but at the time he was primarily interested in early warning, particularly the forward deployment of Soviet aircraft in preparations for an attack. Eisenhower realized that eventually missiles would reduce the significance of such indicators, but in the short term, Soviet aircraft posed the greatest threat of delivering nuclear weapons. At the same time, he believed that the Soviets would not deliberately attack the United States and cause a nuclear war. [37]

Speaking without notes near the end of the summit, Eisenhower surprised everyone with the Open Skies proposal that he introduced by noting, "I have been searching my heart and mind for something that I could say here that would convince everyone of the great sincerity of the United States in approaching problems of disarmament." The proposal was widely endorsed but, as anticipated, received an equivocal response from Soviet premier Nikolai Bulganin, the nominal Soviet leader after Stalin's death. At a tea following the official ceremonies, Nikita Khrushchev, first secretary of the Communist Party, came up to Eisenhower and said, "No, no, no, no! You are trying to look into our bedrooms." Eisenhower told Goodpaster, as they rode back from the meeting, "At that moment, I knew who was really in charge of the Soviet delegation; it was Khrushchev." This observation proved correct. In 1958, Khrushchev officially succeeded Bulganin as premier.

The Soviet leadership had been in flux since Stalin's death. Lavrentiy Beria, head of the security services, had been executed. Premier Malenkov had been demoted by the Central Committee in favor of Bulganin. But the Geneva Summit meetings confirmed to Eisenhower that Khrushchev held the real power in Moscow. Thus, Eisenhower focused his attention on building a relationship with Khrushchev. In doing so, Eisenhower consistently demonstrated respect for the Soviet Union. Similarly, the Soviets took steps to demonstrate personal respect for Eisenhower. Marshal Georgy Zhukov had been brought out of domestic exile and was now serving as defense minister. Zhukov and Eisenhower met for a lengthy private lunch. [38]

While respectful, Eisenhower did not withhold his views of the shortcomings of communism and was not above piquing the Soviet delegation. For example, during the summit Eisenhower held a reception in honor of Andrei Gromyko's birthday and included Bulganin, Khrushchev, and Molotov. For the party, Eisenhower had vodka served in water goblets, with a piece of ice floating. Perhaps an intentional breach of custom, the large size of the glasses was intended to show the American way of drinking vodka. The Soviets were surprised and sipped it cautiously, except for Bulganin, who drank his quite manfully. During the party, Gromyko sat stone-faced through the entire affair. President Eisenhower noted that he was a little surprised by Gromyko's behavior. To that Goodpaster replied, "Well, sir . . . My grandmother used to say, if you can't say something pleasant, keep quiet, and Gromyko didn't know anything pleasant to say." On balance, however, Eisenhower was successful in establishing an initial relationship with Khrushchev.[39]

These experiences enabled Goodpaster to further understand Eisenhower's success in dealing with other leaders. The president was skilled in judging the character of others and made great efforts to understand their perspectives. Personal relationships of all kinds mattered greatly. The experience also impressed Goodpaster with Eisenhower's broad concept of security in terms of defense, deterrence and arms control, rather than the more typical one-dimensional approach of focusing almost entirely on an arms buildup being called for at the time.[40]

FRENCH INDOCHINA, VIETNAM (1954)

Before Goodpaster joined the White House staff, the NSC and the JCS debated how to deal with the deteriorating French position in Indochina, beyond the already substantial military assistance program. National policy included Indochina among certain countries of such strategic importance that the United States would probably be compelled to intervene militarily if threatened seriously. Supporting studies even concluded that nuclear weapons might be used effectively. Other studies estimated huge costs of intervention requiring substantial increases in the defense budget, extending terms of service for draftees, and activating National Guard units.[41]

In January 1954, the French insisted that they would pull out of Indochina unless the United States participated directly in the war. President Eisenhower, however, was "bitterly opposed" to U.S. ground forces becoming involved because the Vietnamese would transfer their hatred of the French to the Americans. Furthermore, he argued that the Indochina War would absorb our troops by divisions. By April, with French forces besieged at Dien Bien Phu, Eisenhower emphasized there was "no possibility whatever of U.S. unilateral intervention in Indochina." Congressional support was judged "impossible."[42]

The French garrison fell on May 7, 1954. France signed an armistice agreement in July 1954 creating separate states of Cambodia, Laos, and Vietnam, with Vietnam temporarily divided along the 17th parallel with the North under control of Ho Chi Minh and the Vietminh communist movement, and Ngo Dinh Diem, a Catholic from the North, gaining control in the South after a referendum.

After the split, Eisenhower was faced with a decision as to whether to provide aid to Diem. Previously, the United States had been underwriting about 40 percent of French war efforts in Indochina. Goodpaster noted that while the situation in Vietnam continued to deteriorate, Secretary of State Dulles was inclined to back Diem. Dulles said he was thinking in terms of a limited commitment of helping build a constabulary force rather than a twenty-division force. Joint Chiefs chairman Admiral Radford responded that the Joint Chiefs were thinking in terms of a five-and-a-half light-division force and a militia totaling about 220,000 personnel and costing $400 to $500 million in the first year. Dulles went on to note that we would pull out advisors and support if the situation could not be brought under control. [43]

Dulles asked Goodpaster if he knew of any appropriate senior military officers who might be sent to Vietnam to assess the situation. Goodpaster suggested General Lawton Collins. Dulles then raised the issue with Eisenhower, suggesting that it would be interesting to determine the prospects for South Vietnam as an independent country. [44]

Eisenhower agreed and engaged General Collins to make an assessment of the quality of the government of South Vietnam, the prospects for building an army capable of defending the country, and what it would take in training and equipment from the United States. Collins concluded it was not certain that South Vietnam could form a viable society and nation, but there was at least a reasonable chance it could be done. Such efforts would require training and equipment from the United States. Eisenhower decided to go ahead and approved a military assistance program for South Vietnam. By this point, Goodpaster was involved in a process of correlating U.S. purposes and power in Vietnam, a challenge that would haunt him for nearly two decades. [45]

At this stage, however, Goodpaster noted that Eisenhower was thinking of Vietnam in terms of the Cold War and a limited commitment; he did not want to tie down U.S. forces in small wars on the periphery of the Soviet Union. These views are reflected in several Goodpaster memos of discussions between the president, Army chief of staff Maxwell Taylor and JCS chairman Admiral Radford in the context of the Joint Strategic Objectives Plan. Eisenhower believed that the United States would not get engaged with major ground forces in small wars, keeping these forces available for larger-scale hostilities when greater U.S. interests were at stake. Radford agreed, noting that if the situation in Vietnam deteriorated, we would certainly not move in with large numbers of Army forces. The main Army task there was military assistance to build up the indigenous forces. [46]

PRESIDENT EISENHOWER'S HEART ATTACK (1955)

One of the key roles Goodpaster played was ensuring continuity of leadership after the president suffered a heart attack on September 24, 1955. As the "man with the briefcase," Goodpaster had to ensure that necessary decisions could be made in a timely manner by competent, legal authority. While the law and planned procedures detailed how to handle emergency situations, Goodpaster, with Sherman Adams, determined the appropriate workload for the president during his six-week recovery. Goodpaster also coordinated more closely than before with Vice President Richard Nixon. [47]

In undertaking this responsibility, Goodpaster became close to Mamie Eisenhower, who was understandably concerned that the president not be overtaxed by his workload. After the president was released from the hospital, arrangements were made for him to recuperate at their farm in Gettysburg. A secure phone was installed, and Goodpaster flew up daily by helicopter to meet with the president, while Sherman Adams visited on a weekly basis. [48]

In balancing the demands of the office of the president and Eisenhower's health, along with the desires of his wife and family, Goodpaster was able to develop a "close, loving relationship" with Mamie. She would ask Goodpaster for help in reducing stress on the president and, on one occasion, asked if it would be possible to build a small room next to the Oval Office where the president could relax, read, and paint pictures without returning to the main White House residence. Goodpaster had the outer office space remodeled, creating the president's study, much to the chagrin of the White House architect, but useful for the president. [49]

During Eisenhower's illness, Goodpaster was also in close, very private contact with Vice President Richard Nixon. Goodpaster kept Nixon well informed so he could assume the presidency should that become necessary. This was a very sensitive matter because of concerns that Nixon might be too ambitious and move aggressively to take charge. [50]

This problem did not arise, however, and the leadership crisis worked out well. Goodpaster developed a high regard for Nixon. Goodpaster saw Nixon in operation at every cabinet and NSC meeting. In Goodpaster's view, Nixon had an excellent sense of strategy. [51]

However, Eisenhower suffered several more serious illnesses that caused him to worry about his ability to function as president, especially if a national emergency occurred while he was incapacitated. After the third such occasion in November 1957 and consultations with the attorney general and a few others, he prepared a letter that noted his concerns and delegated to Vice President Nixon the authority to decide that presidential power should be transferred, at least temporarily, to the vice president. Goodpaster would have been, no doubt, a key participant in helping decide if such a transfer were to become necessary. [52]

Many years later, Goodpaster concluded that Nixon's contributions to the Eisenhower administration had not been appropriately recognized. Unfortunately, that problem was compounded by President Eisenhower in remarks at the end of a press conference when he was asked about the specific things that he called on Vice President Nixon to do. Eisenhower decided to end it with a little quip, saying something along the lines of, "Well, give me until next week and I will come up with a few of the things." Despite Eisenhower's attempt at humor, it was widely reported that he was unable to think of anything that Nixon had done. That hurt Nixon badly in both a personal and public sense. Eisenhower regretted his remark. The incident made a deep impression on Goodpaster, who observed that it's very dangerous to try to make a humorous remark publicly because it may be misinterpreted or deliberately misused. He later termed it "a good learning point."[53]

TAIWAN STRAIT CRISES (1955, 1958)

In the 1950s, Asia was a Cold War tinderbox. The cease-fire in Korea had ended the hostilities but resulted in the world's most heavily defended border on both sides and frequent provocations. After Korea, the most immediate threat was the Taiwan Strait, where the last chapter in China's civil war was still being written. United States forces were involved in both cases.

After initially declaring in January 1950 that the United States would not intervene in the Chinese civil war as fighting continued for control of many islands along the coast, the invasion of South Korea in June 1950 caused Truman to send the Seventh Fleet into the Taiwan Strait to defend Taiwan.

At one level, this task was fairly straightforward, with the United States providing arms for Chiang Kai-shek's forces and providing naval forces to deter any attempted invasion of the main island. The latter role was not very demanding, given the minimal Chinese communist amphibious and naval capabilities.

The problem was compounded in August 1954, however, by Generalissimo Chiang Kai-shek's defense strategy that included establishing a vulnerable seventy thousand-man garrison on several small islands, including Quemoy and Matsu, just a few miles from the Chinese mainland but one hundred miles from Taiwan. President Eisenhower understood the difficulty of defending and supplying the large force on the small islands, and Goodpaster noted Eisenhower's efforts to persuade Chiang Kai-shek to use the islands as outposts for early warning of an attack while reducing his forces there substantially. But Chiang was reluctant because he was also aware that a confrontation over the islands might draw the United States into direct conflict with Red China. Furthermore, he had strong backing for this position from the powerful anticommunist China lobby in the United States.[54]

After Premier Zhou Enlai called for the liberation of Taiwan, China began shelling Quemoy and Matsu in September 1954. This, in effect, demanded a response from the United States. Admiral Radford, chairman of the Joint Chiefs of Staff, advised the president to defend Taiwan by attacking Chinese airfields and coastal installations if necessary. Congressional pressure, including that from the Senate majority leader, William F. Knowland, urged a strong defense. In December 1954, Congress passed a mutual defense treaty, committing the United States to help with the defense of Taiwan. Eisenhower, however, was aware of how incidents could escalate and draw the United States and the Soviet Union into war because of agreements to help defend Taiwan and Communist China, respectively. Thus, Goodpaster noted, the president refused to escalate tensions while remaining deliberately vague about whether the United States would take direct actions to defend the small islands. [55]

After some of the more lightly defended islands fell to the People's Liberation Army (PLA), Eisenhower wanted an assessment of the feasibility of defending Quemoy and Matsu. In particular, he wanted to discuss the situation in detail with the responsible commander, Admiral Felix Stump, commander in chief, Pacific (CINCPAC). At the same time, however, Eisenhower did not want to inflame the issue by calling Stump back to Washington. Instead, he sent Goodpaster for a very private meeting with Stump. Goodpaster reported back that if the Chinese did not attack Quemoy and Matsu in the next ten days, Chiang Kai-shek's forces should be able to build up defenses sufficient to hold the islands against assault with U.S. support, presumably not involving the use of nuclear weapons. [56]

For the next ten days, Eisenhower and Goodpaster watched the situation very closely and, once the reinforcement of defenses was completed, rested a bit easier. At about that time, Congress passed a resolution granting the president authority to use whatever force he deemed necessary in the defense of Taiwan, including Quemoy and Matsu. [57]

The congressional resolution also drew attention to the possible use of nuclear weapons in the defense of those islands. This question was raised at one of the president's weekly press conferences on March 23. The week before, Eisenhower had remarked that he saw no reason why they shouldn't be used. This remark fed fears of war around the world. Just before the conference, Jim Hagerty, the president's press secretary, passed on an urgent message from the State Department advising the president to say as little as possible about Taiwan, to which Eisenhower replied, "Don't worry, Jim, if the question comes up, I will confuse them." It did and he did. In his response, Eisenhower proved his mastery at obfuscation:

> The only thing I know about war was two things: the most changeable factor in war is human nature in its day-by-day manifestation; but the only unchanging factor about war is human nature. And the next thing is that every war is going to astonish you in the way it occurred and the way it is carried out. So that for a man to predict, particularly if he had the responsibility for making the decision, to predict what he is going to use, how he is going to do it, would I think exhibit his ignorance of war; that is what I believe. So I think you just have to wait, and that is the kind of prayerful decision that may someday face a president. [58]

Syntax aside, it was successful in a highly charged political atmosphere. Goodpaster, later reflecting on Eisenhower's response, thought the response was also "militarily sound. . . . In war nothing is certain, but the only thing that is certain is that it will not occur in just the way you expect. And the press wondered, what did he say? That was his way of dealing with this." The more important lesson for Goodpaster was Eisenhower's skill at publicly threatening Beijing with nuclear weapons while not undermining his position domestically.[59]

The crisis was defused as both China and Taiwan backed down from the confrontation. The United States exerted quiet pressure on Chiang Kai-shek, while the Soviet Union exerted similar pressure on China. Other nations added their influence as well to urge peaceful settlement.

Three years later, the pattern was repeated as Mao Zedong declared that "East wind is prevailing over the West wind." Communist China's People's Liberation Army began shelling Quemoy and Matsu again on August 25, 1958, as Mao vowed to seize the islands and invade Taiwan. President Eisenhower met with the Joint Chiefs and Goodpaster to discuss contingency plans and options, then, speaking at a press conference on August 27, asserted that he alone would decide on the use of nuclear weapons.[60]

Once again, pressure behind the scenes worked. Goodpaster noted that after sending Dulles to Taiwan and endorsing a joint communiqué announcing "full solidarity in the face of Chinese Communist armed attacks, Eisenhower also sent private letter to Chiang Kai-shek urging a declaration that "restoring freedom to the Mainland Chinese depends principally on the minds and hearts of the Chinese people, and not the use by your Government of force."[61]

Chiang Kai-shek soon began reducing his one hundred thousand–man garrison on the islands, and China agreed to limit shelling to every other day and use mainly shells with propaganda leaflets, permitting resupply convoys on the off days. By 1958, the interests of the superpowers in avoiding nuclear war were, if anything, even greater than earlier, as their arsenals and delivery means increased.[62]

SUEZ AND HUNGARY (1956)

Crises are studied one at a time, but Goodpaster learned that in fact they are often part of a series of events unfolding simultaneously. For example, in 1956, the Suez Canal and Hungary crises presented such challenges. On October 20, 1956, Eisenhower and Goodpaster began what the president later termed "the most . . . demanding three weeks of my entire Presidency." Although most accounts focus on the president, Goodpaster was involved each day, playing key roles in keeping the president informed by anticipating questions, drafting and dispatching many of the president's communications, and following up on decisions. [63]

Both of these crises had the potential of escalating to full-scale war with the Soviet Union. Furthermore, President Eisenhower was in poor health. After his slow recovery from his heart attack in September 1955, Eisenhower continued to have painful intestinal problems that resulted in major surgery in June 1956. On top of that, the crises coincided with the stress of the final weeks of his reelection campaign. His political opponents focused on Eisenhower's age, his history of life-threatening illnesses, and his lack of support for America's key allies: Britain, France, and Israel.

By 1956, peace in the Middle East was increasingly precarious. Border clashes between the Israelis and Arabs threatened to escalate. At the same time, the Soviet Union was making inroads with promises of arms and attractive financing for domestic projects. While Soviet initiatives were growing, Arab nationalism was pressuring Britain and France to remove their forces from the region. These developments portended major shifts in the complex military balance in the Middle East.

To deal with this situation, President Eisenhower had developed a balanced strategy to promote peace between Israel and the Arab states and block Soviet inroads. His Middle East policy was outlined in NSC 5428, approved on July 23, 1954. A derivative, Plan ALPHA, involved a comprehensive peace effort that included resolution of boundary disputes, access to water and holy places, assistance to Israel and Palestinian refugees, and help for Egypt to construct the Aswan Dam. While the Eisenhower administration was open to aiding Egypt, congressional support was questionable, especially given the likely costs and opposition from Israel. [64]

The Aswan Dam was a high priority for Egypt's Gamal Abdel Nasser to build domestic support after seizing power in 1954. The dam was an ambitious effort designed to help with flood control along the Nile River, create a 350-mile long reservoir that would help irrigate 1.3 million acres, and provide more than half of Egypt's electrical energy, but it was also beyond Egypt's ability to finance independently. Thus, Nasser sought financial aid from the United States and the World Bank.

Goodpaster noted that part of Eisenhower's Middle East policy involved efforts to manage the military balance, particularly by coordinating military assistance programs. These efforts built on the 1950 Tripartite Declaration following the war to establish Israel, in which the United States, Britain, and France agreed to support any victim of aggression in the Middle East and coordinate their military assistance programs for the region. At the same time, Eisenhower opposed efforts by the European powers to reestablish control in their colonies after World War II. In particular, he pressured Britain into signing an agreement with Egypt in 1954 to relinquish control of the Suez Canal Zone and withdraw British troops, then numbering about eighty thousand, by June 18, 1956. The British stipulated, however, that the bases would be made available to the British if it became necessary to defend the canal against foreign aggression. Furthermore, the Suez Canal Company remained under the operational control of an international company with British and French commercial interests.

Eisenhower's efforts to resolve the clash between European colonialism and Arab nationalism by peaceful measures were undermined by Nasser's efforts to involve the Soviet Union and the People's Republic of China. After Nasser reached an agreement for Soviet military equipment (thinly disguised as trading Egyptian cotton for Czechoslovak arms) and recognized Communist China, the United States delayed reaching an agreement with Egypt on funding for the Aswan Dam and, in July 1956, withdrew the offer. Goodpaster coordinated implementing the NSC decision, and the administration cited insufficient support in Congress to provide aid to Egypt.[65]

Nasser was surprised and bitterly disappointed by the withdrawal of U.S. funding for Aswan. On July 26, Nasser announced that he was nationalizing the Suez Canal. That move threatened vital British and French interests. Britain depended on the canal, with two-thirds of its oil transiting the canal. The previous year, about fifteen thousand British ships and sixty thousand British troops used the canal. Both Britain and France began preparing for war, while Eisenhower urged restraint.[66]

Goodpaster noted how skillfully Eisenhower framed the problem. The president, while still recovering from surgery, separated the issues of ownership and operation of the Suez Canal and broadened the scope of the problem to include other nations that used the canal. This approach allowed Egypt to exercise sovereignty while also allowing canal users a voice in its operation. At the same time, Eisenhower repeatedly and privately warned British and French leaders that the United States would not condone military action unless all peaceful means of settling the dispute were exhausted.[67]

While reluctantly going along with Eisenhower's proposals for negotiations, the British, French, and Israeli leaders began planning secretly for military operations to seize control of the Suez Canal and overthrow Nasser. Part of British, French, and Israeli planning included efforts to deceive the United States about their war plans. On October 23, British prime minister Anthony Eden, French premier Guy Mollet, and Israeli prime minister David Ben-Gurion met in France to finalize plans to seize the canal, beginning with an Israeli attack quickly followed by British and French forces ostensibly sent to separate Israeli and Egyptian forces. Apparently, these leaders assumed that the United States, once faced with allies locked in combat, would tacitly endorse or at least not oppose their operations, particularly during the final days of the U.S. election campaign.[68]

The deception was successful. U.S. intelligence was clearly aware of British, French, and Israeli military preparations, but judged they would not be used unless negotiations broke down. In mid-October the buildup of British and French forces in Cyprus and Malta seemed well beyond political posturing. U-2 surveillance flights detected sixty French *Mystere* aircraft at Israeli airfields. This was at odds with the French reporting of the delivery of twenty-four aircraft under the terms of the Tripartite Declaration. Israel increased border incidents with Jordan to divert attention in that direction.[69]

On October 27, the CIA warned that massive mobilization had put Israel on a war footing. Eisenhower was aware of the high costs of the scale of preparations undertaken by Israel, Britain, and France. Furthermore, high levels of military readiness could not be sustained for long. Eisenhower cabled his concerns to Ben-Gurion. The following day, intelligence reported that over the last 48 hours, British transport ships in the region had increased from 30 to 63, and French transports were up from 3 to 21 ships. At the recommendation of Dulles, Eisenhower ordered the evacuation of U.S. noncombatant citizens from Jordan, Israel, and Egypt. The president had anticipated such a need and ordered contingency planning in August. Goodpaster coordinated with the Pentagon, and the evacuation began on October 31 using eight U.S. Navy ships and several U.S. Air Force transport aircraft. The operation was completed by November 3 with the evacuation of about three thousand Americans.[70]

On October 29, 1956, while Eisenhower was campaigning in the South, Goodpaster notified him that Israeli forces had launched a major attack against Egypt. Goodpaster also reported that the British indicated they were trying to restore order between the Israelis and Egyptians in the Suez area. Within hours, Britain and France issued an ultimatum for Egypt and Israel to cease fighting and withdraw from the Canal Zone, providing a thinly veiled pretext for their planned invasion.[71]

Eisenhower was furious. He told Goodpaster to assemble the NSC principals and get the British ambassador to come to the White House immediately. The British ambassador, Sir Roger Makins, had been recalled to Britain a few days earlier, probably because he was one of several senior British officials who were opposed to the military intervention.[72] When the British chargé d'affaires arrived, Eisenhower insisted that he be told exactly what the British were up to; the chargé d'affaires said he would see what could be done and left.

With Goodpaster and the NSC principals, Eisenhower made his views of the situation clear. He said, "These people have made an awful mess of things . . . nothing justifies double-crossing us. . . . We must make good our word [to aid the victims of aggression under the 1950 Tripartite Declaration], . . . And if they think this is going to affect my candidacy, that I'm somehow to support them, they've chosen the wrong man." What also upset Eisenhower was the apparent lack of a reasonable endgame for their use of military force. Goodpaster raised the question of the Soviet position, noting that the situation might provide new opportunities for Soviet intervention, so consideration should be given to what might be done to forestall such action. [73]

As Goodpaster was leaving the office, Eisenhower told him to check with the State Department. When Goodpaster informed State Department officials about the conversation and planned meeting, they thought a meeting would be a mistake. It would look as though we were ganging up on Nasser. Goodpaster, in reporting back to the president, knew that Eisenhower didn't take criticism easily, but he saw the logic of State Department concerns. The president agreed and said, "All right, we'll call them and we'll cancel the idea of a meeting, but we've got to talk this through and look at how we can bring it to an end immediately." Eisenhower then questioned his advisors about how to best do that. He also sent an advisor to the United Nations to explore alternatives. [74]

Eisenhower was contacted by British leaders, including Churchill, during the crisis, urging him to support their efforts. In discussions with Goodpaster, however, Eisenhower remained convinced that Britain was reacting mainly on emotions. Eisenhower told Goodpaster that the British had told him: "If we're going to go down, we're going to go down fighting." Eisenhower added, "Unless they think it through and tell us how they are going to get out of this, how they are going to bring it to an end, we can't consider supporting them." This fundamental point of thinking through how to end a conflict made a lasting impression on Goodpaster. [75]

Concurrently, another crisis was unfolding in Hungary. During the previous year, the Warsaw Pact had been formed, binding Hungary and other Eastern European countries to the Soviet Union at a time when reform movements were growing in central and Eastern European communist parties. Reformists, including Imre Nagy in Hungary and Gomulka in Poland, were becoming increasingly popular and influential.

On October 23, a large demonstration in Budapest grew rapidly with encouragement from the U.S.-supported Radio Free Europe. This led to the fall of the government the next day, with Nagy emerging as prime minister. Fighting spread throughout the country as local rebels seized control and executed several communist leaders. On October 28, Nagy announced a cease-fire, dissolved the secret police, announced amnesty for participants in the uprising, promised reform, and called for negotiations for the withdrawal of Soviet forces from Hungary. On November 1, Nagy released political prisoners, including the popular Cardinal Mindszenty, and declared that Hungary would withdraw from the Warsaw Pact.

Eisenhower told Goodpaster that it was unclear what the Soviets were going to do, but the United States should work to see if this could be resolved without the Soviets removing the revolutionary government with armed force. Goodpaster observed that Nagy had signed his own death warrant by indicating Hungary was leaving the Warsaw Pact and might try to join NATO. To try to prevent this, Goodpaster suggested passing word to the Soviets that there could be no question of Hungary coming into NATO. Eisenhower agreed, but they were never sure that that message got through in time, even if it was unlikely to deter a Soviet intervention.[76]

Even during multiple crises, the affairs of government continued to grind on with many other issues brought to the daily attention of the president. Furthermore, the closing days of the election added to an already heavily burdened schedule. For example, on November 1, Goodpaster advised the president that British and French aircraft were bombing Egyptian airfields and a major British-French invasion force had embarked for Egypt on about one hundred ships, while Israeli forces were advancing toward the Suez Canal and Nasser had blocked the canal by sinking ships. Furthermore, oil pipelines had been cut, threatening a shortage that would impact the United States. Goodpaster also noted a new JCS report on the effects of a Soviet nuclear strike on the United States. This report was a follow-on study to the NSC's January 1956 Net Evaluation of a US-USSR nuclear weapons exchange. The JCS report estimated that a surprise Soviet attack would destroy the federal government and inflict casualties on 60 to 70 percent of the American forces in the United States. In addition, the damage to transportation, energy, manufacturing, finances, and the labor force would be devastating.[77]

The more Eisenhower learned about the likely effects of nuclear war, the more determined he became to prevent such a catastrophe. By mid-afternoon on November 1, Eisenhower called in Goodpaster and others to begin work on a major speech he was to deliver that evening in Philadelphia. By 6:30 p.m., when the president departed from Union Station by train, the speech was not yet finalized, and staff with typewriters accompanied him. Before a crowd of eighteen thousand in Philadelphia, Eisenhower noted:

> The United States cannot and will not condone armed aggression—no matter whom the attacker and no matter who the victim. We cannot—in the world any more than in our own nation—subscribe to one law for the weak, another law for the strong; one law for those opposing us, another for those allied with us. There can be only one law or there will be no peace.[78]

Eisenhower's distinctive leadership manner was evident in dealing with these crises. His public persona remained calm, even with the added heat of a political campaign. Publicly, he emphasized principled, reasonable approaches. Goodpaster noted, however, that privately Eisenhower did not hesitate to play hardball and exert pressure, even on allies. Eisenhower was keenly aware of U.S. influence through oil and international finances. For example, the British pound was pegged to the U.S. dollar, and soon after hostilities were initiated, there was a run on the pound. This put the British foreign reserve holdings at risk, and Britain was faced with devaluing its currency, with devastating consequences for the economy. When Britain tried to withdraw funds from the International Monetary Fund (IMF) to re-build reserves, the United States quietly blocked the request. Britain was also faced with the curtailment of oil supplied through the Suez Canal, and the president delayed ordering U.S. assistance. President Eisenhower also in-structed Treasury Secretary George Humphrey to be prepared to sell British government bonds that the United States had accumulated in partial payment of Britain's World War II debt. Saudi Arabia joined in the pressure by halting oil shipments to Britain and France. Other NATO allies joined with the United States in refusing to provide oil unless Britain and France agreed to withdraw their forces from Egypt. These were not hasty, ad hoc decisions on the part of the president. He had anticipated problems in the Middle East, and Goodpaster had coordinated studies about oil dependencies, international finances, and other influential factors as early as July.[79]

Eisenhower's principled approach was effective in gaining support at the United Nations. The United States, having condemned the Soviet interven-tion in Hungary, was not going to condone the Israeli, British, and French invasion of Egypt. On October 30, the United States submitted a resolution to the Security Council calling for an Israeli withdrawal from the Sinai. The resolution was vetoed by Britain and France. The United States persisted and raised the issue in the General Assembly using the 1950 "Uniting for Peace" Korean War precedent. On November 2, the General Assembly approved the U.S. resolution calling for an immediate cease-fire, withdrawal of forces, and an arms embargo. British public opinion shifted dramatically against Eden, dooming his leadership.[80]

Deep into the crises, Eisenhower lost his key foreign policy advisor, John Foster Dulles. On the night of November 2, Dulles was taken to Walter Reed Army Hospital for surgery on a cancerous colon tumor. Throughout the crises, as his health was deteriorating, Dulles was in nearly constant contact with the president, shuttling between Washington, London, Geneva, and the UN in New York. Undersecretary of State Herbert Hoover Jr. became the acting secretary of state and met with the president and Goodpaster the following morning. With the British and French armada still about two days from Egypt, Eisenhower began work to establish a Canadian-led UN police force to separate the belligerents. Eisenhower recommended that the UN Secretary General, Dag Hammarskjöld, be authorized to form the UN force and that it not include any troops from the five permanent members of the Security Council. U.S. Ambassador to the UN Henry Cabot Lodge Jr. worked successfully to get Eisenhower's concept approved by the UN Gen-eral Assembly on November 3.[81]

Meanwhile, on November 4, Goodpaster briefed that the Soviets intervened in Hungary with 12 divisions, reinforcing the five Soviet divisions already in country. With about 200,000 troops and 4,000 tanks, they seized control of key facilities, and installed János Kádár as head of government and the Communist Party. Fighting continued throughout the country, but the outcome was not in doubt.

Eisenhower had concluded earlier that the United States, even with help from NATO allies, would not likely be able to reverse the Soviet occupation and that any such efforts risked starting a much broader war that could involve nuclear weapons. A recent U.S. Army study had anticipated an uprising in Hungary and advised against military intervention by the United States. Now, with the bulk of British and French combat power concentrated in the Mediterranean, the prospects were even dimmer for NATO to contest successfully the Soviet invasion.[82]

The president asked Goodpaster to look into what promises had been made by U.S. officials to Hungarians regarding military support in the event of any uprising. After checking, Goodpaster reported to the president, "Sir, all we can get are very dusty answers, [there were] many discussions that were very close to at least an implication that we would intervene militarily." Goodpaster further noted that his personal view was that "our CIA people went beyond policy guidance in promising support. . . . Our policy was to encourage [Hungarians] and keep their hopes of liberty alive. But there had been no basis whatever for a promise of military support."[83]

The United States raised the Hungarian issue in the United Nations Security Council in late October and, in response to a plea from Nagy at the outset of the Soviet invasion, pushed for a resolution calling for a Soviet withdrawal. The Soviet Union vetoed the resolution, but it was then sent to the UN General Assembly, where it passed. Nevertheless, within a few days the Soviets had consolidated control and the Kádár government refused to acknowledge UN efforts.

On November 5, Goodpaster informed the president that British and French paratroopers had landed at Port Said, Egypt, A few hours later, Eisenhower received a disingenuous message from Soviet premier Bulganin proposing that the United States and the Soviet Union join forces to restore peace in the Middle East; there was no way the United States would side with the Soviet Union in a war against allies. At the same time, Bulganin warned the leaders of Britain, France, and Israel that the Soviet Union was determined to use force if necessary to crush the aggression. Eisenhower met with Hoover, Goodpaster, and a few others to respond to the Soviet ultimatum in ways that would clearly communicate that the United States would oppose with force any Soviet intervention. Eisenhower also directed the Joint Chiefs to provide an airlift for the UN forces and place the U.S. 6th Fleet on full alert. Initially, it was not clear to the fleet whether they should be prepared to block the British and French or defend against Soviet air and submarine attacks. With this clarified, U.S. warships were directed to intersperse themselves with British and French ships so that an attack on one would be an attack on all under the terms of NATO's Article 5. Eisenhower also directed his chief of staff to contact congressional leaders to be prepared to meet with him soon after the election, assuming he was reelected, for initial talks about calling Congress back in session. By election eve, the stress was taking its toll on the president. Eisenhower called in his doctor, who found that the president had elevated blood pressure, an irregular heartbeat, a headache, and abdominal pain. [84]

On election day, November 6, the president was up by 6:30 after very little sleep. His doctor found an infection at the site of the president's earlier abdominal surgery. Shortly thereafter, Goodpaster informed the president that the main British and French invasion force had landed at Port Said and Port Fuad. Next, the CIA director briefed Eisenhower on a special National Intelligence Estimate completed in the early morning, but already outdated because of the British and French landings. The estimate concluded that it was unlikely that the Soviets would risk general war over the Suez crisis. The director also shared intelligence that the Soviets had told the Egyptians that they intended to do something to end the hostilities. Eisenhower approved continued U-2 flights over Israel and Syria, but directed that there be no overflights of the Soviet Union. Shortly after 9 a.m., the president, Mrs. Eisenhower, and his doctor left by car to vote in Gettysburg. Meanwhile, Goodpaster was receiving reports in the White House that the situation was deteriorating. Russians reportedly were arriving in Egypt with "special [nuclear] weapons," and Soviet troops were massing on the border with Turkey. In the Black Sea area, the Soviets had two thousand jet fighters and five hundred bombers. Goodpaster consulted with the JCS chairman about recalling the president, and they decided to send a helicopter to pick him up after he voted. The Soviets did not intervene, and within hours, Eden caved in to domestic pressure and the persistent, private pressure from Eisenhower and announced a unilateral cease-fire effective midnight London time. French and Israeli leaders were furious, especially because the full occupation of the Canal Zone had not yet been accomplished. Nevertheless, they too agreed to the cease-fire. [85]

Eisenhower won reelection by a landslide, although the Democrats won the majority in both houses of Congress. Early on November 7, the president was called by Eden, who wanted to fly immediately to Washington with French premier Mollet, to discuss new intelligence about Soviet efforts in the Middle East. Eisenhower was initially attracted to the idea of reconciling relations, but soon realized that such a meeting would be premature before British and French forces had been withdrawn. Soon after the call, the president met with Goodpaster, Hoover, and Treasury Secretary Humphrey, all of whom agreed that there was good reason to distrust the British and French; such a visit would be premature and send the wrong signal. Eisenhower then called Eden and told him that the timing for such a meeting was "very, very bad." Eden asked if Eisenhower would call Mollet, and the president advised Eden to do that. When Eden noted that Mollet would be making a public statement on the visit within the half hour, Eisenhower responded that Eden had better call Mollet right away. Shortly after the call, Eisenhower visited Dulles at Walter Reed Hospital. Dulles agreed with postponing any meeting and making it contingent on completing the withdrawal of British and French forces. Eisenhower followed up with a cable to Eden to that effect. The same day, Israeli prime minister Ben-Gurion announced before the Knesset that he rejected the UN resolution calling for UN forces to replace Israeli forces then occupying the Gaza Strip, the Sinai Peninsula, and the entry to the Gulf of Aqaba. Furthermore, Ben-Gurion declared the 1949 armistice agreement with Egypt was "dead and buried." Eisenhower dispatched a blunt letter to Ben-Gurion calling for Israel to comply immediately with the UN resolution. He also had Hoover convey a stern message to the Israeli chargé d'affaires. At this point, Nasser had not yet agreed to the UN resolution, but informed the U.S. ambassador not to worry, that Egypt would not accept Soviet involvement in Egypt, noting that he did not trust any of the big powers and would continue the struggle against foreign domination. [86]

The fragile cease-fire held, but the Suez crisis continued to simmer for several weeks. The Soviet Union and China announced they were signing up volunteers to send to Egypt. A Soviet MiG fighter shot down a British reconnaissance plane over Syria. The British, French, and Israelis dragged their feet implementing the details of the withdrawal. U.S. forces remained on high alert worldwide. Eisenhower unblocked British access to funds at the IMF and arranged for U.S. oil to be made available to them. Also, efforts were undertaken to remove scuttled ships blocking the canal, repair sabotaged pipelines, and reestablish oil supplies.

Eisenhower's priority soon shifted to preventing dissolution of Europe in the aftermath of the debacle. The president focused on restoring Arab oil markets in Europe in addition to providing U.S. assistance. This fundamental shift illustrated for Goodpaster how Eisenhower's monumental personal anger could be quickly subordinated to his better judgment on what actions needed to be taken for the good of the country. [87]

Goodpaster also noted that in dealing with these crises, Eisenhower was courageous in using U.S. power against America's closest allies. He resisted pressure from friends and allies, including Winston Churchill. He resisted pressure to support Israel at a time when it would have been politically expedient. Throughout the process, he kept congressional leaders informed. Eisenhower's personal leadership, selfless sense of duty at the risk of his own health, and independent thinking made indelible impressions on Goodpaster.

Reflecting on the period years later, Goodpaster noted that Eisenhower characteristically "was slow to pick up the sword." Eisenhower hated war.[88]

GOODPASTER PROMOTED

In 1956, Colonel Goodpaster was considered, along with hundreds of other well-qualified colonels, for promotion to brigadier general. As the promotion board reviewed the files, paying particular attention to the Officer Efficiency Reports (OERs), they had to notice that Goodpaster's recent reports were different. They were signed by his rating officer but had no endorsements or review by officers above the rating officer. In Goodpaster's case, his rating officer and immediate supervisor was Dwight D. Eisenhower, president of the United States and the commander in chief. In his OER, Eisenhower noted that Goodpaster "is one of the finest, most resourceful and effective staff officers I have known." One could not have a stronger endorsement in the Army. Goodpaster was promoted to brigadier general on January 1, 1957.[89]

SPUTNIK (1957)

When the Soviets launched the first satellite into space, "Sputnik," on October 4, 1957, Goodpaster noted that President Eisenhower was not particularly surprised or concerned. Eisenhower said, "Hell, we've been worrying about that long-range rocket for the last three or four years. There's nothing in this that we haven't anticipated."[90]

The United States had for several years been working on a satellite program that the president was determined should be a scientific program that would share information broadly. The administration decided to keep this space launch and satellite effort separate from military programs and established NASA to manage such programs.[91]

While the reaction inside the White House was almost dismissive, referring to Sputnik as a "space-based basketball," the public reaction was near panic. Within thirty-six hours, Sherman Adams met with the president and Goodpaster and said, "We have to do something." The next morning, Adams brought James Killian, president of the Massachusetts Institute of Technology (MIT), to the White House to meet with the president. Killian noted that the American scientific community was also upset about not being first into space. Early in his administration, Eisenhower had established an advisory panel of leading scientists and engineers; he now thought that this role should be elevated by creating the position of the "president's science advisor." He wanted Killian to take the job. Killian was surprised and reluctant, but agreed to do it. Eisenhower had high regard for the scientific community and had longstanding close personal ties with many members. So his immediate reaction to the Sputnik problem was to ensure that they had better access to the president through Goodpaster.[92]

But it took about thirty-six hours for the president to realize that something more definitive was needed. He then authorized the Army to use the Redstone rocket to launch a satellite, which they did in January 1958 under the leadership of Werner von Braun. Unlike Sputnik, "Explorer I" carried a scientific experiment that resulted in the discovery of the Van Allen radiation belt. This took "most of the edge off the problem."[93]

In Goodpaster's view, this was "one time when Eisenhower got public opinion wrong, but it didn't take him long to correct." Goodpaster noted that during an NSC meeting on the topic, the president was advised that even U.S. allies needed to be reassured that the United States had not been surpassed scientifically and militarily by the Soviet Union. Eisenhower knew, according to Goodpaster, that there would be calls for "astronomical" increases in defense spending and greater federal funding for science education, but he misjudged the extent to which the American public feared that the Soviet Union was gaining intellectual superiority over the United States.[94]

FORWARD DEPLOYMENT OF U.S. FORCES

Eisenhower was well aware of the critical role of U.S. forces abroad in several collective security arrangements, especially with NATO members, Japan, and Korea. At the same time, he believed the allies should share the burden, and he frequently expressed concerns about reducing U.S. forward deployments. For example, from the time he was the first NATO SACEUR, Eisenhower believed that the deployment of four additional U.S. divisions in 1951 was a temporary measure until the European members could build up their forces. After becoming president, he still held to that idea. At one point, Eisenhower commented to Goodpaster, "I just don't seem to make any progress getting our troops out of Europe. . . . Our policy is to cut those troops down. I'm going to issue an order to get those troops out of there."[95]

Goodpaster responded, "Mr. President, before you do that, I'd better tell you that it's true you have always had this in mind, but if you look at your policy documents, they do not call for removing those divisions from Europe." Eisenhower replied, "Well, that just can't be. I don't believe it. I won't accept it." In reply, Goodpaster suggested, "All right sir, I'll get the papers. I'll have to show you." An increasingly agitated Eisenhower told Goodpaster, "I don't want to see the papers. I just don't have any doubt in my mind at all. Foster Dulles is coming over this afternoon, I'll check with him."

Dulles arrived, joining Eisenhower and Goodpaster in the Oval Office. The first thing the president said was that Goodpaster had been telling him that in spite of his view that those units were just to cover a period of great danger and it was our policy to bring them out, the established policy documents didn't provide for that. Eisenhower then said, "Foster, I want you to tell him he's wrong." Dulles, thought briefly, then responded, "Well, Mr. President, it isn't just as simple as that. As a matter of fact, I'll have to say he's right." Eisenhower interjected, "Say no more."

Yet they continued to discuss the situation, and Dulles convinced Eisenhower that withdrawing a large part of our forces would be very damaging to our position in Europe, to stability and confidence. Nevertheless, Eisenhower still held the view that eventually the United States should reduce forces as the European allies took on a larger share of the burden. This was consistent with Eisenhower's overall concept of avoiding a series of U.S. troop deployments around the Soviet periphery as much as possible, Goodpaster noted in a memo to the Joint Chiefs. Instead, local forces should assume the primary responsibilities for defense.[96]

Eisenhower expressed similar concerns about U.S. forward deployed forces in Asia where, from time to time, incidents of rape, murder, and other crimes involving off-duty U.S. servicemen created strong anti-American backlash exacerbated by status-of-forces agreements that protected U.S. personnel from local jurisdiction. In one case in 1957, pressure from the Japanese government led the United States to waive jurisdiction. Goodpaster noted that similar concerns in Korea and the Philippines led the president to review the desirability of maintaining U.S. forces in the Far East. Despite the problems, however, he again decided to keep U.S. forces forward deployed until they could be replaced by local forces.[97]

Goodpaster realized that the debate about overseas deployment of U.S. forces would be an ongoing issue in U.S. national security policy.

LEBANON (1958)

The Middle East was an important theater in the Cold War from the outset. Tensions created by old rivalries, religious conflicts, and colonial legacies were exacerbated by the competition between East and West. For the United States, the region was viewed mainly in terms of communist efforts to gain influence. The Suez Crisis in 1956 created a vacuum in Western influence following the withdrawal of British and French forces from Egypt. In early 1957, President Eisenhower launched an effort to gain a strong declaration of U.S. policy that, after much debate, led to a joint resolution of Congress in March establishing the Eisenhower Doctrine and pledging U.S. support to any Middle East nation threatened by communism.[98]

Goodpaster also noted the intensification of the Cold War, posing the greatest threat since the Korean War, mainly due to increased Soviet influence on the Syrian regime and its neighbors. The governments in Turkey,

Iraq, Jordan, and especially Lebanon were under pressure to reduce their relations with the West.[99]

The Eisenhower Doctrine was soon put to the test. In early 1958, Syria joined with Egypt to form the United Arab Republic while also becoming increasingly close to the Soviet Union. A few weeks later, King Faisal of Iraq and his second cousin, King Hussein of Jordan, formed a pro-Western federation called the Arab Union. This move quickly led to a coup in Iraq in which the king and other pro-Western leaders were killed. Meanwhile, in the middle of this turmoil, Lebanon, with its fragile political balance, was endangered with activist infiltrators, especially from Syria, and domestic unrest over efforts to gain an unprecedented second term for the pro-Western president.[100]

On July 14, Goodpaster reported that the Lebanese president, Camille Chamoun, requested immediate American and British intervention to help stabilize the situation. Chamoun was uncertain of the loyalty of his army, comprised of Muslim and Christian troops with divided loyalties.[101]

Eisenhower, after quick consultation with his advisors and congressional leaders, decided to intervene with overwhelming force and a clear mission. He ordered three Marine battalions to land beginning at 3 p.m. the following day, followed by two Army airborne battle groups from Germany. Within a few days, Goodpaster reported that Operation BLUE BAT put more than 14,000 U.S. troops in Lebanon to provide security for the government. The president also increased the alert level of more than 1,100 Strategic Air Command (SAC) aircraft and deployed SAC tanker aircraft to forward locations, in a move to signal the Soviet Union that the United States was serious. In addition, part of the 82nd Airborne Division was alerted for possible movement.[102]

Eisenhower then called British Prime Minister Macmillan and notified him of the decision. Macmillan was fully supportive and offered to make British forces in nearby Cyprus available should they be needed. Next, the president called for an emergency meeting of the UN Security Council the following morning.[103]

A key unknown was the reaction of Lebanese forces. The chief of staff, General Faud Chehab, had been reluctant to order the 9,000-man Army to put down rebels in Beirut, perhaps waiting to see how the unrest would play out. Also, the loyalty of the 2,500-man gendarmerie was uncertain. But, after some initial hesitation, Chehab decided to throw his chips in with the Americans in the face of clearly overwhelming odds.

At first glance, Eisenhower's snap decision to intervene in Lebanon was surprising even to Goodpaster. Why risk getting directly involved in the complex network of entangling Middle East conflicts? But, as Eisenhower noted, this, as is often the case, was the least bad option. Eisenhower had to decide to get involved directly or not in responding to the Lebanese request.

That was the hand he was dealt. But he was not playing just a two-handed game. He saw more than a half dozen other important players in the game.

The main players included Lebanese President Chamoun, a Maronite Christian who was sharing power with a Muslim prime minister. Eisenhower and Chamoun had developed a personal relationship while sharing their experiences with heart problems; earlier, Eisenhower had asked Dr. Paul Dudley White to examine Chamoun. Nevertheless, Chamoun was part of the problem. He had contributed to unrest in Lebanon by not squelching rumors that he intended to seek an unprecedented second term in office. [104]

In this game, Nasser was a major concern for Eisenhower because Nasser was the leading proponent of Arab unity. Nasser appealed to strong anticolonial sentiments in the Middle East that could easily be translated into anti-Western positions in the Cold War. Furthermore, Nasser was developing closer Egyptian relations with the Soviet Union.

Khrushchev was Eisenhower's main adversary, but Eisenhower knew Khrushchev held a much weaker hand in Lebanon. The Soviets could not match U.S. power projection forces in this area with the U.S. Sixth Fleet positioned in the eastern Mediterranean. With Eisenhower's quick decision, U.S. troops were already on the ground before Khrushchev could react. In addition, U.S. aircraft had ready access to several airbases in the region, and Goodpaster confirmed that a strong strategic reserve was on standby.

General Kassim, head of the recent coup in Iraq, was relatively unknown. In seizing power, he announced Iraq's withdrawal from the Baghdad Pact, established relations with the Soviet Union, and cut off oil exports to Jordan. Eisenhower wanted to deter Kassim from any thought of moving into Kuwait, so the president sent a U.S. Marine regiment to the Persian Gulf. [105]

Prime Minister Macmillan was an old friend with whom Eisenhower had served in World War II. Macmillan agreed to send 2,200 British paratroopers from Cyprus to Jordan to help stabilize the situation. Eisenhower helped resupply the British troops and arrange overflights of a reluctant Israel—still harboring resentment over British support for the Arabs during the struggle to create an Israeli state from the British-administered Palestinian Mandate.

Goodpaster also passed on information about several other players, including the United Nations, in the Lebanon game that required Eisenhower's attention. Eisenhower, mainly through Ambassador Henry Cabot Lodge Jr., dealt almost daily with the Security Council and the General Assembly. The United States made the case for acting in response to a legitimate request from a head of state. However, a U.S. proposal for a United Nations peace-keeping force was blocked by the Soviet Union. Eventually the crisis was resolved after stability was restored, elections were held in Lebanon with President Chamoun turning over power to the duly elected General Chehab, and a UN General Assembly resolution was passed in which the Middle East states pledged not to interfere in the internal affairs of other neighboring states.

On October 25, 1958, after less than four months and with only one man killed from a sniper, U.S. forces withdrew from Lebanon. No Lebanese civilians or combatants were killed during the operation. In achieving this outcome, Ambassador Robert Murphy, Eisenhower's personal envoy in the crisis, played a critical role negotiating with Chamoun, Nasser, Kassim, and other key players.[106]

General Maxwell Taylor, the U.S. Army chief of staff, urged the president to broaden the mission of U.S. forces to go after rebels in the mountains around Beirut, but Eisenhower did not want U.S. forces to become bogged down in a civil war. The president insisted that they be able to withdraw quickly if necessary.

At the time U.S. forces landed, Nasser was in Yugoslavia and undoubtedly surprised. He flew immediately to Moscow for consultations and soon realized that the Soviets were in no position to counter the U.S. move effectively. As a result, Nasser's behavior changed accordingly. The threat of a group of united, pro-Soviet Arab countries was averted.[107]

For Goodpaster, the Lebanese crisis was a useful example of a carefully limited U.S. military intervention.

CUTLER LEAVES THE WHITE HOUSE

After serving as the president's special assistant for national security affairs for nearly four years, Robert Cutler left the White House and was replaced by Gordon Gray. On his departure, Cutler sent a letter to President Eisenhower commending Goodpaster for his work. Cutler noted: "I don't think I ever knew a fellow who could get to the heart of a subject quicker, retain so much of its substance in his mind, and work at such top speed, and all the time keep his good humor. . . . The serenity of his intellectual process is fortified by his integrity and his courage. . . . He is as good a soldier and as good a man as I ever knew."[108]

BERLIN CRISIS (1958–1959)

Berlin was a focal point of East-West tension throughout the Cold War. Nearly every administration was challenged with a crisis that threatened to escalate into World War III. In addition to routine harassment, pressure increased on the Eisenhower administration when Premier Khrushchev, on November 10, 1958, announced that he intended to sign a peace treaty with East Germany at an early date, setting in motion the basis for terminating the Allied occupation of Berlin. Khrushchev later proposed that Berlin become a free city under United Nations administration and called for the complete withdrawal of Allied forces from Berlin within six months. [109]

Goodpaster was aware that previously, in 1952, the Soviets had closed the inner German border in an effort to stem the exodus of Eastern European citizens. Nevertheless, Berlin remained an attractive escape route. West Berlin became a haven for refugees, especially professionals and intellectuals, fleeing from communist rule. It was, as Khrushchev termed it, "a bone in his throat" and he hoped to exploit differences among the Allies to force a withdrawal.

For Eisenhower, the six-month ultimatum posed several problems. U.S. policy linked Berlin to the issue of the overall status of Germany. The United States strongly supported the position of West German Chancellor Adenauer, who was adamant about German sovereignty, West Germany's association with the West, and German reunification. Adenauer strongly objected to any Allied dealing with East German officials because it implied recognition of a divided Germany under Soviet control. British and French leaders generally agreed with the United States and at least tacitly opposed withdrawal of Allied occupation forces from Berlin. At lower levels of government, however, particularly in Britain, there was interest in cooperating with the East Germans. [110]

However, Goodpaster noted that Eisenhower was strongly opposed to such cooperation. Specifically, Eisenhower was determined that "we should make it clear to the Russians that we consider this no minor affair. [We should] avoid beginning with white chips and working up to the blue, we should place them on notice that the whole stack is in play." [111]

In addressing the crisis, Eisenhower maintained close contact with British Prime Minister Harold Macmillan, French President Charles de Gaulle, German Chancellor Konrad Adenauer, and Soviet Chairman Nikita Khrushchev. Eisenhower refused to join a summit-level meeting unless there were tangible assurances of progress on this and other East-West relations, but he did agree to a conference at the foreign ministers' level.

At the same time, Eisenhower wanted to ensure that the situation did not escalate during a time of frequent provocations on both sides. Goodpaster passed the president's concerns on to Defense, State, and the CIA. Shortly thereafter, a Soviet trawler operating off the coast of Newfoundland cut some transatlantic phone cables. U.S. Navy personnel boarded the Soviet ship and directed it to a nearby port. During investigation of the incident, the Soviets stated that the damage was accidental. [112]

In March 1959, Secretary of State Dulles became ill again and was replaced by Christian Herter on April 18, just before the foreign ministers' conference on Berlin. Eisenhower knew that negotiations with the Soviets would be difficult and was concerned that the Allies were "too soft on this issue." [113]

The foreign ministers met in Geneva for several weeks without results; if anything, the Soviet position hardened. Eisenhower thought perhaps one way to deal with Berlin and related problems would be to arrange for a more informal meeting with Khrushchev during a visit to the United States. The possibility of such a visit arose following the opening of a Soviet exhibition in New York and a U.S. exhibition in Moscow. The opening of the Soviet exhibition was attended by First Deputy Premier Kozlov and resulted in some positive exchanges during his visit in June. Similarly, Vice President Nixon attended the Moscow opening of the U.S. exhibition and held the famous "kitchen debate" with Khrushchev.[114]

Eisenhower approved sending an invitation to Khrushchev for a visit, but it was conditioned on the Soviets removing the ultimatum over Berlin. However, when State Department officials came to the White House to discuss the visit, Eisenhower was very upset to learn that the invitation had been sent without the condition. Khrushchev accepted the invitation and Eisenhower was compelled to follow through with the visit.[115]

In the meantime, Eisenhower insisted that Goodpaster be present at every meeting he had with Secretary Herter. Eisenhower sensed that Herter's hearing was not good because Herter had missed a few things in their initial talks, and Eisenhower wanted to make sure they both had an accurate understanding of what transpired. That task fell to Goodpaster. After each session, Herter would stop by and check with Goodpaster to be sure that he had correctly understood the president.[116]

Adenauer and de Gaulle were upset when they learned that Eisenhower and Khrushchev would be meeting without them. To help mollify their concerns, Eisenhower traveled to Bonn, Paris, and London three weeks before Khrushchev's visit. Eisenhower assured the Allied leaders that he would not offer any new proposals, nor would he represent the West in discussions.

In Paris, Eisenhower found de Gaulle generally supportive on Berlin but opposed to NATO's integrated command structure. De Gaulle withdrew the commitment to put the French fleet under the SACEUR in wartime, arguing that the ships were needed to maintain the lifeline to Algeria. De Gaulle also would not allow basing NATO aircraft with nuclear weapons in France without veto power over their use. Finally, he proposed a Big Three coalition with the United States and Britain to deal with worldwide security concerns.[117]

Khrushchev arrived at Andrews Air Force Base on September 15, 1959, for a twelve-day visit. Eisenhower was anxious to build a personal relationship with the Soviet leader and, hopefully, defuse the Berlin crisis. The following day, after exchanging initial remarks, Eisenhower invited Khrushchev for a helicopter tour of Washington. Khrushchev, however, declined the offer. Eisenhower said he was very disappointed because there were a number of things he wanted to point out. Khrushchev, somewhat surprised, asked, "Oh would you be in the helicopter?" Eisenhower replied, "Well, of course." Khrushchev said, "In that case, I would be delighted to go." Khrushchev's initial hesitation suggested to Goodpaster the extent of the distrust that Eisenhower had to bridge.[118]

Following Khrushchev's ten-day tour of the United States, Eisenhower, accompanied by Goodpaster, took Khrushchev to Camp David. After several long discussions, Eisenhower was able to gain a degree of Khrushchev's trust. At one point, Khrushchev noted that Soviet generals often came to him asking for more weapons and equipment because of American arms and asked Eisenhower if he had the same problem with American generals. Eisenhower answered, "Yes, of course, that's what they do, and that's why I've put a limit on our forces." Goodpaster noted in later discussions between the president and the JCS chairman that Eisenhower concluded that Khrushchev's complaints about the huge costs of military expenditures provided an opportunity to pursue arms control negotiations.[119]

Khrushchev very much wanted a summit meeting, but Eisenhower would not agree to attend while under the threat of an ultimatum. On the final day of their meetings, Khrushchev finally said, "Well, we don't regard it as an ultimatum and we'd be prepared to change that." Eisenhower replied, "Fine, we'll put that in the communiqué." Khrushchev, said, "Oh no, we cannot do that." Then Eisenhower countered that the deal was off, no summit. But Khrushchev interjected, "No, we will agree to that, but that can only be done after I have returned to the Soviet Union."[120]

Later, while discussing the exchanges with Goodpaster, Eisenhower explained that Khrushchev could not make such a statement while he was out of the country. He didn't know whether he would be arrested when he got back and thrown out of office because he obviously had gone beyond what had been agreed to by the Politburo. But once he returned, he was able to get the rest of the Soviet leadership to agree to a summit meeting while removing any time limit on when they might sign a peace treaty with East Germany. This new Soviet position made the future of Berlin once again the subject of major power negotiations, rather than vulnerable to unilateral action on the part of the Soviet Union.[121]

President Eisenhower waited forty-eight hours after Khrushchev left before announcing their understanding. And Khrushchev confirmed it in Moscow, thus defusing another Berlin crisis, at least for the time being.[122]

Goodpaster now better understood the critical, complex role that Berlin played in the Cold War competition.

U-2 PROGRAM (1954–1960)

In mid-1954, President Eisenhower commissioned a review of the technologies that could strengthen national security capabilities to avert a surprise attack, from the standpoint of both weapons and intelligence operations. This review was conducted by a technological-capabilities panel led by James Killian, president of MIT, with oversight by the National Security Council. [123]

Out of this effort emerged the idea for a very-high-altitude, long-range reconnaissance aircraft, the U-2. Edwin Land, the head of Polaroid, led the development of camera technology capable of photographing weapons, troops, and other important details with high resolution from seventy thousand feet. Kelly Johnson, from Lockheed's secret research and development facility, later known as the "Skunk works," led development of the airframe. The combined technologies promised early warning of troop buildups for surprise attack, information on new weapons development and testing, and the levels of production of military equipment.

In approving the project on November 22, 1954, Eisenhower insisted on "very, very tight secrecy" and that the project be managed by the CIA rather than the Air Force or Department of Defense. In addition to security concerns, Eisenhower did not want to have military personnel in the cockpit of what the Soviet leadership might view as an instrument of war. The president approved the program because the country needed the information, but he was apprehensive, warning, "Someday one of these machines is going to be caught, and we're going to have a storm." Eisenhower insisted that every mission be authorized personally by him, and he exercised tight control through Goodpaster. [124]

Goodpaster made these arrangements with Richard Bissell, the CIA project manager, and Dulles. They met in the Oval Office where Bissell would lay out the maps and explain the proposed routes and targets. After considerable discussion and a certain amount of soul searching, Eisenhower would reject or authorize missions to be accomplished within a specified period of days. Goodpaster was then responsible for liaison with Bissell to ensure that any planned flights were conducted within the authorized time frame unless bad weather required reconsideration of the deadline. The U-2 provided very valuable information during Suez and other crises, as well as leading to more accurate estimates of Soviet bomber inventories and evidence of new programs in development such as intercontinental ballistic missiles (ICBMs). [125]

However, the U-2 surveillance program over the Soviet Union came to an abrupt, unfortunate ending that Eisenhower described as one of his worst experiences. On May 1, 1960, May Day, a Soviet surface-to-air missile brought down the U-2 piloted by Francis Gary Powers, who parachuted safely and was captured. Goodpaster soon regretted not urging that the window be closed before May 1 because of the traditional Soviet May Day celebrations that featured huge military parades in Moscow. Earlier, the State Department had recommended against flying a U-2 after May 1 because the timing was close to the upcoming Paris Summit scheduled for May 16.[126]

Goodpaster also regretted not pressing the CIA harder on the U-2 program assumptions. The president was assured that neither the plane, with its sensitive imaging equipment, nor the pilot would survive an intercept. Those and other key assumptions about the limits of Soviet air-defense missile technology valid for four years, right up to the last mission. Like Eisenhower, Goodpaster had doubts from the outset, particularly after they were informed initially that the plane could not be picked up on radar. Indeed, the first U-2 flight was picked up on Soviet radar.[127]

During the night of May 1, 1960, Goodpaster received a call that a U-2 was overdue and presumed lost. He called the president at Camp David the next morning with the news. Eisenhower was concerned, commenting, "Winds are likely to blow." He and Goodpaster had always considered the possibility of losing a U-2, and Eisenhower noted, while weighing the issue, "You know that this is resented very deeply by the Soviets."

The cover story in the event a plane was lost was that it was a NASA high-altitude weather aircraft operating out of Adana, Turkey, on a mission to obtain data on air turbulence. On May 5, Khrushchev announced that an American reconnaissance aircraft had been shot down deep inside Soviet territory. The following day, before the Supreme Soviet, he announced that the pilot had been captured and confessed to intelligence collection.[128]

President Eisenhower then had to acknowledge the true nature of the flight, noting that it was necessary to prevent a surprise attack like Pearl Harbor. While there was some early criticism from senators aspiring to the presidency and columnists Drew Pearson and Walter Lippman, Eisenhower's explanation satisfied most Americans.[129]

Khrushchev, however, was in no position to be forgiving. After the meeting with Eisenhower at Camp David, Khrushchev had taken some personal risk to promote the possibility of reducing tensions and invited Eisenhower to visit the Soviet Union. Now this was politically impossible.

Eisenhower arrived in Paris on May 15, the day before the planned summit, and met with de Gaulle and Macmillan. He was surprised to find that Khrushchev had sent a note to both the French and British leaders indicating that he would not participate in the summit unless President Eisenhower apologized. Specifically, Khrushchev demanded that Eisenhower denounce the U-2 incident, renounce any similar acts in the future, and pass severe judgment on those immediately responsible. Eisenhower told de Gaulle and Macmillan that he would not apologize.[130]

Despite the incident, Khrushchev came to Paris, and the four leaders met on May 16. Khrushchev immediately launched into a scripted tirade. Eisenhower responded that the United States had no aggressive intent and such acts were required for national security. De Gaulle noted that during the meeting, a Soviet satellite was flying overhead. After Khrushchev left the meeting, de Gaulle commented privately to Eisenhower, "Whatever happens, we are with you."[131]

Goodpaster talked with Eisenhower about the U-2 incident many times, "especially the high price that we had paid." The Soviets canceled the invitation for the president to visit the Soviet Union. Eisenhower had hoped to accomplish a great deal during the trip, including reductions in tensions and in the arms race. For Goodpaster personally, the U-2 incident was painful. He felt he had let the president down by not pressing harder on the assumptions—that was his responsibility.

CUBA (1960–1961)

Castro-led revolutionary forces overthrew the Batista government in late 1959. By 1960, there was no doubt in the White House that Castro was working against the United States. In response, the CIA initiated some operations in support of opposition groups, but they had little effect. In discussing this situation with Goodpaster in February 1960, President Eisenhower noted: "If we're going to take action against Cuba, I want to see a plan; I want to see it well thought out." Eisenhower encouraged broad thinking, including things that might be "drastic." He gave that task to Gordon Gray for study by the NSC staff's 5412 Group, a subcommittee set up under NSC 5412/1 to review covert-action proposals.[132]

The resulting plans involved continuing support for opposition in Cuba, radio broadcasts, and forming a battalion of about five hundred Cuban exiles that would be available, trained, and ready for a contingency. The battalion could be brought to Cuba in case there was an uprising against Castro, and an opposition government needed protection. Under the plan, the "first requirement" was the creation of a publicly declared "responsible, appealing and unified Cuban opposition to the Castro regime."[133]

In March 1960, Allen Dulles briefed President Eisenhower, Goodpaster, and the NSC principals on the plan. Eisenhower was very concerned about maintaining secrecy while gathering and training the battalion. He advised limiting American contacts with the group to only two or three people, getting the Cubans to do most of the work. Richard Bissell added that the opposition group would raise funds for the operation on their own. Eisenhower approved the plan and advised anticipating all likely Cuban reactions and preparing responses. He was concerned about the safety of about ten thousand Americans in Cuba and on the U.S. naval base at Guantanamo.[134]

After the briefing, Goodpaster privately raised his concern with the president that if such a group were set up, it might develop a momentum of its own for intervention. Eisenhower was agitated at the remark and snapped back, stating that would not happen "while I'm here." Goodpaster replied, "Well sir, that's the problem. You won't be here very long." The president looked at Goodpaster for a moment, clearly very angry, but then gained control and said, "Andy, you're right, and we've got to be sure that doesn't happen." Yet, as Goodpaster later put it, "in fact, it did happen."[135]

U.S. relations with Cuba continued to deteriorate and the U.S. embassy country team in Havana concluded that there was no hope of establishing satisfactory relations with the Castro government. By November, Eisenhower's fears that the plan would become known were realized. Undersecretary of State Douglas Dillon reported during NSC discussions that the operation was no longer secret, but known all over Latin America and discussed in UN circles. Eisenhower commented that even if the training and preparations were known, the main thing was to not let the U.S. role be visible; there would be no training in the United States. The president also realized that the disparate groups opposed to Castro had not come together and lacked an appealing leader. Thus, Eisenhower decided that it was not yet possible to recognize a government in exile.[136]

Castro escalated tensions on January 2, 1961, when he announced that the United States had to reduce its embassy to no more than eleven personnel, the same number of Cuban diplomats currently in the United States. Furthermore, this reduction had to be completed within forty-eight hours. The U.S. embassy noted that it would be impossible to maintain operations at that level and recommended severing diplomatic relations. President Eisenhower approved the recommendation after consulting with his NSC and Dean Rusk, President-elect Kennedy's secretary of state designate. Castro reacted defiantly to the rupture in relations, according to Dulles.[137]

The Eisenhower administration briefed Kennedy and Rusk on the situation and planning for Cuba. By January 1961, about five hundred Cuban exiles had been recruited and were in training. Planners noted that conditions in the training camps were difficult and would probably result in large-scale desertions if the recruits were not used relatively soon. Because of such concerns and pressure from the local government to wrap up the training, planners estimated operations should be launched in the latter half of February, up to March 1. Planners also noted that there was a critical shortage of pilots and aircrew. Air support was critical for the success of the initial operations. The planners recommended the operation be abandoned if policy restrictions did not provide for adequate tactical air support. Furthermore, they raised the question of whether President-elect Kennedy concurred in the operations; if not, preparations should cease.[138]

On January 10, 1961, the *New York Times* ran a front-page article, "U.S. Helps Train an Anti-Castro Force at Secret Guatemala Base." In discussing the article with Goodpaster, the president decided to make no public comment. Eisenhower thought that the cover story for the operation—that it was merely an extension of conventional training—was too weak and unconvincing. [139]

After Eisenhower left office, the premise of the plan changed from sending in a battalion *after* an uprising to sending in a larger unit, a brigade, *beforehand* to precipitate such an uprising. President Kennedy was skeptical of the plan and directed several changes to minimize appearances that the United States was orchestrating a landing as a pretext for an invasion. As the planning underwent revision almost continuously until the operation was launched, important details, especially air support, were not well coordinated, and the Bay of Pigs landing was a disaster. As Goodpaster explained it, "Between Eisenhower's grip on the planning and preparations, and the presentation of the issue to President Kennedy, there was a change of concept. And that was not made clear to President Kennedy." [140]

THE EISENHOWER-KENNEDY TRANSITION (1960–1961)

Each new administration organizes the White House staff somewhat differently to accommodate different personalities and priorities. When the shift is from one political party to the other, the changes may be even more consequential.

Although the Democrats won the close election, and President Eisenhower later felt some regret that he had not supported the Nixon campaign more strongly, the president also believed that it was his duty to aid the new administration to ensure a smooth transfer of power. He met twice with President-elect Kennedy, who came away from the first meeting appearing very pale and somber after learning about the challenges he was about to face. At that meeting, Kennedy told President Eisenhower that he would like Brigadier General Goodpaster to stay for a time to assist in the transition. Eisenhower told Kennedy that he knew Goodpaster was eager to get back to troop duty and he didn't know whether he would want to stay. Kennedy insisted that it was very important to him and that his staff was not clear as to Goodpaster's duties and wanted to be sure there were no gaps. The issue arose again at their second meeting. President Eisenhower repeated Goodpaster's desire to return to troop duty, to which Kennedy responded, "Well, you know, I could order him back if I had to." [141]

President Eisenhower told Goodpaster after the meeting, "You've got to stay." Goodpaster understood that he really did not have a choice, but was concerned that it had already been seventeen years since he was last with troops and that continued assignments in Washington removes one from the Army mainstream—leading troops in the field. Nevertheless, he began preparing for his role in aiding the transition.

Goodpaster consulted with President Eisenhower about the transition and the practice of allowing those in an outgoing administration to take all their papers with them. Goodpaster asked for permission to provide copies of papers on the key issues that were still in process. Eisenhower agreed. [142]

Goodpaster was the only member of the White House staff asked to remain for the transition. He met with Kennedy and suggested an approach that would involve working with the transition team and new staff so that every function he performed for President Eisenhower was assigned to some specific individual on the new White House staff. Kennedy agreed, and Goodpaster remained for about two months after the inauguration.

Near the end of the process, Goodpaster told President Kennedy that the one thing he was "uneasy about" was Kennedy's decision to divide responsibilities among several individuals, with each reporting separately to the president. No one person had the kind of overall responsibility for national security affairs from the perspective of the president comparable to Goodpaster's role. In addition to providing a morning briefing to the president on intelligence that had arrived overnight, along with a summary of important diplomatic cables and a report from the Defense Department on any exchanges between the chiefs and the field commands, Goodpaster was responsible for arranging meetings on national security issues that required the president's attention, ensuring that all of the responsible heads of agencies and other experts were represented and were prepared to discuss the issue in depth. Finally, Goodpaster would ensure follow-up until the issue was resolved.

The danger that Goodpaster alluded to was that assigning key functions such as intelligence to different members of the staff meant that these individuals were likely to adopt the perspective of the respective agencies and not be sensitive to how issues were interrelated. Goodpaster was particularly aware of how the CIA, with both intelligence and covert operations responsibilities, could pose problems for the president. When Goodpaster told Kennedy that this division of labor could be a problem for him in the future, Kennedy acknowledged that but was very confident and said that he could handle it.

The reorganization of the Kennedy White House went well beyond eliminating the position held by Goodpaster. For example, the NSC Operations Coordination Board and other support structures were eliminated because the new staff thought they were an unnecessary paper mill that slowed down action. They wanted to move more quickly with less time spent on deliberations.

Before Goodpaster left the White House, President Kennedy assured him, "I know you want to get back to troops and I will see that a position is held for you." Kennedy had also spoken to Eisenhower about ensuring Goodpaster's assignment to troop duty. Eisenhower had been assured by the Army chief of staff that Goodpaster would return to troop duty.

In the meantime, the CIA asked Goodpaster to arrange a briefing for President Kennedy by Major General Edward Lansdale, who was then the Deputy Assistant Secretary of Defense for Special Operations. He had served in the Office of Strategic Services (OSS) during World War II and then played a key role in developing the Philippine Army capabilities to fight *Hukbalahap* insurgents after the war. From 1954 to 1957, Lansdale served on the U.S. military mission in Saigon and became a key advisor to President Diem.[143]

Goodpaster made the arrangements and joined in the meeting. Lansdale noted that an insurgency was growing in South Vietnam. The government had clamped down on religious sects and various other autonomous groups in an effort to promote more unity. The government believed they were being successful. Lansdale concluded that "the U.S. should recognize that Vietnam is in critical condition and should be treated as a combat area of the Cold War, as an area requiring emergency treatment." That briefing and other information led President Kennedy and his staff to develop a counterinsurgency approach to Vietnam that went beyond the Eisenhower military assistance program.[144]

Shortly after he left the White House, Goodpaster received a letter from President Kennedy thanking him for helping with the transition. Kennedy noted, "It is easy for me to see and understand why President Eisenhower placed so much confidence in your judgment and ability."[145]

President Eisenhower's confidence in Goodpaster was reflected in annual performance reports to the Army. In his May 1960 report, Eisenhower noted that Goodpaster "has constantly assumed new and increasing responsibilities. Many of these have been in connection with my trips abroad; I have relied greatly on General Goodpaster's judgment in their planning and upon his informed advice in the new and varied situations that always arise in my talks with leaders of other countries." In his last report, January 20, 1961, Eisenhower summed up, "There are no words of mine adequate to describe my admiration for General Goodpaster's abilities, intelligence, dedication to duty, and performance. He is outstanding in every respect. . . . I have been associated with him for many years, for the past six in a most intimate fashion. . . . To my mind he is eminently qualified and will eventually attain the highest positions the military establishment has to offer."[146]

Those six years for Goodpaster provided incomparable experience to learn firsthand about collaborative leadership and best practices in national security affairs. Eisenhower mentored Goodpaster on a daily basis, setting high standards, making principled decisions, and always putting the country first. Eisenhower was neither a "hawk" nor a "dove."

Figure 8.1. Goodpaster at Desk Next to Oval Office, White House, 1954. Official photo. *Source*: Courtesy of the George C. Marshall Library

Figure 8.2. Goodpaster and Eisenhower, White House, 1954. Official photo. *Source*: Courtesy of the George C. Marshall Library

Figure 8.3.   Goodpaster, Eisenhower, and Eisenhower's personal secretary, Ann Whitman. Official photo. *Source:* **Courtesy of the George C. Marshall Library**

NOTES

1. Goodpaster, Mandel interviews, January 15, 2002, tape 10.

2. Goodpaster wrote daily synopses of intelligence and diplomatic items reported to the president. See, for example, Goodpaster memos, White House, Office of the Staff Secretary, Subject series, Alphabetical subseries, box 14 Intelligence Briefing Notes, Vol. I, 1958 through

January 1961, Vol. II; also Goodpaster memos are in the National Security, International Meeting, Cabinet, Ann Whitman, and other series at the Eisenhower Library.

3. The scope of Goodpaster's work is best documented at the Eisenhower Library in the White House, Office of the Staff Secretary papers. Also see, Greenstein, *The Hidden-Hand Presidency*, 134, 145.

4. Goodpaster, Mandel interviews, January 15, 2002, tape 10.

5. Eisenhower, *Waging Peace*, 319.

6. See for example, various Goodpaster memos, White House, Office of the Staff Secretary; Subject Series; Alphabetical Subseries; box 14, Intelligence Briefing Notes. Vol. 1 (1), 1958 through January 1961 Vol. II (7), Eisenhower Library. Goodpaster's foreign travel with President Eisenhower is listed on a security clearance questionnaire, SF 86, Goodpaster Papers, box 40, file 2, Marshall Library. Also see Goodpaster's handwritten notes on NSC meetings, such as on Dien Bien Phu, Geneva, etc., White House, Office of the Staff Secretary, Records, NSC, box 1, folder 2, Eisenhower Library.

7. Goodpaster, Mandel interviews, January 15, 2002, tape 12.

8. Eisenhower in May 4, 1956, enclosure to Goodpaster's efficiency report, Goodpaster Papers, box 54, file 3, Marshall Library; also see Greenstein and Immerman, "Effective National Security Advising: Recovering the Eisenhower Legacy," *Political Science Quarterly* 115, no. 3 (2000): 335–45.

9. Susan Goodpaster Sullivan, telephone interview with author, June 27, 2010.

10. Goodpaster, Mandel interviews, tape 12.

11. Ibid. Also see Goodpaster Memo, March 13, 1956, *FRUS 1955–1957, National Security Policy*, 238–41.

12. Ibid. Also see Goodpaster-drafted Memo, Eisenhower to Wilson, January 5, 1955, PDDE, XVI, 1488-1491; Public Papers of the Presidents, January 5/6, 1955, WH/LOC.

13. Goodpaster Memo, April 2, 1956, White House, Office of the Staff Secretary, Subject series, DoD subseries, box 4, JCS; Goodpater Memo, November 4, 1957, *FRUS 1955–1957, National Security Policy*, 622; and Goodpaster Memo, November 4, 1957, *FRUS 1955–1957, National Security Policy*, 624.

14. Eisenhower, *Waging Peace*, 244–51.

15. Goodpaster Memos, February 10 and February 14, 1956, White House, Office of the Staff Secretary, Subject series, DoD subseries, box 4, JCS, Eisenhower Library; also Goodpaster Memo to Twining, February 14, 1956, Twining Papers, box 92, Office File/Chief of Staff 1956, "White House," Library of Congress.

16. Ibid. Goodpaster Memo, May 14, 1956, *FRUS 1955–1957, National Security Policy*, 301–2.

17. Ibid., 251.

18. Ibid., 253.

19. Goodpaster Memo, March 15, 1956, White House, Office of the Staff Secretary, Subject series, DoD subseries, box 4, JCS, Eisenhower Library.

20. Goodpaster Memo, January 11, 1961, White House, Office of the Staff Secretary, Subject series, DoD subseries, box 4, JCS, Eisenhower Library.

21. Net Evaluation Committee reports are in NSC Presidential Records, Intelligence Files, box 1, Eisenhower Library; Goodpaster, Mandel interviews, tape 14.

22. Goodpaster Memo, November 2, 1959, White House, Office of the Staff Secretary, Subject Series, Alphabetical subseries, Instructions to Commanders, box 14; and Goodpaster Memo, May 16, 1957, Atomic Energy Matters, box 5, Presidential Actions, Eisenhower Library.

23. NIEs represent the most authoritative judgment of the entire intelligence community including the CIA, the Defense Intelligence Agency, the State Department's Bureau of Intelligence and Research, the National Security Agency, and another half dozen or more national intelligence organizations. NIEs are limited to the most important subjects, and copies are provided to the intelligence committees of the House and Senate, ensuring that the political opposition is aware of their judgments. As a result, they are usually taken more seriously than intelligence reports produced by one of the intelligence organizations.

24. Goodpaster, Mandel interviews, January 16, 2002, tape 12.

25. Goodpaster Memo of Conference, June 19, 1959, *FRUS, 1958–1960, Vol. III, National Security Policy; Arms Control*, doc. 59 and doc. 58; Also see Thomas, *Ike's Bluff*, 181, 212, 215.

26. Hagerty Diary, January 4, 1956, *FRUS 1955–1957, National Security Policy*, 5.

27. Goodpaster Memo, December 1, 1954, *FRUS, Western European Security, 1952–1954, Part 1*, doc. 279, 532–33.

28. Ibid.

29. Goodpaster Memo, April 24, 1958, White House, Office of the Staff Secretary, Subject series, Alphabetical subseries, box 5, Atomic Energy Matters, Presidential Actions, Eisenhower Library; Goodpaster Memo, December 1, 1954, *FRUS, National Security Affairs, 1952–1954, Part 2*, 1576–77.

30. Goodpaster, Mandel interviews, tape 10. The first U.S. thermonuclear weapon test was in 1952; the Soviet Union tested one in 1955.

31. "Atoms for Peace" speech at www.eisenhower.research.gov.

32. Ibid. and IAEA website.

33. Ann Whitman Diary, February 6, 1956, *FRUS, 1955–1957, Vol. XX, Regulation of Armaments, Atomic Energy*, 316.

34. Goodpaster Memo, February 6, 1956, *FRUS, 1955–1957. Vol. XX, Regulation of Armaments, Atomic Energy*, 318; Goodpaster Memo, September 17, 1956, *FRUS, 1955–1957, Vol. XX, Regulation of Armaments, Atomic Energy*, doc. 155.

35. Goodpaster Memo, April 7, 1958, *FRUS 1958–1960, Vol. III, National Security Policy, Arms Control, and Disarmament*, 62–65.; Cutler Memo, April, 1958, Ibid, 65–66; Editorial Note, Ibid., doc. 14.

36. Goodpaster, Mandel interviews, January 16, 2002, tape 14. Also see Smith, *Eisenhower in War and Peace*, 667–71.

37. Ibid.; Goodpaster Memo, July 16, 1955, *FRUS 1958–1960, Vol. III, National Security Policy, Arms Control, and Disarmament*, doc. 174; Goodpaster Memo, July 12, 1958, Ibid., doc. 163.

38. Ibid.; Thomas, *Ike's Bluff*, 172–179. Also see Hagerty Diary entry of conversation with Eisenhower and Goodpaster, February 8, 1955, *FRUS, 1955–1957, Soviet Union, Eastern Mediterranean*, 23.

39. Goodpaster, Mandel interviews, January 16, 2002, tape 14.

40. Goodpaster, Soapes interview, January 16, 1978.

41. Memo of NSC Meeting, January 8, 1954, *FRUS 1952–1954, Vol. XIII, Part 1, Indochina*, doc. 499; Memo of NSC Meeting, April 6, 1954, *FRUS 1952–1954, Vol. XIII, Part 1, Indochina*, doc. 705. Also see Ronald Spector, U.S. Army in Vietnam series, *Advice and Support: The Early Years, 1941–1960*, 191–214.

42. Ibid.

43. Goodpaster Memo, October 31, 1954, *FRUS, 1952–1954, Indochina, Part 2*, 2198–99. Also see Goodpaster Memo, January 31, 1956, *FRUS 1955–1957, Western Europe, Canada*, 626–28.

44. Goodpaster, Mandell interviews, February 11, 2004, tape 18. Also see Goodpaster, interview by Richard D. Challenger, January 11, 1966, John Foster Dulles Oral History Project, Princeton University Library, 34–35.

45. Ibid.

46. Goodpaster Memo, May 14, 1956, *FRUS 1955–1957, National Security Policy*, 301–2. Also see Goodpaster Memo, May 24, 1956, *FRUS 1955–1957, National Security Policy*, 311–12.

47. Goodpaster, Mandel interviews, January 16, 2002, tape 15.

48. Ibid.

49. Ibid.

50. Goodpaster, Mandel interviews, February 12, 2004, tape 22.

51. Ibid.

52. Eisenhower, *Waging Peace*, 233–34.

53. Goodpaster, Mandel interviews, February 12, 2004, tape 22.

54. See *FRUS, 1952–1954, East Asia, Pacific, Part 1*, 740–50; Goodpaster Memo, October 29, 1954, *FRUS, China and Japan, Part 1*, 814–22.

55. Ibid.

56. Goodpaster Memo, March 11, 1955, *FRUS 1955–1957, Vol. II, China*, 360, 366; Goodpaster, Mandel interviews, January 16, 2002, tape 13; MFR, March 14, 1955, PDDE, XVI, 1532–33.

57. Ibid.

58. Eisenhower as quoted in Thomas, *Ike's Bluff*, 160–61.

59. Goodpaster, Mandel interviews, tape 14; Goodpaster Memo, May 12, 1965, in which Eisenhower contrasts his secret threats to China that he would use nuclear weapons in Korea if the fighting failed to stop and his public threats during the Taiwan Strait crisis, Eisenhower File, Lyndon B. Johnson Library, hereafter LBJ Library.

60. Goodpaster Memos, August 11, September 30 and October 15, 1958, Office of the Staff Secretary, Subject Series, DoD subseries, box 4 JCS, Eisenhower Library. Also see Thomas, *Ike's Bluff,* 300.

61. Eisenhower Letter to Chiang Kai-shek, October 24, 1958, OSS, International Series, box 4, China, Eisenhower Library.

62. Goodpaster, Mandel interviews, tape 14.

63. Eisenhower, *Waging Peace,* 58. Kingseed, among other scholars, noted that Goodpaster was "ever-present" during important meetings involving Eisenhower. Kingseed, *Eisenhower and the Suez Crisis of 1956*, 90.

64. For well-documented accounts of the Suez crisis, see David Nichols, *Eisenhower 1956*, 2011, and Kingseed, *Eisenhower and the Suez Crisis of 1956*.

65. *FRUS, 1955–1957, Vol. XV*, no. 473, 861–64; *FRUS, 1955–1957, Vol. XIX*, no. 54, 188–92; NSC 291st Meeting, July 19, 1956, B8, Eisenhower Library.

66. Nichols, *Eisenhower 1956*, 113, 131–34.

67. Goodpaster Memo, July 28, 1956, *FRUS 1955–1957, Suez Crisis*, 26. Also see pp. 5, 12, 27, 62, 69, 77, 241, 366. Also see Goodpaster talk, "Eisenhower as Statesman," December 8, 1978, Goodpaster Papers, box 71, file 15, Marshall Library.

68. Kingseed, *Eisenhower and the Suez Crisis of 1956*, 68, 74, 81, 84, 85, 103.

69. Ibid.

70. Ibid., 80, 83, 84, 87, 88, 108.

71. Goodpaster, Mandel interviews, January 16, 2002, tapes 14, 15.

72. Anthony Nutting, Eden's personal secretary, resigned over the issue, Mountbatten and Macmillan also were opposed. See Kingseed, *Eisenhower and the Suez Crisis of 1956*, 84–85.

73. Goodpaster Memo, October 29, 1956, *FRUS, 1955–1957, Suez Crisis*, 839. Goodpaster, Mandell interviews, January 16, 2002, tapes 14, 15; Nichols, *Eisenhower 1956*, 203, 204; Kingseed, *Eisenhower and the Suez Crisis of 1956*, 88, 89, 103.

74. Goodpaster Memo, *November 7, 1956, FRUS, 1955–1957, Suez Crisis*, 143; also in PDDE, XVI, 2371.

75. Goodpaster, interview by Richard D. Challenger, January 11, 1966, John Foster Dulles Oral History Project, Princeton University Library, 38.

76. Ibid.

77. Net Evaluation Committee Reports, OSS, DoD, box 1, and NSC Presidential Records, Intelligence Files, box 1, Eisenhower Library. Also see Chairman's Staff Group to Radford, November 1, 1956, RG 218, Records of U.S. JCS, Chairman's File, Radford, B 38, file 381, Net Evaluation 1956, National Archives, cited in Nichols, *Eisenhower 1956*, 225. Also, Kingseed, *Eisenhower and the Suez Crisis of 1956*, 103.

78. Address in Convention Hall, Philadelphia, November 1, 1956, Public Papers of the Presidents, no. 283, 1066–74, cited in Nichols, *Eisenhower 1956*, 226.

79. Nichols, *Eisenhower 1956*, 251 and Kingseed, *Eisenhower and the Suez Crisis of 1956*, 94, 97.

80. Nichols, *Eisenhower 1956*, 202, 211, 223, 226,

81. Ibid., 233–35.

82. U.S. Army, "Hungary, Resistance Activities and Potential," January 1956, in *The 1956 Hungarian Revolution: A History in Documents,* George Washington University, National Security Archives, 2002-11-04.
83. Goodpaster, Mandel interviews. MacArthur Memo, November 13, 1956, *FRUS, 1955–1957, Eastern Europe,* 435.
84. Nichols, *Eisenhower 1956,* 244–46.
85. Kingseed, *Eisenhower and the Suez Crisis of 1956,* 120–21; Gaddis, *Now We Know,* 173.
86. Nichols, *Eisenhower 1956,* 258–60.
87. Goodpaster Memo, November 21, 1956, *FRUS, 1955–1957, Near East: Jordan-Yemen,* 404–5.
88. Nichols, *Eisenhower 1956,* 90. Eisenhower's hatred of war was emphasized by members of his White House staff, including Eugene Rossides, Douglas Price, and Roemer McPhee at a meeting with the author at the Eisenhower Institute, October 14, 2013.
89. Eisenhower in Goodpaster's Officer Efficiency Report, July 6, 1955, Goodpaster Papers, box 54, Marshall Library.
90. Goodpaster, Mandel interviews, tape 15.
91. Eisenhower in Memo of Conversation, October 8, 1957, *FRUS, 1955–1957, United Nations and General International Matters,* 755.
92. Goodpaster, Mandel interviews, tape 15.
93. Ibid.
94. Ibid.
95. Goodpaster, interview by Richard D. Challenger, January 11, 1966, John Foster Dulles Oral History Project, Princeton University Library, 12. Also see Goodpaster Memo, October 2, 1956, Office of the Staff Secretary, Subject Series, DoD subseries, box 4, JCS, Eisenhower Library.
96. Goodpaster Memo, February 17, 1956, White House, Office of the Staff Secretary, Subject series, DoD subseries, box 4, JCS, Eisenhower Library.
97. Goodpaster Memos, May 28, 1957 and July 23 1957, *FRUS, 1955–1957, Japan,* 333. Also see pp. 315–16.
98. Eisenhower, *Waging Peace,* 178–82.
99. Goodpaster Memo, September 7, 1957, *FRUS, 1955–1957, Near East: Jordan-Yemen,* 685–86.
100. Eisenhower, *Waging Peace,* 262–70.
101. Ibid.
102. Ibid., 275–76. Goodpaster Memos, July 15, July 19, October 15, October 31, 1958, Office of the Staff Secretary, Subject Series, DoD Subseries, box 4, JCS, Eisenhower Library.
103. Ibid.
104. Ibid., 265.
105. Ibid., 265–72.
106. See Goodpaster memos on Lebanon crisis, such as July 15, July 19, October 15, White House, Office of the Staff Secretary, Records of Carroll, Goodpaster, Subject Series, DoD Subseries, box 4, JCS September 1959 folder, Eisenhower Library. Also see Newton, *Eisenhower,* 272.
107. Eisenhower, *Waging Peace,* 288.
108. Cutler to Eisenhower, July 10, 1958, Goodpaster Papers, box 54, file 4, Marshall Library.
109. Eisenhower, *Waging Peace,* 329–30, 333.
110. Ibid., 351–52.
111. Goodpaster Memo, December 17, 1958, OSS, Records, International Series, box 5, Berlin, Eisenhower Library; Goodpaster Memo, February 27, 1959, PDDE, 1378–79.
112. Eisenhower, *Waging Peace,* 356.
113. Goodpaster, Mandel interviews, tape 14.
114. Ibid.; Eisenhower, *Waging Peace,* 404.
115. Goodpaster, Mandel interviews, tape 14; Eisenhower, *Waging Peace,* 405–7.
116. Ibid.

117. Ibid.; Eisenhower, *Waging Peace*, 426–27.

118. Goodpaster, Mandel interviews, January 16, 2002, tape 14; Eisenhower, *Waging Peace*, 438.

119. Goodpaster, Mandel interviews, January 16, 2002, tape 14. Goodpaster memo, September 28, 1959, White House, Office of the Staff Secretary, Subject Series, DoD Subseries, box 4, JCS, Eisenhower Library.

120. Goodpaster, Mandel interviews, January 16, 2002, tape 14.

121. Ibid.

122. Goodpaster Memo, December 17, 1958, OSS, Records, International series, box 1, Berlin, Eisenhower Library; Eisenhower, *Waging Peace*, 447–48.

123. Ibid., 544.

124. See examples: Goodpaster, memos for record, July 5, 6, 7, 1956, December 18, 1956, White House, Office of the Staff Secretary, Subject series, Alphabetical subseries, box 14 (Intelligence Matters), Eisenhower Library; Goodpaster, Mandel interviews, January 16, 2002, tape 13 and Eisenhower, *Mandate for Change*, 425.

125. Eisenhower, *Waging Peace*, 547n; Goodpaster Memo, May 28, 1956, *FRUS, 1955–1957, Soviet Union, Eastern Mediterranean*, 105; Goodpaster Memo, April 11, 1959, OSS, Records, Subject Series, Alphabetical subseries, box 15, Intelligence Matters, Eisenhower Library.

126. Goodpaster memo, March 7, 1958, White House, Office of the Staff Secretary, Subject series, Alphabetical subseries, (Intelligence Matters), box 14; Eisenhower Library; Goodpaster Memo, December 18, 1956, *FRUS, 1955–1957, Soviet Union, Eastern Mediterranean*, 142; Goodpaster, Mandel interviews, January 16, 2002, tape 13.

127. Ibid.

128. Eisenhower, *Waging Peace*, 548.

129. Goodpaster, Mandel interviews, January 16, 2002, tape 13.

130. Eisenhower, *Waging Peace*, 553–56.

131. Ibid.

132. Gray, Memo of Conference, February 17, 1960, Document 454, *FRUS, 1958–1960, Vol. VI*, Cuba; Goodpaster, Mandel interviews, January 16, 2002, tapes 15 and 16; NSC Presidential Records, Intelligence Files, box 1, (NSC 5412 Actions), Eisenhower Library.

133. President's approval of policy of regime change is noted in Goodpaster Memo, November 9, 1959, White House, Office of the Staff Secretary, International Series, box 4, Cuba, Eisenhower Library. Also see paper by 5412 Committee, March 16, 1960, "A Program of Covert Action Against the Castro Regime," *FRUS, 1958–1960, Vol. VI*, doc. 481 and CIA Policy Paper, same title, March 17, 1960, OSS, International Series, box 4, Cuba, Eisenhower Library.

134. Goodpaster Memo of Conference, March 17, 1960, *FRUS, 1958–1960, Vol. VI*, doc. 486; Goodpaster Memo, March 18, 1960, OSS, Subject series, Alpha. Subseries, box 15, Intelligence Matters, Eisenhower Library.

135. Goodpaster, Mandel interviews, January 16, 2002, tapes 15 and 16.

136. Memo of NSC Meeting, March 10, 1960, *FRUS, 1958–1960, Vol. VI*, doc. 474; Memo of NSC Meeting, November 29, 1960, *FRUS, 1958–1960, Vol. VI*, doc. 613.

137. Telegram, U.S. Embassy to State, January 3, 1961, *FRUS, 1961–1963, Vol. X*, doc. 1, Memo for Record, January 3, 1961, *FRUS, 1961–1963, Vol. X*, doc. 3; Memo of Conversation, January 3, 1961, *FRUS, 1961–1963, Vol. X*, doc. 4; Editorial Note, *FRUS, 1961–1963, Vol. X*, doc. 11.

138. Memo Hawkins to Esterline, January 4, 1961, *FRUS, 1961–1963, Vol. X*, doc. 9.

139. Memo Merchant to Herter, January 10, 1961, *FRUS, 1961–1963, Vol. X*, doc. 15.

140. Planning and deliberations for the Bay of Pigs during the Kennedy administration are detailed in *FRUS, 1961–1963, Vol. X*, doc. 231, 232, 233, 26, 27, 28, 30, 32, 35, 40, 46; CIA IG Survey, Lyman Kirkpatrick to John McCone, "Inspector General Survey of the Cuban Operation," October 1961, cited in Michael Warner's article, "The CIA's Internal Probe of the Bay of Pigs Affair, Center for the Study of Intelligence, undated; Goodpaster, Mandel interviews, January 16, 2002, tapes 15 and 16.

141. Goodpaster, Mandel interviews, February 11, 2004, tape 16; Goodpaster Memo, November 21, 1960, following meeting with Ted Sorenson, Kennedy's special counsel at which Goodpaster was asked to stay on; Wilton B. Persons Papers, box 1, Eisenhower Library; Eisenhower, *Waging Peace*, 712–16.

142. Eisenhower, Diary entry, December 6, 1960, PDDE, XXI, 2189–95.

143. Editorial Note, *FRUS, 1961–1963, Vol. 1, Vietnam 1961*, 12, cited in Goldstein, *Lessons in Disaster*, 52.

144. Goodpaster, Mandel interviews, February 11, 2004, tape 18.

145. Kennedy to Goodpaster, March 16, 1961, Goodpaster Papers, box 54, file 4, Marshall Library.

146. Eisenhower to Secretary of the Army, May 31, 1960, and January 20, 1961, Goodpaster Papers, box 54, files 1–18, Marshall Library.

Chapter Nine

Commanding an Infantry Division (1961–1962)

During the long period that Goodpaster was away from the Army mainstream, many of his mentors had retired. Furthermore, he had missed serving in the Korean War. Goodpaster knew that his prolonged absence could make him somewhat of an outsider. While the Army considered it necessary at some point for officers to gain experience on high-level staffs in Washington, so-called purple assignments, too much time in Washington was frowned upon. Such officers were often stigmatized as being political, implying that they earned their promotions more through pandering to politicians than through demonstrating their military competence.

Goodpaster need not have worried about his future in the Army. One could not receive a stronger endorsement in the Army than six years of excellent ratings by Eisenhower, the commander-in-chief and a revered soldier.

Goodpaster was returning to a much different Army from the one in which he served seventeen years earlier. It was a Cold War army focused mainly on defending Europe with undernourished NATO allies. Specifically, the main focus of the Army was on defending the Fulda Gap in Germany, while badly outnumbered and outgunned by Soviet and Warsaw Pact forces that also had the advantages of initiative—choosing the time and place of attack—and geography, with much shorter distances to supply and reinforce forward forces.

It was also an Army in transition. General Maxwell Taylor had recently reorganized the Army into "pentomic" divisions with five battle groups that could be quickly reconfigured according to changing missions by changing the mix of infantry, armor, and mechanized forces in a battle group. The new structure was designed in part so that troops could be more easily dispersed on a battlefield with nuclear weapons. These changes were controversial.[1]

3ᴿᴰ INFANTRY DIVISION (APRIL 1961–OCTOBER 1961)

After leaving the White House in April 1961, General Goodpaster was assigned as assistant division commander of the 3rd Infantry Division, a position he would hold for six months. En route to his new assignment, Goodpaster visited Fort Benning, home of the Infantry School, Fort Knox, home of the Armor School, and Fort Leavenworth, home of combined arms schooling. He talked with Army leaders about the changing Army, especially newer technologies such as helicopters and other challenges.[2]

Dossy settled the family into Army housing in Wurzburg, West Germany. Their older daughter Susan was in her first year of college at Wellesley. Younger daughter Anne was entering her teens and enrolled in the post school.[3]

Goodpaster joined the division at Hohenfels, a major training area in Germany. As the assistant division commander, he was responsible for training and alert readiness; the division needed to meet planned contingency deployments on short notice. Goodpaster also supervised the handling of personnel issues such as general courts martial and elimination of soldiers determined to be unfit for further service.[4]

Joining one of the battle groups in the field brought back memories of Italy and the 48th Engineers. In a jeep at night on a muddy road, with pouring rain, foul weather felt very much the same. He also noted that the battle group and battalion commanders were wound tight as a drum. He soon attributed this to the current "Zero Defects" fad that the Army had adopted from business schools. As a result, virtually anything that went wrong was a black mark against the commander.[5]

After his first week on the job, Goodpaster had an officers' call in the informal setting of the officers' club. There he noticed that, at the end of every week or at the end of every training exercise, he found it useful to look back and ask, "If I were doing this again, is there something I could do differently and could do better? Now when you do that, the answer can be either yes or no. If the answer is yes, then I could reflect on it and give some thought to how I could do this a little better. If the answer is no, then, if I am really serious about it, it means I had attained perfection. That is something that hasn't been seen on earth in two thousand years." This kind of thinking seemed to resonate with the officers. That encouraged them to loosen up and think for themselves rather than be overly reliant on checklists. As a result, they were able to take more initiative in leading their units.

Goodpaster added: "Now look, you're down here. This is the time to make mistakes. Don't make that a habit, but if you see that something could be done better in retrospect, learn from that. And see that your unit learns from that. Enjoy the time that you're here." And they did.[6]

While Goodpaster encouraged independent thinking at every echelon, he also insisted on units meeting high standards in training. When a unit was called out on a practice alert and failed to meet the standards, it was alerted again the following night and so on until it passed. Word quickly spread through the division that substandard performance was not tolerated.[7]

Another major challenge Goodpaster faced was cross-organizing the battalions into battle groups in the Pentomic division. Traditionally, the same battalions were part of the same regiment, where they trained together, got to know one another well, and worked as a team. Under the Pentomic structure, the composition of a battle group could change, depending on the mission; some could be allocated more tanks when the mission so required, for example. While certainly more flexible, the Pentomic structure sacrificed team building and had other significant deficiencies. Eventually the Army returned to a more traditional structure.

In August 1961, the division was alerted to send a combat-ready, reinforced rifle company to Berlin as part of a battle group moving by road across the East German border. These orders were triggered by President Kennedy's rebuff of a Soviet ultimatum to withdraw Allied forces from Berlin. On August 13, 1961, East Germany, under Soviet direction, began sealing the border with West Germany and constructing what became known as the Berlin Wall. This was done mainly to help staunch the flow of East Germans to the West. By that time, nearly 20 percent of the East German population had fled, particularly younger people, along with doctors, teachers, engineers, and other professionals. Premier Khrushchev was determined to remove the Berlin thorn in 1961, but recognized the risk that such efforts could lead to full-scale nuclear war. Khrushchev aptly characterized Berlin "as the most dangerous spot in the world."[8]

This move was also seen as a possible challenge to Western access to Berlin, so President Kennedy sent Vice President Johnson and retired General Lucius Clay (commander of U.S. forces during the Berlin airlift) to Berlin on August 19. They were on hand to greet a convoy of nearly 500 vehicles with 1,500 troops of the 1st Battle Group of the 18th U.S. Infantry that had been sent by road 110 miles across East Germany. The convoy stretched nearly 100 miles and arrived without incident. While the test was successful, Berlin would remain a bellwether throughout the Cold War.

In judging Goodpaster's performance, his division commander expected that it would take Goodpaster time to adjust to troop duty after nearly seventeen years since he commanded a battalion in Italy. Instead, the commander found that Goodpaster "proved to be immediately and fully effective. . . .

[He] contributed innovations in planning, control and coordination which were highly effective in supervising newly decentralized training and testing."[9]

8TH INFANTRY DIVISION (OCTOBER 1961–OCTOBER 1962)

In October, he was selected to command the 8th Infantry Division and promoted to major general. A proud part of the division's history was captured by the motto, "These are my credentials." That referred to the reply by the assistant division commander, Brigadier General Charles D. W. Canham, during the battle for the port of Brest following the Normandy invasion. After months of bitter fighting, on September 19, 1944, Canham entered the German command bunker, demanding the surrender of German forces. Lieutenant General Herman Ramcke, the German commander, replied through an interpreter that he wanted to see Canham's credentials. Ramcke was stalling for time so that his final report could be sent by radio, but Canham, annoyed by the arrogance of this more senior German general, motioned to his battle-hardened soldiers in the doorway, and replied, "These are my credentials."[10]

Soon after getting settled into their home in Wurzburg, Dossy and the family moved to Bad Kreuznach, West Germany. This process of fitting furniture into new quarters and adjusting to new schools, new neighbors, new shopping, new medical care, and a myriad of other necessary details of daily life had become routine by this point.

Shortly after Goodpaster took command of the division, his chief of staff, Jack Wright, advised him that he should become airborne qualified because part of the division was airborne. To better exercise leadership, Wright suggested, Goodpaster needed to train and fight with all the soldiers in the division. So, at age 46, Goodpaster went to airborne school for three weeks of intense training, culminating in his making five jumps in one day and thereupon receiving his paratrooper wings.[11]

As a division commander, Goodpaster had his hands full with a myriad of administrative details, but his main job was to lead soldiers. His approach to leadership involved spending as much time as possible with the troops. For example, while on a field exercise during the winter with very deep snow, very cold temperatures, and the wind blowing like hell, the captain in command of a mechanized infantry company pitted against a German Panzer Grenadier outfit was surprised to find the division commander walking along the defensive perimeter, talking to the troops, asking questions about their fields of fire and personal questions as well. The captain's soldiers were very impressed to see a general joining them in the snowdrifts and caring about what they were doing. The captain never forgot Goodpaster's leadership example, which served him well; he retired as a three-star general.[12]

Goodpaster could also come down hard on his battle group commanders. In one such incident, Goodpaster was overheard reprimanding Colonel Glover Johns at his retirement ceremonies for disregarding instructions from division staff about troop duties and billeting arrangements. Apparently, Goodpaster was angry about commanders focusing on the interests of their own unit at the expense of others, fostering an attitude of "we versus they," rather than working together as a team. Goodpaster had seen this attitude and behavior before, often reflected in disdain for staff officers by some commanders, and it set a bad example for subordinate commanders. [13]

Colonel Johns was especially angered by the timing of the reprimand at his retirement ceremony. In a letter to David Hackworth, one of his company commanders, Johns noted that Goodpaster's behavior was "so incredibly thoughtless" that it made him wonder at the man's ability "in anything that requires subtle thinking . . . he damn sure couldn't lead a squad of real soldiers to the PX for a cup of coffee." Johns disparaged Goodpaster for being an engineer rather than an infantry officer and having served in the White House. Johns also acknowledged his own "uncanny ability to alienate my immediate superiors." [14]

Goodpaster and his chief of staff noted the tendency of units to learn much during field training exercises but that the lessons seemed tenuous and would soon slip away. Often, when a unit went on the next exercise, it made the same mistakes and relearned the same things, with little overall progress. [15]

In addressing the training problem, Goodpaster had the division keep very thorough records of all of the skills that needed improving. Using this information, he had specific unit action plans developed. The main focus was the central purpose of the division. He eliminated many things that involved troop time but actually distracted from the mission. Goodpaster put into effect simple guidelines, such as, "Anything that contributes to our central purpose, we will do that. Anything that takes away from it, we're going to be against that." As these action plans were implemented, the division didn't make the same mistakes again. They made some new ones, but they made progress, focusing on the central mission and the ability to accomplish it under all circumstances. The idea caught on, and other division commanders began to put similar approaches into practice. [16]

During his time back with troops, Goodpaster maintained contact with Eisenhower; they shared their experiences of command and training. Goodpaster recalled Eisenhower's concentration on the central mission when they both were involved in establishing NATO's military structure. In Goodpaster's mind, Eisenhower's systematic focus on mission was useful in aligning a wide variety of necessary support functions and resulted in unity of effort and increased the chances of success on the battlefield. In his letters, Eisenhower welcomed the exchanges and would draw on his Louisiana maneuvers experience training divisions for overseas deployment in the early stages of World War II.[17]

In 1962, West German chancellor Konrad Adenauer invited former president Eisenhower to visit Germany. During the visit, Adenauer arranged for a small private luncheon and asked Eisenhower if there was anybody else he would like to have join them, such as the SACEUR or the American ambassador. Eisenhower said that he would only like to have Major General Goodpaster join them. Goodpaster recalled that it was a delightful, relaxed lunch. Aside from his official duties, Adenauer operated a high quality vineyard and stocked an excellent wine cellar. During the lunch, he enjoyed sharing some of his best wine, including a white wine from 1921.[18]

At the luncheon, Eisenhower and Adenauer shared their views about how Europe could be different in the future and the role that Germany could play. The recently formed West German forces were in the process of being integrated into the NATO structure, and the discussion turned to how they would be part of a new Europe and a new Germany. Goodpaster shared some of his thoughts about training and his contacts with German units now commanded by colleagues he had known from the early days at SHAPE.[19]

Unit pride was encouraged by Goodpaster and other commanders, along with competition between units. But sometimes this led to problems. For example, off-duty soldiers from the 8th Infantry Division would sometimes encounter soldiers from the adjacent 3rd Armored Division, and, after a few drinks, there would be fights in bars. Major General Creighton Abrams commanded the 3rd Armored Division, whose plans were integrated with those of the 8th Infantry Division, so Abrams and Goodpaster were often coordinating their efforts, including ways to reduce friction between the divisions. This was not the last time they would serve together.[20]

Goodpaster's corps commander observed him leading the 8th Infantry Division in the field, in garrison, and in social settings. The V Corps commander noted that "there is no other officer-family combination that is contributing more now or will contribute more through leadership, character and ability, to the training, morale, prestige or well-being of the Army. This applies to his relationships with his troops, his officers, and the families . . . as well as the German civilians under his command." Later, the corps commander noted that he particularly respected Goodpaster for his "succinct and sound analysis of important mutual problems." The Seventh Army Commander noted that Goodpaster "is a potential theater commander or Chief of Staff of the Army."[21]

During this tour of duty, Goodpaster was advised that, following his command, he had been selected to be superintendent of the United States Military Academy, West Point, replacing General Westmoreland in that post in the summer of 1963.[22]

In October 1962, however, Goodpaster's division command assignment was curtailed by the Cuban Missile Crisis. President Kennedy recalled General Maxwell Taylor to active duty to serve as chairman of the Joint Chiefs of Staff. General Taylor requested Goodpaster to return and be his assistant and help with his plans for reinvigorating the way the organization of the Joint Chiefs of Staff operated. In particular, Taylor said he wanted Goodpaster to serve as his alter ego on occasions when he was involved in interdepartmental and National Security Council meetings. [23]

Goodpaster's brief experience once again commanding troops provided opportunities to practice his accumulated understanding of leadership. He demonstrated that he genuinely cared for the troops who, in turn, respected his leadership. Together, they functioned effectively as a team. They made mistakes, but they learned from their mistakes.

Figure 9.1.   Commanding General, 8th Infantry Division, 1962. Official photo.
Source: **Courtesy of National Archives and Records Administration (NARA)**

Figure 9.2.   Paratrooper, 1962. Official photo. *Source*: Courtesy of Goodpaster Family

NOTES

1. Andrew Bacevich, *Pentomic Army*, xx.
2. Goodpaster, Mandel interviews, February 11, 2004, tape 16.
3. Susan Goodpaster Sullivan, telephone interview with author, March 2013.
4. Goodpaster, Mandel interviews, February 11, 2004, tape 16.
5. Ibid.
6. Ibid.
7. Goodpaster, Mandel interviews, February 11, 2004, tape 17.
8. Nikita Khrushchev, cited in Kempe, *Berlin 1961,* 244, 12, 4.
9. Commanding General, 3rd Infantry Division, Goodpaster Efficiency Report, October 17, 1961, Goodpaster papers, box 54, Marshall Library.
10. See Michael Doubler, *Closing with the Enemy*, 1994.
11. Goodpaster, Mandel interviews, February 11, 2004, tape 17.
12. Lieutenant General Sam Wetzel, correspondence with author, May 4, 2012.
13. Hackworth, *About Face,* 1989, 403–4.
14. Ibid.
15. Goodpaster, Mandel interviews, February 11, 2004, tape 17.
16. Ibid.
17. Ibid.
18. Ibid.
19. Ibid.
20. Goodpaster, Mandel interviews, February 12, 2004, tape 20.
21. Commanding General, V Corps, Goodpaster Efficiency Reports, August 1, 1962, October 28, 1962, Goodpaster papers, box 54, Marshall Library.
22. Goodpaster, Mandel interviews, February 12, 2004, tape 20.
23. Ibid.

Chapter Ten

The Joint Staff (1962–1967)

After completing a year in command of an infantry division, Goodpaster was called back to Washington in November 1962 to become Special Assistant (Policy) to the new Chairman of the Joint Chiefs of Staff (JCS), General Maxwell D. Taylor. Given the very public differences between President Eisenhower and General Taylor over defense policy, this put Goodpaster in a difficult position.

General Taylor, while serving as chief of staff of the Army from 1955 to 1959, had become increasingly critical of the Eisenhower administration's defense policies that emphasized nuclear weapons at the expense of the Army. Taylor retired in 1959 and published a book, *The Uncertain Trumpet*, making his criticism even more public. Taylor's critique resonated with Senator John F. Kennedy during his 1960 campaign for president and later became an important basis of President Kennedy's subsequent shift in defense policy from the Eisenhower "New Look" to his "Flexible Response."

Of course, Goodpaster was aware of the rift between Taylor and Eisenhower, even though he also knew that both had great respect for each other on a personal level. Given that situation, Goodpaster insisted on reaching an early understanding with General Taylor that he would not be a party to any criticism or attack on Eisenhower. Taylor had anticipated the issue and promised that there would be none of that. [1]

The train of events that led to Taylor's being recalled to active duty as chairman of the JCS began when President Kennedy had been in office only a few months and the operations to overthrow Castro with Cuban exiles in the Bay of Pigs invasion failed dramatically. It was a huge embarrassment for which President Kennedy accepted full responsibility. Although he was briefed on the plans when he became president-elect in November, he was not aware of how the concept had been changed fundamentally from that of the Eisenhower administration. Kennedy appointed General Taylor to head a small group to investigate the failure. The report confirmed Kennedy's suspicions that he had not been well served by the CIA and the Joint Chiefs of Staff. Soon after the report, Kennedy recalled Taylor to active duty, initially making him his military representative in the White House and then appointing him Chairman of the Joint Chiefs of Staff in October 1962.

General Taylor was undoubtedly aware that, in assuming the challenge of leading the Joint Chiefs after the Bay of Pigs debacle, he needed an assistant whom he could trust and who had the ability to work well under pressure. Goodpaster was assigned specifically as Special Assistant (Policy) to the new Chairman, but Taylor wanted him to play a broader role. He wanted Goodpaster to be responsible for briefing him on all issues that were to be discussed at meetings with the service chiefs. Goodpaster had a staff of five officers to help him prepare such briefings for the chairman.[2]

Taylor also wanted Goodpaster to help improve the process by which the Joint Chiefs provided advice to the president. The current process was not timely, in Taylor's view. Finally, Taylor wanted Goodpaster to "dig into" the big issues, including NATO, and particularly Vietnam. Goodpaster found himself in a similar position to the one he had with Eisenhower; the problems of the JCS chairman became Goodpaster's problems.[3]

Soon after returning to the Pentagon, Goodpaster joined General Taylor for a meeting at the White House. Upon their entering the Oval Office, President Kennedy came around his desk and shook Goodpaster's hand, noting that he had kept his promise to give Goodpaster a command. After the briefing, Goodpaster recalled realizing for the first time that the president of the United States was younger than he was; nevertheless, Kennedy impressed Goodpaster.[4]

CUBA, CHINA, AND INDIA

Goodpaster arrived during the Cuban Missile Crisis. An agreement had been reached between Kennedy and Khrushchev on October 28, 1962, under which the Soviet Union would remove missiles and warheads from Cuba in return for a U.S. promise not to invade Cuba and a secret understanding that the United States would also remove certain missiles from Turkey and Italy. In the meantime, the U.S. military was on high alert with strategic bombers on airborne alert ready to strike the Soviet Union, and ships enforcing the naval blockade of Cuba. Plans included landing ninety thousand troops within eighteen days following airstrikes. By many accounts, the United States and the Soviet Union were at the brink of a catastrophic nuclear war.[5]

While Goodpaster and the national security team were focused on the Cuban Missile Crisis, China attacked Indian forces along a disputed border.

After initial Chinese gains in mountainous terrain at elevations of more than fourteen thousand feet, India sacrificed its nonalignment policy and requested military assistance from the United States and others. President Kennedy, at a meeting with Goodpaster and senior NSC leaders, decided to help, but he wanted the United Kingdom to take the lead in organizing a multinational assistance effort. Initially, the United States provided C-130 transport aircraft and sent a military mission to Delhi. [6]

The war provided an opportunity to improve U.S. relations with India at the expense of the Soviet Union, which had been providing military assistance to India. At the same time, however, any U.S. support for India would strain U.S. relations with Pakistan. Meanwhile, on the Sino-Indian border, China declared a cease-fire after seizing territory. Later negotiations demarcated the border, but Sino-Indian tensions remained, and that situation would also continue to engage the attention of Taylor and Goodpaster.

VIETNAM

Vietnam was viewed in terms of a pattern of communist aggression and the "domino theory," the notion that the fall of one state to communism posed an immediate threat to neighboring states. As a senator, Kennedy had voiced such concerns in terms of the "Red Tide of Communism." In his inaugural speech, Kennedy promised to "pay any price, bear any burden, meet any hardship, support any friend, and oppose any foe in order to assure the survival and success of liberty." [7]

These promises were soon tested. The situation in South Vietnam was deteriorating as President Ngo Dinh Diem increasingly failed to stem North Vietnamese infiltration and support of the Viet Cong (VC). Diem also resorted to repression to put down Buddhist and other popular demonstrations. In May 1961, Kennedy approved National Security Action Memorandum (NSAM) 52 establishing the U.S. objective of preventing communist domination of South Vietnam and approving covert actions. He also sent Vice President Johnson to South Vietnam to investigate the situation. In the same time frame, Kennedy ordered the substantial expansion of U.S. Special Forces troops to better deal with such challenges on a global basis. The combination of covert operations and military advisors seemed like a reasonable hedge against communist insurgencies that were challenging friendly governments throughout the Third World, especially with "wars of national liberation" in colonies and former colonies of the European powers. [8]

In Vietnam, the U.S. military assistance effort in 1961 included about two thousand advisors, but the Joint Chiefs of Staff anticipated increasing it substantially and created a new headquarters, Military Assistance Command,

Vietnam (MACV), under General Paul Harkins in 1962. Goodpaster realized Vietnam was becoming a test case.[9]

By 1963, the U.S. advisory effort had grown to about 16,700 personnel. President Kennedy realized that a much larger effort might be required, but also feared that he would not be able to win sufficient public support for such an effort. In October 1963, President Kennedy announced that U.S. forces in Vietnam would be reduced by one thousand advisors by the end of the year and completely withdrawn by the end of 1965. At the same time, planning was underway for covert operations, including raids against the Ho Chi Minh Trail in Laos and North Vietnam, with U.S. support including naval ships.[10]

Kennedy and others were losing confidence in South Vietnamese president Ngo Dinh Diem and his brother, Ngo Dinh Nhu, the secret police chief, who had become wary of increasing American involvement and held secret talks with North Vietnamese representatives, exploring alternatives. On August 29, 1963, President Kennedy approved a coup d'état that resulted in the assassination of Diem and Nhu on November 2, 1963. After the coup, the United States had to support the military-led government in South Vietnam. Without U.S. support, the South Vietnamese government would likely fall to the communists, so the administration shifted toward greater U.S. involvement.[11]

Only a few weeks later, on November 22, 1963, President Kennedy was assassinated. Lyndon Johnson inherited the Vietnam problem along with overall responsibility for maintaining the security of the United States. Despite any personal reservations, Johnson was determined to not lose Vietnam because he feared the same kind of political backlash that had accompanied the earlier "loss of China" to the communists. Further, as a lifelong politician, he understood that he had not been elected president but now was faced with a presidential election in less than a year. On November 26, 1963, Johnson approved NSAM 273, drafted a day before the assassination. The action memorandum provided for drawing down the advisory effort publicly while privately allowing for increases in other military actions, especially covert operations.[12]

In assuming the role of president, Lyndon Johnson kept McGeorge Bundy as his national security advisor and retained most of the White House staff for continuity rather than bring in a new team that would be more familiar and loyal to him personally. The staff soon became aware of how Johnson's style of decision making differed from that of Kennedy. Johnson continued to think much as he did when he was the Senate majority leader. He sought to build consensus among key constituents by managing bureaucratic concerns—in effect, trying to please nearly everyone.[13]

EISENHOWER

Early in his administration, President Johnson asked Goodpaster to keep former President Eisenhower informed on national security developments, particularly Vietnam. Goodpaster agreed and met with Eisenhower regularly, about sixty times over the next four years and spoke by phone on several occasions. Although Vietnam was the focus of most of these discussions, they also covered a wide range of international security developments including NATO, arms control, and crises in countries including the Dominican Republic, Indonesia, Rhodesia, India-Pakistan, Israel, and North Korea. Goodpaster briefed Johnson on these meetings and Johnson always expressed strong interest in Eisenhower's ideas and recommendations. [14]

While President Johnson was undoubtedly interested in Eisenhower's views, Johnson was also eager to avoid having such an influential Republican be openly critical of his policies. Eisenhower understood the sensitive nature of their relationship and did not make public statements that would undermine the president. The relationship went well for both with Goodpaster as the intermediary. The following summer, McGeorge Bundy noted to Goodpaster that "next to the operations in Vietnam themselves, there is nothing more important than the work that President Johnson and President Eisenhower have done over the last 20 months to maintain their close mutual understanding." In particular, Johnson emphasized the continuity in the United States' commitment to Vietnam beginning with Eisenhower in October 1954. [15]

Eisenhower viewed Vietnam and Laos mainly in terms of the Cold War and the domino theory. From the earliest meetings with Goodpaster, Eisenhower advised Johnson to prevent South Vietnam from falling to communism. In particular, after Johnson decided to commit U.S. forces to a combat role, Eisenhower urged Johnson to bring it to a quick conclusion. For example, Goodpaster reported that Eisenhower advised going all out, "swamping the enemy with overwhelming force." Eisenhower would "err on the side of putting in too much." Eisenhower also advised putting the best commander in charge and letting him fight the war, avoiding micromanaging operations from Washington. By way of example, Goodpaster reported that Eisenhower recounted that during the World War II Battle of the Bulge, General Marshall ordered the War Department to not bother Eisenhower and notified General Eisenhower to ignore anything from Washington during the battle. [16]

President Johnson, according to Goodpaster, was grateful for Eisenhower's advice. Johnson would comment, "We're going to see what we can do about this." But the initiative would seem to drain away as Johnson talked to his other advisors. As this pattern evolved, Eisenhower became very concerned about President Johnson and said, "You know that man is at war with himself. He simply cannot make a decision of this character." That phrase stuck in Goodpaster's mind. But both Eisenhower and Goodpaster refused to say anything publicly that would make the president's job more difficult. [17]

GET IN OR GET OUT

On January 22, 1964, the Joint Chiefs sent a memo to the president proposing air strikes against North Vietnam and sending in U.S. combat forces to stem the deteriorating situation in South Vietnam. The Chiefs met with President Johnson on March 2 and further elaborated proposals including the mining of harbors and a naval blockade of North Vietnam; they even proposed using nuclear weapons if China intervened. For Johnson, the meeting was a high-pressure push by the Chiefs to "get in or get out." But Johnson was not willing to make such a decision, particularly before the November election. He did, however, approve Operations Plan (OPLAN) 34A on January 16, 1964, for covert operations against North Vietnam, beginning on February 1. [18]

By the summer of 1964, President Johnson and Secretary of Defense Robert McNamara had decided to install a new team in Saigon—Ambassador Taylor and General Westmoreland. Henry Cabot Lodge Jr., then U.S. ambassador to the Republic of Vietnam and a prominent Republican who was a potential contender for president, had made it difficult for Johnson to disagree openly over how to combat the spread of communism. Furthermore, Ambassador Lodge and General Harkins were at odds, so the country team was dysfunctional. McNamara was also disillusioned with General Harkins, believing him to be overly optimistic in his reporting and reluctant to adopt McNamara's more detailed and systematic approach to managing the problem. [19]

On July 1, 1964, General Taylor was named Ambassador to South Vietnam. He was replaced as Chairman of the JCS by Army general Earle Wheeler, who retained Goodpaster as his assistant. By July, the military assistance and advisory program had increased to include 16,500 troops, and General William Westmoreland had been appointed to take over as Commander, U.S. Military Assistance Command, Vietnam, from General Harkins. By this point, it was clear to Goodpaster that Vietnam had become a top priority. [20]

As a result of these changes, Westmoreland became the primary person responsible for the military effort in Vietnam. He was the leader on the front lines, although he was nominally under Ambassador Taylor and the commander in chief, Pacific Command, Admiral Ulysses S. Grant Sharp, as well as the chairman of the Joint Chiefs of Staff. Nevertheless, Westmoreland was responsible for recommending the strategy and military resource requirements. Traditionally, senior officers in the chain of command were reluctant to second-guess and overrule the commander on the scene, so Westmoreland's views prevailed for the next four years.

THE GULF OF TONKIN INCIDENT

In August 1964, U.S. Navy destroyers were collecting radar and communications emissions near the coast of North Vietnam in the Gulf of Tonkin and were apparently attacked by North Vietnamese torpedo boats. Goodpaster recalled in a subsequent interview that the Joint Chiefs went to great lengths to confirm that attacks had occurred, "Our judgment was as near certain as it's possible to be in circumstances of that kind." Goodpaster also noted that the Chiefs had previously studied a series of options for responding to a North Vietnamese attack in terms of a minimal to a maximum effort. In the study, they agreed, and Goodpaster supported, that a maximum effort was appropriate instead of a gradual escalation. [21]

However, in response to the Tonkin incident, President Johnson, in the middle of a reelection campaign, ordered limited air strikes against naval bases and an oil facility in North Vietnam. Within days, by August 7, 1964, Congress had passed the Gulf of Tonkin Joint Resolution, authorizing the president to undertake military operations in Southeast Asia. The vote was overwhelming.

Subsequently, however, it became clear that the North Vietnamese actions took place within the context of the shelling of North Vietnam by U.S. naval vessels, bombings, and commando raids over the previous several days under the covert-action OPLAN 34A. Further, before the North Vietnamese attack, a U.S. destroyer was directed to move to within four miles of the North Vietnamese coast instead of more typical operations twenty miles or more offshore. Once the destroyer came under attack, the skipper requested that his intelligence collection mission be terminated, but was turned down. The destroyer was soon joined by U.S. fighter-bombers from a nearby aircraft carrier and another U.S. destroyer. [22]

WAR GAMES

The Gulf of Tonkin incident highlighted the internal debate about the appropriate strategy for Vietnam at a time when the administration was facing an election and was under pressure from Republicans including the former JCS chairman, retired Admiral Arthur Radford, for being too timid in security affairs. At the same time, influential Democrats were opposed to deeper involvement in Vietnam.

To help political and military leaders think through such problems, General Taylor was attracted to detailed war games organized by the JCS. He participated frequently and personally invited other senior political and military leaders to join him, including McGeorge Bundy, who frequently represented the White House in the games. Goodpaster was familiar with the games, both as a participant and as the assistant to both General Taylor and General Wheeler, each of whom participated in war games as chairman of the JCS.

During the early 1960s, about four war games were conducted each year, in which political and military leaders were faced with challenging scenarios requiring them to make difficult decisions. The Sigma series focused on Southeast Asia. Others dealt with NATO, the Middle East, and a wide range of security challenges.[23]

These games were designed to explore the possible consequences of alternative strategies, and they enabled leaders at the highest levels to anticipate the kinds of tough choices they might have to make. Control-team experts helped insure that proposed actions were feasible in terms of logistics, transportation, and many other details that might prove problematic, including possible consequences for other allies and adversaries.

The SIGMA II war game was conducted from September 8 to September 17, 1964, building on the Gulf of Tonkin incident and featuring a scenario depicting a general deterioration of the situation in South Vietnam. Participants included National Security Advisor McGeorge Bundy, Assistant Secretary of State William Bundy, CIA Director John McCone, Deputy Assistant Secretary of Defense for International Security Affairs John McNaughton, Deputy Secretary of Defense Cyrus Vance, and the Joint Chiefs of Staff, including General Curtis LeMay. Secretary of Defense McNamara, Secretary of State Dean Rusk, Undersecretary of State George Ball, and Walt Rostow from the State Department's Policy Planning staff observed the game and were briefed on its conclusions.[24]

Goodpaster noted that the SIGMA II war game explored a massive U.S. military escalation, including air strikes against virtually all military and industrial targets in North Vietnam, mining the ports, and the introduction of more than five U.S. Army and Marine divisions to interdict North Vietnam's supply lines and to threaten an invasion of the North. Yet despite the application of such power, it was not clearly decisive; about half of the participants believed that eventually losses and destruction would compel North Vietnam to stop supporting the war in South Vietnam. However, North Vietnam's calculus was clearly the "great unknown." At the same time, players expressed doubt about the "U.S. stomach" for such a large commitment of ground forces to a war in Southeast Asia. A major conclusion of the game was that in the absence of major aggression, a massive U.S. military intervention "appears questionable."[25]

This game built on Sigma I, a similar nine hundred-man-hour high-level effort, conducted April 6 to 9, before the Gulf of Tonkin incident. The Sigma

I scenario also posed a deteriorating situation in South Vietnam, so the U.S./ Blue team was faced with choices of escalation or likely accepting a communist victory. The escalation strategies involved either a gradual buildup of U.S. pressure or a massive, immediate application of U.S. forces that included bombing North Vietnam back into the "stone age." Both approaches were problematic, however. Bombing was not likely to solve the problems in South Vietnam, and U.S. public opinion was a key factor. As one Blue team member put it, "In the end, public opinion is the only decisive factor here." In the game, the United States was branded an aggressor and lost a vote in the UN General Assembly. More importantly, Blue team members did not relish preparing testimony for the secretary of defense and chairman of the JCS to explain to Congress "what this is all about." Other Blue team members argued that if we can impose our will on North Vietnam, then we can take the penalty of world public opinion. The game director concluded that lots of homework and planning was needed to prepare a clear and convincing U.S. policy. Goodpaster got the message.[26]

The war games, along with national intelligence estimates and other studies, documented that the Vietnam situation was well thought through by the mid-1960s. Problems and broad consequences for the United States, allies, neutrals, and adversaries were anticipated. However, experts and policy makers within both the State and Defense Departments disagreed on strategy. Similarly, outside the administration, there was no consensus. The joint resolution of Congress following the Gulf of Tonkin incident provided legal authority for escalation, yet the president was also under pressure to avoid overreacting. And Goodpaster was in the middle of the debate.

JOHNSON REELECTED

In the 1964 election campaign, Johnson faced Senator Barry Goldwater from Arizona, a staunch conservative, who had defeated more liberal candidates for the Republican nomination, with the votes split between New York governor Nelson Rockefeller, Henry Cabot Lodge Jr. of Massachusetts, and Pennsylvania governor William Scranton.

Johnson's campaign painted Goldwater as a dangerous figure, more likely to lead the United States into war because of his strong anticommunist views. Given such a public position, President Johnson was careful not to react too strongly to the Gulf of Tonkin incident, while still demonstrating a quick, "tit-for-tat" limited response.

In November, President Johnson won the election decisively with 61 percent of the vote and carrying 44 states. Democrats also won both houses of Congress, with a 68–32 margin in the Senate and a 297–140 majority in the House of Representatives.[27]

In December 1964, Goodpaster was nominated for promotion to lieutenant general. Confirmation of a third star was initially held up in Congress because the title of his position had been changed from Special Assistant to the Chairman (Policy) to assistant to the Chairman with expanded duties. The Defense Department's Legislative Liaison staff, however, had not briefed congressional staffs on the change in title. Some in Congress feared that this suggested that Goodpaster, as a junior three-star, might preside over more senior four-star officers from other services in the absence of the chairman. Once this concern was resolved, his promotion was confirmed. Shortly thereafter, Goodpaster was notified that he had been selected to command the XVIII Airborne Corps, probably the most desirable assignment for an Army three-star general. However, when President Johnson learned of the proposed assignment, he vetoed it, wanting Goodpaster to remain nearby in the Pentagon.[28]

Meanwhile, events in Vietnam took a fateful turn following the bombing of an officers' billet in Saigon, killing two Americans and wounding thirty-eight. President Johnson initially disapproved a request for retaliatory air strikes. However, in a cable to Ambassador Taylor on December 30, 1964, Johnson noted,

> I have never felt that this war will be won from the air, and it seems to me that what is much more needed and would be more effective is a larger and stronger use of Rangers and Special Forces and Marines, or other appropriate military strength on the ground and on the scene. . . . I am ready to look with great favor on that kind of increased American effort, directed at the guerrillas and aimed to stiffen the aggressiveness of Vietnamese units up and down the line. Any recommendations that you or General Westmoreland make in this sense will have immediate attention from me, although I know that it may involve acceptance of larger American sacrifice. We have been building our strength to fight this kind of war ever since 1961, and I myself am ready to substantially increase the number of Americans in Vietnam if it is necessary to provide this type of fighting force against the Viet Cong.[29]

Westmoreland, in response, concluded that at least 34 battalion equivalents with supporting units, totaling about 75,000 troops, would be needed. Taylor, in reporting this on January 6, 1965, expressed doubt that American ground forces could be decisive in defeating the insurgency. Taylor noted that historically such efforts required a ten-to-one ratio of troops to insurgents, even when the insurgents did not have substantial outside assistance. With porous borders and a shaky political situation in Saigon, the job was too big in the time likely to be available, in Taylor's view.[30]

FATEFUL FORK IN THE ROAD

Given this basic disagreement in Saigon, National Security Advisor Bundy weighed in with the "Fork in the Road" memo to President Johnson in which he argued that the current course of providing military assistance would likely lead to defeat and humiliation. Instead, Bundy argued for taking the course of exerting more U.S. military power, without specifying what this should entail. At this point, Johnson sent Bundy and Goodpaster to Vietnam for a firsthand assessment in February 1965. During his trip, Bundy visited Pleiku, where a recent attack had killed eight Americans and wounded 137. This made a strong impact on Bundy.[31]

On his return, Bundy summarized for the president the situation, the stakes, and the recommended measures to be taken. The situation is "deteriorating, and without new U.S. action, defeat appears inevitable—probably not in a matter of weeks or perhaps even months, but within the next year or so." The stakes, Bundy noted, "are extremely high. The American investment is very large, and American responsibility is a fact of life which is palpable in the atmosphere of Asia, and even elsewhere. The international prestige of the United States, and a substantial part of our influence, are directly at risk in Vietnam. There is no way of unloading the burden on the Vietnamese themselves, and there is no way of negotiating ourselves out of Vietnam which offers any serious promise at present." In conclusion, Bundy recommended a strategy of "graduated and continuing reprisal" as the most promising course. Furthermore, he noted that this judgment was shared by Goodpaster.[32]

Bundy also added a cautionary note:

> At its very best the struggle in Vietnam will be long. It seems to us important that this fundamental fact be made clear and our understanding of it be made clear to our own people and to the people of Vietnam. Too often in the past we have conveyed the impression that we expect an early solution when those who live with this war know that no early solution is possible. It is our own belief that the people of the United States have the necessary will to accept and execute a policy that rests upon the reality that there is no short cut to success in South Vietnam.[33]

In detailing the new policy of sustained reprisal, Bundy envisioned a continuous, graduated air campaign against North Vietnam, tied to the level of Viet Cong violence in the South. He acknowledged that U.S. air losses would be significant and more visible than those suffered by American military advisors in South Vietnam. Yet, he argued, even if such efforts fail to turn the tide of war, the losses would seem "cheap" measured against the "costs of defeat." Furthermore, such a campaign would set "a new norm" for counterinsurgency operations by raising the price for future guerrilla warfare.[34]

A key feature of the policy involved focusing attention in "every forum" on North Vietnam's aggression in the South. Such efforts, hopefully, would help sustain political will in the United States to support the air campaign. At the same time, the policy involved communicating to Hanoi that these efforts were carefully calibrated, not to conquer or destroy North Vietnam, but to be modulated in accord with changes in the level of violence in South Vietnam.[35]

At this key decision point, Johnson again looked to Eisenhower for advice. Goodpaster told Johnson that Eisenhower believed that protecting South Vietnam from communist domination was pivotal to regional security in Southeast Asia.[36]

On February 19, 1965, Johnson accepted Bundy's recommendation for a continuing campaign of air strikes. Westmoreland seized on the decision and recommended a marine expeditionary brigade be deployed to defend the airbase at Da Nang. Taylor objected vehemently, anticipating that deployment of combat forces would ultimately lead to Americanization of the war. Taylor argued, "Once this policy is breached, it will be difficult to hold the line." Taylor predicted that America would then suffer the same fate as France.[37]

Taylor's warning was not heeded, and on March 8, 1965, 3,500 U.S. marines landed in South Vietnam. Given the policy disagreements in Saigon, Bundy urged Johnson to replace Taylor. McNamara and Rusk concurred, and Taylor was recalled several months later. Goodpaster was aware that a fateful line had been crossed.[38]

On March 15, 1965, General Harold K. Johnson, the Army chief of staff, briefed President Johnson on a study that estimated that it would take 500,000 troops five years to win the war.[39] This estimate of requirements seemed high at the time but turned out to be close to the mark. Nearly 550,000 U.S. troops were eventually committed to the war.[40]

In a memo to the president on April 1, 1965, Bundy argued that the cardinal principle of intervention was for the United States not to be a paper tiger. American credibility was the paramount interest. Bundy argued that America's strategic objective did not have to be precisely defined. Coercive leverage, including air strikes, combat forces, and economic carrots, might induce cooperation from Hanoi. "We want to trade these cards for just as much as possible of the following: an end to infiltration of men and supplies, an end of Hanoi's direction, control and encouragement of the Viet Cong, a removal of cadres under direct Hanoi control, and a dissolution of the organized Viet Cong military and political forces."[41]

The same day, April 1, 1965, Johnson approved sending two additional Marine battalions and a Marine air squadron to Vietnam. More importantly, Johnson agreed to increase the Marines' mission from base security to active offensive combat operations against the Viet Cong. On April 13, the president approved the immediate deployment of the Army's 173rd Airborne Brigade and, the following week, Westmoreland recommended increasing troop levels from 33,500 to 82,000. In June, Westmoreland requested an immediate increase of 41,000 combat troops, followed by 52,000, later saying, "The basic purpose of the additional deployments is to give us a substantial and hard hitting offensive capability on the ground to convince the VC they cannot win." Goodpaster knew from his World War II strategic planning experience the far-reaching implications of such a surge. As a minimum, the strategic reserve would need to be reconstituted.[42]

DOMINICAN REPUBLIC

Also, in this time frame of April 1965, the American ambassador in the Dominican Republic called for U.S. forces to protect the lives of Americans and others because of unrest following a military coup. Local police and military forces were no longer able to guarantee security. Furthermore, there were concerns that outside powers were trying to gain control of the rebellion and install a "Castro-like dictatorship."[43]

A Marine expeditionary unit was sent to the main port to assist in the evacuation of Americans and provide local security, but the political situation remained unsettled. Efforts to organize an international military force were moving slowly, so the administration decided to intervene unilaterally. A task force under Lieutenant General Bruce Palmer, commander of the XVIII Airborne Corps, was deployed quickly in Operation POWERPACK. Goodpaster also was aware of the irony that, but for President Johnson's veto, he would have been in command.[44]

One of the more difficult tasks was providing appropriate guidance for Palmer in this sensitive political-military situation. Aware of the unpopular legacy of "American gunboat diplomacy" in Latin America, it was important that U.S. forces not act in a manner that would be viewed as seizing control and installing a puppet leader. In dealing with this challenge, Goodpaster played important roles in helping develop the concept for the operation in which U.S. forces secured the lines of communication between the capital and the main port. This enabled them to control the flow of men, materiel, food, water, and other supplies, thus isolating rebel forces in the capital's inner city until a political solution was reached and elections were held.[45]

GOODPASTER'S VIEWS ON VIETNAM

In most cases, it is difficult to distinguish Goodpaster's personal views from the views of those he was serving such as Eisenhower and Taylor, but there are a few exceptions. Goodpaster's personal views on Vietnam during the early stages of escalation were indicated in a lecture he prepared in May 1965 for the National Defense University. In his talk, Goodpaster noted that, of South Vietnam, our knowledge and skills were inadequate. Furthermore, our plans, policies, decisions, tactics, scale of operations, and organization in the field provided no basis for confidence in achieving a satisfactory outcome. Similarly, in a June 1965 speech at West Point, Goodpaster contrasted the Napoleonic principles of war that seemed to be governing U.S. military thinking about Vietnam (e.g., offensive, mass, and maneuver) with Mao Zedong's and Ho Chi Minh's people's war approach and concluded that the former were not promising in the Vietnam environment. This was typical of Goodpaster's caution to not become overly wedded to doctrine. [46]

In May 1965, Air Vice Marshal Nguyen Cao Ky and General Nguyen Van Thieu toppled the existing government in South Vietnam, resulting in the fifth change in leadership since the November 1963 coup that overthrew President Diem. By mid-1965, Goodpaster noted that the Joint Chiefs were of the view that the situation was desperate. Without the major intervention of U.S. forces, South Vietnam probably would fall within a matter of weeks. [47]

At the same time, President Johnson was under increasing pressure both publicly and from within the administration to seek a peaceful resolution to the war. He decided to test some of these proposals by ordering a secret halt in the bombing campaign while seeking reciprocal restraints from Hanoi. Johnson asked Goodpaster to seek advice from Eisenhower about this initiative, while also noting that he had found Eisenhower's views among the best he had received. After Goodpaster's briefing, Eisenhower thought overall that the bombing halt initiative with peace feelers was a good step, but was not sure that it should be kept secret. Eisenhower recalled that in the case of the Korean War, he passed word secretly to China that if the war did not stop, China would be liable to direct attack, including nuclear weapons. In the case of the Formosa (Taiwan Strait) crisis, he passed the word publicly. Eisenhower acknowledged that he was not in a good position to judge the current situation but thought that if North Vietnam failed to respond to this initiative, then we should hit them heavily, using "everything that flies." But before resuming the bombing, it would be wise to go public and give Hanoi about a week to find a different solution to war. Eisenhower also inquired about the effects of a bombing halt on South Vietnamese morale. Goodpaster noted that the South Vietnamese prime minister had given his general consent to the initiative. [48]

Faced with the proposed rapid escalation of troop requirements, Johnson asked, "How do we extricate ourselves?" He was told by White House staff, "Hope for a settlement lay in stalemating the Viet Cong and keeping the North under pressure." Unsettled by the response, Johnson again turned to Eisenhower for counsel. In June, Goodpaster carried Eisenhower's response recommending not only continued support of South Vietnamese forces but also direct offensive action by American troops. "We have got to win," said Eisenhower.[49]

On June 7, 1965, General Wheeler asked Westmoreland if his request for another 175,000 troops would be sufficient to break the back of the insurgency. Westmoreland replied that they probably would not be sufficient to persuade insurgents that they could not win. In a June 24, 1965, cable to the Joint Chiefs of Staff, Westmoreland added, "The struggle has become a war of attrition. Short of a decision to introduce nuclear weapons against sources and channels of enemy power, I see no likelihood of achieving a quick, favorable end to the war."[50]

By mid-1965, the Chiefs were concerned primarily with defeating North Vietnamese main force units. Unless the North Vietnamese Army (NVA) was stopped, the South Vietnamese stood little chance of defeating the insurgency. Furthermore, Hanoi was in a fight to the finish, and the Chiefs believed that the United States should respond with a full air campaign against North Vietnam and the resupply system through Laos and Cambodia known as the "Ho Chi Minh Trail." McNamara and the president disagreed, preferring instead to gradually escalate military pressure on Hanoi.[51]

As a result of this basic disagreement, the military leaders and Goodpaster were excluded from the Johnson administration's primary policy deliberations on Vietnam. The major forum for deliberations was a series of Tuesday luncheons limited to the president, McNamara, and McGeorge Bundy. Military leaders were not consulted in the decision-making process and were faced with difficult choices of supporting incremental decisions, even though they disagreed with the approach.[52]

The Chiefs and Goodpaster voiced their dissent in private to McNamara. On one occasion, General Goodpaster was representing General Wheeler at a meeting with Secretary McNamara and Secretary Rusk. During the meeting, McNamara indicated how the North Vietnamese would respond to one of the U.S. initiatives. Goodpaster interrupted: "Sir, the one thing you cannot do is program the enemy. We can program ourselves, but you have to understand that the enemy will make his own decision."[53]

CAN WE WIN IN VIETNAM?

President Johnson also asked Secretary of Defense McNamara, "Can we win in Vietnam?" McNamara returned to the Pentagon and posed the question to General Wheeler. In turn, Wheeler tasked Goodpaster on July 2, 1965, for an assessment of the prospects for winning "if we do everything we can."

Goodpaster organized a study involving the Office of the Chairman, JCS, the Chairman's Special Study Group, DIA, J-3 and the Joint War Games

Agency. The report, carefully entitled "Intensification of the Military Operations in Vietnam, Concept and Appraisal," concluded on July 14, 1965, that if the assumptions hold true, "there appears to be no reason we cannot win if such is our will—and if that will be manifested in strategy and tactical operations."[54]

Winning was defined in the Goodpaster study as a range of outcomes with a "maximum" result achieving an end to the insurgency in South Vietnam and a "minimum" outcome ending in containment of the insurgency and an end to the need for the presence of substantial U.S. forces. Years later, Goodpaster described the most likely winning outcome as something similar to that achieved in South Korea: a cease-fire with a substantial, long-term commitment of U.S. forces.[55]

The main assumptions on which the Goodpaster study was based included: (1) that China and Russia would not intervene unless there was an invasion of North Vietnam; (2) that restrictions on the use of force not exceed a land invasion of North Vietnam, the use of nuclear or chemical weapons, and mass bombing of populations; (3) that, once the concept for operations had been approved by higher authority, there would be no further restrictions, restraints or, planning delays; and (4) that the government of South Vietnam would cooperate and the South Vietnamese people or government would not turn against the United States and demand withdrawal.[56]

The study noted, "Essentially, the struggle in Vietnam remains a Vietnamese struggle." The military situation, however, had become increasingly serious, resulting in a steady decline in the security situation. South Vietnamese forces had experienced a 100 percent increase in both soldiers killed in action and desertions over the last year. Leadership was the greatest single weakness within the South Vietnamese forces. War weariness was setting in, and many South Vietnamese commanders were reluctant to assume offensive operations. This was a major factor leading to the introduction of U.S. forces. At the same time, the U.S. air interdiction of supplies and personnel from North Vietnam had "not achieved the purpose intended . . . economic effects of the bombings have been minor," despite ten thousand aircraft sorties to date. North Vietnam "still seems ready and able to endure air strikes at the current level," according to the Goodpaster study.[57]

That study also highlighted the basic split early in the Johnson administration between the military and civilian leadership, a relationship that would become increasingly dysfunctional. The Joint Chiefs of Staff believed that an overwhelming, comprehensive campaign should be conducted. McNamara sided with the White House and disagreed with the Chiefs. The White House concluded that such a massive military effort was not necessary and probably not feasible politically. An all-out approach would require mobilizing several military Reserve and National Guard units for active duty, a politically risky move when the immediate danger to the United States was not apparent.[58]

Goodpaster did not brief the president on his report directly. Instead, McNamara summarized it for the president, noting that the course of action recommended, a substantial buildup of U.S. forces in Vietnam, "stands a good chance of achieving an acceptable outcome within a reasonable time." Nevertheless, Bundy received a full copy of the report.[59] Also, McNamara and Goodpaster took the study for discussions with Admiral Sharp, the commander-in-chief, Pacific, and General Westmoreland. Westmoreland commented that he thought the study was too pessimistic, implying more favorable outcomes were achievable and likely.[60]

The Chiefs and Goodpaster were convinced that the North Vietnamese leaders were totally committed to victory. The Johnson administration, however, judged that the United States would not likely be able to muster the political will necessary to support a sustained, all-out U.S. effort. Thus, the president decided in favor of trying to negotiate an end to VC/NVA efforts to overthrow the South Vietnamese government by a more gradual increase in military pressure—mainly bombing. U.S. military leaders, however, saw no evidence that the North Vietnamese were interested in a negotiated outcome short of gaining control of the south.

Regretfully, the Goodpaster study did not spur a serious debate within the administration about what exactly was meant by "winning" in Vietnam. Thus, objectives and priorities were not clear, and a series of ad hoc decisions were made leading to a level of effort that was not politically sustainable by the United States.

In early August 1965, Goodpaster briefed Eisenhower that planning was underway to provide Westmoreland all the troops he had asked for at a very rapid rate. To do this required careful study about whether the additional troops should come first from increasing the draft or calling up the reserves. The decision was made to extend the terms of service for current enlistees and use an increase in the draft. In part, this was done because reserve forces would still be available in the event of a contingency in Europe. Eisenhower said he was not concerned about the impact in Europe; he would not favor sending large numbers of U.S. forces to Europe, but in the event of hostilities in Europe, we should be, "using every bomb we have."[61]

In that time frame, Eisenhower was thinking along lines similar to the Joint Chiefs. In an early October 1965 meeting with Goodpaster, Eisenhower noted that President Johnson had recently spoken with him about possible further increases in U.S. forces in Vietnam. Eisenhower advised Johnson that having made decisions to engage in combat operations, we must now be sure to deploy enough to win. He would err on the side of putting in too many rather than too few. He thought that overwhelming strength would discourage the enemy as well as keep our own casualties down. In his discussion with Goodpaster, Eisenhower also noted the importance of pacification efforts, and Goodpaster assured him that such was the case. Finally, Eisenhower noted that as American casualties mounted, the public would become more concerned, especially if young draftees were involved. Goodpaster responded that the personnel issue was a matter of careful study for the Chiefs, but, to date, they had not come up with better alternatives than one-year tours in Vietnam. [62]

A week later, on October 19, 1965, Eisenhower asked Goodpaster to call him about a "matter of importance." Eisenhower was concerned that war materiel, such as surface-to-air missiles delivered through Haiphong, was leading to the increased loss of American lives and, therefore, the United States was justified in making a public declaration that the United States would interdict any suspect shipping. [63]

Goodpaster noted that currently the United States was not interfering with Chinese or other shipping. Furthermore, U.S. allies were pressuring the United States to not interfere with shipping. Goodpaster also informed Eisenhower that studies suggested that mining the harbor would be more effective than a blockade. Finally, Goodpaster agreed to pass on Eisenhower's concerns and suggestions to President Johnson. [64]

In January 1966, Goodpaster again discussed the situation in Vietnam with Eisenhower, explaining that during the current bombing halt, a series of quiet initiatives was undertaken by Harriman and other U.S. diplomats that offered to defer a resumption in bombing if there were a reduction in National Liberation Front (NLF) military activity in South Vietnam. [65] Goodpaster noted that the United States government did not have high hopes of a satisfactory North Vietnamese response, and thus bombing would soon be resumed, probably focusing on lines of communication resupplying the sizable VC/NVA forces in South Vietnam. The bombing also might interdict supplies through North Vietnam's ports, principally Haiphong. Eisenhower recalled that he had earlier called for a blockade or quarantine. Mining of the ports, he stated, would probably require a declaration of war. Eisenhower also mentioned that it had been suggested that he organize a group of "old heads" with experience in war to advise the administration. Eisenhower rejected the idea. [66]

By early 1966, an alternative approach for U.S. operations in Vietnam was gaining attention. The concept focused on establishing a few "enclaves" along the coast to secure ports and airfields and support South Vietnamese forces. This concept, however, was rejected by Westmoreland, the Joint Chiefs, and Eisenhower, as Goodpaster reported to President Johnson. [67]

During the summer of 1966, President Johnson asked Goodpaster to join Averell Harriman and Walt Rostow in briefing the National Conference of State Governors. Harriman briefed the governors on efforts to begin negotiations with North Vietnam, Rostow briefed on pacification efforts in South Vietnam, and Goodpaster briefed on the military situation. In meeting with the briefing team before the governors' conference, Johnson advised them to not "overestimate" the situation. In his briefing, Goodpaster noted that at the starting point of direct U.S. involvement in combat the previous year, South Vietnam was very close to collapsing. Subsequently, much progress had been achieved, but it was going to be a long, costly, difficult effort. Much would depend on the South Vietnamese.[68]

NUCLEAR WEAPONS, FRANCE, AND NATO

In addition to Vietnam, nuclear weapons and NATO were frequently part of the national security agenda. The Kennedy/Johnson administration wanted to deemphasize nuclear weapons, in part to mark a departure from the Eisenhower administration's New Look and Massive Retaliation policies in which nuclear weapons played a prominent role. One of the ways this new policy of "Flexible Response" was put into practice was to deemphasize nuclear weapons while emphasizing the ability to defend successfully by conventional means alone.

This created a crisis within NATO while the organization was in the process of developing a new strategic concept. The problem arose when the civilian leadership in the Pentagon sought to exclude nuclear weapons from the NATO strategic concept, and the Joint Chiefs of Staff disagreed. The Chiefs believed that nuclear weapons played an important role in making NATO's deterrence capabilities credible. The existing strategic concept provided West Germany, Italy, and other NATO allies with capabilities to deliver nuclear weapons even though the actual weapons were held under U.S. control, short of war. Thus, the total nuclear capabilities of the alliance were greater than merely those of the United States, Britain, and France. The French, in particular, disagreed strongly with the proposal to change the strategic concept to Flexible Response.[69]

Goodpaster tried to find a compromise. He had worked closely with the French on nuclear weapons issues during the early days of NATO. One of the French colonels with whom he had worked at NATO was by then an advisor to President de Gaulle. Goodpaster, however, could not find a way to reconcile the positions. The administration insisted on Flexible Response. President de Gaulle was incensed. He withdrew French forces from the integrated military command and directed that NATO facilities, including the headquarters, be removed from France.

In discussing these problems with Eisenhower in September 1965, Goodpaster noted that the key issue was to keep Germany as a closely aligned member of the West. He cautioned that if France tried to keep Germany in an inferior position, the danger would increase that those old European antagonisms would arise and divide NATO. Eisenhower agreed and added that the United States had to be careful to not overemphasize the day-to-day issues that were featured in the press. Instead, a carefully considered, well-coordinated approach was needed—one that might not appear brilliant, but would help insure that mistakes would not occur because of failure to consider important aspects of the problem in a timely manner.[70]

But well-coordinated policies were not the hallmark of the Kennedy-Johnson administration. Earlier in the Kennedy administration, an agreement was reached with the Soviet Union to cease testing of nuclear weapons in the atmosphere; however, the Joint Chiefs of Staff were not involved in the negotiations. Nevertheless, their support was critical for congressional ratification, and Goodpaster became involved in trying to negotiate a solution. The issue was very contentious. The Chiefs reluctantly agreed to support the president by setting up a series of "safeguards" specifying actions to be taken if the treaty were breached.[71]

Frustration among the Chiefs was high and, according to Goodpaster, they thought seriously of resigning. But, after talking it through, they concluded that this was not best for the country because it could undermine respect for the principle of civilian control of the military. And, if they resigned, it would look like a form of "mutiny."[72]

HEART ATTACK

At this point in Vietnam, the United States had taken the path of escalation with little hope of a favorable outcome. It was an agonizing path for Goodpaster and others directly involved. In August 1966, Goodpaster became Director of the Joint Staff. The stress was immense. Within a short period, four of the deputy military leaders suffered heart attacks. In addition to Goodpaster, the vice chief of staff of the Air Force, Bill Blanchard; the vice chief of Naval Operations, Claude Ricketts; and the vice chief of staff of the Army, Barksdale Hamlett, all had heart attacks. Admiral Ricketts died, and the others recovered. Later, General Wheeler, the chairman, also had a heart attack.[73]

Goodpaster's heart attack occurred on November 15, 1966. In his words, the "pressure got to him." In addition to Vietnam, he was particularly agitated about the constant fighting between the services. While recovering at Walter Reed Hospital, Goodpaster was barred from reading newspapers. He remained in the hospital for about one month and had another month of recuperation at home.[74]

After his release from the hospital in April 1967, Goodpaster met with General Harold K. Johnson, the Army Chief of Staff, whom Goodpaster considered a good friend. Johnson usually advised generals to retire when they suffered stress-related heart problems because, if they stayed on active duty, they might "pull their punches a little bit," and it also could endanger their lives. In Goodpaster's case, however, the chief agreed to let him continue physical rehabilitation and, on a trial basis, work on some Army planning problems and strategic analyses.

As a result, Lieutenant General Goodpaster was assigned temporarily to the Army staff as director of special studies in the Office of the Chief of Staff. In May, he took on the added responsibilities of senior U.S. Army member of the Military Staff Committee of the United Nations.

Part of his understanding with General Johnson, however, was that the chief would not allow him to be assigned back to the Pentagon on a regular basis. Instead, Goodpaster was soon nominated to become the commandant of the National War College at Fort McNair in Washington, DC.

During the preceding five years Goodpaster learned the difficulties of calibrating power and purpose. While the United States could employ an impressive array of military forces, their ability to achieve decisive outcomes was limited, especially in terms of the kinds of outcomes that General Marshall had taught him, a sustainable peace.

NOTES

1. Goodpaster, Johnson and Ferguson interviews, January 9, 1976; Goodpaster, Mandel Interviews, February 11, 2004, tapes 17, 18.

2. Goodpaster, Mandel Interviews, February 11, 2004, tape 18.

3. Ibid.

4. Ibid.

5. Minutes of NSC Meeting, October 21, 1962, *FRUS, 1961–1963, Vol. XI*, Cuban Missile Crisis, doc. 38.

6. Presidential Meeting Memo, November 19, 1962, *FRUS, 1961–1963, Vol. XXX*, South Asia, doc. 202.

7. www.whitehouse.gov/about/presidents/johnfkennedy.

8. NSAM 52, May 11, 1961, *FRUS, 1961–1963, Vol. I*, Vietnam, 1961, doc. 52.

9. *Military Assistance Command, Vietnam, Command History Chronology*, 1966.

10. Caro, *The Years of Lyndon Johnson*, 401–3.

11. Kennedy to Lodge, August 29, 1963, *FRUS, 1961–1963-Vietnam*, 4:20-22.

12. NSAM 273, November 26, 1963, *FRUS, 1961–1963, Vol. IV, Vietnam*, doc. 331; also see Goldstein, *Lessons in Disaster*, 97–98; Caro, *The Years of Lyndon Johnson*, 403, 532.

13. Goldstein, *Lessons in Disaster*, 219.

14. See more than sixty Goodpaster memos for record, in National Security File, Name File, Eisenhower, box 2, especially count provided in Bromley Smith memo to president, June 11, 1966, LBJ Library, Goodpaster, Mandel interviews, February 11, 2004, tape 19.

15. Bundy Memo to Goodpaster, August 19, 1965, National Security File, Vietnam, box 212, folder 13, Eisenhower Briefings at Gettysburg, 8/65, LBJ Library.

16. Goodpaster Memos for Record, August 3, 1965, October 12, 1965, April 7, 1967, National Security Files, Eisenhower, box 2, LBJ Library; Goodpaster, Mandel interviews, February 11, 2004, tape 19.

17. Goodpaster, Mandel interviews, February 11, tapes 18 and 19.

18. Goldstein, *Lessons in Disaster*, 108; Caro, *The Years of Lyndon Johnson*, 535.

19. McMaster, *Dereliction of Duty*, 57–58.

20. Westmoreland, *A Soldier Reports*, 156. For a contemporary critique of Westmoreland's approach, see General Krulak's "Strategic Appraisal of Vietnam," December 1965, Krulak Papers, LBJ Library.

21. Goodpaster, interview by Joe Frantz, January 21, 1971, 23–25, Oral History Program, LBJ Library.

22. Gillespie, *Black Ops Vietnam*, 24–26.

23. Sigma I-64 and Sigma II-64, JCS War Games, Volume I and II, National Security Files, Agency File, box 30, LBJ Library.

24. Sigma II-64, box 30, folder JCS-War Games, Vol. II (2), C-1–C-4, LBJ Library.

25. Ibid., Tabs D, F, and G, especially G-9, G-14, and G-21.

26. Sigma I-64, JCS War Games, Tab G, especially G-16, G-21, Vol. I, National Security Files, Agency File, box 30, LBJ Library

27. David Liep's "Atlas of US Presidential Elections," www.uselectionatlas.org.

28. Historical Division, JCS, *Chronology of JCS Organization, 1945–1984*, 204; Goodpaster, interview by Joe B. Frantz, June 21, 1971, Oral History Program, LBJ Library, 22, 27.

29. Johnson to Taylor, *FRUS, Vietnam 1964*, 1057–59.

30. Goldstein, *Lessons in Disaster*, 151–58.

31. Ibid.

32. Bundy memo to the president, February 7, 1965, National Security Files, International Meetings and Travel File, folder 1, box 28, LBJ Library.

33. Ibid. 8.

34. Ibid. Annex A, A Policy of Sustained Reprisal.

35. Ibid.

36. Goldstein, *Lessons in Disaster* 161.

37. Ibid., 162–63.

38. Ibid., 164.

39. Ibid.

40. Ibid.

41. Bundy in Memo to the President, *FRUS 1964–1968, Vietnam January–June 1965*, 508.

42. Ibid., 169.

43. Cables from Ambassador Bennett, April 30, 1965, NSF, Dominican Republic, box 38, 1 of 2, and military cables, May 1965, box 50, LBJ Library.

44. Ibid.

45. Ibid.; Goodpaster, interview by Joe B. Frantz, June 21, 1971, Oral History Program, LBJ Library, 28.

46. Goodpaster in "Lecture on New Patterns of Security," May 4, 1965, IV-2, National Defense University Library (NDU), and in Goodpaster address to West Point Conference on the Role of the Military in National Security Policy Formulation, June 24, 1965, 7, NDU Library.

47. Goodpaster, interview by Joe Frantz, June 21, 1971, 26, Oral History Program, LBJ Library.

48. Goodpaster Memo for Record, May 12, 1965, National Security Files, Eisenhower, box 2, LBJ Library.

49. Ibid. 178.

50. Ibid. 190–91.

51. Goodpaster, Mandel interviews, February 11, 2004, Tape 18.

52. Ibid.

53. Ibid.

54. Goodpaster/JCS Study on Vietnam, July 21, 1965, National Security Files, Vietnam Country File, box 20, XXXVII, "Memos," C 7/65, 413, LBJ Library; Goodpaster, Mandel interviews, February 11, 2004, tape 18. Also see *Pentagon Papers as Published by the New York Times* (New York: Quadrangle Books, 1971) 465–75.

55. Goodpaster Study.

56. Goodpaster Study, ii and Annex C.

57. Goodpaster Study, especially pages C-8, I-9, E-6, G-1.

58. Goodpaster, Mandel interviews, February 11, 2004, tapes 18 and 19.

59. Ibid.; *Pentagon Papers*, 475.

60. Goodpaster, Johnson and Ferguson interviews, April 9, 1976.

61. Goodpaster Memo for Record, August 3, 1965, National Security Files, Eisenhower, box 2, LBJ Library.

62. Goodpaster Memo for Record, October 11, 1965, National Security Files, Eisenhower, box 2, LBJ Library.

63. Goodpaster Memo for Record, October 20, 1965, National Security Files, Eisenhower, box 2, LBJ Library.

64. Ibid.

65. The NLF was a combination of the Viet Cong from South Vietnam and the People's Army of Vietnam from North Vietnam.

66. Goodpaster Memo for Record, January 4, 1966, National Security Files, Eisenhower, box 2, LBJ Library.

67. Goodpaster Memo for Record, January 25, 1966, National Security Files, Eisenhower, box 2, LBJ Library.

68. President Johnson, Press Conference, July 5, 1966; Goodpaster, interview by Joe Frantz, June 21, 1971, 31, Oral History Program, LBJ Library.

69. Goodpaster, Mandel interviews, February 11, 2004, tapes 18 and 19.

70. Goodpaster Memo for Record, September 14, 1965, National Security Files, Eisenhower, box 2, LBJ Library.

71. Ibid.

72. Goodpaster, Mandel interviews, February 11, 2004, tape 19.

73. Ibid., tape 18.

74. Susan Goodpaster Sullivan, phone interview with author, June 27, 2010. Also Goodpaster, Mandel interviews, February 11, 2004, tapes 18 and 19.

Chapter Eleven

National War College (1967–1968)

In August 1967, Goodpaster was installed as commandant of the National War College at Fort McNair in Washington, DC, a less stressful job while he recovered from his heart attack. The Joint Chiefs of Staff needed to confirm his appointment, because the commandant of the National War College was a joint service position under the JCS. The Chiefs concurred, noting that the college could use some revitalization. The job called for a two-star flag officer, so three-star Lieutenant General Goodpaster was the most senior officer to hold that position. [1]

The job was a good fit for Goodpaster, given his strong interest in promoting intergovernmental cooperation, his high level experience on the joint staff, and his academic credentials. The National War College was founded in 1946 after World War II revealed the need for greater understanding between the civilian and military components of government and among the military services.

After becoming commandant, Goodpaster concluded that the National War College lacked a clear purpose and its curriculum seemed to lack integrating themes. After discussing the matter extensively with faculty and staff, Goodpaster gained consensus that the purpose was to contribute to solving the difficult problems of implementing U.S. national security policy. Goodpaster thus focused the college on preparing students for responsibilities found at the level of a three-star general or admiral on the service and service-secretary staffs, as well as in the major unified and specified commands. [2]

Goodpaster and the faculty also sought to stimulate intellectual curiosity, independent thought, and the capacity to think objectively. Intellectual freedom was encouraged. There were no "approved" or "school" solutions. Students were exposed to the different experiences and viewpoints of others. [3]

To move the institution further along, Goodpaster guided the development of the first Curriculum Objectives Plan, which provided a concise description of mission, objectives, philosophy, and goals of the college. Curriculum changes included initiating the Individual and Electives Study Program that constituted about one-third of the total curriculum. This allowed students to broaden their knowledge and fill gaps, recognizing the broad diversity in background and experience among the 140 students. The curriculum changes also allowed for greater flexibility in writing "think pieces" and taking voluntary seminars on economics, international law, religion, Marxist thought, and the history of strategic thought.[4]

The guest-speaker program included addresses by General Eisenhower, Senator Henry Jackson, Senator Hugh Scott, General Wheeler, General H. K. Johnson, Admiral Thomas Moorer, Dean Rusk, Nicholas Katzenbach, Sol Linowitz, Clark Clifford, Paul Nitze, Harold Brown, Richard Helms, and more than twenty other senior military and political leaders from the United States and abroad.[5]

Before long, however, Goodpaster was called back to the Pentagon—without being assigned—to conduct two studies estimating the results of a cessation of the bombing of North Vietnam. These studies were also to recommend how, when, and under what terms to reduce or cease the bombing of North Vietnam.[6]

In January 1968, when North Korea seized the *USS Pueblo*, General Wheeler contacted Goodpaster at President Johnson's request with several key questions for General Eisenhower, including what actions should be taken and how Congress should be associated with these actions. Goodpaster raised the questions with Eisenhower, who advised that the staff consider every possible action and share these ideas with the congressional leadership. Eisenhower thought that a quarantine might be appropriate, but it was important to act quickly, while the event was still fresh in people's minds. The United States should not make any threats that could not be backed up, so a key question was whether we would be prepared to use nuclear weapons. Of course, everything possible should be done on the diplomatic front including possibly calling for a UN General Assembly special session if anything useful might result. Eisenhower also recommended intensifying bombing of North Vietnam to let it be known that these developments were related.[7]

PARIS NEGOTIATIONS

In the spring of 1968, after returning from a trip to Africa with War College students, Goodpaster got a call from the White House saying that President Johnson wanted him to serve on a delegation that would enter into negotiations with the North Vietnamese. A meeting was arranged at the White

House for the president to meet with the five delegation team members—Ambassador-at-Large and former governor Averell Harriman, who would head the delegation; Clark Clifford who replaced McNamara as secretary of defense on February 29, 1968; Deputy Secretary of Defense Cyrus Vance; Assistant Secretary of State for East Asia and the Pacific Philip Habib; and Lieutenant General Andrew Goodpaster, representing the Joint Chiefs of Staff.[8]

Goodpaster believed that South Vietnam was strong enough relative to their adversaries that talks could be undertaken without endangering South Vietnamese security. Goodpaster, however, was concerned about prolonged negotiations similar to those experienced during the Korean War, but he envisaged two possible favorable outcomes: one was political accommodation that was acceptable to the South Vietnamese leadership, the other a de facto stalemate in which most of the fighting was moved away from South Vietnam population centers.[9]

Harriman was not new to the problem. With his broad range of political experience including as ambassador to the Soviet Union, he was selected in 1966 to explore negotiations. At that time, Soviet leadership was passing from Khrushchev to Kosygin, and China was in turmoil with the Cultural Revolution. Harriman judged that Moscow and Beijing would not allow North Vietnam to be defeated, but perhaps did not care as much about South Vietnam to risk escalation of the war. He explored options including linking U.S. actions in NATO to Soviet efforts to persuade Hanoi to negotiate.[10]

At the White House meeting, delegation members were provided with a background paper that had been prepared for the president. Johnson reviewed the paper and asked if there were any questions. The ensuing discussion soon highlighted a basic division between Harriman and Goodpaster. Harriman insisted that the negotiations would be badly damaged if our troops in Vietnam were engaged in an all-out offensive, thus there needed to be some restraint on the part of U.S. forces. Goodpaster argued that it was very important to the Joint Chiefs of Staff and to the MACV commander that there be no interference with the conduct of operations in Vietnam for the purpose of offering unilateral concessions to the North Vietnamese. President Johnson agreed with Goodpaster, noting that "there would be none of that." Harriman came back to the issue twice more, and the third time, the president put his hand alongside his face and winked at Goodpaster and again said, "No, we wouldn't do that." Goodpaster considered that a key part of the presidential guidance for the delegation—no unilateral concessions. Also part of his guidance was that Goodpaster would stay in touch with the Joint Chiefs of Staff but was responsible only to the president. Goodpaster made it clear that he would not be under the policy direction of Ambassador Harriman.[11]

On the flight to Paris on the secretary of defense's aircraft, Harriman, Clifford, and Vance began to discuss how to bring the war to an end in ways that seemed to depart from the president's guidance, at least in Goodpaster's view. Harriman insisted that the purpose of the delegation was to "end this war—to get the best terms we can, but to end the war." Goodpaster objected strongly, arguing that the president's instructions were to negotiate but to not in any way compromise putting "maximum pressure" on the enemy. As the exchange became more heated, Harriman became angry with Goodpaster's insistence that the ambassador was exceeding his mandate.[12]

The dispute between Harriman and Goodpaster reflected President Johnson's dilemma in prosecuting the war. Johnson wanted to support the Joint Chiefs of Staff's efforts to put maximum pressure on North Vietnam, while at the same time the president supported Harriman and others who wanted to negotiate an end to the war. While these approaches were not mutually exclusive, how they were pursued was critical from Goodpaster's perspective, in order to achieve the kind of outcome he had posited in his 1965 study of the prospects for an independent, viable South Vietnam. Furthermore, since there were no South Vietnamese delegates at the talks, Goodpaster was concerned that their interests were not being well represented.

During negotiations in Paris, the problem became worse from Goodpaster's standpoint. He was convinced that senior delegation members were undercutting the president's guidance of putting maximum pressure on North Vietnam. On one occasion, Ambassador Harriman contacted the Russians, and when Goodpaster asked him what that was about, Harriman said it was very private and not to be disclosed. Goodpaster told Harriman that such initiatives did not conform to his guidance and so informed the chairman of the Joint Chiefs of Staff. Soon thereafter, instructions were sent to Harriman to keep Goodpaster fully informed of any such contacts.[13]

The delegation meetings with the North Vietnamese went nowhere. The North Vietnamese each had a small packet of notecards with quotations from Americans and others about the illegal nature of U.S. aggression. It was soon apparent to Goodpaster that the North Vietnamese had no interest in bringing the war to an end other than by their gaining complete control of South Vietnam. Thus, the meetings were perfunctory. There were, however, some interesting conversations over tea after the meetings. In these exchanges, Goodpaster learned just how determined the North Vietnamese were. One of the North Vietnamese representatives noted to him, "We defeated the French in Paris and we plan to defeat your country in Washington."[14]

The North Vietnamese seemed to be stalling; they were awaiting the outcome of the November elections in the United States after President Johnson announced that he would not seek another term. After six weeks of futile talks, Goodpaster came away believing that any notion that negotiations would allow the continued existence of a separate, independent South Vietnam was simply an illusion.[15]

Goodpaster returned from Paris in time for the National War College graduation. During his short tenure, Goodpaster took every opportunity to speak to the students. In these talks, he stressed the importance of having a clear purpose in whatever position one is serving. "If you don't know where you want to go, you're not likely to get there." The 1968 War College class appreciated Goodpaster's care for their interests and his sage advice. The class made General Goodpaster an honorary member.

The class of 1968 included Lieutenant Colonel Brent Scowcroft, a future national security advisor for President George H. W. Bush. Scowcroft and Goodpaster became lifelong friends and collaborators on national security studies.

Goodpaster's War College assignment was curtailed in early July 1968 when he was selected to become the deputy commander in Vietnam.

During his short tenure both as commandant and negotiator, Goodpaster insisted on a clear understanding of purpose and then focusing all efforts accordingly. While easy in theory, this proved more difficult in practice.

Figure 11.1. Goodpaster & Westmoreland, 1967. Official photo. *Source*: Courtesy of the George C. Marshall Library

NOTES

1. Goodpaster, Mandel interviews, February 11, 2004, tape 19.
2. Ibid.; The National War College Yearbook, the 1968 *Rotunda*, 9.

3. Goodpaster, Mandel interviews, February 11, 2004, tape 19, *Rotunda,* 9.

4. National War College Commandant's Annual Report, 1967–1968, 4.

5. Ibid.

6. Goodpaster, interview by Joe Frantz, June 21, 1971, 34.

7. Goodpaster Memo for Record, January 29, 1968, National Security Files, Eisenhower, box 2, LBJ Library.

8. Goodpaster, Mandel interviews, February 12, 2004, tapes 19 and 20.

9. Goodpaster, interview by Joe Frantz, June 21, 1971, 40.

10. Harriman memo, September 1966–May 1967, National Security File, Country File, Vietnam, box 212, LBJ Library.

11. Ibid.

12. Goodpaster interview cited by Mark Perry in *Four Stars*, 196. Also see Sorley, *A Better War*, 90–91, and Goodpaster, Mandel interviews, tape 20.

13. Goodpaster, Mandel interviews, February 12, 2004, tape 20.

14. Goodpaster, Mandel interviews, February 11, 2004, tape 18; Goodpaster, interview by Joe B. Frantz, June 21, 1971, Oral History Program, LBJ Library, 39.

15. Goodpaster, Mandel interviews, February 12, 2004, tape 20.

Chapter Twelve

Vietnam (1968–1969)

The Tet Offensive in 1968 was a seminal event. A cease-fire for the Tet Lunar New Year had been announced by both sides several months prior to the holidays, but on January 30, 1968, the National Liberation Front (NLF) launched attacks throughout South Vietnam in thirty-six of forty-four provincial capitals and five of the six largest cities as part of the largest military offensive launched by either side up to that time. Most of the attacks were defeated quickly but, in a few cases, including the attack on Hue, a major cultural center and former capital of Annam, the battle lasted for several weeks before the NLF forces were defeated. The Viet Cong forces in particular suffered heavy losses, and the offensive failed to achieve its objective of spurring an uprising of the South Vietnamese people against their government. It dealt a blow, however, to American political will that would eventually prove fatal.

Planning for the Tet Offensive originated in the spring of 1967 at a time when most trends had turned unfavorable for the NLF. Casualties were high, American bombing was destroying much of the North Vietnamese infrastructure, and there were doubts among several northern leaders about their ability to sustain the military efforts in the South. The communist leadership was badly divided on how to pursue the war. One line of thought argued that pursuing the war in the South was undermining the viability of the North, which was the top priority. According to this view, South Vietnam and the United States could not be defeated militarily; thus, large-scale military efforts should be scaled back and more emphasis placed on smaller-scale guerrilla war, political efforts, and a protracted struggle. An alternative perspective held that the governments of South Vietnam and the United States were very unpopular, and a general offensive would attract popular support in the

South, resulting in a decisive victory. The second view was adopted only after many of those holding the first view were arrested.[1]

In November 1967, General Westmoreland and Ambassador Ellsworth Bunker returned to Washington for consultations and to help make the case for substantial additional American military involvement in the war. On November 21, Westmoreland noted in a speech at the National Press Club that the communists were unable to mount a major offensive. A few months earlier, a classified Special National Intelligence Estimate had created considerable controversy by highlighting differences between MACV and CIA estimates of the enemy order of battle. The CIA estimated a total of about 430,000 troops, whereas the MACV total was about 300,000. The main difference was that the CIA total included the Viet Cong infrastructure (VCI), a cadre that General Westmoreland argued was not part of the main- and local-force military formations. Nevertheless, the VCI inflicted a large share of the friendly casualties. This information was shared with members of Congress serving on committees with a need to know and raised doubts about the credibility of the MACV strategy of attrition and, more importantly, about whether the war was indeed being won.[2]

The Pentagon and MACV measures of the war, including body count, ratios of combatants killed, and improvements to local conditions in South Vietnam, detailed in the comprehensive Hamlet Evaluation Surveys, seemed inconsistent with the large and growing enemy order of battle. Operations research, at the core of McNamara's Pentagon, was discredited. McNamara resigned as secretary of defense and was replaced by Clark Clifford on February 29, 1968.[3]

Another policy reassessment in early March 1968 highlighted the long-standing differences on Vietnam within the administration. General Wheeler and the Joint Chiefs of Staff pressed Westmoreland to request two hundred thousand more troops, which would force the president to call up strategic reserves from the National Guard and Reserve forces.

Mainly because of the Tet Offensive, February 1968 proved to be the deadliest month in the war for the United States, with 16,592 soldiers killed. By this time, the draft had made the war an increasingly personal and unpopular issue in the United States as inductions rose from about 82,000 in 1962 to more than 296,000 in 1968. Furthermore, the economic costs of the war were mounting for the United States at a time when the country was in a severe monetary crisis. Finally, faced with growing antiwar sentiment and challenges from Robert Kennedy and Eugene McCarthy for the Democratic Party nomination, President Johnson announced on March 31 that he would not seek a second term in office.[4]

Those in the administration who had been hawkish on the war became increasingly skeptical about the costs and likely outcome of escalating U.S. military involvement in the war. President Johnson decided that U.S. efforts should be capped at 549,500 troops, and South Vietnam should assume increasing responsibility for the war. In his March 31 address, Johnson announced a unilateral halt in bombing north of the 20th parallel in North Vietnam in an effort to persuade North Vietnamese leaders to begin negotiations on ending the war. However, there was no reciprocal concession by North Vietnam.[5]

In July 1968, Goodpaster was assigned as the deputy commander of MACV and promoted to four-star general. This was part of a change in leadership in which General Creighton Abrams, the former deputy commander, replaced General Westmoreland as the commander of MACV in June, with Westmoreland becoming the Army chief of staff. One of Westmoreland's first official acts as chief of staff was Goodpaster's promotion ceremony.[6]

In sending him off, President Johnson said that he had been informed that, with Westmoreland becoming the Army chief of staff and with Abrams and Goodpaster in Vietnam, he had the foremost commanders in terms of professional capabilities. Goodpaster knew Abrams from their days at West Point and held him in high regard. They had next met when they were both division commanders in Europe. Abrams commanded the 3rd Armored Division while Goodpaster commanded the adjacent 8th Infantry Division in the early 1960s. More recently, Goodpaster would often see Abrams when he visited Vietnam. As a result, Goodpaster had great confidence in Abrams.[7]

Before he went to Vietnam as the deputy commander, Goodpaster was aware that the Vietnam War was increasingly unpopular in the United States. As trends in political will became increasingly unfavorable, the current approach to the war was becoming unsustainable. Furthermore, Goodpaster noted in his monthly briefings to Eisenhower that the military effort in Vietnam had stretched the United States to a dangerous point. The strategic reserve was exhausted, and it was not feasible politically to reconstitute the reserve from National Guard and Reserve forces.[8]

With a lack of consensus in Washington, Goodpaster was pleased to find that he and General Abrams shared similar views on the war. They soon agreed on a new strategic concept that focused on building South Vietnamese capabilities and went to work harmoniously.[9]

The new concept, outlined in the MACV Strategic Objectives Plan, assumed that the incoming Nixon administration would move to disengage U.S. forces well before the government of South Vietnam was capable of handling security, political, and economic challenges independently. Thus, MACV planners focused on the immediate challenge of securing the most important population centers before U.S. troop withdrawals would begin, probably not later than July, 1970.[10]

With the assumption that U.S. forces had reached their peak, the new strategic concept called for a better integrated approach with increased priorities of strengthening the South Vietnamese Army and local government. Bombing focused on preventing North Vietnam from building up the forces and logistics necessary for major attacks. [11]

In formulating the strategy, one of Goodpaster's roles was to sound out the new Nixon administration to insure that the initiative under the new strategy of constant pressure would not be undermined by negotiation-related restraints, except in the context of mutual withdrawals by North Vietnamese forces. [12]

Also, in implementing the new strategy, Goodpaster's role was to improve Vietnamese professional skills and leadership, as well as eliminating or working around incapable Vietnamese commanders. He traveled extensively throughout the country, meeting with division commanders and leaders of local and regional forces. Abrams often met with the senior South Vietnamese military leaders and President Thieu. By late 1968 and early 1969, General Goodpaster believed that President Thieu was on target with his acceleration of the pacification program to extend security and South Vietnamese control in the countryside. [13]

Abrams and Goodpaster met weekly with the senior staff to discuss the situation in detail and determine what actions were needed; they were both very action-oriented leaders. The meetings also included the air deputy, General George Brown; the Naval deputy, Admiral Elmo "Bud" Zumwalt; and William Colby, the CIA deputy for CORDS (Civil Operations and Revolutionary Development Support). Every three to four weeks, the senior staff met with the four corps/field force commanders in charge of operations from I Corps in the north to IV Corps in the southern delta. [14]

By this time, MACV was a major multinational command with more than 525,000 U.S. troops and operational control over another 70,000 troops from seven allied countries. The latter category, called Free World Military Assistance Forces, included major contingents from South Korea, the Philippines, Thailand, Australia, and New Zealand, along with smaller contributions from Taiwan and Spain.

Unlike the dysfunctional political-military relationship in Washington, the MACV staff and the American embassy staff worked well together. General Abrams and Ambassador Bunker set the example. General Goodpaster worked with one of Bunker's assistants to send regular cables back to the staffs at the State Department and Defense Department, providing assessments of the situation based on their meetings with military and political leaders in the field. The new cables also paved the way for better coordinated support from Washington. [15]

After President Nixon took office in early 1969, the policy of Vietnamization of the war became the top priority. This policy involved turning over to the Vietnamese nearly all of the responsibilities for ground-combat operations. Abrams and Goodpaster worked diligently to make a reality of what was an implicit, lower level objective prior to that time. For example, the South Vietnamese had no heavy weapons, such as 155mm artillery. Abrams decided to deactivate some American artillery and pass the weapons to the South Vietnamese. Such moves demonstrated that the United States was serious about Vietnamization, and the South Vietnamese began to prepare themselves to take on a much larger direct burden in the conduct of the war. Nevertheless, Vietnamization was a daunting task that involved turning over a $30 billion per year war effort on relatively short notice to a country with a GDP of a few billion per year. [16]

Abrams and his staff were aware of the growing political opposition to the war in the United States but believed that this could be mitigated by the orderly transfer of responsibilities for combat operations to South Vietnamese forces. Accordingly, within a few years, U.S. roles would be reduced mainly to advisory, training, and military assistance personnel. [17]

In getting to know the current generation of American troops, Goodpaster became aware of the impact on the armed forces of the dramatic social changes underway at home. Drug use was an increasing problem, particularly in support units at large bases. The Army was expanding to meet the added requirements of the Vietnam War, and standards were lowered for soldiers and officers. The controversial "Project 100,000" was launched in October 1966 to provide poorly educated individuals training and opportunities. More than three hundred thousand individuals who scored low on the Armed Forces Qualification Test and would otherwise have been rejected for service were enlisted under this program. [18]

The growing unpopularity of the war and increasing racial tensions added to the challenges of leadership. There were incidents of soldiers "fragging" (assassinating) their own officers and senior noncommissioned officers. Twelve-month tours of duty for most soldiers and officers caused a huge turnover in personnel, with the associated loss of continuity and knowledge of the local area. Despite these challenges, Goodpaster was confident that units were well led for the most part and capable of performing their missions. [19]

In December 1968, President-elect Richard Nixon requested that Goodpaster return to Washington and serve as his military advisor during the presidential transition. As he departed, Goodpaster was reasonably confident that South Vietnam could evolve to a status similar to South Korea's, as an independent country facing a serious threat, but bolstered by its relationship with the United States and others. Goodpaster left Vietnam feeling optimistic that the corner had been turned.

ORGANIZING THE NIXON WHITE HOUSE NATIONAL
SECURITY AFFAIRS

For the next four weeks, Goodpaster's principal duty was to work with Bryce Harlow and Henry Kissinger to organize the security structure for the Nixon administration. According to Kissinger, Goodpaster was the architect and produced a meticulous NSC structure similar to the Eisenhower system that allowed the president to consider multiple options rather than being presented with a single option. [20]

Also, Goodpaster argued strongly that the various supporting committees should be chaired by somebody on the White House staff, with the highest level committees chaired by the national security advisor. The State Department adamantly opposed that structure with two of Goodpaster's good friends, Alex Johnson and Elliot Richardson, leading efforts to retain State Department chairmanship of key committees, thus controlling the agenda. Goodpaster, drawing on his JCS and White House experience, argued that, to be effective, key committees should be chaired by a representative of the president. Goodpaster explained that if a State Department official was chairing a committee, it would be less likely to gain Defense Department support than if it were headed by the president's national security advisor. The debate was finally brought to William Rogers, who was to become secretary of state, and to Nixon. Goodpaster's recommendation prevailed, and Henry Kissinger was named to chair the key committees. [21]

After his inauguration, President Nixon asked Goodpaster for his views on Vietnam. One journalist reported in January 1969 that Goodpaster told Nixon that "he can expect a good outcome in Vietnam in return for a reasonable display of patience and sturdiness." By this time, however, there were growing doubts about the willingness of the American public to pay the price for another large, indefinite commitment of U.S. forces similar to that in Korea. [22]

Figure 12.1. Goodpaster & Abrams. Official photo. *Source*: Courtesy of National Archives and Records Administration (NARA)

During early 1969, Goodpaster also visited Eisenhower frequently at Walter Reed Army Hospital where the former president was suffering from congestive heart failure. Goodpaster's last visit was the day before Eisenhower died on March 28, 1969. Goodpaster found Eisenhower continuing to be alert and interested in world affairs, especially NATO. Eisenhower was particularly pleased to hear that Goodpaster might soon be leading NATO forces.[23]

NOTES

1. Lien-Hang Nguyen, "The War Politburo: North Vietnam's Diplomatic and Political Road to the Tet Offensive," *Journal of Vietnamese Studies* 2, no. 1–2 (2006): 15–16, 24.

2. Dougan and Weiss, *Nineteen Sixty-Eight*, 22, 66.

3. For an interesting view of the problems of measuring progress in Vietnam, see Daddis, *No Sure Victory*.

4. Johnson, *The Vantage Point*, 389–92; Induction Statistics, U.S. Selective Service website, www.sss.gov, accessed December 14, 2014.

5. In approving an increase in the authorized strength for MACV of 24,500, the new ceiling was set at 549,500 but was never reached. Westmoreland had requested an increase of 206,000 troops, along the lines suggested by Wheeler.

6. Goodpaster, Mandel interviews, February 11, 2004, tape 19.

7. Goodpaster, Mandel interviews, February 11, 12, 2004, tapes 20 and 21.

8. Goodpaster Memo for Record, February 14, 1968, National Security Files, Name Files, Eisenhower, box 2, LBJ Library; Goodpaster, Johnson and Ferguson interviews, April 9, 1976.

9. Goodpaster, Mandel interviews, February 12, 2004, tape 20.

10. Graham Cosmas, U.S. Army in Vietnam series, *MACV, The Joint Command in the Years of Withdrawal, 1968–1973*, 136.

11. Goodpaster, Johnson and Ferguson interviews, April 9, 1976.

12. Ibid., 245; Goodpaster, Mandel interviews, February 12, 2004, tape 20.

13. Goodpaster, Mandel interviews, February 12, 2004, tape 20.

14. Ibid., tapes 20 and 21.

15. Ibid., tape 21.

16. Ibid., tape 20. Also see the 1969 MACV Strategic Objectives Plan, Army War College Library.

17. Mandel interviews, February 12, 2004, tape 21; Kissinger, *White House Years*, 41, 46.

18. Assistant Secretary of Defense, Manpower and Reserve Affairs, "Project 100,000," September 1968.

19. Ibid. Also see the report by the Assistant Secretary of Defense for Manpower and Reserve Affairs, "Project One Hundred Thousand: Characteristics and Performance of 'New Standards' Men," September 1968.

20. Kissinger, *Years of Renewal*, 75.

21. Goodpaster, Mandel interviews, February 12, 2004, tape 22.

22. Joseph Alsop in the *Washington Post*, January 17, 1969, as reported in *Current Biography* 1969, 172.

23. Goodpaster, interview by Joe B. Frantz, June 21, 1971, Oral History Program, LBJ Library, 35.

Chapter Thirteen

SACEUR NATO (1969–1974)

In early 1969, President Nixon informed General Goodpaster that he was recommending him to be the next SACEUR. Nixon also said that he would send a message to the leaders of the other NATO allies asking for their agreement with the assignment. In May, President Nixon announced his nomination, and Goodpaster's appointment was soon confirmed.[1]

General Goodpaster assumed command of U.S. forces in Europe several months before he took command of the allied NATO forces in Europe. The intervening three months gave Goodpaster an opportunity to coordinate with the current SACEUR, General Lyman Lemnitzer, on the transition, a pattern that Lemnitzer had followed when he succeeded General Norstad. In discussions with Goodpaster, Lemnitzer stressed two issues: (1) dealing with the French withdrawal from the NATO integrated military structure and (2) dealing with strong pressures to reduce the military contributions in nearly every country.

On the first issue, Lemnitzer advocated unofficial arrangements for French forces to operate within the NATO structure. Goodpaster agreed and thought it was best to let the French make the approach and, over a period of time, establish working relationships that would facilitate French contributions in the event of war.

They also discussed the unresolved issues of NATO nuclear planning and preparations. Both Lemnitzer and Norstad before him had argued with civilian leaders in the Pentagon who had pressed for NATO to rely on conventional defense. This, Lemnitzer thought, was not feasible.

Goodpaster was also told to expect continuing pressure to reduce contributions to NATO forces. The Belgians were likely to approach him with the idea of pulling their units back across the Rhine, and the Canadians were planning to make deep cuts in their forces. Both Lemnitzer and Goodpaster were aware of some behind-the-scenes talks involving Pentagon officials and Congress about reducing the American forces in NATO by thirty thousand troops. The latter would pose a major problem because U.S. forces in NATO had already been drained substantially by requirements to send forces to Vietnam. Finally, Lemnitzer noted that persistent efforts on his part to improve communications among the disparate NATO forces had achieved some progress, but poor communications remained a serious problem.[2]

On July 1, 1969, General Goodpaster became the Supreme Allied Commander, Europe, NATO's top military position. This seemed a particularly appropriate career capstone, given his role in organizing NATO's military structure in the early 1950s. Goodpaster, as had his predecessors, now commanded in three capacities: NATO forces as SACEUR; U.S. forces as US-CINCEUR (United States Commander-in-Chief, European Command); and Quadripartite Forces (United States, British, French, and West German) under the Live Oak headquarters, a separate organization that dealt with crises in Berlin involving Allied occupation forces dating back to the end of World War II.

While all three commands were interrelated, each posed a unique set of problems. Berlin, for example, had frequently been the focal point of Cold War confrontations. By this time, Quadripartite plans for Berlin operations had been leaked to the Soviets by a French agent. Thus, Goodpaster had to assume that subsequent plans had been compromised while also being prepared to brief the U.S. president on alternative options and priorities should another Berlin crisis arise.[3]

FRANCE AND NATO

The resignation of President Charles de Gaulle in April 1969 presented opportunities to improve both U.S. and NATO relations with France. Goodpaster's staff was eagerly looking for ways to bring the French back into NATO's integrated efforts. While not wanting to stifle initiative, Goodpaster was concerned that the staff not get too far in front of the issue because, as he put it, NATO could easily find itself "buying the same horse quite a number of times and then it would turn out not to be there." While NATO was certainly open to cooperation, the initiative should come from the French, in his view.[4]

To help him stay abreast of the evolving French positions on NATO, Goodpaster was informed by his old friend, Lieutenant General Vernon "Dick" Walters, the U.S. military attaché in Paris. For example, Walters noted a recent French military exercise for a French-only defense for a war in Europe. French officers confided with Walters that the notion was political posturing, but military nonsense.[5]

After de Gaulle's public split with the Alliance, France had remained involved quietly with NATO in several important ways, such as being part of the air defense network. Also, arrangements were worked out whereby the French shared their contingency plans with NATO, although NATO plans were not shared with the French, at least officially.[6]

Goodpaster was aware of several other examples of quiet progress in working with the French, such as planning by his Central Army Group (CENTAG) staff, headed by a German officer. When Goodpaster was briefed on plans premised on cooperation with French forces should the NATO defenses fail, he observed that it would be better if planning were based on the association of French forces *before* NATO defenses failed. Goodpaster urged his planners to talk to their respective governments to see what could be worked out, and changes were then planned accordingly. Such initiatives continued, but it was not until 2009 that France officially rejoined NATO's integrated military command.[7]

NATO STRATEGY

Goodpaster was eager to have President Nixon provide a personal and strong endorsement of NATO, so he invited the president to meet with NATO commanders in September 1970 at the Allied Forces South Headquarters in Naples, Italy. Nixon told the assembled commanders and political leaders that although many voices can be heard in the United States, policy can only be established by the president. He further noted that the U.S. commitment to NATO was indispensable to any viable European defense policy and that Europeans could be assured that there would be no unilateral withdrawal of U.S. forces.[8]

A few weeks later, Goodpaster discussed NATO strategy in more detail with Nixon at an NSC meeting on the subject. Goodpaster described the strategy to deter war and, should deterrence fail, defend the allies. It was based on a limited conventional defense capability with medium risk and medium cost. The other major options were: a full conventional defense capability would provide a lower risk but at much higher cost; or a "tripwire" (token ground forces that could trigger a nuclear response) capability would involve high risk at lower cost.[9]

The military balance increasingly favored the Warsaw Pact. As Kissinger noted, the Warsaw Pact had a major advantage in ground forces, including two and one-half times the number of tanks. This disparity was not redressed by NATO's having the edge in naval and air forces and logistics.[10]

MANSFIELD AMENDMENT

Debate on reducing contributions to NATO had intensified in December 1969 when U.S. senators Mansfield, Fulbright, and Kennedy appeared at a NATO Council meeting in Brussels, where they asserted that "forthcoming considerable cuts in American forces in Europe were inevitable." The pronouncement, Goodpaster noted, "came like a cold water shower upon the heads of NATO Defense Ministers already worried by the impending Canadian withdrawals."[11]

Addressing the House Foreign Affairs Committee in February 1970, General Goodpaster quoted an old military adage about reinforcing success. He added, "At the least, we should not imperil it. There are not so many successes around today that we can afford to throw any one of them away." The NATO alliance was a success, he said, and went on to say it was obvious that the more conventional forces are reduced, the greater is the need for an early nuclear response and the lower is the nuclear threshold. As the Soviets closed the nuclear gap, the need for conventional forces in place in Europe was continuing or increasing, not decreasing.[12]

In early 1971, Senate Majority Leader Mike Mansfield introduced an amendment to the Defense Authorization Bill to reduce U.S. forces in NATO by half. In May 1971, President Nixon asked Goodpaster to return to Washington immediately and work with him to block the amendment. Goodpaster left that night, flew back to Andrews Air Force Base and went by helicopter, landing on the White House lawn, just after a meeting on the problem had begun. President Nixon had assembled influential Republicans and Democrats with extensive NATO experience to mobilize bipartisan support. Those present included Dean Acheson, Averell Harriman, Alfred Gruenther, Lauris Norstad, Lyman Lemnitzer and several others. Senior administration officials present included Secretary of State Bill Rogers, Secretary of Defense Melvin Laird, and National Security Advisor Henry Kissinger.[13]

The Senate appeared to be lined up with about 60 in favor and 35–40 against. One administration official noted that it would take enormous persuasion to beat the amendment. General Gruenther noted that businessmen were telling him that the Mansfield amendment would save $14 billion. General Norstad argued that many Americans believed our troops had been in Europe too long. General Goodpaster, however, pointed out that NATO forces already had been reduced by 120,000 over the last eight years, and we must avoid any further major cuts in a short period of time. Goodpaster stressed that the key issue was alliance solidarity. If the United States acted unilaterally, allies would not work together, and old quarrels would reignite. NATO served to suppress those tendencies. Furthermore, the possibility of the dissolution of NATO "petrified Germany's allies," Goodpaster noted.[14]

Goodpaster later recalled discussions about some Democrats in the Senate who were willing to fight against the amendment but wanted to be assured that after taking a strong public stand, they would not be made vulnerable by the administration later agreeing to more modest reductions. Nixon said no; indeed, he planned to oppose any reduction in troops very firmly. He would reduce U.S. forces only in consultation with allies and in light of Soviet reductions. [15]

Nixon next sent Goodpaster to talk to Senator Mansfield. In his meeting with the senator, Goodpaster argued that NATO, or something like it, was essential to the security of the United States and that American participation in NATO was vital for NATO to be successful. Mansfield said he agreed. Goodpaster then added that an American contribution at substantially the current level was necessary. Major reductions by the United States would trigger similar reductions by other allies and the promise of future deployment of forces from the United States was not a credible alternative. At that point, however, Mansfield said, "Nevertheless, there's an awful lot of pressure to reduce our forces." The discussion ended in a stalemate. [16]

The issue continued to be fought largely behind the scenes. Goodpaster argued persuasively that U.S. forces were the glue that held NATO together. Another senator later told Goodpaster that he and others had signed on to the amendment thinking that it would never come to a vote. When it did on May 19, 1971, much of the earlier support evaporated and, it was defeated by a vote of 61–36. That vote also helped Goodpaster successfully avert Canadian plans to reduce their NATO contribution and the Belgian proposal to redeploy forces as well.

The battle, however, continued to be fought within the Defense Department. Soon after taking command as SACEUR, Goodpaster set his staff to work on how best to compensate for any reductions in NATO forces. The obvious response was for other nations, including the United States, to make up the differences. When word of this reached the Pentagon, there was a suggestion that Goodpaster needed to be straightened out on the role of SACEUR in matters of U.S. force commitments. [17]

When he learned of these exchanges, Goodpaster contacted General Wheeler, the Chairman of the Joint Chiefs of Staff, and told him he understood that SACEUR was accountable to NATO, not the United States, and it was the SACEUR's responsibility to analyze and make force recommendations to NATO. That was the way NATO operated under General Eisenhower, and Goodpaster saw no reason that this should not continue. Goodpaster pointed out that these were matters of considerable policy importance and said he would talk to the president if there were any difficulties. General Wheeler, aware of Goodpaster's close personal relationship with Nixon, assured Goodpaster there would be no problems in the Pentagon regarding the independent role of the SACEUR. [18]

General Goodpaster also viewed NATO as part of the broad, interrelated network of U.S. alliance relationships. Thus, when the issue of control of the China seat in the United Nations arose, pitting the Republic of China (Taiwan), a U.S. ally, against the communist government on the mainland, the People's Republic of China, Goodpaster argued privately with West European political leaders that supporting Taiwan's continued control of the China seat was in their best interests. Goodpaster, however, was unsuccessful in stemming the tide of countries establishing diplomatic relations with Beijing. After Kissinger's secret visit to Beijing, Taiwan's control of the China seat at the UN became untenable, and Beijing won a General Assembly vote on the issue in 1971.[19]

ALLIANCE DEFENSE IN THE 1970S

In his first speech as SACEUR to NATO parliamentarians, General Goodpaster recalled Winston Churchill's famous Iron Curtain speech in which Churchill noted that he did not believe the Russians wanted war but rather wanted to obtain the fruits of war without bearing the costs of war. In like manner, Goodpaster said, within the Atlantic Alliance there were apparently some who wanted the fruits of peace without the costs of peace. Goodpaster concluded, noting that, "Simply stated, if the Alliance is to avoid having to meet the terrible cost of war, then it must pay the much more modest costs for peace."[20]

A major Goodpaster concern was decreasing Allied commitments to NATO, but he also was worried about the increasing military threat. During 1970, Soviet and Warsaw Pact forces conducted three major military combined arms and naval exercises: DVINA in March, OKEAN in April, and COMRADES IN ARMS in October. Each exercise was the largest of its kind since World War II.[21]

General Goodpaster worked closely with the Secretary General of NATO, Manlio Brosio,[22] a brilliant, experienced Italian diplomat, to find a positive way to put NATO to work in addressing these concerns. Drawing on Eisenhower's early experience at NATO, Goodpaster and Brosio took the analytic initiative to reframe the political debate. They established the Alliance Defense for the Seventies program to use every means possible to improve the effectiveness and efficiency of the resources provided to NATO by the member states. This shifted the debate from cutting back support to looking for improvements and initiatives for more effective use of funds. This program was a high priority for Goodpaster during his first year and a half.[23]

Another early concern of General Goodpaster's was setting appropriate priorities for NATO. Whereas many commanders focus almost entirely on the adversary, General Goodpaster concluded that the threats to NATO from within were at least as serious as those from outside and that he was in a stronger position to deal with problems posed by the allies. Goodpaster knew that in NATO it takes a concerted effort by all to achieve anything, but a single unwilling or self-seeking member can greatly obstruct or endanger the rest.[24]

NATO's main missions were deterrence, defense, and allied solidarity. Of the three, Goodpaster devoted most of his efforts to the problem of allied solidarity.[25] While at first glance this might appear to be a third-order priority, in fact, it was his most pressing problem. NATO forces were continuously under serious threat of being reduced further by political leaders in the United States and Europe at a time when the capabilities of Soviet and Warsaw Pact forces were increasing.[26]

Goodpaster also recognized that NATO military capabilities were far less than the sum of the parts contributed by members of the Alliance. Better interoperability was essential to increasing these capabilities, so he made standardization a high priority for NATO forces. In particular, he emphasized the need for improved and more standardized communications within NATO forces. Such communications would be critical during a war in which much larger Warsaw Pact forces would also have the advantages of picking the time, place, and manner of attack. Under these circumstances, NATO's key to successful defense would be its agility, while Warsaw Pact forces were locked into set attack plans. NATO's agility depended upon timely communications for effective command and control.[27]

DÉTENTE

The geopolitical environment General Goodpaster faced had several crosscurrents. The Cold War competition was heated in Latin America and Southeast Asia, particularly in Vietnam. Efforts at liberalization in Czechoslovakia's "Prague Spring" had been squashed by Warsaw Pact intervention. Simultaneously, there were several initiatives to reduce East-West tensions. "Détente" became an increasingly attractive policy along with the new West German government's "*ostpolitik*" initiatives to improve cooperation with East Germany. These efforts also coincided with several allied nonaggression pacts with the Soviet Union, the ongoing Conference on Security and Cooperation in Europe (CSCE), the Strategic Arms Limitations Talks (SALT), and other negotiations intended to reduce East-West tensions and the likelihood of war.

While supportive of efforts to reduce the chances of war, General Goodpaster was concerned about the dubious assumptions and lack of rigorous analyses underpinning the concept of *détente*. He was worried that arms-control agreements might be based more on hope than reality and about a "tendency to assume that it is safe to reduce Western forces *unilaterally* or drawback from forward deployments," without careful study of the risks. [28]

In particular, General Goodpaster was concerned about the potentially adverse impact on NATO's military capabilities of negotiations on mutual and balanced force reductions (MBFR). He commissioned detailed analyses of the implications of MBFR for NATO. The studies highlighted key asymmetries in the military balance, including Soviet advantages in numbers of forces and geographical advantages in any redeployment of forces. Indeed, he noted that if the negotiations resulted in more balanced forces, then the required reductions would necessarily be much larger for the Warsaw Pact. Goodpaster insisted that MBFR negotiations be conducted on the principle of undiminished security. The Soviets initially opposed the idea of balanced reductions. [29]

Within the administration, the debate pitted arms-control advocates against Goodpaster and others working for a stronger NATO. Eventually, the matter came to a head in choosing which issue should have priority; the United States could not continue to push for both NATO force improvements and MBFR simultaneously. Goodpaster won the debate, at least initially, to make every effort to get force improvements while slowing the rush toward MBFR. [30]

Goodpaster also engaged the debate by noting that détente must be based on reducing and removing the causes of tensions, not merely their symptoms. Détente for NATO was in addition to defense and deterrence, not instead of them. Such thinking enabled him to incorporate détente into NATO's missions, while keeping attention on the implications of détente for allied deterrence and defense. [31]

In this charged political environment, Goodpaster managed to introduce some humor. He loved a "well-turned" phrase, so when the saying "Better Red than dead" became popular, particularly in Europe, Goodpaster countered with "Better neither than either." This alternative appealed in NATO circles because it translated well into German *"lieber keins als eins."* [32]

President Nixon was interested in Goodpaster's views on the changing geopolitical environment and instructed Goodpaster to return to Washington regularly and meet with him to discuss the situation in Europe and global security issues. This involved several meetings during the first year and about twice a year during the rest of Goodpaster's tenure. [33]

Such direct consultations between the president and the SACEUR were not unusual because of the special access of SACEUR to European leaders. In setting up NATO, General Eisenhower established a precedent that the SACEUR, as a first priority upon assuming command, would visit the political leaders of the allies to establish and maintain personal relationships and discuss views on the alliance. Succeeding SACEURs followed suit, staying in close touch with European leaders. [34]

On one occasion, when Goodpaster had returned for consultations in the Pentagon, he called the White House to arrange a meeting with the president and was advised that the president was very busy and might not have time for a meeting. Goodpaster said to just pass on his regrets that they would not be able to meet, because this was his final day in Washington. About ten minutes later, Goodpaster received a call to meet the president in the old Executive Office Building. When they met, Nixon outlined his plan of action for the Middle East. Although at that time, this region was not part of Goodpaster's area of responsibility, Nixon wanted to discuss his ideas. Goodpaster was very impressed with the president's thinking, which he termed "brilliant" and reflective of a deep understanding of the problems in the Middle East. The encounter provided Goodpaster with background information when the region was later added to his area of responsibilities. [35]

The meeting next turned to the president's NSC structure, which Goodpaster had helped establish. Goodpaster suggested that Colonel Lincoln, who was retiring from his teaching position at West Point, be appointed head of the Office of Emergency Preparedness. Such an appointment would allow Lincoln to participate in NSC meetings and bring his experience and wisdom to bear on the problems. Nixon agreed and appointed Lincoln to the position. [36]

MIDDLE EAST WAR (1973)

Nixon's Middle East initiative was derailed by the Watergate scandal and the 1973 Arab-Israeli War. During Ramadan and on Yom Kippur, October 6, 1973, Egypt and Syria attacked Israel and were soon joined by forces from other Arab countries. Soviet and U.S. involvement was triggered by their agreements to provide military equipment to the belligerents, the Soviets to Syria and Egypt and the United States to Israel. A Soviet merchant ship was sunk by Israeli warships, and the Soviets sent destroyers, minesweepers, and landing craft with naval infantry to the Syrian coast, resulting in further exchanges of fire with Israeli forces. In addition, seven Soviet airborne divisions were alerted for deployment. [37]

The United States, in turn, placed its forces on higher alert and began resupplying Israel with military equipment from Europe. This involved Goodpaster in his role as Commander-in-Chief, U.S. Forces in Europe. Admiral Moorer, chairman, JCS, called Goodpaster to coordinate airlift support involving four C-5A and twelve C-141 aircraft every twenty-four hours, plus providing F-4 fighter aircraft. Most of the European allies were not cooperative and were unwilling to provide overflight rights. As a result, only Lajes Air Base, in the Portuguese Azores Islands, was available for refueling flights between the United States and Israel. [38]

When the United States met with some reluctance on the part of Germany to permit Israeli shipping concerns to pick up U.S. military equipment at German ports, General Abrams, the Army chief of staff, was furious and responded, "They're our God damn tanks and we'll do anything we want with them." The issue was quickly resolved, the tanks were sent, and Soviet and U.S. leaders soon agreed to avoid a superpower confrontation and supported the UN-brokered cease-fire on October 25, 1973.[39]

The White House and Goodpaster were mainly concerned about the direct intervention of Soviet forces, particularly after Israel apparently violated the cease-fire and encircled Egyptian forces in the Sinai. A threatening message from Leonid Brezhnev to Nixon came at a time that Kissinger noted there was "no functional president" in Soviet eyes because of the Watergate scandal. Nevertheless, U.S. forces were placed on higher levels of alert and a brigade in Europe was readied for deployment.[40]

The crisis also served to highlight the influence of the OPEC (Organization of Petroleum Exporting Countries) cartel on the United States and on NATO allies. In response to U.S. aid to Israel, OPEC declared an oil embargo in October 1973. Oil prices quadrupled, gasoline was rationed in the United States and elsewhere, inflation spiked, a global recession ensued, and unemployment rose. The resulting tensions further strained relations between the United States and several NATO allies. Goodpaster would later recall 1973 as characterized by "disunity, disarray, disagreement, and mutual recrimination." Faced with pressure from Arab oil producers, several allies chose to "save their own skins . . . and sit on the sidelines." He judged the overall performance of NATO during the crisis in uncompromising terms, "To call it ignominious would be to indulge in unwarranted flattery."[41]

TACTICAL NUCLEAR WEAPONS

Nuclear weapons were a very sensitive issue in Europe and consumed much of Goodpaster's attention. During the 1960s, Secretary of Defense McNamara was frequently quoted as saying we had no plans for the use of tactical nuclear weapons. In 1962, when McNamara was visiting U.S. troops in Europe and Goodpaster was the acting V Corps Commander, Lieutenant General Bonesteel, commanding VII Corps, called Goodpaster and informed him about McNamara's visit and apparent misunderstanding about tactical nuclear weapons. When McNamara met with Goodpaster, Goodpaster explained that, while tactical nuclear weapons were not part of the U.S. Single Integrated Operations Plan (SIOP) for strategic nuclear war options, they were an important part of deterrence. This news did not sit well with McNamara who had been deemphasizing nuclear weapons in the new administration's Flexible Response strategy.[42]

By the time Goodpaster became SACEUR, the political environment in Europe was even more hostile to nuclear weapons. Efforts by Sol Zuckerman, a prominent British pioneer in operations research and scientific advisor to the Allies in World War II on strategic bombing; Lord Mountbatten, former British defense chief; and others had terrified the British, Germans and other Europeans that Europe would be completely devastated in a nuclear war, leaving nothing but a graveyard. [43]

As a result, General Goodpaster developed planning approaches that were tightly controlled to limit collateral damage. The planning addressed the purposes and types of weapons and how they would be delivered. In congressional testimony, Goodpaster made the point that the initial, limited use of tactical nuclear weapons would not necessarily result in uncontrolled escalation. Nevertheless, the Soviets would have to calculate that control of Europe was worth risking the destruction of the Soviet Union. [44]

General Goodpaster also discussed tactical nuclear weapons with President Nixon, noting that after more than six years of a split in U.S. policy between the Pentagon and SACEUR, agreement had finally been reached that tactical nuclear weapons provided an important contribution to deterrence. U.S. weapons had much lower yields than the Soviet weapons and thus could potentially be used on the battlefield without risking massive collateral damage, while also possibly avoiding escalation to a full-scale nuclear war. This made them more credible, increasing the likelihood that the Soviets would not risk an attack. Goodpaster also noted that the tactical nuclear weapons stockpile was in need of modernization after ten years of neglect. [45]

NATO strategy called for developing capabilities for a ninety-day conventional war on the assumption that attacking Soviet/Warsaw Pact forces would run out of steam by that time, and a stalemate would develop. A 1970 United States NSC report, however, concluded that there was only about a fifty-fifty chance that NATO forces could defend effectively even against an attack launched without Soviet mobilization; thus tactical nuclear weapons might be needed earlier than ninety days. [46]

Kissinger, in addressing the problem, noted that even with seven thousand tactical nuclear weapons in Europe, no one could win a nuclear exchange. The weapons were mainly serving as a deterrent, and ambiguity and uncertainty about their use was part of deterrence. When Nixon asked why, if no one can win a tactical exchange, would we escalate to a strategic exchange that no one could win? Kissinger replied that he had written a book on the subject and still did not know the answers. [47]

At a subsequent meeting on U.S. nuclear policy, Kissinger described the dilemma as, "We have an agreed NATO doctrine for the use of ten weapons, after that Goodpaster will do what he feels necessary." Kissinger further noted: "On the one hand, we want the Soviets to think the situation might get out of hand, while on the other hand, we want to persuade them not to let it get out of hand. . . . I think they will be looking for excuses not to escalate."[48]

VIETNAM

During this time, Goodpaster also played a role in keeping secret Kissinger's early negotiations with North Vietnamese diplomat Le Duc Tho. Kissinger's trips to Europe could be credibly explained as visits to NATO. On January 27, 1973, the Paris Peace Accords were signed, calling for a cease-fire in place, the withdrawal of American forces within sixty days, the release of American prisoners of war, negotiations between the Viet Cong and government of South Vietnam to allow self-determination through free and democratic elections under international supervision, and the peaceful reunification of Vietnam. The accords did not, however, require the withdrawal of North Vietnamese forces from South Vietnam.[49]

President Thieu had not been informed of the talks and was furious. But he eventually accepted the terms after strong pressure from the United States and a secret understanding that U.S. support would be provided if needed. Thieu had no choice.

In June 1973, Congress passed the Case-Church Amendment to the Defense Authorization Bill prohibiting any further U.S. military operations in Vietnam, Laos, or Cambodia after August 15, 1973, unless the president received approval in advance from Congress. The amendment had been defeated in August 1972 but was reintroduced after the reelection of President Nixon and passed in the Senate by a vote of 64–26 and in the House by 278–124, margins greater than the two-thirds majority required to override a presidential veto. U.S. air support was halted on August 15, which, in General Goodpaster's view, severely undermined the chances of achieving an independent South Vietnam.[50]

The Vietnam War continued to touch General Goodpaster personally. While he was SACEUR, his daughter Anne and her two children came to stay with her parents at *Chateau Gendebien*, the SACEUR's quarters, while her husband was serving in the Army in Vietnam.[51]

CYPRUS CRISIS

NATO solidarity was threatened by the prospects of war between Greece and Turkey. On July 20, 1974, the Turkish invasion of Cyprus followed a coup engineered by the Greek-military-led "colonels" regime. In the coup, Cypriot president Archbishop Makarios was replaced by a leader favoring union with Greece. After the invasion, the Greek military regime collapsed and a UN-brokered cease-fire was established in Cyprus in August 1974.

In the meantime, the Greek government announced that it was withdrawing Greek forces from NATO. This was counter to the major U.S. objective of keeping NATO together by discouraging war between Greece and Turkey. To help defuse the crisis, General Goodpaster communicated directly with Greek and Turkish leaders, urging them to avoid any clash between their forces on the border. The crisis, he told them, must not escalate, or the costs to both countries would be very high. Indeed, a ship carrying U.S. military assistance to both countries was already in nearby waters.[52]

PLANNING FOR RETIREMENT

About five months before General Goodpaster retired, General Norstad came to see him and, over lunch, they talked about retirement. Norstad, a former SACEUR, advised Goodpaster to begin his planning because retirement is a great change. Norstad recommended some rules for retirement:

> One, when you retire, don't do nothing, because that's ruinous. Two, don't do anything you don't want to do. That's a privilege you haven't had until now. Three, when you retire, devote one-third of your time to *pro bono* work, because you have an obligation to convey your experiences and let people draw some lessons from that; devote one-third to remunerative work, because if somebody pays you, even if it's not much, that says it's real; and devote one-third to your wife. You certainly owe it to her.[53]

WATERGATE AND AN AWKWARD CHANGE OF COMMAND

The Watergate scandal set in motion a series of events that led to a most unusual change of command at SHAPE. Investigations of the break-in of Democratic National Committee Headquarters offices at the Watergate Hotel and Apartment Complex on June 17, 1972, led to the resignation of President Nixon on August 9, 1974, after evidence of his involvement in the Watergate scandal pointed to his likely impeachment. During this time frame, Nixon and Vice President Spiro Agnew were reelected, but evidence increasingly implicated senior White House officials in the scandal. Furthermore, Agnew, next in line for the presidency, was independently being investigated by the Justice Department for extortion, tax fraud, and conspiracy. General Alexander Haig, Nixon's chief of staff, pressured Agnew to "go quietly . . . or else." Agnew resigned on October 10, 1973, and was replaced as vice president by Gerald Ford, formerly the House minority leader.[54]

Haig was at the center of making arrangements for the transfer of power from President Nixon, but Haig was also part of the problem. Driven by his MacArthur-like personal ambition, he wanted to remain in the White House. He had developed too many detractors, however, especially during his meteoric rise. Serving initially as Henry Kissinger's military assistant, Haig had been promoted rapidly from colonel to four-star general in about three years. Especially in the Army, Haig earned a reputation for intimidating others, firing capable subordinates and striking fear in those under and around him. He often seemed inordinately angry. Few, if any, senior political and military officials wanted Haig to remain. At this critical stage of the Nixon transition, Haig could not be fired, but he had to be removed from Washington.[55]

The SACEUR position became the least-bad option. Goodpaster was scheduled to retire at the end of his tour as SACEUR in the spring of 1975, so ending his assignment several months early was considered embarrassing but necessary. Goodpaster, however, was not consulted in advance about the move. It is unlikely that Goodpaster would have favored Haig being appointed to such an important position. Senior NATO officials also shared the view that Haig was not a good choice for the job. The British and French representatives, in particular, did not hide their disdain for Haig.[56]

Before the controversy, on one of his trips to Washington near the end of his tour, General Goodpaster talked about his tenure with General Abrams, who was then chief of staff of the Army. Abrams said they would like to think of Andy's retirement in the spring of 1975. Goodpaster said that would be fine with him and added that he had been at NATO long enough to accomplish most of what he was capable of doing.[57]

In the early fall of 1974, Goodpaster got a call from Brent Scowcroft on the NSC staff, advising him that General Alexander Haig would soon be replacing him as SACEUR. This was a great surprise to Goodpaster. He was not aware until later that this move was part of behind-the-scenes negotiations for the transfer of power to Vice President Ford.[58]

Goodpaster was embarrassed because earlier he had been called by some allied commanders who said they had heard that Goodpaster had requested retirement. He replied that this was not the case. Evidently, before Goodpaster got the call from Scowcroft, the White House had sent out a message to foreign leaders saying that Goodpaster had requested retirement and that General Haig would take over as SACEUR, part of the formality of gaining allied agreement on any new SACEUR.[59]

The clumsy affair got worse. The White House set Sunday, December 17, 1974, for the SACEUR change of command, with a concomitant change of U.S. European Command (EUCOM) in Stuttgart, Germany, a month earlier. At the time of the EUCOM change, Goodpaster was recovering from surgery and did not attend the ceremony, so it became an assumption of command rather than a change of command. Goodpaster claimed that he did not want to publicize his operation, but clearly he was deeply angered by the manner in which he had been treated. General Goodpaster's absence, of course, was noticed and portrayed in the press as shunning General Haig. The later change of command at SHAPE was a very private, unpublicized ceremony, with General Haig arriving without fanfare and using a side door entrance.[60]

General Goodpaster retired the same day, December 17, 1974, after more than thirty-five years of service. During those years, the Goodpaster family had moved thirty-six times.[61]

GOODPASTER'S CONTRIBUTIONS TO NATO

In reflecting on his tour at NATO, General Goodpaster considered among his most important accomplishments stopping the erosion of NATO troops while building the capabilities of the forces deployed. The drawdown in U.S. forces in Europe abated after U.S. troops began withdrawing from Vietnam in 1969 as part of the Vietnamization policy.[62]

Goodpaster had also made arrangements for French forces to fit into NATO defenses if that should be necessary, while not requiring the French publicly to reverse de Gaulle's decision and rejoin NATO's political structure. In welcoming the more positive French attitude toward NATO, Goodpaster was careful to not lose sight of the need for a quid pro quo involving access to French pipelines, communications, and forces being committed to the alliance.[63]

As for the contentious nuclear program, Goodpaster had instituted planning for the selective employment of tactical nuclear weapons that provided flexibility to impede Warsaw Pact attacks at a very early stage.

In exercising command, Goodpaster had emphasized the notion of "wielding the force" during exercises. He had learned this approach from Eisenhower, who said that, at the time of decision, "plans are nothing but planning is everything." Therefore, at such decision points, commanders should employ the force in the best possible way, not hold slavishly to plans. Exercises provided important training for commanders to be ready to wield the force.

Improvements in NATO communications had remained regrettably meager. Efforts had continued to be delayed by high-level studies because of the commercial implications of procuring new equipment. Goodpaster observed that NATO's cumbersome processes delayed General Lemnitzer's Communications Improvement Plan '67 until it would more likely become the Communications Improvement Plan '76. Goodpaster compared NATO's cumbersome approval procedures to something like the old British slow bicycle race, in which young ladies would ride bicycles for short distances, about thirty yards, in lanes, to see who could finish last without putting a foot down or falling over.[64]

Strategy was at the center of Goodpaster's thinking throughout his tenure as SACEUR. He wanted it to be clear in his mind and in those of his staff and commanders, about "what to do, how to do it, and what to do it with" so that all problems and proposed initiatives could be evaluated in that context. One of his methods of keeping focused on strategic thinking was to speak often before war colleges, where he would be exposed to challenging questions. Goodpaster would often ponder these questions after such visits and put his staff to work on these problems. [65]

Goodpaster's collaborative leadership style also was notable. He engaged systematically a wide range of political and military leaders that contributed to better understanding of important issues and priorities. For example, on his periodic trips to Washington, Goodpaster made it a point to call on each of the service chiefs for an exchange of views. [66]

NEXT STEPS FOR RETIREMENT

Although surprised and no doubt disappointed with the abrupt nature of his retirement, Goodpaster was not unprepared. He recalled General Norstad's advice on retirement that included consideration of the Wilson Center in Washington as a place to reflect and write about what he had learned that might be of interest to future generations.

Figure 13.1. **NATO's Supreme Allied Commander, Europe, 1969-1974. Official photo.** *Source*: **Courtesy of National Archives and Records Administration (NARA)**

NOTES

1. Goodpaster, Mandel interviews, February 12, 2004, tape 21.
2. Ibid., tape 22.
3. Editorial Note, *FRUS, 1969–1976, Vol. XL, Germany and Berlin, 1969–1972,* doc. 34.

4. Minutes of National Security Council Review Group, May 22, 1969, *FRUS, 1969–1976, Vol. XLI, Western Europe, NATO, 1969–1972*, doc. 128; Ibid., Kissinger to Nixon Memo, March 10, 1970, d.142; Goodpaster, Sorley interview, December 3, 1985, Washington, DC.

5. Goodpaster, Sorley interview, December 3, 1985, Washington, DC.

6. Ibid.

7. Ibid.

8. Report on NATO Commanders Conference, Naples, September 30, 1970, *FRUS, 1969–1976, Vol. XLI, Western Europe, NATO, 1969–1972*, doc. 48.

9. Minutes of NSC Meeting, November 19, 1970, *FRUS, 1969–1976, Vol. XLI, Western Europe, NATO, 1969–1972*, doc. 53.

10. Minutes of NSC Review Group Meeting, June 16, 1970, *FRUS, 1969–1976, Vol. XLI, Western Europe, NATO, 1969–1972*, doc. 42

11. Hinteroff, "NATO and Spain," *NATO's 15 Nations*, April–May, 1970, 67.

12. Goodpaster remarks to House Foreign Affairs Committee, February 17, 1970, Goodpaster Papers, box 30, NDU Library.

13. Minutes of Legislative Interdepartmental Group Meeting, May 12, 1971, *FRUS, 1969–1976, Vol. XLI, Western Europe, NATO, 1969–1972*, doc. 62; White House Memo for Record, May 13, 1971, Ibid., doc. 63.

14. Ibid.

15. Goodpaster, Sorley interview, December 3, 1985, Washington, DC.

16. Ibid.

17. Ibid.

18. Ibid.

19. Goodpaster in meeting with President Nixon and Dr. Kissinger, Oval Office, August 7, 1972, White House Tape 763-12, www.nixonlibrary.gov.

20. Goodpaster remarks to North Atlantic Assembly, Brussels, October 18, 1969, Goodpaster Papers, box 24, NDU Library.

21. Goodpaster remarks at the Royal United Services Institute, London, December 16, 1970, Goodpaster Papers, box 24, NDU Library.

22. Brosio was a veteran of World War I and had fought in the Italian underground in World War II and was former minister of defense and ambassador successively to the Soviet Union, the UK, the United States, and France; NATO secretary general 1964–1971.

23. Ibid., tape 22; also see Lewis Sorley's chapter, "Goodpaster," in Robert Jordan's *Generals in International Politics*, 123–49.

24. Goodpaster in the speech "Role of the Military in National Security Policy Formulation," June 24, 1965, West Point, NDU Library.

25. Author's analysis based mainly on the Goodpaster in Special Collections Data Base, National Defense University (NDU) Library. See for example, documents 11900, 11878, 11888; Sorley, "Goodpaster."

26. Sorley, "Goodpaster," 124.

27. Sorley, "Goodpaster," 144.

28. Goodpaster, *Interests and Strategies in an Era of Détente*, U.S. Army War College, 1975, 6.

29. Goodpaster speech at Harvard, April 25, 1975, Goodpaster Papers, box 39, files 3, 4, Marshall Library and Goodpaster Special Collection, document 174, NDU Library.

30. Memo Smith to Kissinger, July 12, 1971, *FRUS, 1969–1976, Vol. XLI, Western Europe, NATO, 1969–1972*, doc. 69.

31. Sorley, "Goodpaster," 137.

32. Susan Goodpaster Sullivan, interview with author, June 27, 2010.

33. Nixon White House Tapes, especially 763-12 and 857-5 (part b), Nixon Library; Sorley, "Goodpaster," 137.

34. Ibid.

35. Ibid.

36. Ibid.

37. SNIE 35/36, October 6, 1973, *FRUS, 1969–1976, Vol. XXV, Arab-Israeli Crisis and War, 1973*, doc. 98.

38. Telecon Moorer and Goodpaster, October 15, 1973, *FRUS, 1969–1976, Vol. XXV, Arab-Israeli Crisis and War, 1973*, doc.185.

39. Goodpaster remarks to the Council on Foreign Relations, New York, November 14, 1973, NDU Library, Group 28. Also see Goodpaster as quoted by Sorley in *Generals in International Politics*, 140–41.

40. Memo For Record, CJCS Memo, NSC/JCS Meetings, October 24–25, 1973, *FRUS, 1969–1976, Vol. XXV, Arab-Israeli Crisis and War, 1973*, doc. 269.

41. Ibid.

42. Goodpaster, Sorley interview, December 3, 1985, Washington, DC.

43. Ibid.

44. Ibid.

45. Goodpaster in meeting with President Nixon, Oval Office, February 15, 1973, White House Tape 857-5 (part b), www.nixonlibrary.gov.

46. Minutes of NSC Review Group Meeting, June 16, 1970, *FRUS, 1969–1976, Vol. XLI, Western Europe, NATO, 1969–1972*, doc. 42.

47. Ibid.

48. Minutes of Verification Panel Meeting, August 9, 1973, *FRUS, 1969–1976, Vol. XXXV, National Security Policy, 1973–1976*, doc. 22.

49. Goodpaster, Mandel interviews, February 12, 2004, tape 22.

50. Ibid., tape 23. For a detailed analysis of the consequences of congressional actions on Vietnam, see Hunt, *Losing Vietnam*, 3, 35, 101, 111, 126, 164, 167, 170, 253, 276, 298.

51. Susan Goodpaster Sullivan, phone interviews with author, June 27, 2010, March 25, 2013.

52. Minutes of Meeting of Washington Special Action Group, August 14, 1974, *FRUS, 1973–1976, Vol. XXX, Greece; Cyprus; Turkey, 1973–1976*, doc. 131.

53. Goodpaster, Sorley interview, December 3, 1985, Washington, DC.

54. Agnew, *Go Quietly . . . or Else*, 190.

55. Charles W. Dyke, Lt. General, USA (ret.), formerly Executive Assistant to the Secretary of the Army during the Nixon transition, interview with author, February 25, 2014, Washington, DC. Haig was replaced as White House chief of staff by Donald Rumsfeld. Haig served as secretary of state for seventeen months under President Reagan in 1981–1982 and ran for president in the 1988 Republican Party primaries.

56. Ibid.

57. General Abrams letter to Goodpaster, September 30, 1973, Goodpaster Papers, box 16, NDU Library.

58. Goodpaster, Mandel interviews, tape 23 and Scowcroft, interview by author, June 10, 2010, Washington, DC.

59. Goodpaster, Mandel interviews, tape 23.

60. Ibid. Galvin (military assistant to SACEUR in 1974), in undated memo to Sorley. Goodpaster developed two hernias as a result of airborne training rather late in his life. He underwent the surgery to correct both of these problems before he retired.

61. Goodpaster, Mandel interviews, tape 24.

62. Ibid.

63. Goodpaster remarks to Seventh Army Commander's Conference, Heidelberg, Germany, December 11, 1969, in Goodpaster Papers, Group 30, NDU Library.

64. Goodpaster remarks to Ends of the Earth Club, London, May 21, 1970, Goodpaster Papers, box 23, NDU Library,

65. Goodpaster in Sorley interview, December 3, 1985, Washington, DC.

66. Admiral James Holloway, former chief of Naval Operations, interview with author, January 31, 2014.

III

Collaborative Leadership

By age fifty-nine, Goodpaster had attained one of the two highest positions imaginable for an Army officer, command of NATO forces in Europe (the other being chief of staff of the Army). Also, by this point, Goodpaster had established a broad international network of influential friends and acquaintances—a network that would prove instrumental in bringing power to ideas and ideas to power.

More importantly, Goodpaster had developed an approach for dealing with national security problems based on his experience with what worked well and poorly. His approach was collaborative—a style that reflected a strong capacity to engage effectively the necessary people to work in concert to achieve the best possible outcomes. In particular, Goodpaster's collaborative leadership exemplified exercising influence through reason.

Using this method and network, Goodpaster continued to be active in national security affairs for another three decades. The balance of this book outlines the nature and scope of his work during his final three decades.

These times also brought fundamental changes in the security environment. The Cold War ended with the collapse of the Soviet Union. The Berlin Wall fell, and Germany was united. This changing environment called for rethinking national security policies, and Goodpaster continued to be an important player.

His story over these next thirty years included many achievements that, taken together, "changed the face and the soul of our country," as President Reagan noted.[1]

NOTE

1. Ronald Reagan, in commendation awarding the Presidential Medal of Freedom, March 26, 1984, White House website.

Chapter Fourteen

Woodrow Wilson Center (1974–1977)

Soon after he retired on December 17, 1974, Goodpaster met again with General Norstad, who suggested that Goodpaster not make any commitments until he had talked to officials at the Woodrow Wilson International Center for Scholars in Washington, DC.

The director of the center, Dr. James Billington, knew of Goodpaster by reputation and had met him on several occasions. Billington invited him to join the center with the expectation that Goodpaster would produce a book. The collegial atmosphere of the center, with frequent, informal discussions among the international scholars, would be mutually beneficial. Goodpaster would have an opportunity to reflect and write as well as make valuable contributions to discussions at the center.[1]

Goodpaster accepted the invitation and became a senior fellow at the Woodrow Wilson Center in 1975. He enjoyed discussions with others at the center and began writing his book, a process he completed in about eighteen months.

VIETNAM

On April 30, 1975, Saigon fell. After holding on for nearly two years following the withdrawal of U.S. forces, South Vietnam was unable to sustain the effort without American funds, logistics, communications, intelligence, and critical air support, especially since North Vietnam was receiving increased support from its patrons. Goodpaster attributed the downfall mainly to the 1973 act of Congress denying further American support to South Vietnam despite promises of support by U.S. officials at the highest levels.[2]

General Goodpaster maintained that an outcome similar to that achieved in South Korea had been well within the military capabilities of the United

States and South Vietnam, but the Case-Church Amendment sealed the fate of South Vietnam. The withdrawal of U.S. support also called into question the reliability of the United States in supporting other U.S. allies. As a result, the fall of South Vietnam was a major setback for the United States in the Cold War. The Vietnam tragedy set the scene for Goodpaster's reflections on his thirty-five years of service.[3]

FOR THE COMMON DEFENSE

General Goodpaster's choice for the title of his book, *For the Common Defense,* was not surprising. In his early days as a debater in high school and college, Goodpaster learned to ground his analyses and arguments in terms of first principles and the most authoritative sources. In the case of his book, the title was taken from the preamble to the Constitution, which succinctly defines the purpose of United States armed forces—the common defense of the people.

Goodpaster framed the book as:

> an opportunity to review, reappraise and reshape contributions of American military power to national security after the tumult of the Vietnam war years. . . . [This is] not only an opportunity, but an obligation . . . evolving problems abroad with adversaries, allies and the uncommitted are inexorably bringing past solutions into question . . . recent years set America at cross-purposes with ourselves . . . left much of the American public and its leaders unconvinced and uneasy about the essentiality, adequacy, and appropriateness of security policies and defense programs.[4]

In the preface, Goodpaster established his framework for strategic thinking as the process of "correlating power and purpose." Matching appropriate power with clearly defined purpose, according to Goodpaster, began with analysis of a threat in terms of the extent of risk to specific national values and national interests that require protection.

Much of Goodpaster's later writing reflected this analytic point of departure focusing on national interests. The term "national interest," however, had been invoked too often to justify action without carefully considering the relative importance of the threat and, as he put it, understanding the extent to which the American people really care and are willing to make the sacrifices required. The sense of sacrifice, however, was narrowed with the end of the draft during the Vietnam War, and the concomitant advent of the all-volunteer Army changed fundamentally the sense of national sacrifice associated with military intervention.

Goodpaster realized that the United States could not and should not try to take on all the security challenges facing the nation. Thus, before undertaking a military intervention, Goodpaster proposed determining how much impact the United States would likely have on the situation within the resource limits the American people were likely to make and sustain. Vietnam, he noted, did not meet that test. Security policies must keep costs commensurate with expected benefits. Goodpaster also believed analysis should address the likely consequences if the United States did not act. [5]

In either case, intervention or not, outcomes are uncertain. They depend to a significant degree on the skill with which political and military leaders use resources. Goodpaster thought that the post–World War II American record in this respect had been disappointing. He acknowledged that adversaries had been skillful in targeting American vulnerabilities. Implicitly, he suggested that the United States had not understood adversaries as well as some of them had understood us. [6]

His book did not advocate fundamental changes in the existing framework of security policies—a combination of defense, deterrence, and détente. It did, however, point out the critical importance of adapting to the rapidly changing security environment, especially in terms of technological change. [7]

No one of the existing policies alone was sufficient in providing adequate or economical security, Goodpaster wrote, but all were necessary for an effective and sensible security posture. Furthermore, the changing security environment required regular reassessments of security policies. Reassessments also disclosed instances where policies were somewhat incompatible, such as anti-ballistic missile defense and détente. [8]

From his experience as SACEUR, Goodpaster also provided interesting observations on the connections between defense and deterrence. He cited a Soviet scholar who commented in 1969 that there had been no day in the last twenty years in which NATO could have defended itself successfully. While perhaps true, Goodpaster conceded, that observation also made the point that deterrence must have safeguarded the peace in Europe. Soviet leaders must have concluded that they could not have attacked NATO successfully. Thus, despite all the shortfalls and weaknesses in NATO's defense posture, the Soviets "saw costs, risks, and uncertainties that made any notion of attack unappealing." [9]

NATO's military posture, however, did not deter Soviet military intervention in Hungary in 1956 and Czechoslovakia in 1968. Had those satellite regimes fallen, the Soviet military buffer in Eastern Europe would have been lost, and multiparty systems could have ultimately undermined the Soviet regime.

These cases point out how the lack of more robust military capabilities helped to avoid risky military interventions. That was consistent with President Eisenhower's willingness to forego massive military buildups in favor of nuclear deterrence, a lesson still fresh in Goodpaster's mind.

Goodpaster nevertheless acknowledged the defense planners' dilemma of never knowing just how much defense spending was enough. Again, his White House experience made him very sensitive to the tendency among the military services to consistently seek more funding. [10]

Goodpaster was impressed with President Nixon's 1970 "New Strategy for Peace" because it provided a comprehensive and systematic framework for determining force posture. The approach was not implemented, however, mainly because of Pentagon opposition. Goodpaster noted that the NSC's Defense Program Review Committee was ideally suited to correlate purpose and power, with the president closely involved. The Pentagon, however, viewed it as an attempt to usurp internal management functions. [11]

In one of his conclusions, Goodpaster noted that much remains to be done to "assure that military power is in fact the instrument or agent of policy— and not its determinant, or an independent force in itself." His conclusion is reminiscent of Eisenhower's warning about the dangers posed by the military-industrial complex. Throughout the book, the strong influence of Eisenhower's thinking and their common experiences are evident.

Reviews of the book were generally positive. Some noted that much of what Goodpaster pointed out was obvious, implying that they expected something more profound from someone with such an esteemed reputation. [12]

While Goodpaster was at the Wilson Center, he also was engaged in several other efforts. For example, Vice President Nelson Rockefeller named him as his staff assistant on the Commission on the Organization of Government for the Conduct of Foreign Policy, also known as the Murphy Commission. This was a three-year, $3 million study initiated by Congress. Goodpaster reported on how the Eisenhower White House engaged with Congress in conducting foreign affairs. In particular, Goodpaster emphasized that because the NSC staff functioned as advisors without operational responsibility, they should not appear before Congress. Instead, that role was more appropriate for the principal NSC members. [13]

GOODPASTER AT THE WOODROW WILSON CENTER

Dr. Billington was pleased with Goodpaster's contributions to the center. "I cannot stress enough what a great person of principle he was," he said, recalling their association several years later. "Not because of any one thing, but a unique combination of extraordinary integrity, unshakable courage, and extraordinary modesty." Billington cited Eisenhower referring to Goodpaster as the "gold standard." [14]

Several years later, when Billington visited Goodpaster at West Point during his tenure as superintendent, Billington noticed the exceptionally high regard the cadets had for Goodpaster. This was during controversial times following the cheating scandal and the introduction of women. Yet Billington commented that he could not imagine any other college president held in such high regard in the 1970s.[15]

In reflecting on the tragedy of Vietnam, Goodpaster, like his mentors, avoided placing blame for mistakes. Instead, he thought carefully about the lessons to be learned. His conclusion was the simple but profound idea that the essence of national security affairs was the ongoing process of correlating purpose and power. In this process, no amount of foreign military power could compensate for weak local government. Foreign military power could only provide a temporary measure of security. Aspiring to greater purposes required sustained political and economic investment to build strong, and hopefully good, local government. Eisenhower's intervention in Lebanon was an example of a purpose with limited military security compared to the broader purposes of the Marshall Plan in Europe and the development of viable governments in Korea and Taiwan.

Unfortunately, Goodpaster's lessons were not well learned. In discussing the situation prior to the 2003 Iraq war with the author, Goodpaster was concerned that the challenge had not been well thought through. He noted that the United States was a big country and could afford to make mistakes, but in this case, he thought we may be pressing our luck. Regime change was likely to be more difficult than simply replacing Saddam Hussein with Iraqi exiles. Winning the peace would require power sharing among the Sunni, Shia, and Kurdish communities; managing reinvestment in, and proceeds from, the oil sector; as well as orchestrating troubled relations with Iran, Syria, and Turkey—a daunting agenda for any new government.[16]

THE CITADEL

Near the end of his time at the Wilson Center, Goodpaster was approached by General George Seignious with an invitation to come to The Citadel as a distinguished professor. Seignious was a friend who had followed Goodpaster in several assignments, and a person Goodpaster held in very high esteem. Now Seignious, also retired, was president of The Citadel, The Military College of South Carolina.[17]

The prospect appealed to both Goodpaster and Dossy. So, after finishing work at the Wilson Center, they moved to Charleston. They found it a lovely city, with wonderful people. Soon, Goodpaster was well ensconced in the work of The Citadel.

During the 1976 Thanksgiving holidays, Goodpaster got a call from the Chief of Staff of the Army, General Bernard Rogers, with whom he had served on the Joint Chiefs of Staff.[18] Rogers said that he and the Vice Chief of Staff, General Walter T. "Dutch" Kerwin, had been talking about what to do about West Point because the superintendent was leaving after exposure of a large-scale cheating scandal. Rogers asked Goodpaster what he thought about calling a retired officer back to active duty for the job. Goodpaster told him he thought that might be a good idea. Then Rogers said, "If we ask you to come back at the grade of three star-general, would you consider it?" Goodpaster replied "My response is immediate and affirmative." Rogers interjected, "But you haven't asked your wife." Goodpaster said, "I don't have to ask her. I know what she would say." Rogers concluded by saying that the assignment was not final, but he and Kerwin were thinking along those lines. Goodpaster then told General Seignious that he might be leaving The Citadel. A month later, Goodpaster was told that the Army wanted him to take on the job of fixing West Point.[19]

NOTES

1. Goodpaster, Mandel interviews, February 12, 2004, tape 23.

2. Goodpaster, Mandel interviews, February 12, 2004, tape 20; Ellsworth Bunker, Oral History Interviews, LBJ Library; Sorley, *A Better War*, 358, 364, 373.

3. Goodpaster, concluding remarks at Symposium on National Defense into the 21st Century, February 1997, as recorded by Earl H. Tilford for the Strategic Studies Institute, June 6, 1997, 37, accessed on DTIC database.

4. Goodpaster, *For the Common Defense*, vii.

5. Ibid., 17, 18.

6. Ibid.

7. Ibid., 39.

8. Ibid., 53, 54.

9. Ibid., 62.

10. Ibid., 65.

11. Ibid., 152.

12. Reviews of *Common Defense* are in Goodpaster Papers, box 53, folder 16, Marshall Library;

13. Benjamin Welles, "Congress, Commissions and Cookie-Pushing," *Foreign Service Journal* (January 1976): 11.

14. Billington interview.

15. Ibid.

16. Goodpaster in conversations with the author, January 2003. Also see Policy Paper, "Wining the Peace: Managing a Successful Transition in Iraq," Atlantic Council and American University, January 2003.

17. Goodpaster, Mandel interviews, February 12, 2004, tape 23.

18. Colonel Rogers had been executive officer for the chairman, Joint Chiefs of Staff, 1962–1966, when Lieutenant General Goodpaster was assistant to the chairman, JCS, General Taylor, in 1962–1964, then for General Wheeler.

19. Goodpaster, Mandel interviews, tape 23. Date of phone call corrected by Susan Goodpaster Sullivan, who received the call, correspondence with author, November 30, 2013.

Chapter Fifteen

Superintendent, West Point (1977–1981)

THE CRISIS

In mid-1976, West Point was put in a deep crisis by the worst cheating scandal in the academy's nearly two hundred-year history. The institution was under increasing pressure from lawyers of accused cadets, parents, and members of Congress at a time when there was already significant anti-military sentiment following the Vietnam War. These feelings combined to embolden certain congressmen, who argued that West Point should be eliminated in favor of other, much less expensive, sources of commissioned officers.

The scandal was precipitated in the spring of 1976, when an instructor in the Department of Electrical Engineering noted, in grading take-home exams involving about eight hundred cadets, that a cadet had indicated that he had received help on a problem. The instructor reviewed other papers to see if the person providing the help had acknowledged giving help. In the course of his examination, the instructor found a disturbing similarity in answers. Eventually 152 cadets were found guilty of cheating.[1]

The cadets found guilty, except for those who resigned, were referred to representation by military lawyers before a hearing by a board of officers. These defense counsels petitioned the secretary of the Army, Martin Hoffman, for an investigation, alleging that officials at West Point were trying to limit the damage of the scandal when, in fact, the problem was much broader and included a pervasive web of uncoordinated honor violations ranging from toleration of cheating to bribing members of the Honor Committee.[2]

Secretary Hoffman initially declined to order such an investigation, but the superintendent, Lieutenant General Sidney Berry, on May 23, 1976, appointed an internal review panel to conduct a broad investigation. Time was critical because graduation was only a few weeks away and most of the Honor Committee would be graduating. On August 23, 1976, Hoffman announced that an outside special advisory panel, headed by Frank Borman, a West Point graduate, former astronaut (Apollo 8), and head of Eastern Air Lines, would similarly look into the problem. Hoffman also commissioned another report by Bland West, deputy general counsel for military and civilian affairs, and Hugh Clausen, chief judge of the United States Army Court of Military Review.[3]

The Borman Commission report concluded that cheating on the electrical engineering exam was widespread and indicative of pervasive attitudes that encouraged cadets to "beat the system." The commission also criticized the requirement for a unanimous vote to find a cadet guilty. There was evidence of at least one dishonest former Honor Committee member who "fixed boards."[4]

Bad news travels fast, particularly when fanned by lawyers who challenged the lack of specific statutory authorization for honor code procedures and outcomes. The Army, in particular the chief of staff, General Bernard Rogers, knew that something extraordinary was needed to deal with this serious challenge to West Point. Rogers turned to Goodpaster because of his exceptionally high and widely held esteem.

GOODPASTER TAKES COMMAND

On June 1, 1977, at age sixty-two, General Goodpaster was recalled to active duty to serve as superintendent of the United States Military Academy at West Point. For Goodpaster and Dossy, the call to be superintendent was a "reprise late in life." Earlier, in 1963, while commanding the 8th Infantry Division, he had been informed that he would succeed General Westmoreland as superintendent. Both he and Dossy were delighted with the prospect of returning to West Point. That assignment, however, was preempted by the Cuban Missile Crisis when General Maxwell Taylor called on Goodpaster to become his assistant on the Joint Staff.[5]

This time, before moving to West Point, Goodpaster wanted to ensure that there was full agreement on his mandate. To do this, he drew on a lesson he learned from General Eisenhower upon assuming command of NATO. Eisenhower asked President Truman to send him a letter expressing Eisenhower's authority over American forces so that there would be no doubt that Eisenhower had complete command authority over U.S. forces assigned by all three services. Now Goodpaster had a similar exchange of letters with the then secretary of the Army, Clifford Alexander. During the process, Alexander, a lawyer, asked General Rogers what was meant by giving Goodpaster broad authority to do the things he believed in—a broad, general mandate to take whatever action necessary to fix the system, not just address the specific cheating episode. Rogers replied that he didn't have to worry about that; he had full confidence in Goodpaster's judgment.[6]

Goodpaster also clarified with the Army leadership that his assignment was for an extended but indefinite period, so that any opposed to his changes could not merely wait him out. Goodpaster told Secretary Alexander and General Rogers that any time they wanted to do something different from what he believed, they should let him know and inform him who his successor would be so that the changeover could be done systematically.[7]

General Rogers offered to seek congressional approval to bring Goodpaster back on active duty as a four-star general to serve in a three-star position. Goodpaster replied that that would not be necessary, as he did not want to create a precedent and would accept a reduction in grade.[8]

Before moving to West Point, Goodpaster began preparing for the challenge by meeting with the outside West Point Study Group commissioned by General Rogers to conduct a comprehensive study of all aspects of cadet life that may have contributed to the cheating problem and provide recommendations. The study group was co-chaired by three brigadier generals: Jack Merritt, Hillman Dickinson, and Jack MacMull. The broad approach of the study group coincided with Goodpaster's thinking. In addition, the brief study by the Borman Commission also helped inform Goodpaster of the problems he was facing.

Goodpaster further consulted with his many friends in the academic community. Some of these scholars had become administrators, including college presidents, such as Bill Bowen, the president of Princeton. Dr. Bowen shared his experiences in leading an academic institution with Goodpaster. While Princeton was obviously different from West Point, they shared many similar challenges in dealing with students, faculty, and alumni.[9]

General Goodpaster assumed responsibility for leading West Point on June 13, 1977. At the change-of-command ceremony, Goodpaster noted in his brief remarks that the purpose of West Point was to provide cadets with a high quality intellectual, military, physical, and ethical experience. That would be the central goal guiding their collective efforts. The challenges would be faced with resolution, integrity, human understanding, and "not the least, with good humor and good will. Our common standard will be excellence. Our common inspiration will be duty, honor and country."[10]

The Goodpasters quickly settled into Quarters #100, the superintendent's quarters on the Plain at West Point. The new superintendent found a few skeptics at the academy who doubted that a cheating scandal on that scale could have occurred. However, most of the faculty, staff and cadets, Goodpaster noted, "knew something was wrong, but didn't know how to get a handle on it." Goodpaster would not participate in minimizing the problem. He insisted, "Let's agree that it did occur and it wasn't 200. It was probably

400 and there may have been 800. And that's the challenge we have and that's what we're going to set out to correct." Goodpaster was, in part, referring to those who were aware of cheating but tolerated it, also a violation of the Honor Code.[11]

SCOPE AND NATURE OF THE PROBLEM

West Point felt like "Grimsville" to Goodpaster. Cadets, staff, and faculty were caught up in a dismal situation. They knew the situation was dire and somebody had to be at fault. They were angry and, without a clear target to blame; they were upset with just about everybody.[12]

Goodpaster soon became convinced that institutional failure had contributed to the massive honor violation. It was not just a problem of a few bad apples spoiling the bunch. West Point, too, had failed to meet its responsibilities. He noted that much of the West Point community, including faculty, staff, and cadets, had lost sight of the purpose of the academy. They did not have a clear identification with the mission and, as a result, were pursuing their own interests at the expense of more important parts of the West Point experience.[13]

Unhealthy interpersonal competition was at the core of the problem. Competition was always an important aspect of life at West Point, but Goodpaster found it had become focused on promoting oneself at the expense of others rather than competing within oneself for improvement. In his view, West Point, and probably the Army in general, had taken the wrong path; "They were very unwisely over-emphasizing interpersonal competition." He noted that competition may be healthy or unhealthy and that the role of senior leadership is to decide where the dividing line begins to be crossed and the system gets corrupted.[14]

Similarly, in his view, the plebe system had been abused. The system was inherently stressful, requiring plebes to learn how to take orders, work hard, and pay attention to details. Too many upper classmen lost sight of West Point's purposes and had exercised authority in senseless and sometimes vicious ways, thus abusing their authority.

The combination of failure to identify with the institutional mission and unhealthy interpersonal competition was manifested in poor attitudes among the cadets. Particularly counterproductive was a widespread sense of "we-they," pitting cadets against each other and against the institution.

Goodpaster's problem was not limited to the West Point community. Congress also had ideas about how West Point should be managed, and there continued to be some members interested in eliminating the academy altogether because of its higher costs compared to the Reserve Officers Training Corps (ROTC) and Officers Candidate Schools (OCS). Others advocated replacing West Point with a single-year postgraduate training program like Britain's Sandhurst. [15]

GOODPASTER'S APPROACH

Goodpaster was well aware of how much society had changed since his cadet years. Among the many changes, he noted in particular that individualism was more highly valued. He understood that his challenge was not simply a matter of strengthening old practices, but rather that changes must center on the youth of the day. [16]

Goodpaster's first step was to gain consensus on the purpose of West Point. After convening several meetings and holding many individual discussions throughout the West Point community, he settled on this formulation:

> West Point exists to provide cadets with an academic, military, physical and moral-ethical experience of such high quality that it can serve as a bedrock on which they, as future military leaders, will develop the capability, in due time, to take responsibility for the security and well-being of our country. [17]

Given this common understanding of the purpose, a series of committees was established to determine how best to provide an integrated experience incorporating each of the four disciplines: academic, military, physical, and ethical. Other committees were added to deal with more specific concerns, such as cadet life. Each committee had representatives from all relevant parts of the West Point community, including faculty, staff, athletic teams, chaplains, legal advisors, and cadets from all four classes. Goodpaster reminded the committees that their work must center on the cadets; they were the final product by which the contributions of West Point would be measured in meeting the needs of the Army and the nation.

With that guidance in mind, the entire West Point team went to work. Goodpaster made it clear from the start that changes were not going to be imposed from the top. He charged his subordinates to generate proposed actions and, with his approval, put them into effect. Recalling his experience working for General Marshall, he did not attempt to dictate the answers to problems. Instead, he put talented people to work, considered carefully what they recommended, and discussed ideas in a collegial way. [18]

Goodpaster also established a policy board to address broad policy issues, much as the National Security Council had functioned under President Eisenhower. In this forum, Goodpaster wanted to draw on the views of representatives from all parts of the West Point community having stakes in the issue. While this decision created an influential, broad-based group that rivaled the powerful Academic Board and opened new opportunities for change, it also created problems because the delineation of authority was not clear between the two boards. With overlapping jurisdiction, sometimes it was not clear which board should have primary responsibility for making recommendations for reform.

Goodpaster also was concerned that he not become distracted by the many responsibilities associated with day-to-day operations and running the post that also fell under the superintendent, so he sought and was granted authority to create the position of deputy superintendent. As a result, a brigadier general, first Charles Bagnal, then Arthur Brown, was assigned to manage the West Point facilities and garrison. This freed Goodpaster to concentrate fully on the cadet experience.[19]

Much of the approach was organized around the central issue of cadet time. Each of the four pillars, and their many subcomponent programs, competed for scheduling. There was a sense that cadets were overscheduled but underworked. And, as they were given more choices, cadets would often opt for things they enjoyed over more difficult work that they needed.

CHANGING AN INSTITUTION

Soon after Goodpaster took charge, the West Point Study Group completed its report and submitted it to the Army chief of staff. General Rogers called Goodpaster and said, "I've got the report now; what do I do with it?" Goodpaster responded, "Bernie, send it to me with a one-sentence [note] that I should take such action on it as I deem appropriate." And that's what Rogers did.[20]

Goodpaster incorporated the study group report and recommendations into a broad-based process of instituting change. More than 150 recommendations were reviewed by the committees at West Point, and nearly all were adopted. These reforms resulted in strengthening the authority of the superintendent, mainly at the expense of the Academic Board, which had become the most powerful component of the institution.[21]

More importantly, the committees and the West Point community increasingly identified with the overall purpose of the academy. They began to think like a team with a common goal. Goodpaster began to notice a change in the climate at West Point, turning away from an us-versus-them environment to one of "we're all in this together." He found that development very encouraging but was careful not to delude himself by noticing mainly positive indicators.

Academics

Goodpaster found the general attitude of cadets toward academic study unsatisfactory. They did not take their studies seriously; many were satisfied to get by with a minimum effort. One indicator of the problem was that many cadets who ranked high in academic standing had declined to wear stars on the collar of their uniform, traditionally signifying outstanding academic achievement. Peer pressure created an atmosphere in which it was not cool to be a scholar. [22]

He held the Academic Board primarily responsible. He found the board to be experienced, highly qualified, and deeply dedicated. However, some of the "old bulls" had become accustomed to being in complete control and found it difficult to accept change, particularly if the impetus came from those outside their departments. [23]

In opening up the process, Goodpaster brought in junior faculty and outsiders to discuss a broad range of academic issues, including cadet attitudes toward their studies. Goodpaster controlled the agenda, but believed the Academic Board's advice should essentially govern in academic matters. Academic freedom, he noted, was an important principle at first-rate institutions. [24]

The transformation process was not easy. The Academic Board had gained broad power over the years and had lost focus on the overall development of the cadet. As a result, its influence needed to be trimmed and refocused. Part of this effort involved greater participation in academic affairs by the commandant, who was responsible for military training, as well as the chief of staff and the deputy superintendent. [25]

In reviewing the curriculum, Goodpaster noted that there was a void in terms of preparing cadets for service in high levels of government. He recommended a course on American institutions, which was adopted. Not surprisingly, his direct intervention in the curriculum met with resistance and came at the cost of reducing the military history course from two semesters to one. The new American institutions course was interdisciplinary with responsibilities for teaching shared among three departments: Behavioral Sciences, Social Sciences, and History. That arrangement, combined with resentment over Goodpaster's personal intervention, eventually undermined the course. With no single department as an advocate, the course was later dropped. [26]

The major challenge for the curriculum was to get the right balance between math, science, and engineering versus the humanities. The Academic Board struggled with pedagogy and the mix of courses, determining that greater depth could be achieved with fewer courses while still retaining the broad balance that had served graduates well over the years. Class periods were reduced in length and, as noted, military history was reduced from a two- to a one-semester course. Foreign language courses also were reduced, while math and science courses were strengthened.

The new curriculum reduced the number of courses from forty-eight to forty and reduced the load from six courses each semester to five. It also reduced the number of required courses and increased the number of electives. Cadets were allowed to choose different areas of concentration for their studies, which eventually became different majors. Cadets with exceptionally heavy loads were allowed to defer one course until the summer. The semester break was shifted earlier, before Christmas, and a midyear graduation was added for a small number of cadets. [27]

Goodpaster believed that he should not personally intervene in these deliberations. He understood that the power of his suggestions, as noted in the American institutions course, was difficult to resist. In most cases, he kept an open mind. As long as the issues were fully vetted, he accepted the advice of his dean and the Academic Board. During Goodpaster's tenure, the Department of Behavioral Sciences and Leadership was established. The new department took over responsibility for courses on leadership that had been previously part of military training under the commandant. [28]

Soon after his first year at the academy, Goodpaster was informed that President Carter wanted to see him about heading up the Arms Control and Disarmament Agency (ACDA). Goodpaster met with Carter and did something that he had never done before or after: he refused a presidential request. Goodpaster told Carter that he really did not think that was something he should do because the job was incomplete at West Point and cadets would be shocked by his departure. If the president would excuse him, he would like to continue at West Point. Goodpaster recommended General George Seignious for the position as ACDA director. President Carter, a Naval Academy graduate, understood the importance of Goodpaster's role at West Point and appointed General Seignious to the job. [29]

Back at West Point, Goodpaster was still engaged in efforts to achieve the right balance between science and the humanities. It was part of a long-standing debate over the West Point curriculum that involved numerous internal and external review panels. Traditionally, the curriculum emphasized thinking in terms of engineering. Leading colleges in science and engineering required a heavy load of these courses. On the other hand, most of the panels argued for more courses in the humanities. The West Point Study Group even got feedback from Army commanders in the field about the quality of thinking of recent graduates, suggesting that West Point's emphasis on mathematics fostered mental rigidity in a chaotic world filled with problems for which there were no precise solutions. [30]

During this period, Goodpaster was called by Admiral Hyman Rickover, the father of the nuclear-powered Navy who, with more than fifty-five years of service, was still on active duty and counted President Carter as one of his students. In addition to his interest in the nuclear Navy, Rickover had a longstanding concern about education. He told Goodpaster that he had been talking to President Carter about the need for the service academies to focus more on math, science, and engineering. By this point, Rickover was aware of the trend at West Point to add more social science courses to the curriculum, a trend with which he obviously disagreed.[31]

Goodpaster replied to Rickover that, while it was important to provide a solid foundation in math, science, and engineering, it was also important to equip students well to understand and deal with human beings. Rickover dismissed his remarks, but Goodpaster persisted, arguing that leadership is very important to West Point; cadets must learn how to lead and work well with others. Rickover disagreed, maintaining that studies should concentrate on science and engineering. Goodpaster told Rickover, "Admiral, I want you to know that we're not planning to do it that way here." Rickover threatened, "Well, I talked to the President about it." Goodpaster retorted, "Well, if you talk to him further, you'll understand how we feel about it."[32]

A few weeks later, Rickover called Goodpaster and asked whether he had thought about the issue any more. Goodpaster replied that, even with further thought, he had arrived at the same conclusion: balance was necessary in the curriculum. "We think we have the balance about right and that's what we'll continue to do." That was the last he heard from Rickover. Goodpaster refused to be swayed by Rickover; Goodpaster was convinced of the need to provide cadets with both what he called "technological literacy" and a good understanding of human nature.[33]

Goodpaster also wanted to teach while he was superintendent. Initially he presented classes on security affairs, including "Strategy, Soldiers and Statesmen." He enjoyed teaching very much, but quickly found that his schedule did not permit him to prepare and teach a course in the manner that it should be presented. He did, however, continue to drop in on classes and join in discussions.[34]

Despite the many demands on his time, Goodpaster was careful to meet regularly with congressmen and discuss their concerns about West Point. These efforts were successful in forestalling initiatives to drastically restructure the academy or close it completely.

Military

Goodpaster acknowledged important differences between military training and academic education. Nevertheless, he viewed the two processes as complementary. The academic approach emphasized the pursuit of knowledge through open inquiry and academic freedom, whereas the military approach existed within a structure that emphasized a sense of mission. In both cases, however, individuals had to think for themselves and find solutions to complex problems.[35]

Because of the unique military context, individuals had to develop competence in decision making under conditions of great physical and mental stress. They needed to understand their own behavior and the implications of their leadership in taking responsibility for those they led. Military training at West Point must put "Iron in their soul," according to Goodpaster.

Thus, Goodpaster believed that building a sense of responsibility was a fundamental requirement of military training. As Eisenhower had pointed out to him, the traditional distinction made between commanders and staff officers missed the central point: the main issue was how one handled responsibility. One must learn to perform assignments in a responsible way, not by merely going through the mechanics. Good officers excel in both staff and command positions.

The cadet chain of command was part of this process of learning to take responsibility for others, but it had become corrupted. Selection for leadership positions was based in part on a peer-review process that factored into class standing in a "General Order of Merit" that also included academic and physical performance. The General Order of Merit determined the order in which cadets selected their branch of service and their relative order of consideration for promotion in the Army after graduation.

After detailed study, the committees recommended and Goodpaster approved changes in the General Order of Merit, reducing the role of peer reviews and using a behavior-based rating scheme. The system had been corrupted by cadets who, in some cases, purposely gave low ratings to their peers who were trying to do the right thing, creating a kind of negative peer pressure. Additionally, the system distracted cadets from the goal of education.[36]

Goodpaster also found that the plebe/fourth class system had often been abused by some upper class cadets in subjecting plebes to nonsensical hazing. The system, in Goodpaster's view, was intended to teach cadets about leadership by first requiring them to follow orders so that they would know what it is like to be on the lowest end of a chain of command. Over the course of their first year, plebes should have evolved from the tightly administered discipline experienced in the first few months of Beast Barracks to more self-discipline. Instead, Goodpaster found a tendency for some upper classmen to mistake harsh methods for higher standards.[37]

In reorienting the situation, Goodpaster emphasized positive leadership in which the upper class cadets (juniors and seniors) were responsible for motivating lower class cadets (freshmen and sophomores) in positive ways to do well. A key part of this process was learning how to handle authority well while still very young. Most people had not had this kind of experience in their teenage years. Goodpaster made clear to the commandant, the Tactical Department, and the cadets the responsibility that they all had for finding ways to build positive leadership.

Part of this effort included studies of stress and determining which sources of stress were necessary and healthy, such as time deadlines and high work standards, and which were nonessential and counterproductive. The positive leadership effort also changed the role of the tactical officers from mainly enforcing discipline and high standards to teaching of military heritage, standards of professional behavior, counseling, and sharing of their personal experiences as a junior officer in the Army. These changes led to further innovation and eventually became the Cadet Leader Development System instituted in 1986–1991 under Superintendent Dave Palmer.[38]

Goodpaster also had some problems with faculty members who thought the principle of academic freedom extended to second-guessing the decisions of the superintendent in the military area. Part of the problem seemed to come from military lawyers. He clarified the distinction between academic freedom, individual legal rights, and military authority at an Officers' Call of the West Point community. He pointed out that he was the commander, and he expected his decisions to be implemented. His decisions were legal and within the scope of his legal authority. He did not expect opposition or undercutting once decisions were made.

A major challenge was in breaking the counterculture and making the cadet chain of command responsible for the social organization of the corps. Peer pressure from some bad actors in many of the cadet companies was promoting unhealthy attitudes toward academics, ethics, and the chain of command. That had to be reversed and required considerable time and effort, but eventually it happened and proved to be a major step toward restoring high ethical standards at the academy.[39]

Physical

Physical training and athletics were also a central part of the West Point experience. The rigors of combat demanded high levels of physical stamina, and competitive sports were somewhat analogous to battle. Indeed, General Douglas MacArthur, West Point's superintendent from 1919 to 1922, institutionalized the key role of sports at West Point, noting, "Upon the fields of friendly strife are sown the seeds that, upon other fields, on other days, will bear the fruits of victory."[40]

The main issue for Goodpaster regarding physical training and athletics was the priority they should receive in terms of the demands on cadet time. He also had to deal with a football coach who was increasingly at odds with the institution as he tried to arrange for a contract extension.[41]

In both cases, the problems were studied in detail by representatives from all parts of the West Point community and consolidated into a concept paper on how physical training and intercollegiate sports should best fit into cadet life. This required some rethinking, particularly on the part of coaches who may have thought more in terms of winning at any cost. That was not the primary goal of the academy and when winning came into conflict with ethics or the best use of cadet time, it became a secondary consideration.

Football was part of the problem. Army football had a strong tradition. Teams in the 1940s and into the 1960s had achieved top national ranking, with several players named to All-American teams and even winning Heisman Trophies. But, as college football became a big business, Army found it increasingly difficult to recruit top-level players who could pass the entrance requirements and were willing to undergo the rigors of cadet life, including a demanding academic schedule and a requirement to serve several years in the Army after graduation, especially in times of war, which was increasingly the case.[42]

The choice was clear: football players would either be an integral part of the Corps, with all the duties and responsibilities that entailed, or be excused from many of the routine requirements. Goodpaster had played football and understood well the tradition and importance of Army football. He endorsed a schedule that included some of the best teams in the country because it gave Army players a chance to compete against the best. The same was true in other sports. But Goodpaster and the West Point community reached a consensus confirming that the pursuit of winning should not compromise the full West Point experience that shaped *all* graduates.

Part of this process involved affirming the success of several minor sports in competing at the national level, and also acknowledging the benefits of intramural sports. Changes involved bringing the admissions process into the open for critique by representatives from the entire West Point community. This helped satisfy concerns that the athletes who were sought by coaches were also able to meet the academy's academic and other standards.[43]

In implementing changes to the physical-training program, Goodpaster approved the selection of a new director of intercollegiate athletics (DIA) and a new football coach. The Athletic Board was also transformed into a more cohesive team rather than a collection of advocates for individual programs.

None of these changes were easy. The football coach did not leave without creating controversy. Alumni objected to selecting someone from outside the West Point community as the new DIA. But Goodpaster led the process by holding individuals and groups responsible and keeping their focus on the ultimate objective of producing leaders for the nation. The tradeoff of requiring football players to participate in the full West Point experience, however, meant that West Point would not likely have top-level teams. Goodpaster's choice frustrated many influential alumni, including senior Army leaders who were eager to see Goodpaster step down as soon as possible.[44]

Ethics

Goodpaster of course saw his top priority as restoring the honor system, and he acknowledged that this was his most difficult challenge. While difficult and never complete, he understood that honor was central to the role of the academy and to the nation. Goodpaster had ample experience in the White House and on the Joint Staff to understand the critical importance of military leaders telling the whole truth when providing advice.[45]

In taking responsibility for ethical and moral training at West Point, General Goodpaster was careful to exercise the kind of leadership that elicited willing and genuine responses from the cadets. He understood that one could not gain the desired commitment to honorable behavior by edict or fiat.[46]

Goodpaster approached ethical training as a process, beginning with the plebes on their first day and expanding their thinking and responsibilities about ethics and morals over the next four years. The initial focus was on what Goodpaster called the "simple negatives" that "a cadet does not lie, cheat, steal, or tolerate those who do." But, as he put it, "That's just the price of admission." Honorable behavior in word and deed involved much more taking of personal responsibility than just staying within the narrow regulations of the honor code; it involved carrying out the purpose of the institution. By instilling thinking along these lines, the honor system also complemented the notion of duty.[47]

As cadets become officers and rise to senior positions, Goodpaster believed, they need moral courage to stand up for what they know is right, even if it involves personal cost to them and their careers. So Goodpaster hoped to move the honor system beyond the "simple negatives," but he was to be largely frustrated. He looked into reinstituting absence cards posted in each room indicating whether each person not present was on an authorized absence, and the system of verbal "all rights" also indicating that a cadet was on authorized business. But these practices proved no longer feasible. Cadet privileges had become so extensive and were given unconditionally, so it was impossible to go back to a system that tied granting of privileges to the honor commitment.

Goodpaster believed that the goal of non-toleration had not made sufficient progress. He noted that, even after nearly four years of work on the honor system, cadets continued to try to find ways to close their eyes to honor violations by others. If there was any doubt in their mind as to whether somebody lied or cheated, they were reluctant to report it. Toleration remained the weakest area of the honor system. Nevertheless, it was consistently reaffirmed by cadet committees and outside panels as being essential to the process of ethical development. As former superintendent General Sidney Berry noted, non-toleration required each cadet to be an active participant in the honor system, and it inculcated in cadets the higher loyalties and keen sense of duty required by the profession of arms.[48]

The non-toleration of unethical behavior at West Point goes back a long way. Early efforts to train cadets to place loyalty to the mission and organization above their personal ties includes an 1820 battalion order that has since become known to all cadets:

But an officer on duty knows no one—to be partial is to dishonor both himself
and the object of his ill-advised favor. What will be thought of him who exacts
of his friends that which disgraces him? Look at him who winks at and over-
looks offenses in one, which he causes to be punished in another, and contrast
him with the inflexible soldier who does his duty faithfully, notwithstanding it
occasionally wars with his private feelings. The conduct of one will be vener-
ated and emulated, the other detested as a satire upon soldiership and honor.[49]

The non-toleration issue reflects the natural tension between preserving
personal relationships and subordinating them for a greater good. The easier
choice is always to not tell on your friends, but that is not the right choice at
West Point. And it is the kind of choice that cadets must be exposed to early
and often, because they will certainly face it during their careers in the Army.

Part of Goodpaster's approach to this problem was to shift the focus from
the individual to the behavior. Throughout his tenure, he tried to get the
cadets to change the wording of the honor code from "nor tolerate those who
do" to "nor tolerate such conduct in others." This would allow the superintendent more discretion in tolerating such conduct than the cadet honor committee. For example, the superintendent might find mitigating circumstances
such as lack of experience with the system on the part of a plebe or lack of
intent or impulsive action immediately corrected. Furthermore, by Army
regulation, the superintendent was required to take such factors into consideration in making a final determination about dismissing a cadet found guilty
of an honor violation by the Honor Committee.[50]

The cadets, however, insisted that they owned the honor code and there-
for wanted to exercise control. They would not agree to change the code
along the lines the superintendent suggested. Goodpaster decided it was more
important to retain cadet commitment than to impose change from above.

Nevertheless, in practice, mitigating factors were considered. In making
his final decisions on honor cases, Goodpaster would draw on input from the
Honor Committee regarding mitigating factors. Often individuals accused
would note that they did not intend to violate the code. For example, in cases
of plagiarism, they neglected to footnote work that was not their own because
of haste or oversight, although an objective observer could see it otherwise.[51]

Throughout his tenure, Goodpaster understood that the challenges of the
honor system were not amenable to being solved in any definitive sense.
There would always be more work to be done because cadets were young
and because the standards went far beyond prevailing general practices in
society.

In other efforts to move the honor system beyond the simple negatives,
Goodpaster instituted a broader honor concept that involved making good on
promises and standing up for what you believe in. He wanted to instill more
deeply the notion of being forthright in word and deed by planting the seeds

that would result in a lifelong process of growing integrity. While it gained some support, the expanded concept did not survive long after his tenure.

A report by the Honor Committee during Goodpaster's final year showed substantial improvement. In most areas, the honor system was judged to be in good health. Goodpaster was satisfied that no issues had been neglected. Some issues were not fully resolved, such as cadet borrowing, which could amount to stealing under certain circumstances. Plagiarism, too, continued to present problems because some cadets still felt that some faculty would use charges of plagiarism against cadets they did not like. Nevertheless, open discussions of the situation improved overall understanding. The biggest problem, however, continued to be toleration of unethical behavior.[52]

Priorities

Academic development, Goodpaster noted, was critically important. Yet military development was the reason for West Point's existence. In addition to being a necessary part of the profession of arms, physical development was essential to understanding the mind-body connection. And ethical development remained the cornerstone of the West Point experience.[53]

Given the importance of all four disciplines, academic, military, physical, and ethical, Goodpaster was constantly under pressure to establish priorities. When citing all four components in his frequent speeches and informal talks, he would often refer to the pillars in the same order; that implied a relative priority. While generally thought of in this order, Goodpaster noted that it was not useful to say academic development is number one because of the interrelated nature of the disciplines. Furthermore, when making specific decisions in which different disciplines came into conflict, as they inevitably did, Goodpaster was aware that the consequences of a particular decision might impact the core components of the other disciplines.[54]

While all four disciplines were important and complementary, they still competed for cadet time, facilities, funds, and support. In attempting to integrate competing priorities, Goodpaster commissioned a study led by Colonel Schilling that detailed the tasks and subtasks associated with each of the four areas of cadet development. When looking at the details, however, it became clear that no algorithm could be written to determine which task had priority over others under all circumstances. Instead, the study concluded, and Goodpaster agreed, that priorities were best determined by using detailed information, especially about linkages, to formulate a process of consultation and deliberation bringing together people of primary responsibility and concerned others to determine how best to handle specific competing demands.

The policies and decisions resulting from the many committees, discussions, studies, and concept papers were reflected in the updated *Regulations of the United States Military Academy* and subjected to review by the Department of the Army, Congress, the Board of Visitors and many others who watched closely how Goodpaster was handling the transformation.

WOMEN AT WEST POINT

The introduction of women at West Point began the year before Goodpaster arrived, and there were still tensions remaining. Lieutenant General Sidney Berry, the previous superintendent, had prepared thoroughly for the transition, but this dramatic change in the culture was met with resistance from some officers and cadets. When Goodpaster heard of misgivings about the changes, he held a meeting of the entire command and made it clear that he would make the introduction of women successful and would remove anyone who was not prepared to accept women at West Point. [55]

Goodpaster added that, indeed, this was the law of the land. Under the U.S. Constitution, women were entitled to the same rights as men. He argued that we had women in the Army, including female officers, therefore women should have equal opportunity for professional development. The United States had learned from experience that the "separate but equal" approach does not work. For all these reasons and more, the decision to integrate women at West Point had been made. There would be no going back.

Nevertheless, the path was not easy for the early female cadets and the Goodpaster administration. Every detail of cadet life had to be addressed to determine how best to handle the integration. For example, yearling (sophomore) summer training at Camp Buckner included living in Spartan barracks, so initially women were housed in separate barracks. But the men and women worked side by side in their integrated units, so it was subsequently decided that it was better for all for men and women in the same unit to live in the same barracks with partitions. [56]

DRUGS

General Goodpaster met with each class separately at the beginning of each academic year and shared his vision for the coming year. In these talks, he made it clear that "drugs and those who use them have no place at West Point." He also gave the same message to the staff and faculty. Early in his tenure, he received feedback that officers in the Law Department were discussing the issue with cadets and suggesting that, because society had become increasingly tolerant of drug use, it was unreasonable to enforce a no-drug policy at West Point. [57]

Goodpaster, however, was not open to changing his policy. Drug use was against the law, and he was obligated to uphold the law. Furthermore, he was aware that drug use by Army officers serving in sensitive positions, such as units with nuclear weapons, could endanger national security and could not be tolerated. He made it clear, repeatedly, that anybody who could not abide by the policy should not be serving under his command.

OPERATION TEAMWORK

Near the end of his second year, Goodpaster thought further steps were needed to get cadets to take more responsibility for their own development. Surveys indicated that cadet attitudes continued to reflect a sense of "we and they," and that disturbed Goodpaster. So he organized "Operation Teamwork" with a series of groups: one under the superintendent, one under the deputy superintendent, one under the commandant and one under the dean. Each group would have representatives from all parts of the West Point community, including senior and junior faculty, cadets from each class, the Honor Committee, intercollegiate athletics, and other such areas.[58]

Each group examined all four core disciplines, academic, military, physical, and ethical, to determine which issues caused antagonism toward the system. These issues were then discussed in detail, and in most cases, this led to better understanding of why things were done in certain ways. And in some cases, changes were made to alleviate unnecessary annoyances. Once it became clear that this process was more than a forum for discussion and could produce real changes, the community began to function more as a team with a common mission, and cadet attitudes improved.

In several cases, the groups produced concept papers that identified specific needs and ways to achieve them. Committing them to writing made the ideas more precise, minds became more focused, and widespread debate was stimulated, resulting in much better understanding of important concepts.[59]

One of the concept papers addressed the notion of duty. One cadet observed that, although "duty" was part of the motto "Duty, Honor, Country," it was not well understood. The resulting concept paper was a good example of cadets, working with staff and faculty, taking responsibility and mastering a subject. In this case, they analyzed the progressive development of a sense of duty by taking on more personal responsibility and gaining a commitment to the mission.

The objective of duty was for individuals to find satisfaction in a job well done. This went against the trend in society toward more individualism, but cadets came to understand that selfishness also undermines the teamwork that is necessary for a successful Army. These and other concept papers, including one on honor, were provided to cadets in notebooks to add to their professional libraries.

One of the ways Goodpaster monitored the extent to which Operation Teamwork was improving cadet attitudes was through a series of informal social gatherings for all first classmen (seniors) that he and Dossy hosted at their quarters. These buffet dinners provided many opportunities for him to talk with nearly every member of the class on an informal basis, and he found that the concepts were indeed taking root. In such settings, Goodpaster noted changes in facial expressions and tone of voice that conveyed that cadets were much happier and less sullen than he had witnessed initially.[60]

Another approach Goodpaster used was to have the senior class prepare a State of the Corps report, providing another means of bringing concerns to the attention of the leadership. The first report was bitter, but it provided the kind of feedback Goodpaster wanted. After a large share of the "gripes" were dealt with, or at least explained to a reasonable degree of satisfaction, the next report reflected much less animosity toward the institution.

RETURN TO RETIREMENT

After four years of reform led by Goodpaster, General Edward "Shy" Meyer, chief of staff of the Army, decided that it was time to return leadership of West Point to the contemporary generation. Meyer sent General John Vessey, the vice–chief of staff, to West Point to discuss the transition with Goodpaster. Vessey had a high regard for Goodpaster but had some trepidation about the task because of the awkward manner of Goodpaster's transition as SACEUR. Vessey was delighted, however, to find that Goodpaster was fully supportive of the transition. Goodpaster, as noted earlier, had indicated at the outset to General Rogers that he would not stay a day longer than he was needed, and he was true to his word.[61]

When the class of 1981 graduated in June after experiencing four transformative years under Goodpaster's leadership, they made him an honorary member of their class. The class made Dossy an honorary member as well.

After graduation, Goodpaster turned the responsibility for leading West Point over to Lieutenant General Willard Scott. In his brief remarks at the change-of-command ceremony, Goodpaster noted that West Point no longer felt as grim as when he had first arrived. Indeed, West Point had been put back on course. Nevertheless, in meeting privately with General Scott, Goodpaster cautioned that work remained. In particular, he noted that the honor system was always a work in progress and should be closely monitored.[62]

Indeed, the more than two hundred-year history of West Point can be divided into two parts: before 1976 and after 1976 because of the transformations in leadership and character development initiated by Goodpaster, according to a leading scholar on the subject.[63] His contributions changed the institution, the Army, and many others well beyond. Goodpaster emphasized that leadership was far more than just telling others what to do and using intimidation for compliance. Instead, he promoted positive leadership by drawing people into doing a job willingly and effectively. This did not involve a soft kind of leadership by which one tries to gain popularity, but a "hard, fair, but hard" leadership that set very high standards in the pursuit of the organization's mission. Goodpaster's leadership initiatives were developed further and institutionalized in the Cadet Leader Development System under Superintendent Dave Palmer in 1986–1991.

Similarly, Goodpaster's reforms in ethics and the honor code led to new approaches to character development at West Point. Goodpaster fostered progressive character development beyond the "simple negatives" of behaviors that were not condoned—lying, cheating, and stealing—to positive behavior that exemplified personal integrity. He planted seeds that he hoped would lead to growing personal integrity over a lifetime by both knowing what is right and having the courage to do what is right. Goodpaster understood that standards for integrity should increase commensurate with one's increasing responsibilities. Such standards cannot be mandated or easily learned from textbooks. They evolve mainly from examples, mentoring, and personal experience in trying situations that help individuals develop values of honor, ethics, and integrity.

In formulating these reforms, General Marshall served as an important model for Goodpaster. Marshall's selfless integrity was the gold standard. Goodpaster, in turn, set the standard for the next generation. His many contributions were acknowledged by the awarding in 1984 of the Presidential Medal of Freedom with the citation that described him accurately as a lifelong leader who changed the face of the nation.

NOTES

1. Jorgenson, "Duty, Honor, Country and Too Many Lawyers," *American Bar Association Journal* (April 1977): 564–67. Also see Betros, *Carved from Granite*, 56–62.
2. The Honor Code requires reporting any knowledge of lying, cheating or stealing, in addition to direct participation.
3. Jorgenson, "Duty, Honor, Country"; Sorley, *Honor Bright*, 107.
4. Ibid.
5. Goodpaster, Johnson interviews, March 7, 1988, Washington, DC.
6. Goodpaster, Mandel interviews, February 12, 2004, tape 23.
7. Ibid., tape 24.
8. General Jack Merritt, interview with author, May 11, 2013, Arlington, VA.
9. Goodpaster, Johnson interview, March 10, 1988, Washington, DC.
10. Goodpaster, remarks at change-of-command ceremony, June 13, 1977, West Point Library.
11. General Jack Merritt, interview with author, May 11, 2013.
12. Goodpaster, Mandel interviews, February 12, 2004, tape 23.
13. Goodpaster, Johnson interview, March 7, 1988.
14. Ibid.
15. Goodpaster, Mandel interviews, February 12, 2004, tape 24.
16. Goodpaster, Johnson interview, March 7, 1988.

17. Goodpaster interview, "Goodpaster + Two: West Point Today" *Army* (June 1979): 14–15.

18. Ibid.

19. Brown, Art, phone interview with author, March 2, 2012.

20. Goodpaster, Mandel interviews, February 12, 2004, tape 23.

21. Goodpaster, Johnson interview, March 7, 1988; Betros, *Carved from Granite*, 61.

22. Ibid.

23. Ibid.

24. Goodpaster, Mandel interviews, February 12, 2004, tape 24.

25. Goodpaster, Johnson interview, March 7, 1988.

26. Ibid.

27. Ibid.

28. Ibid.

29. Goodpaster, Mandel interviews, February 12, 2004, tape 24.

30. Betros, *Carved from Granite*, 148.

31. Goodpaster, Johnson interviews, March 10, 1988, Washington, DC.

32. Goodpaster, Mandel interviews, February 12, 2004, tape 24.

33. Ibid.

34. Ibid.

35. Ibid.

36. Goodpaster, Johnson interview, March 7, 1988.

37. Ibid.

38. Goodpaster interview in "Goodpaster + Two: West Point Today" *Army* (June 1979): 14–24.

39. Goodpaster, Mandel interviews, February 12, 2004, tape 24.

40. MacArthur, *Reminiscences*, 82. Similarly, the Duke of Wellington is alleged to have said that the battle of Waterloo was won on the playing fields of Eton.

41. Goodpaster, Johnson interview, March 7, 1988.

42. Ibid.

43. Ibid.

44. Ibid.

45. Goodpaster, Johnson interview, March 7, 1988.

46. Ibid.

47. Ibid.

48. Sorley, *Honor Bright,* 79, 107–20.

49. Major Worth, commandant of cadets (1820–1828), cited in Sorley, *Honor Bright,* 80.

50. Goodpaster, Johnson interview, March 7, 1988.

51. Ibid.

52. Ibid.

53. Goodpaster in letter to alumni, *Assembly*, June 1981.

54. Goodpaster, Johnson interview, March 7, 1988.

55. Goodpaster, Mandel interviews, tape 23.

56. Goodpaster, Johnson interviews, March 7 1988.

57. Ibid.

58. Ibid.

59. Ibid.

60. Ibid.

61. John Vessey, interview with author, January 27, 2014.

62. Goodpaster, Mandel interviews, tape 23.

63. Lance Betros, interview with author, May 22, 1976. Betros is the author of a history of West Point, *Carved from Granite: West Point Since 1902.*

Chapter Sixteen

Bringing Ideas to Power (1974–2005)

Goodpaster approached his second retirement with Norstad's advice in mind about dividing his time into roughly thirds. However, instead of working for remuneration, Goodpaster donated much of his time to pro bono work leading national security think tanks. Also, family and friends were very important to him. He attended weddings, graduations, baptisms, and birthdays of children, grandchildren, and a first great-grandchild. As his daughter Susan noted, "He had quite a record of caring."[1]

Another high priority for Goodpaster was continuing to inform debates on national security affairs. Although no longer in positions of authority, General Goodpaster would continue to address persistent national security problems and identify new opportunities. With a collaborative style of leadership, he organized small groups of influential experts to produce recommendations on important policy issues, bringing nonpartisan, collective wisdom to policy makers. In so doing, Goodpaster brought power to ideas and ideas to power. This chapter highlights examples of these ideas.

UNFINISHED BUSINESS: DEFENSE DEPARTMENT REFORM AND THE GOLDWATER NICHOLS ACT

The inability of the services to work together was a long-standing concern of General Goodpaster dating back at least to his tour in the White House. Even though the idea of unity of effort was a widely accepted principle of war, it was not widely practiced in the Pentagon because of the insularity and political power wielded by the individual services. Institutional interests usually trumped conceptual efforts when it came to the battle of the budget. The many efforts by Truman and Eisenhower to change the political-military system resulted in modest improvements, but serious shortcomings remained.

By the 1980s, Jim Locher, a congressional staffer, described the problem:

> The Pentagon badly needed reform. . . . Decision making had become so convoluted, fiefdoms so powerful and inbred, lines of authority so confused, and chains of command so entangled that the military hierarchy had repeatedly failed the nation. Third-rate powers and terrorists had humiliated America. Tens of thousands of troops died needlessly. Unprecedented levels of defense spending were not making the nation more secure. [2]

Goodpaster, having witnessed such problems firsthand for much of his career, agreed with the need for reform. In June 1983, he joined with former Secretary of Defense Melvin Laird as vice-chairmen of a project on reforming the Defense Department. The twenty-four-month effort was designed to provide recommendations to political leaders taking office after the next election, in November 1984. The project was based at the Center for Strategic and International Studies (CSIS) and involved a working group of seventy-five influential defense experts including Goodpaster. [3]

The comprehensive review resulted in a sixty-page report, "Toward a More Effective Defense," produced in February 1985, and a 250-page book with the same title containing the supporting papers was published later that year. The report made a strong case for the need to improve the effectiveness and efficiency of defense plans, acquisitions, and operations. [4]

The study and recommendations were endorsed by six of seven living former secretaries of defense—only Secretary Rumsfeld declined. Harold Brown, Clark Clifford, Melvin Laird, Robert McNamara, Elliot Richardson, and James Schlesinger noted in the foreword the "serious deficiencies in the organization and managerial procedures of the U.S. defense establishment." This level of bipartisan support opened the way for conservative members of Congress to join in the debate, despite strong objections from the Navy and other senior administration officials. [5]

The project coincided with Senator Barry Goldwater's decision to team with Senator Sam Nunn in a bipartisan investigation of defense reform. On December 5, 1984, General Goodpaster briefed Senator Goldwater on the CSIS study and found Goldwater quite receptive to the need for serious reform. Goldwater had maintained close ties with the military since 1930, when he was commissioned a second lieutenant in the Army reserves. After serving in World War II, he remained in the Arizona National Guard and was promoted to the rank of major general in the Air Force reserves. During the briefing by Goodpaster, Goldwater recognized many of the problems from his own experience. [6]

Two days after President Reagan's second inauguration, *The New York Times* featured a front-page article on the study, noting that a diverse group of experts, including influential members of Congress had agreed to push for a sweeping restructuring of American military operations. The article noted that the study concluded that "the current military organization is paralyzed by rivalries between the Army, Navy, Air Force and Marine Corps and is the underlying cause of bloated budgets, poor combat readiness and a lack of coordination in operations."[7]

General Goodpaster was called to testify at the Senate Armed Services Committee Goldwater-Nunn hearings on defense reform on December 4, 1985. As a former SACEUR and commander of U.S. European Command, Goodpaster underscored the fundamental weakness of the JCS system. Goodpaster, along with other former commanders-in-chief of combatant commands, made it clear that these commands were unified in name only. They lacked authority commensurate with their responsibilities to conduct joint operations.[8]

Despite strong opposition, particularly from Secretary of the Navy John Lehman, the Senate passed the Goldwater Defense Reorganization Act on May 7, 1986. The House passed an earlier reform bill in November and a version that went further than the Senate's, the Nichols Defense Reorganization Act, on August 5, 1986. The differences were reconciled in the Goldwater-Nichols Defense Reorganization Act, sent to the president on September 12, 1986. On October 1, 1986, President Reagan signed the bill into law, making the most dramatic changes in military structure and authority since the Eisenhower reforms of 1958.[9]

The Goldwater-Nichols Act made several important contributions to better integrating the capabilities of the separate services into more effective joint military operations. Goldwater-Nichols strengthened the previously ambiguous role of the secretary of defense by declaring, "The secretary has sole and ultimate power within the Department of Defense on any matter on which the secretary chooses to act." The act also established the JCS chairman as the principal military advisor, replacing the corporate-style JCS in which agreement was reached only after a slow process on "least-common-denominator documents that every chief would accept but few secretaries of defense or presidents found useful." In addition, the act established a vice-chairman of the JCS as the second ranking officer among the Joint Chiefs.[10]

Goldwater-Nichols strengthened the commanders-in-chief of the combatant commands. It established clear lines of authority and responsibility over subordinate service component commanders. The chain of command went from the president to the secretary of defense to the combatant commanders, with the JCS, including the chairman, deliberately removed.

While the Goldwater-Nichols Act held great promise for improving the effectiveness of U.S. joint military operations, Goodpaster knew that such sweeping changes would meet with resistance and be difficult to impose.

Therefore, he continued to take every opportunity to influence changes in the direction of more effective joint military operations.

COMMISSION ON INTEGRATED LONG-TERM STRATEGY (1986–1988)

The Commission on Integrated Long-Term Strategy (CILTS) was a dream team of distinguished strategic thinkers with a broad mandate to recommend changes in national security policies and practices. They had time, access, and resources to address the full range of security issues. The central challenge for national security officials was then, and remains, orchestrating the broad and diverse security efforts of the government in a constantly changing geopolitical and technological environment. Thus, the commission was aptly named, "Integrated" and "Long-Term."

The commission brought together more than a dozen of the nation's top strategic thinkers, co-chaired by Fred Iklé and Albert Wohlstetter, and including Andrew Goodpaster, Henry Kissinger, Zbigniew Brzezinski, Samuel Huntington, Joshua Lederberg, John Vessey, Anne Armstrong, William Clark, W. Graham Claytor Jr., James L. Holloway III, and Bernard Schriever. Working group chairs included Andrew Marshall, Henry Rowen, Charles Wolf, and Paul Gorman.[11]

The commission met monthly for about fifteen months, then met more frequently to finalize the main report, "Discriminate Deterrence," published in January 1988. Not surprisingly, the commission concluded that U.S. strategy was badly in need of greater integration to deal more effectively with the "never-ending trade-offs in defense planning." Major elements, including nuclear weapons, conventional forces, advanced technologies, arms control, and security assistance, were too often addressed independently. Further, the United States needed more credible responses to aggression, not a posture based mainly on indiscriminate destruction with nuclear weapons.[12]

Goodpaster played a leavening role in the discussions through balancing arguments by strong proponents of a particular view. One of the more contentious issues was the Strategic Defense Initiative, with some members arguing for substantial increases in funding and early deployment of a ballistic-missile defense system. Others, including Goodpaster, were more cautious and, in the final report, the commission recommended "evolutionary development" and a broader policy objective of gaining and maintaining advantages in military technology.[13]

Not surprisingly, most of the recommendations pointed out that the problems were more institutional than conceptual. Security assistance programs, for example, were micromanaged by Congress with administration requests repeatedly underfunded and up to 86 percent of military assistance earmarked by Congress for five countries without regard to national security strategies and priorities. Israel and Egypt received 62 percent of the military-assistance funds. Furthermore, Congress frequently blocked funding for certain countries to send military leaders to courses in the United States.[14]

In addition to meetings of the full commission, Goodpaster played an important role in guiding the commission's Third World Conflict working group. He suggested that their efforts be structured around three questions: (1) What are our objectives? (2) What concepts should guide us in pursuing these objectives? (3) What means shall we apply?[15]

Interestingly, at a time when much of the Cold War competition was focused on the Third World, the working group recommended that U.S. involvement in Third World conflicts be "seldom and minimal." Criteria for intervention should include determining if the United States could succeed rapidly with minimal cost and minimal damage.[16]

The commission also pointed out that crash programs and spikes in budgeting were notoriously inefficient, and, ultimately, defense spending had to be sustainable for the long haul without damaging the economy. This notion was reminiscent of President Eisenhower's strong efforts to reduce defense spending early in the Cold War.[17]

The immediate impact of the commission was modest. Secretary of Defense Casper Weinberger and Secretary of State George Schultz read it as endorsing most of their programs and priorities.[18] Nevertheless, it also served to cause the national security community to think in ways that were more integrated and longer term. All of the commission reports were read at the most senior levels because those principals could not afford to be surprised by the views of such a distinguished group, particularly if the recommendations bolstered the positions of the opposition, either political or institutional. Such concerns ensured that commission reports were carefully studied by the staffs of the principals to determine the likely consequences of commission recommendations for institutional areas of interest. The end of the Cold War, however, soon undermined the direct impact of the report, even though the basic critique of U.S. strategy remained valid.

The longer-term impact of the commission was in nudging a wide range of security debates in the right direction. As Goodpaster noted with the Solarium Project, such efforts of collective wisdom moved debates beyond overly simplistic political rhetoric. For example, earlier debates had been framed in terms of "Massive Retaliation" versus "Flexible Response," or "for" versus "against" the war in Vietnam. By avoiding such simplistic policy formulations, the collective wisdom of the commission contributed to the ongoing process by which new studies build on the best studies of the past. Cumulatively, they continued to argue for more integrated, longer-term strategies.

COMMISSION ON AMERICA'S NATIONAL INTERESTS (1996)

The term *national interest* was commonly used to justify desired programs without much careful thinking about the details and the relative importance of competing programs. For many leaders, national interests were basic and obvious and did not require much analysis. But Goodpaster gave the concept close attention throughout his career. In 1996, he co-chaired the Commission on America's National Interests to help sort out truly vital interests at a time of confusion in the post–Cold War era when nearly everything was purported to be in the national interest. [19]

Goodpaster liked to think of priorities among various military, economic, humanitarian, environmental, and other interests in terms of Eisenhower's poker chip analogy of blue, red, and white chips. Blue chips were reserved for those vital interests when the survival of the United States was at stake. Red chips were for important interests that would affect national well-being, but were not vital. White chips represented lesser interests and involved lower levels of resource allocations such as economic aid and humanitarian assistance. While such distinctions were intuitively obvious, in practice Goodpaster noted that such choices had proven more problematic because they involved difficult trade-offs with other American interests.

One of the reasons Goodpaster insisted on careful prioritizing of national interests was to avoid overcommitting resources to problems that were lower priority, as had often been the case. Similarly, by according top priority to the ultimate purpose, the chances were lessened that efforts would be diverted to lower priority interests.

NUCLEAR WEAPONS

Few, if any, people had more experience than Goodpaster in dealing with nuclear weapons at the policy and command levels. He participated in the initial Joint Staff study on nuclear forces soon after the first use of the atomic bomb in 1945. In the early 1950s, he was involved in the first efforts to incorporate nuclear weapons into NATO planning. During more than six years in the White House, Goodpaster saw how nuclear weapons were factored into decisions on Korea, Indochina, Berlin, the Taiwan Strait, and several other crises. As a division commander in Europe, he had firsthand experience with planning and training for the use of tactical nuclear weapons. And as NATO's SACEUR, he understood the critical role of nuclear weapons in deterring the Soviet Union.

After retirement, Goodpaster was frequently called on by the Defense Science Board, the national nuclear weapons laboratories, and many others for his expertise on a wide range of issues related to nuclear weapons. Furthermore, Goodpaster was one of the first to draw attention to how the end of the Cold War changed fundamentally the security context and required rethinking the role of nuclear weapons. The threat posed by conventional arms was reduced substantially with the breakup of the Soviet Union and disbanding of the Warsaw Pact. NATO no longer had to rely on nuclear weapons to augment conventional forces.[20]

In opening a new debate on nuclear weapons, Goodpaster argued that the primary purpose of nuclear weapons for the United States was to deter their use by others. They were not appropriate for deterring chemical and biological weapons as was implied in combining them all under the term *weapons of mass destruction*. Given the critical yet limited purpose of nuclear weapons, Goodpaster concluded that the main objective for the United States was the fewest weapons in the fewest hands.[21]

He immediately ran into opposition from those interested in maintaining robust nuclear capabilities as a hedge in a new era of uncertainty. He knew institutions with a vested interest in nuclear weapons would resist change, but he persisted in engaging the debate through a series of discussion groups and policy papers. As part of these efforts, Goodpaster produced a series of reports known collectively as the Atlantic Council's "Further Reins on Nuclear Arms" series that tipped the debate in favor of reducing Soviet and American nuclear inventories in the early post–Cold War period. The buildup of these weapons had been driven mainly by targeting requirements, redundant survivability, and technology, all of which resulted in continuing demands for increasing nuclear arsenals.

Goodpaster's work provided new ways of thinking about nuclear inventories. In particular, he identified the criteria necessary to safely reduce Soviet and American nuclear weapons to progressively lower levels. For each lower level, Goodpaster identified the necessary additional conditions for such reductions to be undertaken without reducing security.[22]

In addressing the prospects for reducing to a "zero level" of nuclear weapons, Goodpaster took a middle path between the nuclear abolitionists— whose ultimate goal he shared—and the skeptics—whose prudence he respected. Goodpaster acknowledged that the United States was bound by treaty to work toward the elimination of nuclear weapons, but he concluded that the international security required for abolition to work had to be first built and sustained before nuclear stockpiles could be reduced to zero. Drawing down arsenals on a pragmatic, negotiated, multilateral basis could go a long way toward building the necessary trust while still providing mutual security and hedging against a breakout by one or more nations.[23]

Goodpaster encouraged taking advantage of the once-in-a-lifetime opportunity presented by the end of the Cold War to pursue a five-power nuclear agreement to reduce American, Russian, British, French, and Chinese weapons to the lowest possible levels. He feared that, absent such an agreement, the Cold War restraints would give way to new strategic arms races in volatile regions, notably the Middle East and East Asia.

In 1996, Goodpaster collaborated with General Lee Butler, a recently retired Air Force general and formerly commander-in-chief of the Strategic Air Command. As SAC commander, Butler was responsible for a large share of the U.S. nuclear strike capability delivered by bombers and intercontinental missiles. A speech by Butler at the National Press Club and an open letter signed by Goodpaster and sixty other generals and admirals from around the world, including Russia, gained widespread media attention. The news focused on their call for eliminating nuclear weapons rather than on the details about how that might be achieved and the time required to build the necessary levels of trust. As a result, Butler and Goodpaster were discredited in the eyes of many who considered any ideas about eliminating nuclear weapons naïve.[24]

RUSSIA

At age seventy-four, five years before the collapse of the Soviet Union, Goodpaster initiated a series of semiannual meetings between leading Soviet strategic thinkers and former senior U.S. officials from the Atlantic Council. On the Soviet side, Goodpaster drew on relationships with Soviet military leaders that he had developed during his tenure as SACEUR and continued to foster. These meetings helped U.S. officials understand the problems facing the Soviet Union and accord its leaders the proper respect at a time when cooperation with the United States was highly controversial. Goodpaster was also interested in transforming thinking about NATO among Russian military leaders.[25]

Goodpaster saw in the Gorbachev initiatives opportunities for transforming the basic security structure of the world. Gorbachev announced a new military doctrine of "reasonable sufficiency," calling for much lower Soviet military requirements. Intrigued by the possibility of major reductions in Soviet forces, Goodpaster found that there was no serious planning underway in the Department of Defense or State Department anticipating the implications of deep cuts in Soviet forces, so he organized a delegation of senior retired U.S. officials, including Brent Scowcroft, to engage Soviet counterparts and recommend appropriate U.S. responses. These meetings produced an Atlantic Council policy paper in April 1989 recommending radical restructuring of NATO and Warsaw Pact forces to roughly equal levels of no more than 50 percent of current NATO strength. That argument gained attention and tipped the debate in favor of taking seriously the Gorbachev initiatives.[26]

Subsequently, after the split-up of the Soviet Union ended the Cold War, Goodpaster made the case for better relations with Russia to establish a more sustainable peace. To do this, he sought to forge an "overarching framework" for a nonadversarial, more positive relationship between the United States and Russia. With agreement on such a fundamental purpose, specific problems, such as missile defense and intellectual property, would be less likely to threaten overall relations.

As part of this framework, Goodpaster advised President Clinton to bring Russia into Europe constructively, using NATO's Partnership for Peace program. Then, only after Russia had "firmly anchored itself with the West—or definitely failed to do so," should NATO consider full membership to Eastern European states. Unfortunately, NATO expansion moved forward before a constructive relationship with Russia was seriously attempted. [27]

IN DEFIANCE OF SENILITY

In his later years, a few skeptics began to question privately General Goodpaster's wisdom, particularly after his involvement with those advocating the elimination of nuclear weapons. Yet shortly before his eighty-ninth birthday, Goodpaster demonstrated his thinking was little diminished when he had an insightful op-ed piece published in *The New York Times*. On the fiftieth anniversary of General Marshall's accepting the Nobel Peace Prize, Goodpaster, who had helped Marshall draft his speech, reminded readers of the wisdom of Marshall's vision and pointed out its relevance to contemporary problems. [28]

In his speech, Marshall had emphasized the interdependent relationships between peace, security, economic prosperity, and democracy. In particular, Marshall noted, "Democratic principles do not flourish on empty stomachs and that people turn to false promises of dictators because they are hopeless." Goodpaster added that the genius of the Marshall Plan was in the United States listening to the hopes and needs of the countries of Europe, including West Germany, rather than imposing its own ideas at the outset. [29]

In 2003, Goodpaster noted that the debate over aid to Iraq and Afghanistan was often too shortsighted. Funds spent to date on rebuilding Iraq "may prove to be just a down payment for the peace and prosperity in the region that must be our enduring aim." As Marshall well understood, judicious economic aid and mutual defense commitments serve both humanitarian and national security interests; they help build a sustainable peace. [30]

BRINGING IDEAS TO POWER

In addition to the foregoing activities, Goodpaster was chairman of the Atlantic Council, president of the Institute for Defense Analyses, president of the Eisenhower Institute, and a founding member of the Committee on the Present Danger. He was also president of the United States Strategic Institute and served on several national commissions. The number and scope of these efforts indicate how active Goodpaster remained after retirement from the Army. He had an extensive network of contacts that enabled him to organize some of the best minds and most influential people to address many of the most important challenges. Goodpaster knew that the government was mainly focused on immediate problems and had little time for thinking about the future. This provided a useful opportunity for Goodpaster to continue to make a difference. It also provided an opportunity for him to engage and mentor mid-level government officials in working groups that included many of the former senior officials the younger officers had read about in their studies. He usually avoided the spotlight and continued to be influential.[31]

Goodpaster also played a key role in raising funds for these efforts. His reputation and association with a project greatly increased the chances that donors would invest in the project. Through these many efforts, Goodpaster's reputation grew for his collaborative method and engaging manner of bringing ideas to power.

No matter the challenge, Goodpaster was always on call when the government needed his help, but sometimes the task proved impossible. For example, in 1979, President Carter responded to the Soviet invasion of Afghanistan with several measures including covert funding to opposition groups, an embargo of grain sales to the Soviet Union, and withdrawing United States participation from the Soviet-hosted Olympic Games. Carter also appointed General Goodpaster as his special envoy to deal with related issues. On one of these missions, Goodpaster was sent to Argentina to meet with the president to discourage the ruling military junta from replacing U.S. grain exports to the Soviet Union. The Argentine leaders were not consulted on the unilateral U.S. grain embargo and told Goodpaster that they wanted the United States to stop denouncing human rights violations in Argentina and resume military sales that had been blocked by the U.S. Congress. Goodpaster was in no position to negotiate such demands, and a few weeks later Argentina signed a five-year trade agreement with the Soviet Union that included cooperation in nuclear energy as well as grain sales.[32]

Figure 16.1. Goodpaster at Army War College, 1975. Official photo. *Source*: Courtesy of the George C. Marshall Library

NOTES

1. Susan Goodpaster Sullivan, note to author, March 25, 2013.
2. Locher, *Victory on the Potomac*, 4.
3. Ibid., 167.
4. Ibid., 169; CSIS Defense Organization Project, *Toward a More Effective Defense* (Washington: CSIS, Georgetown University, 1985) and Barry M. Blechman and William J. Lynn, eds., *Toward a More Effective Defense: Report of the Defense Organization Project,* (Cambridge, MA: Ballinger, 1985).

5. Locher, *Victory on the Potomac*, 171.
6. Ibid., 216.
7. Bill Keller, "Overhaul Is Urged for Top Military: A Panel Seeks to Expand Power of Chairman of Joint Chiefs," *New York Times,* January 22, 1985, 1.
8. Locher, *Victory on the Potomac*, 381.
9. Ibid., 419, 428, 433. Also see rebuttal of Lehman by Ike Skelton, "We're Not Trying to be Prussians," *Washington Post*, June 16, 1984, A13.
10. General Colin Powell, cited in Locher, *Victory on the Potomac*, 439.
11. CILTS Report, "Discriminate Deterrence," January 1988, 1.
12. Ibid., 6.
13. John Vessey, interview with author, January 27, 2014; CILTS Report, "Discriminate Deterrence," 52.
14. CILTS Report, "Discriminate Deterrence,"16.
15. CILTS Third World Conflict Working Group Report, "Supporting U.S. Strategy for Third World Conflict," June 1988, 16.
16. Ibid., 20, 22, 27–28.
17. CILTS Report, "Discriminate Deterrence," 2–3, 58.
18. John Vessey, interview with author, January 27, 2014.
19. Andrew J. Goodpaster, Robert Ellsworth, and Rita Hauser, Co-Chairs, Graham Allison lead author, Commission on America's National Interests, Belfer Center, Harvard University, 1996.
20. Andrew J. Goodpaster, "Tighter Limits on Nuclear Arms," Atlantic Council Consultation Paper, 1992, 6.
21. Former Secretary of Defense William J. Perry coined this term. See Andrew J. Goodpaster's Atlantic Council Occasional Paper, "Shaping the Nuclear Future: Toward a More Comprehensive Approach," 2.
22. Article VI of the Treaty on the Non-Proliferation of Nuclear Weapons, signed July 1, 1968, entered into force March 5, 1970.
23. Goodpaster, "Shaping the Nuclear Future; and Goodpaster, "Tighter Limits on Nuclear Arms."
24. See Craig Cernielio, "Retired Generals Re-Ignite Debate Over Abolition of Nuclear Weapons," *Arms Control Today* (November/December 1996).
25. Ibid. 5.
26. Don Oberdorfer, "An Old Warrior Rocks the Boat," *Washington Post*, April 30, 1989, C2.
27. Goodpaster to Clinton, July 13, 1995, Goodpaster Papers, box 99, folder 2, Marshall Library.
28. Goodpaster, "George Marshall's World, and Ours," *New York Times*, December 11, 2003, A43.
29. Ibid.
30. Ibid.
31. For several examples, see Goodpaster Papers, Marshall Library.
32. Paarlberg, "Lessons of the Grain Embargo," *Foreign Affairs* 59, no. 1 (Fall 1980): 153.

Chapter Seventeen

Connecting the Past and Future (1974–2005)

Goodpaster was both future oriented and well grounded in the past. His values included education and honoring the sacrifices of fellow soldiers. With such efforts, Goodpaster helped prepare future generations for the challenges that lay ahead. This chapter provides examples of his work with educational and heritage institutions.

THE GEORGE C. MARSHALL FOUNDATION (1974–2005)

General Goodpaster regarded General Marshall as the outstanding Allied military leader of World War II and the greatest person he had ever met. Thus, when asked to join the Board of Trustees of the George C. Marshall Foundation just after his retirement in 1974, he readily accepted and remained active until shortly before his death in 2005. In 1993, he was elected chairman of the board and served in that capacity until 2000, when he became chairman emeritus. Goodpaster considered it "a privilege and an honor." He wanted to make whatever contribution he could to "the continued legacy of General Marshall."[1]

The Marshall Foundation was established in 1953 at the urging of President Truman. Located in Lexington, Virginia, on the campus of Virginia Military Institute (VMI), Marshall's alma mater, the foundation perpetuates the legacy of George Marshall by maintaining a research library and housing a collection of Marshall papers and other important documents for research by scholars and students. The foundation also sponsors educational programs that promote the ideals exemplified by General Marshall. It honors individuals who, like General Marshall, exhibit courage, selfless service, and outstanding leadership. The foundation operates the Marshall Museum at VMI and supports the *Journal of Military History*, a quarterly publication of the Society for Military History.

Of course, none of this is possible without funding. Over a quarter century, General Goodpaster played a key role in raising funds for the foundation and its many activities. Not surprisingly, he led by example, quietly making frequent, generous personal financial contributions to the Marshall Foundation, and over these many years, General Goodpaster accepted many offers to speak and donated related stipends to the Marshall Foundation.[2]

After the end of the Cold War, Goodpaster effectively used his roles as chairman of the Marshall Foundation and vice-chairman of the Atlantic Council to work with the council's affiliated organizations throughout Europe to help establish the George C. Marshall European Center for Security Studies in June 1993. The Marshall Center, operated in Garmisch, Germany, by the U.S. European Command, was designed to create a more stable security environment through the development of democratic institutions and relationships, especially in the field of defense. Senior and junior diplomats, military leaders, scholars, and other officials from more than 110 countries have participated in Marshall Center courses and seminars.[3]

After General Goodpaster's tenure, the foundation established the Andrew J. Goodpaster Award to honor his life and service as a "Champion of the Marshall legacy, an American hero and extraordinary public servant."[4]

AMERICAN VETERANS CENTER (1995–2003)

General Goodpaster was an early supporter of the World War II Veterans Committee and its successor, the American Veterans Center. The center was formed in 1978 to honor the legacy of American veterans through oral histories and civic events so that their stories would not be forgotten. During the fiftieth anniversary of World War II, for example, the center produced a weekly series of radio broadcasts commemorating key developments in each week of the four-year war, drawing on World War II chronicles and collaboration with the National Archives and Radio America.[5]

In 2006, the center merged with the National Vietnam Veterans Committee and expanded its scope to include veterans from all American wars. The center organized the National Memorial Day Parade in Washington and hosted an annual conference at which General Goodpaster became the keynote speaker, beginning in 1995, and was invited back each year in this capacity for the next eight years. He often reminded the audience of mostly young people that World War II was won by people their age or younger. In these presentations, as in his other efforts to support the legacy of veterans,

General Goodpaster exuded integrity and was seen as exceptionally modest with no personal agenda.[6]

In 2007, the center established the "Andrew J. Goodpaster Prize and Lecture" to honor "soldier-scholars" who undertake groundbreaking work in military scholarship. The prize honors the legacy of General Goodpaster, one of the early soldier-scholars. Recipients of the Goodpaster Prize have since included Lewis Sorley, Dave Palmer, and Carlo D'Este.

EISENHOWER COLLEGE (1975–1982)

General Goodpaster's first experience on the board of trustees of a small liberal arts college taught him important lessons about the critical role of fundraising for educational and nonprofit institutions. In 1975, while Goodpaster was at the Wilson Center, General Norstad and General Gruenther convinced him he should join them on the board of Eisenhower College. This appealed to Goodpaster because the college was intended to be a national, living memorial to General Eisenhower. At the same time, Goodpaster was aware that the college was in deep financial difficulty.

Eisenhower College opened on September 5, 1968, with about three hundred students. Fundraising was largely successful and included a $5 million congressional grant, but the construction and operating expenses generally exceeded income. Over the next several years, a number of fundraising initiatives met with only modest success, including controversial efforts in Congress to provide about $8 million from the sale of proof sets of Eisenhower commemorative silver dollars.[7]

A major setback occurred on March 28, 1969, when General Eisenhower died at Walter Reed General Hospital after a prolonged illness. Thereafter, giving by friends and admirers of the general slowed markedly. When Goodpaster joined the board of trustees in 1975, the college was thus in a precarious financial state. Furthermore, the problem was compounded as enrollment declined, and news spread that the college might be forced to close. To help with the situation, General Norstad urged Goodpaster to become chairman of the board. Goodpaster declined the leading role, but agreed to serve on the board. Norstad had been tireless in his efforts to raise funds for the college, but he suffered a stroke just before Goodpaster's first board meeting.[8]

In 1979, General Goodpaster found himself personally occupied with the challenges of running a college as superintendent of West Point. He nevertheless remained loyal to the Eisenhower family, especially in the aftermath of Mamie Eisenhower's death in November 1979, and he remained on the board of Eisenhower College.[9]

General Goodpaster assisted fundraising by arranging meetings with prominent individuals and encouraging their support. In 1979, the board agreed to a merger with the Rochester Institute of Technology (RIT), but the merger failed, and in July 1982, the board decided to close Eisenhower College.

In April 1984, General Goodpaster signed an affidavit stating that the former trustees of Eisenhower College believed that the new Eisenhower Institute was the appropriate recipient of the assets of Eisenhower College because the assets were almost exclusively accumulated as a memorial to General Eisenhower. RIT settled the issue by providing about $1.2 million to the Eisenhower Institute.[10]

Dr. David Dresser, a former vice president and dean of students at Eisenhower College and author of a 799-page history, *Eisenhower College: The Life and Death of a Living Memorial,* wrote, "When General Goodpaster was chosen and accepted the position of national chairman, he very quickly enlisted the aid of such notables as William Rogers, William Scranton, and Walter Thayer, so the campaign might have had a chance if it had just gotten off the ground." By that time, however, it was too late.[11]

ST. MARY'S COLLEGE OF MARYLAND (1987–1999)

Despite his disappointing experience on the board of Eisenhower College, General Goodpaster agreed to join the Board of Trustees of St. Mary's College of Maryland in 1987 at the urging of his friend, Paul Nitze, who also served on the board. Goodpaster served for the next twelve years. As vice-chair of the board, General Goodpaster was instrumental in raising the national stature of the institution by helping transform the college into a model of public-private partnership in higher education. International programs were expanded to allow students to study in Britain, Italy, Gambia, Thailand, Vietnam, and China. General Goodpaster was the "undisputed conscience of the Board," in the opinion of the college president.[12]

General Goodpaster, as chair of the Academic Affairs Committee, established a new system for faculty compensation based on the midpoint of salaries for a select group of peer institutions. This system created a sense of fairness for compensation and, when disputes arose, the system provided objective, transparent criteria to help resolve differences. The approach was soon extended to provide the basis for staff salaries and has continued in effect. A program for faculty leave of absence was also developed under General Goodpaster's tenure. This program enabled faculty to pursue scholarship opportunities for their continued career development. Goodpaster gained respect from the faculty accordingly, and they were impressed with his knowledge of higher education, his attention to detail, and his willingness to consider changes—a welcome relief from previous boards that struggled under the weight of alumni resistant to change.[13]

During a 1998 college sponsored trip to Guatemala, several students were attacked and five were raped. Part of the response included a comprehensive review of St. Mary's programs of study abroad by a task force led by General Goodpaster. He approached the problem to improve the process, not placing blame, and was particularly attentive to details. The task force recommended changes in policies and procedures for safeguarding students' health and safety and also helped to restore confidence in the study-abroad programs. [14]

General Goodpaster partnered with Ben Bradlee, vice president of *The Washington Post* and chair of the Historic St. Mary's City Commissioners, to promote cooperation between the college and the city of St. Mary's. These efforts led to collaboration on development and building plans that included a $60 million-grant from the State of Maryland for a new visitors' center and other facilities showcasing the seventeenth century heritage of the city and college.

Because General Goodpaster could be counted upon "to do the right thing" and to recognize the many ways in which the college flourished under his "gentle guidance and careful direction," the college established the Andrew J. Goodpaster Leadership and Honor Lecture Series in 1998. The lecture was created at a time when honor was not valued in higher education, according to Dr. Jane M. O'Brien, then the college president. The first lecture was presented by General Brent Scowcroft who, in his opening remarks, called Goodpaster his hero. [15]

In 2005, shortly before Goodpaster's death, the board of trustees announced that a new academic building, the Andrew J. Goodpaster Hall, would be named in his honor. The award-winning building was dedicated the following year at a ceremony that again featured General Scowcroft. The impressive new building houses lecture halls, along with classrooms for psychology and education courses. Goodpaster Hall also features a heritage display in its grand foyer depicting many of General Goodpaster's contributions to the country and his role in launching St. Mary's as a public honors college for the State of Maryland. Goodpaster's granddaughter, Sarah Wilson Nesnow, the family archivist and a graduate of St. Mary's, played the key role in establishing the heritage display featured in Goodpaster Hall. [16]

In recalling General Goodpaster, Dr. O'Brien, former president of St. Mary's, noted perceptively that he was very intelligent, with a "high IQ; but his EQ [emotional intelligence] was extraordinary, off-the-scale." This referred to his combination of personal and social skills that made him particularly effective in dealing with others. [17]

PRESIDENTIAL COMMISSION ON WHITE HOUSE FELLOWSHIPS (1981–1985)

President Reagan invited General Goodpaster to join the Commission on White House Fellows in May 1981. The White House Fellows Program is among the most prestigious leadership and public service programs in the United States. Its purpose is to provide gifted young leaders with firsthand experience in the process of governing the nation. Selected fellows spend one year working full-time with senior White House officials, Cabinet secretaries and other top-ranking government officials. They also participate in round-table discussions with leaders from the private and public sector and travel domestically and abroad to conduct research on U.S. policy. [18]

From about one thousand individuals applying for these fellowships each year, between fifteen and twenty are selected, with each receiving a paid, full-time fellowship. Applicants are selected mainly on the basis of their records of achievement early in their careers, evidence of leadership skills and potential for further growth, ability to work effectively as part of a team, demonstrated commitment to public service, and indications of skills to succeed at the highest levels of the federal government.

In reviewing the applications, General Goodpaster would often be asked by other commission members for his thoughts about the relative strength of applicants from the military. While the program did not entail any specific obligations on participants after their fellowships, the expectation was that they would repay the privilege by contributing to the nation as future leaders. [19]

AMERICAN BATTLE MONUMENTS COMMISSION (1985–1990)

General Goodpaster believed strongly that the sacrifices of others for the sake of future generations should not be forgotten, particular the soldiers with whom he served in World War II.

One way he acted on this was by serving as chairman of the American Battle Monuments Commission and thus taking responsibility for maintaining American military cemeteries abroad. In typical Goodpaster fashion, he did this without pay or publicity.

The commission was established in 1923 under General Pershing to commemorate soldiers who died during World War I and were interred abroad. In addition to overseeing the maintenance and upkeep of cemeteries and memorials to the fallen soldiers, the commission also marked the World War I battlefields where American forces had fought. General Pershing personally chaired the commission and approved personnel assignments as well as all expenditures. Major Dwight Eisenhower was selected for one of those assignments in December 1926. Eisenhower's first job with the commission was to write *A Guide to American Battlefields in Europe*, which was published in 1927.[20]

General Pershing chaired the commission from 1923 to 1948, promising that "time will not dim the glory of their deeds." General George C. Marshall followed Pershing, chairing the commission from 1949 until 1959. General Goodpaster was appointed by President Reagan to chair the commission in 1985 and served in that capacity until 1990.[21]

The commission designed, built, and continues to maintain 24 American burial grounds abroad and 25 memorials that honor the sacrifices of about 218,000 Americans, including 125,000 interred abroad and another 94,000 missing in action during related campaigns, and named on these memorials. The cemeteries are in France, Italy, the United Kingdom, Luxembourg, the Netherlands, Tunisia, Mexico, Panama, and the Philippines, with related memorials in 15 countries.[22]

When General Goodpaster chaired the commission beginning in 1985, the annual budget was about $12 million, with personnel costs accounting for about 75 percent of the funding. In addition to maintaining the cemeteries and memorials, the staff provided personalized services to family and friends, including replying to more than five thousand written inquiries, escorting visitors, arranging for flowers, taking photos of grave sites, and organizing annual Memorial Day, Veterans' Day, and other holiday ceremonies that drew more than ten thousand visitors to some events. Annually, more than eleven million visitors came to these cemeteries. During the mid-1980s, the commission was also in the early stages of planning for the Korean War Memorial to be located on the Mall in Washington, DC.[23]

During his tenure from 1985 to 1991, General Goodpaster made it a priority to visit the Sicily-Rome American Cemetery near Anzio. The cemetery has about 7,900 American grave sites, including nine soldiers he knew from the 48th Engineers. A distinctive feature of the cemetery is a statue of two soldiers entitled "Brothers-in-Arms." In addition to celebrating the bonds among soldiers during war, the statue is a literal tribute to the twenty-one sets of brothers interred there.[24]

It is easy to forget that the outcome of the war was not assured. Goodpaster pointed out that it could have been lost in the Battle of the Atlantic, it could have been lost in the Battle of Britain, and it could have been lost on the Normandy beaches. But it was not, thanks to the sacrifices of the servicemen and women, thousands of whom were buried abroad. Goodpaster was determined that they will not be forgotten.[25]

Serving in such a capacity was a humbling experience. As Eisenhower described it, "humility must always be a part of those whose success is built on the lives of their followers and the sacrifices of their friends."[26]

KNOLLWOOD

During their later years, the Goodpasters lived at Knollwood, a retirement community for military families in Washington, DC. He developed prostate cancer in the mid-1990s and had been treated with radiation. The cancer returned in 2004, and his health declined over the next year. Nevertheless, he remained an active contributor to national security affairs. In late January 2005, for example, he presented insights on the Eisenhower White House at a seminar, "Eisenhower and National Security for the 21st Century," at the National Defense University.[27]

He celebrated his ninetieth birthday, February 12, 2005, at the home of his daughter, Susan, with eleven other family members including his younger daughter Anne, seven grandchildren, and one great-grandson. The following week, he was admitted to Walter Reed Army Hospital. For the next three months he was in and briefly out of the hospital. Andrew J. Goodpaster died on May 16, 2005, in Washington, DC.[28]

Figure 17.1.   Brothers in Arms, Sicily-Rome American Cemetery. Official photo.
Source: **Courtesy of American Battle Monuments Commission**

Dossy, meanwhile, was suffering from dementia and had moved to nursing care at Knollwood in Washington, DC. While dealing with his own physical decline, Andy had continued to care for Dossy—an effort that he described as the most difficult challenge of his life. She died after Andy at

Knollwood on November 29, 2006, with her daughter Susan and son-in-law Roger at her side.

NOTES

1. Goodpaster, Mandel interviews, tape 24; Warner memo to Marshall Foundation Board, May 17, 2005, Marshall Foundation Papers, Marshall Library.
2. Marshall Foundation Papers, Marshall Library.
3. Marshall Center website. www.marshallcenter.org.
4. Marshall Foundation website, www.marshallfoundation.org.
5. James Roberts, president, American Veterans Center, interview with author, September 4, 2012.
6. Ibid.
7. Dresser, *Eisenhower College*, 131, 333.
8. Ibid., 342, 344.
9. Ibid.
10. Ibid., 739.
11. Ibid., 750.
12. Dr. Jane M. O'Brien, president of St. Mary's College, in June 3, 2010 interview and in a June 21, 2010, summary prepared for the author.
13. Ibid.
14. Ibid.
15. Ibid.
16. Ibid. Also, correspondence from Susan Goodpaster Sullivan with author, November 30, 2013.
17. Jane M. O'Brien, president of St. Mary's College of Maryland while Goodpaster was on the board of trustees, phone interview June 3, 2010. For more on emotional intelligence, see Daniel Goleman, *Emotional Intelligence*, 1997, 43–44; and Goleman's *Working with Emotional Intelligence*, 2000, 24–29.
18. White House website, www.whitehouse.gov/about/fellows.
19. James Roberts, member of the commission during Goodpaster's tenure, interview with author, September 4, 2012, Arlington, VA.
20. D'Este, *Eisenhower: A Soldier's Life,* 190.
21. See website: www.abmc.gov.
22. Ibid.
23. American Battle Monuments Commission, Annual Report, FY 1986, 5, 10, 11, 54; Annual Report, FY 1987, 2, 49.
24. Ibid., and Sicily-Rome American Cemetery and Memorial Brochure.
25. Goodpaster cited in Sorley, "Normandy Revisited" *Assembly* (September 1994): 30.
26. Eisenhower, Guildhall Address, London, June 12, 1945. www.eisenhower.archives.gov.
27. Goodpaster in Schowalter, *Forging the Shield*, 207–10.
28. Susan Goodpaster Sullivan, correspondence with author, December 9, 2013.

Chapter Eighteen

The Goodpaster Legacies

"What Would Andy Do?"

There are many lessons that may be learned from Andrew J. Goodpaster. A search of "Goodpaster" in the authoritative *Foreign Relations of the United States* series yields more than one thousand citations consisting mainly of memos he wrote as records of high-level meetings. Similarly, a search of reports in the public version of the Department of Defense Technical Information Center yields more than 350 citations. Goodpaster's fingerprints may be found on a wide range of national security issues throughout the second half of the twentieth century.[1]

The lessons highlighted in this book deal with the ideas and ideals that led Goodpaster to be chosen repeatedly by leaders to participate in national security affairs at the highest levels. These ideas and ideals earned for him a reputation for dependability and integrity. He was chosen because his participation increased the prospects that the challenges would be well thought through and intellectually honest. When faced with such major decisions, Goodpaster would ask himself, "What would Eisenhower do?" He coupled this with his experience in what worked well and poorly in other administrations. As a result, Goodpaster developed a broad-based, richly experienced understanding of best practices in national security affairs.[2]

In reflecting on his close experience with four administrations, Goodpaster found the strengths of each to be instructive, such as Eisenhower's thoroughness, Kennedy's initiative, Johnson's ideals, and Nixon's breakthroughs in establishing new relations. Similarly, each administration had shortcomings, including lack of flexibility, poor coordination, internal disunity, and restrictive tendencies. Goodpaster observed that White House and NSC staffs were especially vulnerable in the early days of their transitions.

Once a new administration was well established, Goodpaster recommended that it reach out in many directions to many sources for new ideas that could lead to breakthroughs in improving relations with adversaries, strengthening ties with allies, and extending good offices to resolve conflicts.[3]

Goodpaster's ideas and ideals have been passed on to the countless individuals he mentored and the organizations he led. His influence has endured because many of those who knew him, when later faced with a difficult situation, asked themselves, "What would Andy do?"[4]

Of course, we can never be certain what Goodpaster would do, but a summary of his approach to analysis and decision making—the Goodpaster mind, method, and manner—illustrate what Andy might do.

THE GOODPASTER MIND: HABITS OF CAREFUL REASONING

First and foremost, Goodpaster would contribute independent thinking to the process. He could be counted upon to think through the problem well without falling into the traps of routine or group thinking. He was rigorous; he thought like a mathematician and engineer. (His doodles on the margins of papers would sometimes include calculus equations.) Goodpaster sought to understand the key variables and how each contributed to the best solution.

Goodpaster was adept at concentrating on the problem at hand, cutting to the heart of a situation, and recognizing the decisive elements. In addition, Goodpaster rejected politically expedient but simple solutions to complex problems. Furthermore, Goodpaster was not ideological; he was neither a hawk nor a dove.

Goodpaster's thinking cannot be easily reduced to a single set of principles. Although he was systematic and rigorous in his thinking, he rejected rigid, static, formulaic approaches. He noted that "old guidelines will be of limited application. Of greater value will be *habits of careful reasoning* and a *sense of responsibility*."[5]

Interestingly, he chose the term *habits* rather than *principles* or *guidelines*. The distinction is important because he was aware that one can become overly reliant on principles and doctrine and not do the kind of careful reasoning that is essential to good strategic thinking. Goodpaster was aware of the dangerous tendency to apply doctrine—wisdom about what usually works in general situations—without examining carefully the uniqueness of each situation.

Instead, Goodpaster advocated thinking through the distinctive aspects of a problem and how it differed in important ways from other, similar problems. He also stressed the need to continuously reassess the constantly changing strategic environment. These habits reduced the chances of doctrine-induced blind spots and failures to adapt to important changes.

Goodpaster would place the problem in context by framing it at the highest appropriate level of analysis, such as global, and then take a long-term view. This strategic perspective facilitated discovery of linkages that otherwise might have been missed from an operational viewpoint. This big-picture perspective also reduced the chances of unintended consequences.

While working for General Marshall, Goodpaster learned to think several steps beyond the immediate challenges of winning the war toward how to win the peace. Marshall and other leaders were painfully aware of how the seeds of World War II were sown by the failure to conclude World War I with a sustainable peace. Thus, Marshall instilled the habit of thinking through problems thoroughly among his staff. "Winning the peace" became shorthand for Goodpaster's integrated thinking through the long-term political, military, economic, and other consequences that must converge to achieve *desirable, feasible, and sustainable outcomes.*

Serving in Marshall's command post also introduced Goodpaster to a concise analytic framework that included carefully defining the problem, providing the appropriate background context, comparing options, noting dissenting positions, and recommending the best choice. General Marshall required that problems be analyzed comprehensively and yet summarized succinctly. Marshall admonished his staff officers: "Don't just bring me a problem, think it through."

This process helped ensure that all relevant factors and perspectives, including the views of the harshest critics were considered (e.g., the Navy or certain members of Congress). The resulting recommendations were clear and concise. Goodpaster noted that the strategic concept for fighting World War II could be summarized on a single page.

Another prominent characteristic of Goodpaster's strategic analysis was thinking in terms of interests and priorities. To distinguish relative levels of national interest, Goodpaster often used the Eisenhower poker chip analogy of blue chip, red chip, and white chip priorities. Blue chips were reserved for truly vital interests when national survival was at stake. One did not bet all-in with blue chips for a red chip problem unless a critical situation warranted. One of the main reasons Goodpaster insisted on careful consideration of prioritizing national interests was to avoid overcommitting resources to problems that were of lower order priority.

Priorities for Goodpaster ultimately were determined based on their relative importance in terms of national interest. He noted that whenever faced with a security problem, Eisenhower thought first in terms of the national interests at stake. Could a compelling case for military intervention be made to the American public? Thus, he avoided the mistake of considering political will as an afterthought.

In 1996, Goodpaster co-chaired the Commission on America's National Interests to help determine the truly vital interests at a time of confusion in the post–Cold War era when nearly everything was purported to be in the national interest. Goodpaster also understood the need to integrate a series of interrelated priorities so that a priority-one effort did not automatically trump a priority-two effort.

Goodpaster recognized that some problems were intractable and that often there were no good choices. Nevertheless, decisions had to be made. While determining which options were most desirable, Goodpaster also insisted on careful analysis to ensure the options under consideration were indeed feasible, especially economically, and likely to be supported by the American public over the longer term.

THE GOODPASTER METHOD: CORRELATING PURPOSE AND POWER

While in a strict sense, there was no Goodpaster Method, there certainly was a distinctive Goodpaster approach that he applied to a wide range of problems. He avoided relying on any single framework that would limit thinking, and he rejected the notion that any particular method would apply to all situations. Instead, he emphasized a dynamic process of *correlating purpose and power.*

Both parts of the purpose and power equation would receive careful attention from Goodpaster. The purpose would be clear, and the power would have a reasonable chance of achieving the purpose. Furthermore, if multinational efforts were envisaged, then a coalition mandate would be developed in parallel.

Goodpaster was well aware of the limits of military power and covert action. His early education, including the Navy's "Sound Military Decisions," inclined him to examine options closely in terms of cause and effect. From this perspective, Goodpaster viewed power in broad terms, especially noting how Eisenhower was careful to not overestimate the significance of military capabilities at the expense of political and economic factors. And the Vietnam War taught Goodpaster that power is not based on simple measures of the military balance such as kill ratios, firepower, mobility, and technology. Ultimately, power is the ability to influence behavior.

The Goodpaster process of *correlating purpose and power* would often involve convening a team of independent thinkers to address a carefully defined problem with the precise kind of collective wisdom that he experienced in the Solarium Project. Such a process, particularly at the beginning of a new administration, would examine the strategic options carefully and allow the president to decide the path forward in the presence of all of the senior national security authorities, ensuring that the new team were all on the same page. Furthermore, Goodpaster would strongly advise an administration to separate policy and operations by assigning responsibilities to different individuals and groups. Otherwise, as Marshall and Eisenhower pointed out, daily operations tended to overcome policy and longer-term planning. As a result, individual, short-term decisions might not contribute to long-term goals.

After an administration had its bearings, Goodpaster would likely structure subsequent decision making in the Eisenhower mode of "each in the presence of all." This approach involved bringing together all of the major stakeholders and experts to discuss an important issue and to "let each in the presence of all bring to bear his facts and his views and let a course of action be resolved." Goodpaster would also shape the discussion in terms of "what's best for America," encouraging participants to rise above their parochial interests.

Of critical importance was a fundamental rule that important facts or views not be withheld from responsible officials. That approach ensured that important decisions would not be made with key participants "frozen out of discussions." In bringing together responsible officials and experts, Eisenhower and Goodpaster insisted that silence could not be used to indicate either consent or dissent. This policy ensured that cautious voices were also heard.

Goodpaster would also ensure that Congress was involved. Members provide critical linkages with the American public and control the purse strings. One approach of engaging Congress that Goodpaster was fond of describing involved the president calling in the Republican and Democrat leadership and, after briefings, asking each of the congressional leaders, "Are you with me or against me?" In any event, Goodpaster would give careful consideration to what the American people would likely support.

Goodpaster also would likely reflect Eisenhower's strong belief that:

> War is a matter of teamwork, and teamwork is not possible among people that are mutually suspicious. I will put it stronger than this: perfect teamwork can be achieved *only* among friends.[6]

In particular, Goodpaster would insist that there should be only one commander in a theater, with authority clearly established, so there was no question as to the right to handle the three services as he or she saw fit.

THE GOODPASTER MANNER: ENGAGING

Goodpaster would have likely led national security efforts in a collaborative style characterized by intellectual honesty. In particular, his emotional intelligence was termed "off the scale," referring to his rare combination of personal and social skills that made him effective in dealing with others, especially those who did not work well together. His traits included empathy, trust-worthiness, conscientiousness, initiative, adaptability, political awareness, and several other attributes that enabled him to motivate and influence others to collaborate on achieving the best outcome for the country.

Many aspects of Goodpaster's effective collaborative leadership style have been captured by colleagues. Some recollections:

> Goodpaster was the "voice of calm reason." He was accustomed to working under great stress. He kept cool in tense, highly charged situations. While the tension in others would tend to narrow their focus, Goodpaster was able to remain open and think clearly. His strong self-discipline held his emotions in check.[7]

As a former U.S. ambassador to NATO described him,

> [General Goodpaster] always carried with him a "zone of quiet" that was infectious in calming the most troubled spirits and the most difficult circum-stances. He spoke under the turmoil, not over it, with his precise, understated logic, taking apart the complexities of argument and then reassembling the key elements with clarity and coherence; and he was listened to, always.[8]

Other similar aspects of Goodpaster's character were noted by his NATO colleagues, several of whom had known him since the founding days of NATO. Much later, during his final round of visits before completing his tour as SACEUR, General Goodpaster's allied colleagues presented him with a copy of a famous sixteenth-century print by Albrecht Dürer depicting a knight, death, and the devil. Goodpaster's comrades said this was how they thought of him as the *knight without fear and beyond reproach.*[9]

Indeed, his courage was unquestioned, and his behavior was "beyond reproach." These characteristics were the hallmark of Goodpaster's reputa-tion for moral integrity. They were critical and too often missing in others when the chips were down and leaders were urgently facing momentous decisions. As one participant in the Bay of Pigs crisis (at which Goodpaster *was not* present) noted, "I felt again the lack of moral integrity which I believe is the central guide in dealing with these difficult questions, particu-larly when individuals are tired, frustrated and personally humiliated."[10]

GETTING THE JOB DONE: GOODPASTER ON LEADERSHIP

Deciding and planning what to do is only 5 percent of the challenge accord-ing to General George S. Patton, while 95 percent of the effort involves getting the job done.[11] Goodpaster looked at getting the job done mainly in terms of leadership. The essence of leadership, according to Goodpaster was, "taking responsibility and getting results." Goodpaster learned that taking full responsibility for an issue forced one to consider the impact of decisions in broad terms and over the long run; it gave one a very personal stake in the outcome. In taking responsibility, he thought about who would be affected in positive and negative terms, and who would pay what price. Taking responsibility also obviated blaming others when efforts failed.

Getting results, for Goodpaster, was ultimately what mattered. Although he argued that mankind was built for action, Goodpaster was not impulsive. When under pressure, he often quoted Eisenhower's admonition, "Let's not make our mistakes in a hurry." Goodpaster thought things through but was sensitive to becoming bogged down by studies, the classic "paralysis by analysis." He kept his eye on the ball and he got results.

Goodpaster, however, did not always get the results he sought. He was disappointed that an "over-arching framework" of relations with Russia was not established before NATO expanded, thus reducing the prospects for long-term peaceful relations. Similarly, Goodpaster's efforts to reduce the role of nuclear weapons did not succeed to the extent that he hoped. Further, his persistent efforts to reduce inter-service rivalry and achieve more integrated strategies met with only modest gains. Yet, had he not failed occasionally, Goodpaster would believe he had not challenged himself sufficiently.

Before he left NATO, several Allied commanders asked Goodpaster to summarize his thoughts on leadership. The main challenge, he noted, was to evoke a desire and a commitment on the part of subordinates to take responsibility for the missions that are assigned.

For Goodpaster, leadership involved caring sincerely for the troops and working to function as a team. It was a simple formula: care = respect; his care for the troops resulted in their respect for him. Establishing this relationship was a necessary step in getting the job done. Goodpaster's actions from his early days as the head of a labor union, through commanding a battalion in combat, to his taking responsibility for the American Battle Monuments Commission, demonstrated his devotion to those who served under him.

Reflecting on his experience in the Pentagon, Goodpaster also advised Allied commanders to work hard to overcome the kind of counterproductive "we-they" cleavages between the services or between military and civilian officials. In overcoming such divisiveness, leaders should focus on gaining consensus on the purpose of the organization and on building a team in which each person saw his or her role as contributing to the team's purpose.[12]

Goodpaster agreed with Eisenhower that good leaders were distinguished by their readiness to take on additional responsibilities; they do more than merely the minimum required. Good leaders were ambitious, but in a selfless way, satisfied by a job well done rather than ambitious for one's own benefit. Good leaders did not seek personal credit for success or blame others for failures.[13]

Goodpaster's views on leadership highlighted seven principles:

1. Clarity of purpose. When the ultimate goal is well defined and clear, every intermediate task should fit into its larger context.
2. Take responsibility. When problems occur, as they inevitably will, one should face them openly, honestly, decisively, and courageously. Don't blame others.
3. Work as a team. Every member must understand their role in accomplishing the mission.
4. Build trust by demonstrating care both up and down the levels of command.
5. Delegate authority and support subordinates. It takes courage to delegate, but delegation encourages responsibility, dedication, and initiative.
6. Reassess old thinking and methods, and be ready to risk forging new directions to meet unique problems.
7. Underlying every principle must be *personal and professional integrity*. Have the courage of your convictions. Be intellectually honest. Don't place demands on others that you would not be willing to accept yourself.[14]

Each new generation of national security officials believes they are facing challenges of unprecedented complexity and uncertainty. However, current challenges are no more daunting than those Goodpaster faced and are similar, to the extent that they need to be well thought through. Goodpaster acquired and practiced these habits over decades of wrestling with such problems. The lessons he learned confirm General Scowcroft's view that Goodpaster is "too important to ignore."

Figure 18.1. **Andrew Jackson Goodpaster, 1915-2005. Official photo.** *Source*:
Courtesy of the George C. Marshall Library

NOTES

1. See www.state.gov/historical documents/frus; www.dtic.mil.
2. Goodpaster, in graduation address at McKendree College, May 19, 1990, in Goodpaster Papers, box 83, folder 24, Marshall Library.

3. Goodpaster, lecture, "Four Presidents and the Conduct of National Security Affairs—Impressions and Highlights," January 1977, in Goodpaster Papers, box 44, folder 12, Marshall Library.

4. One example is Dr. Jane Margaret O'Brien, former president of St. Mary's College of Maryland, who shared this "What would Andy do?" approach to decision making with the author, June 3, 2010.

5. Andrew J. Goodpaster in lecture on New Patterns of Security, iv–2, undated but cleared for delivery by the Department of the Army on May 4, 1965, Goodpaster papers, West Point Library. Italics added.

6. Griffith, *Ike's Letters to a Friend, 1941–1958*, 28–30.

7. General Paul F. Gorman, interview with author, September 27, 2013.

8. Ambassador Robert E. Hunter, U.S. Permanent Representative to the North Atlantic Council, in Jordan, *Unsung Soldier*, 147–48.

9. Susan Goodpaster Sullivan, who inherited the print along with the program of the presentation ceremonies in Bonn, December 3, 1974, interview with author, Alexandria, VA, December 11, 2013.

10. Chester Bowles, Notes on NSC Meeting, April 22, 1961, *FRUS, Vol. X, Cuba, January 1961–September 1962*, doc. 166.

11. George S. Patton, *War As I Knew It*, 357.

12. Goodpaster, Mandel interviews, February 12, 2004, tape 23.

13. Goodpaster, Johnson and Ferguson interviews. January 9, 1976.

14. Adapted from Goodpaster several speeches, such as his "Guideposts for Lives of Service" lecture when he received the George C. Marshall Award from the Association of the United States Army, October 16, 1991, Goodpaster Papers, box 83, folder 25, Marshall Library.

Acknowledgments

This book was a collaborative effort. In conducting research and writing this book, I accumulated huge intellectual and emotional debts to innumerable soldiers, scholars, friends, and family. In particular, I want to acknowledge Ken Weisbrode, my colleague at the Atlantic Council, who first proposed this book. Lewis "Bob" Sorley was a constant source of information, advice, and encouragement. Karen Sullivan, at my side daily helping with editing, was my true companion. Doug Price and his colleagues at the Eisenhower Legacy Council convinced me to write this book and provided valuable support. They also knew Goodpaster firsthand in the White House.

Among the many others I am indebted to are: Christopher Abraham, Marie-Claire Antoine, Richard Baker, Paul Barron, John Berry, Lance Betrros, Suzanne Christoff, Nancy Collins, David Dresser, Charles Dyke, John S. D. Eisenhower, Joe Franklin, Susan Eisenhower, Louis Galambos, Ruth Greenstein, Susan Goodpaster, Paul Gorman, Ruth Greenstein, Josiah Grover, David Haight, Dan Holt, Robert Jordan, Cole Kingseed, Paul Kozemchak, Steven Kramer, Roemer McPhee, Dana Mead, Jack Merritt, Virginia Mulberger, Sarah Nesnow, Roy O'Connor, Margaret O'Brien, Charles Otsott, Dave Palmer, Frank Partlow, Brad Patterson, Douglas Price, Jason Purcell, Elizabeth Radigan, Rozanne Ridgway, Eugene Rossides, Edward Rowny, Brent Scowcroft, Jonathan Sisk, William Y. Smith, William Stofft, Charles Sullivan, Roger Sullivan, James Tobias, Daun Van Ee, John Vessey, Mame Warren, and Robert Watkins. Finally, I would like to thank Alfred Wilhelm, an old Army buddy, who connected me with the Atlantic Council and General Goodpaster.

I regret that I did not begin working on this book sooner so that I might have been able to do more fact checking with General Goodpaster. Nevertheless, any errors are mine, not his.

Selected Chronology of Andrew J. Goodpaster

Year/ Age	Rank/ Position	Events
1915		Born on February 12, in Granite City, IL
1931/ 16	Student	McKendree College, Lebanon, IL; aspiring math teacher
1933/ 18	Laborer	Great Depression forces him out of college; works in St. Louis meat packing plant; elected first president of labor union
1935– 1939/ 20–24	Cadet West Point	Wins competitive appointment; serves on Honor Committee; Brigade Adjutant; graduated second in class; commissioned in Engineers
1939/ 24	2LT/Plt Ldr	A Company, 11th Combat Engineer Regiment, Panama
1940/ 25	1LT	Promoted October 1
1942/ 26	CPT, MAJ Battalion XO	Promoted to Captain on February 24; Major on October 29; Executive officer, 390th Engineer General Services Regiment, Camp Claibourne, LA
1943/ 27	LTC/ Battalion CO	Student at Command and General Staff College; Commander, newly formed 48th Engineer Combat battalion; Camp Gurber, OK; deployed to North Africa and Italy
1943/ 27	LTC/ Battalion CO	Battalion commander, 48th Engineers; earned Distinguished Service Cross, Silver Star, and two Purple Hearts during battles for Monte Cassino; evacuated to Fitzsimmons Army Hospital, CO
1944/ 28	LTC War Dept. Staff	Assigned to Strategy and Policy Group, Operations Division, War Department General Staff, under Col. Lincoln, Gen. Marshall
1945/ 29	LTC War Dept. Staff	Assigned to Advanced Study Group; examined role of nuclear weapons; also Army representative on Joint War Plans Committee
1947/ 32	Student Princeton University	Studied engineering, international relations; received MSE and MA degrees; further study led to PhD in 1950
1950/ 35	LTC Joint Staff	Army representative on Joint Advanced Study Committee
1951/ 36	LTC NATO Staff	Advance party to establish NATO as special assistant to chief of staff; organized intelligence, operations, plans and training; SHAPE Secretariat
1952/ 37	COL NATO Staff	Promoted to colonel; special projects officer; Gen. Eisenhower's Liaison to Three Wise Men
1954/ 39	COL District Engineer	Chief of San Francisco Engineer District (July–October); responsible for Corps of Engineer civil and military projects on West Coast

1954/ 39	COL White House	President Eisenhower's staff secretary and defense liaison officer
1957/ 42	BG	Promoted to brigadier general
1960/ 45	BG White House	Transition advisor to President Kennedy
1961/ 46	BG ADC, 3rd Inf. Div.	Assistant division commander, 3rd Infantry Division Wurzburg, Germany (April–October)
1961/ 46	MG CG, 8th Inf. Div.	Promoted to major general; commanding general, 8th Infantry Division, Bad Kreuznach, Germany; earns parachute wings at age 46
1962/ 47	MG Joint Staff	Special Assistant to Chairman, Joint Chiefs of Staff
1965/ 50	LTG Joint Staff	Assistant to chairman, Joint Chiefs of Staff; promoted to lieutenant general; heads study of prospects for winning Vietnam War
1966/ 51	LTG Joint Staff	Director, Joint Staff, Office of the Joint Chiefs of Staff; suffers heart attack; reassigned to less stressful job
1967/ 52	LTG Army Staff	Director of Special Studies, Office of Army Chief of Staff; Army representative to UN Military Staff Committee
1967/ 52	LTG Cdt	Commandant National War College
1968/ 53	GEN Dep. Commander	Promoted to general; Military advisor, U.S. delegation in negotiations with North Vietnam; deputy commander, U.S. Military Assistance Command, Vietnam
1969/ 54	GEN SACEUR	NATO's Supreme Allied Commander, Europe
1974/ 59	GEN	Retires from the Army
1974/ 59	Board of Trustees	George C. Marshall Foundation, 1974–2005; Chairman 1993–2000
1974/ 59	Assistant to Vice President	Assistant to Vice President Rockefeller on Commission on the Organization of Government for the Conduct of Foreign Policy
1974/ 59	Scholar	Senior Fellow, Woodrow Wilson International Center for Scholars; writes book, *For the Common Defense*
1974/ 59	Professor	Distinguished Professor of Government and International Relations, The Citadel
1975	Board of Trustees	Eisenhower College

1977/ 62	Super- intendent West Point	Called out of retirement to lead West Point after cheating scandal; replaced culture of hazing and intimidation with "positive leadership;" managed integration of women
1981/ 66	Member	President's Commission on White House Fellowships
1983/ 68	Founding Member	Eisenhower Institute; served as chairman; drafted white papers on national security, 1983–2004
1983/ 68	President	Institute for Defense Analyses, trustee, president and senior advisor, 1976–2005
1984/ 69	Recipient	Presidential Medal of Freedom, by President Reagan for "lifetime accomplishments that changed the face and soul of our country"
1985/ 70	Chairman	Atlantic Council of the United States, 1985–1997; board member 1975–2005; organized expert working groups on national security
1985/ 70	Chairman	American Battle Monuments Commission
1986/ 71	Member	Commission on Integrated, Long-Term Strategy
1987/ 72	Board of Trustees	St. Mary's College of Maryland, 1987–1999; commemorated by dedicating new Andrew J. Goodpaster Hall, 2007
1996/ 81	Co-Chair	Commission on America's National Interests
2005/ 90		Died May 16, 2005; interred at Arlington National Cemetery

Sources: Goodpaster papers, George C. Marshall Library, Lexington, VA; Andrew J. Goodpaster file, U.S. Army Center of Military History, Ft. McNair, Washington, DC; Atlantic Council interviews; Goodpaster publications and Goodpaster family archives.

Sources

INTERVIEWS AND ORAL HISTORIES

Billington, James H., phone interview by author, June 18, 2010.

Collins, Arthur S. Jr., interview by Chandler Robbins, April 21, 1982, Alexandria, VA, Senior Officer Oral History Program, U.S. Army Military History Institute, Carlisle Barracks, PA.

Dyke, Charles William, interview by author, February 25, 2014, Washington, DC.

Eisenhower, John S. D., phone interview by author, July 29, 2012.

Eisenhower, Susan, interview by author, March 20, 2012, Washington, DC.

Goodpaster, Andrew J., interview by Richard D. Challenger, January 11, 1966, John Foster Dulles Oral History Project, Princeton University Library.

Goodpaster, Andrew J., interview by Joe Frantz, June 21, 1971, Washington, DC, Oral History Program, LBJ Library.

Goodpaster, Andrew J., interviews by William D. Johnson and James C. Ferguson, January 9–April 30, 1976, Washington, DC, Senior Officers Debriefing Program, U.S. Army Military History Research Collection, Carlisle Barracks, PA.

Goodpaster, Andrew J., interview by Thomas Soapes, January 16, 1978, Oral History for the Dwight D. Eisenhower Library.

Goodpaster, Andrew, J., interview by L. James Binder, reported in article "Goodpaster + Two: West Point Today" *Army*, June, 1979.

Goodpaster, Andrew J., interview by Lewis Sorley, December 3, 1985, Washington, DC.

Goodpaster, Andrew J., interview by James M. Johnson, March 7, 10, 1988, Washington, DC, Oral History of the Superintendency, West Point Library.

Goodpaster, Andrew J., audio- and videotaped interviews by James McCall, July–August 2001, Washington, DC.

Goodpaster, Andrew J., video interviews by Ken Mandel, July-August 2001, January 2002, February 2004, Washington DC.

Goodpaster, Andrew J., interviews by James Billington, Librarian of Congress, for Veterans History Project, American Folk Life Center, Library of Congress, March 18, 2004, Washington, DC, (AFC/2001/001/29916).

Gorman, Paul, interview by author, January 18, 2013, Lexington, VA.

Howe, Fisher, interview by author, June 9, 2010, Bethesda, MD.

Merritt, Jack N., interview by author, April 8, 2009, Arlington, VA, and subsequent phone interviews, 2012.

Nesnow, Sarah [Goodpaster], e-mail exchanges with author, beginning March 23, 2009.

O'Brein, Jane M., e-mail exchanges with author, beginning June 3, 2010.

Palmer, Dave, phone interview by author, August 29, 2013.
Patterson, Bradley, interview by author, March 16, 2010, Bethesda, MD.
Ridgway, Rozanne L., interview by author, July 12, 2012, Arlington, VA.
Rowny, Edward L., interview by author, July 25, 2011, Washington, DC, and subsequent phone interviews.
Scowcroft, Brent, interview by author, June 10, 2010, Washington, DC, and subsequent meetings.
Smith, William Y., interview by author, April 15, 2009, Arlington, VA, and subsequent phone interviews.
Sullivan, Susan Goodpaster, interview by author, March 25, 2013, Alexandria, VA, and several earlier and subsequent phone interviews.
Vessey, John, phone interview by author, January 6, 2014.

ARTICLES AND DOCUMENTS

Annual Report of the Superintendent, United States Military Academy, 1935, 1936, 1937, 1938, 1939.
Goodpaster Papers, George C. Marshall Library, Lexington, VA.
Goodpaster Papers, U.S. Army Military History Institute, Carlisile, PA.
Goodpaster Papers, Special Collections database, National Defense University Library, Ft McNair, Washington, DC.
Goodpaster Reports, Defense Technical Information Center, www.dtic.mil.
Goodpaster Reports, Atlantic Council. During his more than three decade long affiliation with the Atlantic Council, General Goodpaster authored or chaired working groups and delegations that produced more than twenty publications on a wide range of international security issues. Listed below are some examples.
"Shaping the Nuclear Future: Toward a More Comprehensive Approach," *Andrew J. Goodpaster*. January 1998.
"New Patterns of Peace and Security: Implications for the U.S. Military," *Andrew J. Goodpaster*. December 1997.
"When Diplomacy is Not Enough: Managing Multinational Military Interventions," Andrew J. Goodpaster, Report to the Carnegie Commission on Preventing Deadly Conflict, July 1996.
"A Positive Framework for U.S.-Russian Relations: A Possibility for the Next Summit?" Andrew J. Goodpaster. November 1995.
"(Series) Joint Policy Statements with Joint Policy Recommendations and Related Documents on The Future of Ukrainian-American Relations and Russian American Relations in a Pluralistic World," Atlantic Council Policy Papers, June 20–July 1, 1995; December 1995–January 1996; September 1996; March/April 1997.
"The United States, NATO, and Security Relations with Central and Eastern Europe," Andrew J. Goodpaster, Chair; September 1993.
"Further Reins on Nuclear Arms: Next Steps for the Major Nuclear Powers," Andrew J. Goodpaster. August 1993.
"The Future of Russian-American Relations in a Pluralistic World, Joint Policy Statement and Recommendations," Atlantic Council and IMEMO, Russian Academy of Sciences, February 14, 1992, and November 29, 1992.
"Tighter Limits on Nuclear Arms: Issues and Opportunities for a New Era," Andrew J. Goodpaster. May 1992.
"The Future of Russian-American Relations in a Pluralistic World (Phase II-Constructive Interaction), Joint Policy Statement and Recommendations, Atlantic Council and –IMEMO, February 1992, November 1992.
"New Priorities for U.S. Security: Military Needs and Tasks in a Time of Change," Andrew J. Goodpaster. June 1991.
"Gorbachev and the Future of East-West Security: A Response for the Mid-Term," Andrew J. Goodpaster, Atlantic Council Occasional Paper, April 1989.

"The United States and Japan: Cooperative Leadership for Peace and Global Prosperity," Atlantic Council Joint Policy Paper (with Bretton Woods Committee and Japan Center for International Exchange, April, 1989.

"NATO to the Year 2000: Challenges for Coalition Deterrence and Defense," Andrew J. Goodpaster, Chair, Atlantic Council Policy Paper, March 1988.

"U.S. Policy Towards the Soviet Union: A Long-Term Western Perspective, 1987–2000," Andrew J. Goodpaster, Co-Chair, Atlantic Council Policy Paper, March 1987

"U.S. International Leadership for the 21st Century: Building a National Foreign Affairs Constituency," Andrew J. Goodpaster, Co-Chair, Atlantic Council Policy Paper, January 1987.

"Combating International Terrorism: U.S.-Allied Cooperation and Political Will," Andrew J. Goodpaster, Co-Chair, Atlantic Council Policy Paper, November 1986.

"Toward A Consensus on Military Service," Report of the Atlantic Council's Working Group on Military Service, Andrew J. Goodpaster, Co-Chair, Pergamon Press, June 1982 (also published as an Atlantic Council Policy Paper).

"After Afghanistan—The Long Haul: Safeguarding Security and Independence in the Third World," Andrew J. Goodpaster, Co-Chair, Atlantic Council Policy Paper, March 1980.

"Oil and Turmoil: Western Choices in the Middle East," Andrew J. Goodpaster Co-Chair, Atlantic Council Policy Paper, September 1979.

"The Growing Dimensions of Security," November 1977.

Goodpaster, Andrew J. "The Development of SHAPE: 1950–1953," *International Organizations* 9, no. 2, May 1955, 257–62.

———. Review of Maxwell Taylor's *Precarious Security*, *Wilson Quarterly* 1, no. 4, Summer 1977, 146.

Grover, Josiah T. "Andrew J. Goodpaster Jr., 1915–1947: The Making of a Political-Military Officer." Masters Thesis, University of North Carolina Department of History, 2009. UMI #1463822.

Jorgenson, John Harry, "Duty, Honor, Country and Too Many Lawyers," *American Bar Association Journal*, April 1977, 564–47.

Kincer, Alfred, www.6thcorpscombatengineers.com/AlKincer.htm. Website includes the unit history of the 48th Engineers in World War II, "We the 48th," plus many personal anecdotes by 48th Engineer veterans including Kincer.

Sinnerich, Richard Hart. "A Welcome Return to the Guam Doctrine," *Army*, September 2012, 26–27.

Small, Melvin. "The Atlantic Council: The Early Years," History Department, Wayne State University, Report prepared for NATO, June 1, 1998.

United States Military Academy, *Official Register of the Officers and Cadets*, 1935, 1936, 1937, 1938, 1939.

BOOKS

Agnew, Spiro T. *Go Quietly . . . or Else*. New York: William Morrow, 1980.

Ambrose, Stephen E. *Eisenhower: Soldier, General of the Army, President-Elect, 1890–1952*, New York: Simon and Schuster, 1983.

Atkinson, Rick. *The Day of Battle: The War in Sicily and Italy, 1943–1944*. New York: Henry Holt, 2007.

Bacevich, Andrew J. *Pentomic Era*. Washington, DC: National Defense University Press, 1986.

Beschloss, Michael R. *May Day: Eisenhower, Khrushchev and the U-2 Affair*. New York: Harper & Row, 1986.

———, ed. *Taking Charge: The Johnson White House Tapes*. New York: Simon & Schuster, 1997.

Betros, Lance. *Carved from Granite: West Point Since 1902*. College Station: Texas A&M University Press, 2012.

Black, Robert W. *Rangers in World War II*. New York: Random House, Ballantine Books, 1992.

Bland, Larry I., ed. *The Papers of George Catlett Marshall, Vol 4 (June 1943–December 1944)*. Baltimore: Johns Hopkins University Press, 1996.

Blumenson, Martin. *The United States Army in World War II, The Mediterranean Theater of Operations, Salerno to Cassino*. Washington, DC: Office of the Chief of Military History, U.S. Army, 1969.

Brinkley, Alan. *Voices of Protest: Huey Long, Father Loughlin and the Great Depression*. New York: Knopf, 1982.

Brokaw, Tom. *The Greatest Generation*. New York: Random House, 1998.

Chemus, Ira. *Eisenhower's Atoms for Peace*. College Station: Texas A&M University Press, 2002.

Cline, Ray S. *Washington Command Post: The Operations Division*. Washington, DC: Department of the Army, Office of the Chief of Military History, 1951.

Cosmas, Graham A. *U.S. Army in Vietnam Series, MACV, The Joint Command in the Years of Withdrawal, 1968–1973*. Washington, DC: U.S. Army Chief of Military History, 2007.

Daddis, Gregory A. *No Sure Victory: Measuring U.S. Army Effectiveness and Progress in the Vietnam War*. Oxford: Oxford University Press, 2011.

Doubler, Michael. *Closing With the Enemy*. Lexington, KY: University Press of Kentucky, 1994.

Dougan, Clark, and Stephen Weiss. *Nineteen Sixty-Eight*. Boston: Doubleday, 1983.

D'Este, Carlo. *Eisenhower: A Soldier's Life*. New York: Henry Holt, 2002.

Earle, Edward Mead, ed. *Makers of Modern Strategy*. Princeton: Princeton University Press, 1943.

Eisenhower, Dwight D. *At Ease*. Garden City, NY: Doubleday & Co., 1967.

———. *Waging Peace: The White House Years, A Personal Account, 1956–1961*. New York: Doubleday, 1965.

———. *Mandate for Change*. New York, Doubleday, 1963.

Fairbank, John K., Edwin O. Reischauer, and Albert M. Craig. *East Asia: The Modern Transformation*. Boston: Houghton Mifflin, 1965.

Foreign Relations of the United States, Volumes for the Eisenhower through Reagan Administrations. Washington, DC: Government Printing Office, and available at www.state.gov.

Frank, Richard S. *Downfall: The End of the Imperial Japanese Empire*. New York: Random House, 1999.

Franklin, Joseph P. *Building Leaders the West Point Way*. Nashville: Thomas Nelson, 2007.

Gaddis, John Lewis. *George R. Kennan: An American Life*. New York: Penguin, 2011.

———. *The Cold War: A New History*. New York: Penguin, 2006.

Galambos, Louis, ed. *The Papers of Dwight David Eisenhower: NATO and the Campaign of 1952, XII*. Baltimore: Johns Hopkins University Press, 1989.

Garraty, John A. *The Great Depression*. San Diego: Harcourt Brace Jovanovich, 1986.

Gillespie, Robert M. *Black Ops Vietnam: The Operational History of MACVSOG*. Annapolis, MD: Naval Institute Press, 2011.

Goldstein, Gordon M. *Lessons in Disaster: McGeorge Bundy and the Path to War in Vietnam*. New York: Holt Paperback, 2008.

Goodby, James E. *Europe Undivided*. Washington, DC: United States Institute of Peace Press, 1998.

Greenstein, Fred I. *The Hidden-Hand Presidency: Eisenhower as Leader*. New York: Basic Books, 1982.

———. *The Presidential Difference: Leadership Style from FDR to Clinton*. New York: Martin Kessler Books, Free Press, 2000.

Griffith, Robert, ed. *Ike's Letters to a Friend, 1941–1958*. Lawrence: University Press of Kansas, 1984.

Haberman, Aaron L. *Andrew J. Goodpaster Papers, 1930–1997: A Guide*. Lexington, VA: George C. Marshall Foundation, 2000.

Hunt, Ira A. Jr., *Losing Vietnam: How America Abandoned Southeast Asia*. Lexington: University Press of Kentucky, 2013.

Johnson, Lyndon B. *The Vantage Point*. New York: Halt, Rinehart & Winston, 1971.

Jordan, Robert S. *An Unsung Soldier: The Life of Gen. Andrew J. Goodpaster.* Annapolis, MD: Naval Institute Press, 2013.

Kempe, Frederick. *Berlin 1961: Kennedy, Khrushchev and the Most Dangerous Place on Earth.* New York: G. P. Putnam's Sons, 2011.

Kingseed, Cole C. *Eisenhower and the Suez Crisis of 1956.* Baton Rouge: Louisiana State University Press, 1995.

Kissinger, Henry. *White House Years.* Boston: Little, Brown, 1979.

———. *Years of Renewal,* New York: Simon & Schuster, 1999.

Locher, James R. III. *Victory on the Potomac: The Goldwater-Nichols Act Unifies the Pentagon.* College Station: Texas A&M University Press, 2002.

Logevall, Frederick. *Choosing War: The Lost Chance for Peace and the Escalation of War in Vietnam.* Berkeley, CA: University of California Press, 1999.

Marshall, George C. *Infantry in Battle.* Washington, DC: Infantry Journal Press, 1934.

McMaster, H. R. *Dereliction of Duty: Lyndon Johnson, Robert McNamara, the Joint Chiefs of Staff and the Lies that Led to Vietnam.* New York: HarperCollins, 1997.

Miller, Merle. *Ike the Soldier: As They Knew Him.* New York: G. P. Putnam's Sons, 1987.

Mitchell, George C. *Matthew B. Ridgway: Soldier, Statesman, Scholar, Citizen.* Mechanicsburg, PA: Stackpole, 2002.

Mitrovich, Gregory. *Undermining the Kremlin: America's Strategy to Subvert the Soviet Bloc, 1947–1956.* Ithaca: Cornell University Press, 2000.

Naval War College. *Sound Military Decision.* Annapolis, MD: Naval Institute Press, 1942 edition.

Newton, Jim. *Eisenhower: The White House Years.* New York: Doubleday, 2011.

Neustadt, Richard E., and Ernest R. May. *Thinking in Time: The Uses of History for Decision Makers.* New York: Free Press, 1986.

Nichols, David A. *Eisenhower 1956: The President's Year of Crisis: Suez and the Brink of War.* New York: Simon & Schuster, 2011.

Parker, Matthew. *Monte Cassino, The Hardest Fought Battle of World War II.* New York: Anchor Books, 2003.

Patterson, Bradley H. Jr., *The Ring of Power: The White House Staff and Its Expanding Role in Government,* New York: Basic Books, 1988.

Perry, Mark. *Partners in Command.* New York: Penguin Press, 2007.

Pogue, Forrest C. *George C. Marshall: Organizer of Victory.* New York: Viking Press, 1973.

———. *The Supreme Command.* Washington, DC: Office of the Chief of Military History, Department of the Army, 1954.

Rosenau, James N., Vincent Davis, and Maurice East, eds. *The Analysis of International Politics: Essays in Honor of Harold and Margaret Sprout,* New York: Free Press, 1972.

Sheehan, Neil. *Pentagon Papers as Published by The New York Times.* New York: Quadrangle Books, 1971.

Shlaes, Amity. *The Forgotten Man: A New History of the Great Depression.* New York: HarperCollins, 2007.

Showalter, Dennis E. *Forging the Shield: Eisenhower and National Security for the 21st Century.* Chicago: Imprint Publications, 2005.

Skates, John Ray. *The Invasion of Japan.* Columbia, SC: University of South Carolina Press, 1994.

Smith, E. D. *The Battles for Cassino.* New York: Charles Scribner's Sons, 1975.

Smith, Jean Edward. *Eisenhower in War and Peace.* New York: Random House, 2012.

Smukler, William, ed. *We the 48th.* Heidelberg: Brausdruck GMBH, 1945.

Spector, Ronald H. *U.S. Army in Vietnam, Advice and Support, The Early Years, 1941–1960.* Washington, DC: U.S. Army Center of Military History, 1985.

Sorely, Lewis. *A Better War: The Unexamined Victories and Final Tragedy of America's Last Years in Vietnam.* New York: Harcourt, 1999.

———. *Honor Bright: History and Origins of the West Point Honor Code and System.* New York: McGraw Hill Learning Solutions, 2009.

Sprout, Harold, and Margaret Sprout, eds. *Foundations of National Power.* Princeton: Princeton University Press, 1945.

Stoler, Mark A. *George C. Marshall: Soldier-Statesman of the American Century*, Boston: Twayne, 1989.

———. *Allies and Adversaries: The Joint Chiefs of Staff, the Grand Alliance and U.S. Strategy in World War II.* Chapel Hill: University of North Carolina Press, 2003.

Sulzberger, C. Z. *A Long Row of Candles: Memoirs & Diaries, 1934–1954.* New York: Macmillan, 1969.

Thomas, Evan. *Ike's Bluff: President Eisenhower's Battle to Save the World.* New York: Little, Brown, 2012.

Turse, Nick. *Kill Anything That Moves: The Real American War in Vietnam.* New York: Metropolitan Books, Henry Holt, 2013.

Weisbrode, Kenneth. *The Atlantic Century: Four Generations of Extraordinary Diplomats Who Forged America's Vital Alliance with Europe.* Cambridge, MA: DaCapo Press, 2009.

Weigley, Russell. *The American Way of War: A History of U.S. Military Strategy and Policy.* Bloomington: Indiana University Press, 1973.

Index

Able Company, 43, 55; bridge building by, 49–51; establishment of, 38; Mount Porchia attack by, 57

Abraham Lincoln Brigade, 28

Abrams, Creighton, xv, 172, 213; on U.S. tanks, 224; West Point days of, 209

accomplishments, xiii

ACDA. *See* Arms Control and Disarmament Agency

A Company. *See* Able Company

Adams, Sherman, 117, 129, 130

Adenauer, Konrad, 149, 172

Adjutant, West Point, 1939, xi

Administration and Logistics, 25

Advanced Study Group (ASG): Dream Sessions at, 83; Eisenhower meeting with, 82; establishment of, 81; return to, 92

AEC. *See* Atomic Energy Commission

Afghanistan, 271, 272

Agnew, Spiro, 227

Airey, Terence, 101

airlift support, 223

air strikes, 184

air superiority, 60, 73

Alexander, Clifford, 244

Alliance Defense for the Seventies program, 220

Allied leadership, 73

Allied strategic debate, 40–41

Allied tanks, 61

Allies, 36, 60

Amalgamated Meat Cutters and Butcher Workmen's Union, 10

American Battle Monuments Commission, 280–281

American embassy, 210

American gunboat diplomacy, 189

American Military Defense Assistance Program (MDAP), 102

American Veterans Center, 276

Anderson, Dorothy ("Dossy"), 22, 36, 119, 168

Anderson, Jonathan Waverly, 22, 35

Andrew J. Goodpaster Award, 276

Andrew J. Goodpaster Leadership and Honor Lecture Series, 279

Andrew J. Goodpaster Prize and Lecture, 277

Andrews Air Force Base, 150

anti-American backlash, 145

antipersonnel mines, 63

anti-Semitism, 11

antiwar sentiment, 208

appearance, 2

Arab-Israeli War, 223

Arab states, 134

Arab Union, 146

Argentina, 272–273

Armed Forces Qualification Test, 211

Arms Control and Disarmament Agency (ACDA), 250

Army, 29, 167
Army Corps of Engineers, 9
Army Ground Forces, 70
Army swim team, 21
Army War College, 273
artillery fire, 49–51, 58, 60, 62, 64
ASG. *See* Advanced Study Group
Asiatic Security Collaboration Program, 93
assassination, 180
Association of Princeton Graduate Alumni, 92
Aswan Dam, 134
athletics, 20–21. *See also* director of intercollegiate athletics
Atlantic Charter, 79
Atlantic Council, x, 269, 270, 272
Atomic Age, 90
atomic bomb, 78, 80
Atomic Energy Commission (AEC), 124–125
atomic power, 125
"The Atomic Age" (Conant), 81
atomic weapons. *See* nuclear weapons
Atoms for Peace, 125, 126
Attleson, Sergeant, 53
August 1943 Quadrant Conference in Quebec, 40–41
Axis forces, 80

B-17 Flying Fortresses, 64
B-25 medium bombers, 64
Baghdad Pact, 147
Bagnal, Charles, 248
Bailey Bridges, 42–43, 48–49
Baker Company, 38, 55, 57, 60
Balkans, 74–75
Baruch, Bernard, 81
Batista government, 154
Battle of Booby's Bluff, 43n10
Battle of Britain, 281
Battle of the Atlantic, 281
Battle of the Bulge, 181
Bay of Pigs, xiv, 177, 178, 290
B Company. *See* Baker Company
Beast Barracks, 16, 21, 252
Beijing, 133
Beirut, 145, 148
Ben-Gurion, David, 135, 142

Berlin: in Cold War, 148, 151, 216; conference on, 149; Khrushchev on, 148–149; ultimatum on, 150
Berlin Wall, 169
Berry, Sidney, 243, 255
"Better Red than dead", 222
Biddle, Tony, 113
Big Four Summit, 126
Billington, James, 237, 240–241
birth, 5
Bissell, Richard, 152, 154
BLACKLIST, 76
black NCOs, 37
Black Sea, 141
black soldiers, 39
Bohlen, Charles, 64
Bolshevik revolution, 2
bomber-gap, 123
Bonesteel, Charles "Tick", 71, 77
booby traps, 45, 61
Borman, Frank, 244
Borman Commission, 244, 245
Bowen, Bill, 245
Bowie, Robert, 110–111
Bradlee, Ben, 279
Bradley, Omar, 24, 92
Braggs, Oklahoma, 39
Braun, Werner von, 144
Brezhnev, Loenid, 224
bridges, 49–51
Britain, 134, 135, 138–139
British tanks, 55
Brodie, Bernard, 82–83
Brosio, Manlio, 220
Brothers in Arms, Sicily-Rome American Cemetery, 281, 282
Brown, Arthur, 248
Brown, George, 210
Buckley, Lieutenant, 55
Bulganin, Nikolai, 127, 140
Bundy, McGeorge, 180, 181, 187
Bunker, Ellsworth, 208
burial grounds, 281
Burke, Sergeant, 33
Bush, George H. W., 205
Butler, Lee, 270

Cadet Chapel Choir, 22
Cadet Hop Committee, 32n19

Cadet Leader Development System, 253, 261

Cambodia, 128

Camp Claiborne, Louisiana, 36

Camp David, 153

Camp Miles Standish, 40

cancer, 282

Canham, Charles D. W., 170

Carpenter, Scythia, 6

Carr, Edward Hallett, 89

Carroll, Paul T. "Pete", 113, 117

Carter, Jimmy, 250

Case-Church Amendment, 226, 238

Cassino, 64, 65

Cassino Valley, 52–53, 59

Castro, Fidel, 154, 155

casualties: to Baker Company, 60; from Mount Porchia, 57; to Texas National Guard 36th Infantry Division, 62; VCI inflicting of, 208; in Vietnam, 194

Catholic Church, 7

C Company. *See* Charlie Company

cease-fire, 207

CENTAG. *See* Central Army Group

Center for Strategic and International Studies (CSIS), 264

Central Army Group (CENTAG), 217

Central Intelligence Agency (CIA), 118, 119, 157, 208

Chamoun, Camille, 146, 147

character traits, 290

Charlie Company, 38, 46, 48; Mount Porchia attack by, 56–57; Reardon leading, 58; support from, 46

Chehab, Faud, 146, 147

Chiang Kai-shek, 81, 131, 132, 133

China, 3, 81, 192; civil war in, 131, 203; Indian forces attacked by, 178–179; United Nations seat for, 220. *See also* People's Republic of China

Chinese Army, 93

Christmas, 52

Churchill, Winston, 40, 71; Eisenhower contacted by, 137; Iron Curtain speech of, 220; pressure from, 142

CIA. *See* Central Intelligence Agency

CILTS. *See* Commission on Integrated Long-Term Strategy

CINCPAC. *See* commander in chief, Pacific

The Citadel, 241–242

civil engineering, 88

civilians, 23

Civil Operations and Revolutionary Development Support. *See* CORDS

Clark, Mark, 42, 62

Clausen, Hugh, 244

Clay, Lucius, 105, 169

Clinton, Bill, 271

Cold War, ix, xiii, xv, 129, 235; Berlin in, 148, 151, 216; competition in, 221; Laos in, 181; Middle East in, 145; nuclear weapons during, 269; policy for, 110, 111, 126; settlement of, 109; strategy during, xiv

Collins, Lawton, 129

colonial territories, 78

Columbine, 99

combat, 53–54, 65

Combat Command A, 63

Command and General Staff School, 37

commander in chief, Pacific (CINCPAC), 132

Commanding General, 8th ID, 174

Commission on America's National Interests, 268, 287

Commission on Integrated Long-Term Strategy (CILTS), 266

Commission on the Organization of Government for the Conduct of Foreign Policy, 240

Committee on the Present Danger, 272

Communications Improvement Plan, 229

communism, 2; Eisenhower on, 127; expansion of, 80, 97, 109, 179; Johnson, Lyndon B. combating, 182; Middle East threatened by, 145; plans for collapse of, 108

COMRADES IN ARMS, 220

Conant, James, 81, 81–82, 83

concentration camps, 65

Conference on Security and Cooperation in Europe (CSCE), 221

Congress, 100, 245, 266, 289

Conner, Fox, 73, 74

Conservative Party, 104

Containment Team, 108, 114n35–115n36

convoy, 41
CORDS (Civil Operations and Revolutionary Development Support), 210
Corps of Cadets, 21
Corps of Engineers, 29, 30, 113
correlating purpose and power, 288
Coughlin, Charles, 10–11
Council on Foreign Relations, 26–27
counterattack, 59
coup d'état, 180, 189, 190
courtship, 22–23, 23–24
CSCE. *See* Conference on Security and Cooperation in Europe
CSIS. *See* Center for Strategic and International Studies
Cuba, 154, 155
Cuban missile crisis, xv, 173
Cultural Revolution, 203
Current Operations Group, 69
Curriculum Objectives Plan, 202
Cutler, Robert C. ("Bobby"), 107, 118, 148
Cyprus, 147, 226

D-7 bulldozer, 50
Dachau, 65
dance cards, 32n19
Davison, Mike, 22
Dean, Edgar P., 32n32
debate team, 24
Defense Authorization Bill: Case-Church Amendment to, 226; defeat of, 219; from Mansfield, 218
Defense Department, 122, 124, 210; Legislative Liaison of, 186; reforms of, 121, 264
Defense Reorganization Act, 122
Defense Science Board, 268
de Gaulle, Charles, 149, 150, 153–154, 216, 217
Department of Civil Engineering, 88
Department of Defense Technical Information Center, 285
Department of Economics, Government and History, 24
Department of Social Sciences, 85
Desk Next to Oval Office, 159
Détente, 221
Dewey, Thomas E., 105

DIA. *See* director of intercollegiate athletics
Dickinson, Hillman, 245
Dien Bien Phu, 128
Dillon, Douglas, 155
director of intercollegiate athletics (DIA), 254
Discriminate Deterrence, 266
Distinguished Service Cross (DSC), xiv, 56, 63, 67n73, 81
Dominican Republic, 189
Donovan, William, 89
Douglas MacArthur, 29
draft, 193
Dream Sessions, 83
Dresser, David, 278
drought, 10
drugs, 258–259
DSC. *See* Distinguished Service Cross
Dulles, John Foster, 107; death of, 139; Diem backed by, 128; Massive Retaliation from, 126; in Taiwan, 133; on withdrawing troops, 144–145
DuPuy, Trevor, 22
Durbin Castle (ship), 45
Dürer, Albrecht, 290
DVINA, 220
Dzuiban, Stanley, 71

Earle, Edward, 82–83, 88, 90
Eastern Air Lines, 244
East Germany, 221
economy, 122
Eden, Anthony, 135, 139, 141
education, 8, 8–9
Egypt, 134; British-French invasion of, 138, 141; Israel attack of, 136; military-assistance funds for, 267; Port Said in, 140; Soviet involvement in, 142; Syria joined with, 146
XVIII Airborne Corps, 186, 189
8th Infantry Division, 170, 172, 209
Eisenhower, Dwight D., 127, 129, 130, 134, 141, 159, 160, 164n88, 281; admiration of, 158; appointment by, 104; ASG meeting with, 82; Chamoun relationship with, 147; Churchill contact with, 137; on defense spending, 120–121; ideas of, x; intellect of, 74,

110, 120; on inter-service rivalry, 121;
Johnson, Lyndon, B. advice from, 181,
188, 194; Kennedy, John F. transition
from, 156–158; Khrushchev
relationship with, 127, 147; on
leadership, 291; Lebanon intervention
by, 241; mastery at obfuscation of, 132;
meeting of, 81; mentorship from, 95;
Middle East policy of, 134;
monumental personal anger of, 142;
NATO alliance lead by, 98, 99, 125,
219; Nixon joke from, 130; NSC relied
on, 118; on nuclear weapons, 123, 124,
125, 138; personal relationships for,
128; phrase coined by, 104; praise by,
105; presidential run by, 105; reelection
of, 141; relationship with, 106, 119;
resignation of, 107; as SACEUR, 103;
on SHAPE, 101; on South Vietnam,
129; staff secretary and defense liaison
officer created by, 117; staff secretary
of, ix; troops withdrawn by, 144–145;
Truman letter to, 98; visits to, 213
Eisenhower, Mamie, 130, 277
Eisenhower College, 277–278
*Eisenhower College: The Life and Death of
a Living Memorial* (Dresser), 278
Eisenhower Doctrine, 145, 146
Eisenhower Institute, x, 272
11th Engineers, 33–34
emotional intelligence, xiv, 279, 289
Engineer Group, 70
engineering, 9, 11
engineer officers, 33–34
Engineers' perspective, 43n10
ethics, 18, 20, 255. *See also* honor
EUCOM. *See* European Command
Europe, 15, 23, 103; political attitude to
nuclear weapons of, 225; preventing
dissolution of, 142; Vietnam impact on,
193
European Command (EUCOM), 228
European/North African Theater, 39
European Theater, 41
evacuation, 136
Evangeline (ship), 35
Explorer I, 144
extremists, 13n30

Faisal (King), 146
family history, 6
farming, 5
fascism, 80
Fat Man, 78
5th Infantry Regiment, 34
Fifth Army, 52
First Annual Report of the supreme Allied
commander, Europe, 104
First Armored Division, 53, 63
first lieutenant, 34
First Sergeant Buckley, 54, 60
Fitzsimmons Army Hospital, 63, 69
Five Paragraph Field Order. *See*
Operations Order
flash messages, 51, 66n19
flexibility of mind, 72
Flexible Response strategy, 177, 195, 224
football, 8, 21, 254
Ford, Gerald, 227
Foreign Affairs, 108–109
foreign policy, 27
Foreign Relations of the United States, 285
Fort Clayton, 34
For the Common Defense (Goodpaster,
A.J.), 238
Fort Leavenworth, Kansas, 37
Fort McNair, 109
Fort Ord, California, 35
Fortress America, 126
Fort Sam Houston, Texas, 36
48th Engineer Combat Battalion, 60, 63,
64, 281; assignment to, 38; awards
earned by, 65; Fifth Army
acknowledgment of, 52; Presidential
Unit Citation awarded to, 59;
understrength issues of, 40; unification
of, 38–39, 41
Foundations of National Power (Sprout),
88–89
48th Engineer Regiment, 38, 46
foxholes, 46
"fragging" (assassinating), 211
France, 128, 216, 217
Franco, Francisco, 28
Frech, Lieutenant Colonel, 34
Free French Forces, 47
Free World Military Assistance Forces,
210

French Expeditionary Corps, 62
French Foreign Legion, 42–43
French Legion of Honor, 89
friendly fire, 55
Fulda Gap, 167

Gaitskell, Hugh, 104
Garigliano River, 62
gasoline-powered chain saws, 48
general court martial, 39
General Motors, 119
General Order Number 1, 100–101
General Order of Merit, 252
Geneva Summit (1955), 126
George C. Marshall European Center for
    Security Studies, 276
George C. Marshall Foundation, 275–276
German 88mm guns, 46, 58
German bunkers, 53
German Federal Republic, 3
German fighter aircraft, 46
German Messerschmitt 109 aircraft, 48, 60
German Panzer Grenadier, 170
German snipers, 58
German soldiers, 57–58
German submarines, 41–42
German Weimar Republic, 2
Germany, 6, 23, 76, 86n32, 149
Gibraltar, 42
Gilbert and Sullivan, 22
Glee Club, 22
Goldwater, Barry, 185, 264
Goldwater Defense Reorganization Act,
    265
Goldwater-Nichols Defense
    Reorganization Act, 265
Gomulka, 137
Goodpaster, Andrew J., 238, 293. *See also*
    specific topics
Goodpaster, Andrew Jackson, Sr. (father),
    6, 7
Goodpaster, Anne, 87–88
Goodpaster, Susan, 36, 168, 263
Googoo, Sergeant, 55
Gorbachev, Mikhail, 270
graduate education, xvin2, 88
Granite City, Illinois, 5
Granite City High School, 8
Gray, Gordon, 122–123, 148, 154

Great Depression, xiii, 1, 2, 3, 9, 9–10;
    Europe impacted by, 10; product of, 5;
    scholarship on, 91; volatile emotions
    during, 11
Greatest Generation, 3, 95
Greek government, 227
grenades, 56
Gromyko, Andrei, 127
Groves, Leslie, 78
Gruenther, Alfred, 90, 93; dinners with,
    105; on Mansfield amendment, 218;
    SACEUR command by, 107; special
    assistant to, 98
Guantanamo, 154
Guatemala, 279
guerrilla warfare, 187
*A Guide to American Battlefields in
    Europe* (Eisenhower), 281
Gulf of Tonkin, 183
Gulf of Tonkin Joint Resolution, 183
Gustav Line, 47, 60, 61, 62, 63, 64

Hackworth, David, 171
Hagerty, Jim, 132
Haig, Alexander, 227–229
Hamlet Evaluation Surveys, 208
Hammarskjöld, Dag, 139
Hanoi, 188
Harkins, Paul, 180
Harlow, Bryce, 212
Harriman, Averell, 103, 194, 203, 204
Harvard University, 81
hazing, 252
heart attacks, 129, 134, 196, 197
Heisman Trophies, 254
Hermann Goering Division, 60
Herter, Christian, 149, 150
Highway 48, 51; bridge on, 50; building of,
    65; maintenance of, 59; tanks on, 53
Hirohito, Emperor, 77
Hiroshima, 78
History of Soviet Russia (Carr), 89
Hitler, Adolf, 2, 61
Ho Chi Minh, 128, 190
Ho Chi Minh Trail, 180, 191
Hoffman, Martin, 243–244
Hohenfels, 168
honor, 18, 254
Honor Committee, 18, 18–19, 19, 256

Hoover, Herbert, 126
Hoover, Herbert, Jr., 139
House Foreign Affairs Committee, 218
Howitzer yearbook, 28
Hudleston, Edmund, 101
Hukbalahap insurgents, 158
Humphrey, George, 139
"Hundredth Night Show", 22
Hungary, 133, 137, 140
Hunter Liggett (ship), 33
Hunter Packing Company, 10
Hussein (King), 146
Hussein, Saddam, 241
hydrogen bomb, 112, 125

IAEA. *See* International Atomic Energy
    Agency
ICBMs. *See* intercontinental ballistic
    missiles
IMF. *See* International Monetary Fund
Imperial Japanese Navy, 77
independent thought, 72, 169, 286
India, 178–179
Indian Wars, 87, 93n2
Indochina, 128
infantry: fighting for, 53–57; losses to, 50,
    53–54, 59; machine gun units of, 58;
    tactics of, 35
Infantry in Battle (Marshall), 35
Infantry Tank School, 74
Institute for Advanced Study, 89
Institute for Defense Analyses, 272
institutional failure, 246
integrity, 261, 292
intellectual honesty, xv
"Intensification of the Military Operations
    in Vietnam, Concept and Appraisal"
    (Goodpaster), 191–193
intercontinental ballistic missiles (ICBMs),
    152
interment camps, 35
international affairs, 20
International Atomic Energy Agency
    (IAEA), 125
International Monetary Fund (IMF), 139,
    142
International Planning Group, 98–99, 100
international security, 95
international security developments, 181

inter-service rivalry, 80, 119, 121, 291
Iraq, 146, 147, 241, 271
Iron Curtain speech, 220
Israel, 134, 136, 224; military-assistance
    funds for, 267; *Mystere* (aircraft) in,
    135–136; occupation by, 142
Italy, 42, 47

Jackson, C. D., 107–108
Jacobs, Sergeant, 54
James Madison Medal, 92
Japan: Bonesteel facilitation surrender of,
    77; invasion plans for, 77; militarism in,
    3, 28; Pearl Harbor bombing by, 34–35;
    plan for sudden collapse of, 75–76;
    Russia threat by, 3; threat of, 3
JCS. *See* Joint Chiefs of Staff
Johns, Glover, 171
Johnson, Alex, 212
Johnson, Harold K., 188, 196
Johnson, Kelly, 152
Johnson, Lyndon B., 169, 190, 208;
    communism combated by, 182; early
    administration of, 181; Eisenhower
    advice to, 181, 188, 194; reelection of,
    185; in South Vietnam, 179, 180
Joint Advanced Study Committee, 84, 92
Joint Chiefs of Staff (JCS), xiv–xv, 75,
    125; assistant to chairman of, 177;
    estimations by, 128; frustration among,
    196; meeting with, 120; "New Look"
    report from, 110–111; role of, 121,
    121–122; war games organized by,
    183–185
Joint War Plans Coordinating Committee,
    U.S. (JWPCC), 77, 78
Jordan, 147
Jordan, Robert, x
Journal of Military History, 276
judge of character, 54
Juin, General, 62
Julliard School of Music, 8
JWPCC. *See* Joint War Plans Coordinating
    Committee, U.S.

Kádár, János, 140
Kahn, Herman, 83
Karch, Charles A., 11–12
Kassim, General, 147

Katzbeck, Lieutenant, 56
Kennan, George, 83, 108–109
Kennedy, John F., xiv–xv; assassination of, 180; CIA unsupportive of, 178; Eisenhower transition to, 156–158; forces reduced by, 180; "Red Tide of Communism" from, 179; Soviet ultimatum rebuffed by, 169
Kennedy, Robert, 208
Kennedy-Johnson administration, 195, 196
Kerwin, Walter T. ("Dutch"), 241
Kesselring, Albert, 42, 60
Keyes, Geoffrey, 62–63
Khrushchev, Nikita: on Berlin, 148–149; at Camp David, 153; Eisenhower relationship with, 127, 147; ten-day tour by, 150–151
Killian, James, 143, 152
King, Admiral, 40–41
Kissinger, Henry, 212; secret visit to Beijing by, 220; on tactical nuclear weapons, 225; Tho negotiations with, 226; on Warsaw Pact, 217
kitchen debate, 150
Knollwood, 282–283
Knowland, William F., 131
Korea, 131, 163n59
Korean War, 95, 97, 103; Chinese Army in, 93; defense spendings after, 111; level of security during, 107; for NATO, 97–98
Kozlov, Frol, 150
Kwangtung Army, 3
Labour Party, 104
La Follette, Robert M., 11
Laird, Melvin, 264
Lampson, Roy, 111
Land, Edwin, 152
Land & Volk, 99
Lansdale, Edward, 158
Laos, 128, 181
Latin America, 155, 189, 221
leadership, 16, 34, 37, 168, 288–289, 291; action-oriented nature of, 210; Beast Barracks teaching of, 21; collaborative style of, 230, 289–290; disagreement among Allies on, 73; essence of, xvi; formative experiences for, 65; formula for, 291; at NATO, xv, 213, 229;

respect from, xiv; seven principles of, 292; SMD emphasis on, 26; at West Point, xv, 245, 255
League of Nations, 28, 79, 91
Lebanon, 146, 241
Lee, Robert E., 9, 21
Le Feverer, Sergeant, 54
Lehman, John, 265
Lemnitzer, Lyman, 215, 229
life span, 1
limited international scheme, 82
Lincoln, George ("Abe"), xvin3, 70, 84; intervention by, 70; mentorship from, 24–25; Office of Emergency Preparedness appointment of, 223
Lippman, Walter, 153
Liri Valley, 62
Little Boy, 78
Locher, Jim, 264
Lockheed, 152
Lodge, Henry Cabot, Jr., 139, 147, 185
Long, Huey, 10

MacArthur, Douglas, 21, 29, 97, 253
machine-guns, 46, 55
Macmillan, Harold, 146, 147, 149
MacMull, Jack, 245
MACV. *See* Military Assistance Command, Vietnam
The Makers of Modern Strategy (Earle), 89
Makins, Roger, 136
Manhattan Project, 78
manner, xiii–xiv
Mansfield, Mike, 218, 219
Mao Zedong, 81, 133, 190
marriage, 29, 31
Marshall, George C., 35, 70, 72; Churchill on, 71; ideas of, x, 247, 261; invasion pushed by, 37–38; leadership from, xiv; mentorship from, ix, 71–73, 287; Nobel Peace Prize for, 111, 271; retirement of, 81; as secretary of defense, 97
Marshall Museum, 276
Marshall Plan, 241, 271
Massachusetts Institute of Technology (MIT), 143
Massive Retaliation, 126
mathematics, xvin1, 9, 286
Matsu, 131, 132, 133

maximum danger, 102
MBFR. *See* mutual and balanced force reductions
McCaffrey, Barry, 36
McCaffrey, Mary, 35–36
McCarthy, Eugene, 208
McCarthy, Major, 63
McElroy, Neil, 121
McGinnis, Sergeant, 43
McKendree College, 8, 21
McNamara, Robert, 182; report summarized by, 193; on tactical nuclear weapons, 224; on Vietnam, 191
MDAP. *See* American Military Defense Assistance Program
Medal of Honor, 56, 87
Mediterranean theater, 41
Memorial Day speech, 9
memorials, 280–281
Merritt, Jack, 245
Mers El Kebir, 42
methodical strategic thinking, 24–25
methods, xiv
Meyer, Edward ("Shy"), 260
Middle East, 134, 145, 223
midwest roots, 5
Mignano, 47–48, 53
The Mikado (Gilbert and Sullivan), 22
Military Assistance Command, Vietnam (MACV), 179–180; CIA differences with, 208; deputy commander of, 209; increase in strength for, 213n5; Strategic Objectives Plan of, 209
military discipline, 15
military forces, 120
military-industrial complex, 240
military training, 251, 252
mind, xiii
Mindszenty, Cardinal, 137
mine clearing, 43, 46
Mississippi River, 5, 9
MIT. *See* Massachusetts Institute of Technology
Mollet, Guy, 135, 141
Monnet, Jean, 103
Monte Cassino, Italy, xiv, 47
Monte Cassino Abbey, 64
Montgomery, Bernard, 98, 101
Moore, Sergeant, 50

Moorer, Admiral, 223
Morgan, George H., 87, 93n2
mortar fire, 58
Moscow, 36. *See also* Russia; Soviet Union
Mount Camino, 47–48
Mount Porchia: casualties from, 57; control of, 53; first attack on, 54–57; second attack on, 57–58
Mount Trocchio, 60
Mrovka, Paul, 6
Mrovka, Teresa Mary, 6
Munitions and Main Navy buildings, 71
Munson, Orville, 54; fording sites scouted by, 61; machine guns attacked by, 57; Mount Porchia attack by, 54–55
Murphy, Robert, 148
music, 7–8
Mussolini, Benito, 42
mutual and balanced force reductions (MBFR), 222
Mystere (aircraft), 135–136

NAC. *See* North Atlantic Council
Nagasaki, 78
Nagy, Imre, 137, 140
naming lineage, 12n2
Napoleonic principles of war, 190
NASA, 143
Nasser, Gamal Abdel, 134; announcement by, 135; Arab unity promoted by, 147; in Yugoslavia, 148
National Archives, 276
National Defense University, 190
National Guard, 208, 209
National Intelligence Estimate (NIE), 123, 141, 161n23
national interest, 238, 268. *See also* Commission on America's National Interests
National Liberation Front (NLF), 194, 207
National Memorial Day Parade, 276
National Press Club, 270
National Security Action Memorandum (NSAM) 52, 179
National Security Action Memorandum (NSAM) 273, 180
national security advisor, 118

national security affairs: approaches to, ix, 235; best practices for, xiii, xvi; contributions to, x; documents related to, 117–118; nuclear weapons in, 195; think tanks for, 263

National Security Council (NSC), 111, 118; Defense Program Review Committee of, 240; Eisenhower relying on, 118; January 1956 Net Evaluation from, 138; on NATO strategy, 217; note taking for, 119; Operations Coordination Board of, 157; originator of, ix; structure of, 212, 223

National Security Council Report 68 (NSC-68), 102

national security officials, x, 292

national security policy, 107, 266

National Socialist movement, 2

"National Technology and International Politics" (Goodpaster), 90

National Vietnam Veterans Committee, 276

National War College, 81; commandant of, 197, 201; Curriculum Objectives Plan for, 202; guest-speakers at, 202

NATO: Allied Forces South Headquarters of, 217; contributions to, 229–230; Council of, 218; crisis in, 195; Defense Ministers in, 218; de Gaulle on, 150, 217; Eisenhower at, 98, 99, 125, 219; European forces of, 124; France rejoining of, 217; General Order #1 in, xiv; Greek withdrawal from, 227; Hungary joining, 137; interoperability of, 221; Korean War for, 97–98; leadership of, xv, 213, 229; main missions of, 221; military headquarters of, xiv, 98, 100; Nixon endorsement of, 217; nuclear planning of, 215; nuclear weapons at, 112, 229; opposition to, 99; Partnership for Peace program from, 271; poor communication among, 216; possible dissolution of, 218; propaganda against, 99; reductions in, 221; shortcomings of, 239; strategy of, 217, 225; Taft on, 105; threats to, 220–221; troops in, 103, 144; vulnerabilities to, 102; Warsaw Pact gap from, 102

Naval Academy, 15

Naval War college at Newport, 23

Nazi Germany: artillery fire from, 49; Franco support from, 28; Moscow advanced on by, 36; oil supplies to, 40; Poland invasion by, 29; Stalingrad defeat for, 37

Nazis, 2, 2–3

NCOs. *See* noncommissioned officers

Nesnow, Sarah, 279

network of friends, 235

Neutrality Act, 26, 27

New Approach Group, 112

New Deal, 11

New Look, 110–111, 124

"New Strategy for Peace", 240

New York Times, 156, 264, 271

Ngo Dinh Diem, 128, 179, 180; Dulles backing of, 128; Lansdale advisor to, 158

Ngo DinhNhu, 180

Nguyen Cao Ky, 190

nicknames, 6

NIE. *See* National Intelligence Estimate

9th Cavalry, 37

Nitze, Paul, 278

Nixon, Richard, xiv, 130, 150, 222, 223; coordination with, 129; Eisenhower joke about, 130; incoming administration of, 209; NATO endorsement by, 217; "New Strategy for Peace" from, 240; SACEUR recommendation from, 215; on tactical nuclear weapons, 225; Vietnamization policy of, 210–211; Watergate scandal for, 223

NLF. *See* National Liberation Front

Nobel Peace Prize, 111, 271

NOFORN, 112

noncommissioned officers (NCOs), 33

Normandy, 70

Norstad, Lauris, 82, 83, 84, 227

North Africa, 42, 43

North Atlantic Council (NAC), 104

North Atlantic Treaty, 97

North Korea, 202

North Vietnam, 182, 183, 191, 194; bombed infrastructure of, 207; intensified bombing of, 202;

negotiations with, 202–204
North Vietnamese Army (NVA), 191
NSAM. *See* National Security Action
Memorandum
NSC. *See* National Security Council
NSC-68. *See* National Security Council
Report 68
nuclear energy, 125
nuclear war, 124–125, 138
nuclear weapons, 91, 92, 124, 182; Beijing
threatened with, 133; changing design
of, 112; Cold War era of, 269; Conant
on, 81–82; consequences of, 122–123;
debate on, 269; disarmament of, 125,
127; Eisenhower on, 123, 124, 125,
138; Europe attitude for, 225;
experience with, 268; in Korea,
163n59; limited international scheme
for, 82; on national security agenda,
195; at NATO, 112, 229; reduction of,
291; Russia development of, 81–82;
Soviet Union tests of, 97; threats with,
190; U.S. monopoly on, 109; war
changed by, 78, 80, 124; zero level goal
for, 269–270. *See also* tactical nuclear
weapons; weapons of mass destruction
Nuclear Weapons from Pit to Target, 92
Nunn, Sam, 264
NVA. *See* North Vietnamese Army

O'Brien, Jane M., 279
Obstacle 8, 49
Obstacle 13, 55
OCS. *See* Officers Candidate Schools
OEEC. *See* Organization for European
Economic Co-operation
OERs. *See* Officer Efficiency Reports
Office of Defense Mobilization, 122
Office of Emergency Preparedness, 223
Office of Strategic Services (OSS), 89, 158
Officer Efficiency Reports (OERs), 143
Officers Candidate Schools (OCS), 246
oil embargo, 224
OKEAN, 220
Olympic Games, 272
173rd Airborne Brigade, 189
1108th Engineer Group Headquarters, 38,
63
OPD. *See* Operations and Plans Division

OPEC (Organization of Petroleum
Exporting Countries), 224
Open Skies, 126–127
Operation ANVIL/DRAGOON, 65
Operation BLUE BAT, 146
Operation CORONET, 77
Operation DOWNFALL, 77
Operation OLYMPIC, 77
Operation OVERLORD, 41
Operation POWERPACK, 189
Operations and Plans Division (OPD), 69,
70, 84; Norstad director of, 82;
Pentagon Conference Room for, 83;
workload for, 71
Operations Order, 24–25, 26
Operations Plan (OPLAN) 34A, 182, 183
Operation Teamwork, 259–260
OPLAN. *See* Operations Plan
Oppenheimer report, 111
Organization for European Economic Co-
operation (OEEC), 104
Osmeña, Sergio, 79
OSS. *See* Office of Strategic Services
ostpolitik, 221
Oxford Rhodes Scholar, 24

Pacific Theater, 39, 41
Pakistan, 179
Palestinian Mandate, 147
Palestinian refugees, 134
Palmer, Bruce, 189
Palmer, Dave, 261
Panama Canal Zone, 29, 33, 34
paratrooper, 175
parents, 6–7
Paris, 100, 113
Paris Peace Accords, 226
Paris Peace Talks, xv
Paris Summit, 152
Patton, George, 21, 290
Paul, Major General, 84
Pearl Harbor, 34–35, 85n23
Pearson, Drew, 153
peer evaluation, 21
Pentagon, 70, 71, 202; reflections on, 291;
return to, 178; Vietnam war measures
by, 208
Pentomic structure, 167, 169
People's Liberation Army (PLA), 132, 133

People's Republic of China, 135
Pershing, General, 280, 281
PhD dissertation, 90, 91, 92
Philippine Army, 158
Philippines, 79, 85n23
physical training, 253
PINCHER war plans, 78
PLA. *See* People's Liberation Army
Plan ALPHA, 134
Plan RANKIN, 75, 85n28
Plebe, 16–18, 17
Pleven, René, 99
Plowden, Edwin, 104
Plowman, Sergeant, 56
poker chip analogy, 268, 287
Poland, 1, 29
Polaroid, 152
Politburo, 151
Potsdam Conference, 76
Potsdam Declaration, 76
Powers, Francis Gary, 152
Prague Spring, 221
Presidential Medal of Freedom, xv, 261
Presidential Medal of Merit, 89
Presidential Unit Citation, 59
Price, Melvin, 12
Princeton, 1, 87, 92, 245; Department of
    Civil Engineering at, 88; international
    relations studies at, xiv
Princeton Military Studies Group, 89
Project 100,000, 211
promotion: to brigadier general, 143; to
    four-star general, 209; to lieutenant
    colonel, 38; to lieutenant general, 186;
    to major, 36; to SACEUR, 216
propaganda, 99
Prudential Life Insurance Company, 42
Prussian kaiser, 6
psychological implications, 102–103
Pulitzer Prize, 65
Pyle, Ernie, 65
Pytlik, Marianna, 6

Quadripartite forces, 216
Quemoy, 131, 132, 133
quest for knowledge, 7

racial tensions, 37, 39, 211
Radford, Arthur, 183

Radio America, 276
Radio Free Europe, 137
railroads, 48
rains, 46
Ramcke, Herman, 170
rape of Nanjing, 28
Rapido River, 61, 62, 63, 64
Rayburn, Captain, 83
Reagan, Ronald, 264, 280
Reardon, Lieutenant, 51–52, 52–53, 56, 58
reconnaissance, 39, 49, 63
"Red Beach", 65
Redford, Admiral, 128, 131
Redstone rocket, 144
"Red Tide of Communism", 179
*Regulations of the United States Military
    Academy*, 257–258
religion, 7
Republican Party, 105, 107
reputation, xiii, 1
Reserve forces, 208, 209
Reserve Officers Training Corps (ROTC),
    246
retirement, xv, 227, 228, 260
Retirement Board, 70
Richardson, Elliot, 212
Rickover, Hyman, 83, 250–251
Ridgway, Matthew, 92–93, 107
RIT. *See* Rochester Institute of Technology
road maintenance, 52
Rochester Institute of Technology (RIT),
    278
Rockefeller, Nelson, 126, 185, 240
Rogers, Bernard, 241–242, 244
Rogers, William, 212
Roll-Back Team, 108, 109–110
Rome, 60
Roosevelt, Franklin D., 11, 28, 79
Rostow, Walt, 194
ROTC. *See* Reserve Officers Training
    Corps
Rowny, Edward, 19, 24, 26, 71
Rumsfeld, Donald, 264
rum smuggling, 33
Rusk, Dean, 71
Russia, 3, 81–82, 192, 204
Ryder, Charles, 62–63

SAC. *See* Strategic Air Command

SACEUR. *See* supreme allied commander, Europe

Saigon, 186, 237

SALT. *See* Strategic Arms Limitations Talks

Sandhurst, 247

Santjer, Sergeant, 56

Saudi Arabia, 139

Schaefer, Edwin M., 12

Schilling, Colonel, 257

School of Military Government, 75

Schreiner, Sergeant, 55

Schultz, George, 267

science education, 144

Scott, Willard, 260

Scowcroft, Brent, xvi, 205, 228, 270, 279

Scranton, William, 185

Secretary of State, 83

Secretary of War, 74

Seignious, George, 241, 242, 250

Selective Service, 97

Senate Armed Services Committee Goldwater-Nunn, 265

Senator Wherry, 100

756th Tank Battalion, 63

753rd Tank Ballalion, 62

Seventh Fleet, 131

71st Artillery Brigade, 49

severe head wound, 59

SHAPE. *See* Supreme Headquarters, Allied Powers Europe

Shockley, William, 77

shoulder wound, 59

Showalter, Bud, 49

shrapnel wound, 63

Sigma I, 184–185

SIGMA II, 184

Silver Star, 50, 59, 67n73

singing, 8, 9, 20, 22

Single Integrated Operations Plan (SIOP), 224

Sino-Indian tensions, 179

SIOP. *See* Single Integrated Operations Plan

situational awareness, 25

6th Armored Infantry Regiment, 53

SMD. *See* sound military decisions

Society for Military History, 276

Solarium Project, 267; instructions to, 108; meetings for, 107–108; participation in, xiv; purposes of, 110; strategies of, 108

soldier-scholars, ix, xiv, 84

sound military decisions (SMD), 25, 25–26, 26, 288

"The Sources of Soviet Conduct" (Kennan), 108–109

South Korea, 131

South Vietnam, 129, 190, 204, 210; insurgency in, 158; Johnson, Lyndon B. in, 179; military leaders of, 210; NLF attack of, 207; Taylor ambassador to, 182; verge of collapse for, 195; Viet Cong negotiations with, 226

Soviet Union, 28, 140, 141, 142; Afghanistan invasion by, 272; Arab-Israeli War role of, 223; Atlantic Council meetings with, 270; bombers produced by, 123; collapse of, 235, 271; leadership transition in, 203; military capabilities of, 122, 220; nuclear weapons of, 97, 122–123, 127, 196; periphery around, 145; after Stalin's death, 127; U-2 surveillance flights over, 152, 153, 154; ultimatum from, 169; U.S. relations to, 107, 140, 178

Spanish Civil War, 23, 28

Special Forces, U.S., 179

Special National Intelligence Estimate, 208

Special Study Group, 83–84

Specker, Sergeant, 55–56

SPG. *See* Strategy and Policy Group

Sprout, Harold, 82–83, 88, 88–89, 91

Sputnik, 143

staff secretary and defense liaison officer, 117

Stalin, Joseph, xiv, 40, 76, 107, 127

Stalingrad, 37

Standard Oil, 11

Stassen, Harold, 125

State, War, Navy Coordinating Committee (SWNCC), 83

State Department, 126, 210, 212

State of the Corps report, 260

State of the Union address, 121

Stern, Sergeant, 57

Stevenson, Adlai, 107

Stimson, Henry, 74, 79–80, 85n23
St. Mary's College of Maryland, 278–279
Strategic Air Command (SAC), 112, 146
Strategic Arms Limitations Talks (SALT), 221
Strategic Defense Initiative, 266
strategic thinkers, 82–83
"Strategy, Soldiers and Statesmen" course, 251
Strategy and Policy Group (SPG), 70, 70–71, 74–75, 75
Stump, Felix, 132
sudden collapse plans, 75–76, 86n32, 108
Suez Canal, 29, 133, 135, 139, 142, 145
Suez Canal Company, 134–135
supreme allied commander, Europe (SACEUR), xii, xv, 231; Eisenhower as, 103; Haig as, 228; leaders of, 107; lessons from, 239; Nixon recommendation for, 215; political leaders visited by, 222; responsibilities of, 219; tour as, 290
Supreme Headquarters, Allied Powers Europe (SHAPE), 98; Eisenhower vision for, 101; Gruenther last year at, 112; operation control for, 100–101; Watergate scandal impact on, 227
Supreme Soviet, 153
surface-to-air missiles, 194
surgery, 63
surveying, 11
swimming, 21
SWNCC. *See* State, War, Navy Coordinating Committee
Syria, 142, 146

T-2 tank retriever, 50
Tactical Department, 18, 252
tactical nuclear weapons, 224, 225
tactics, 71
Taft, Robert A., 97, 105, 111
Taiwan Strait, 131, 133, 163n59
Task Force Allen, 53
Task Force C, 109, 110
Taylor, Maxwell, xiv–xv, 148, 177, 188; ambassador to South Vietnam role of, 182; Army reorganized by, 167; assistant to, 173
TCC. *See* Temporary Council Committee

technology, 90, 91, 152
Temporary Council Committee (TCC), 103, 104
X Corps, 62
Tet Offensive, xv, 207, 208
Texas National Guard 36th Infantry Division, 62
Thames, Lieutenant, 56, 58
Thieu, Nguyen Van, 190, 226
thinking, 286–287
3rd Armored Division, 172, 209
3rd Infantry Division, 168
Third Army Headquarters, 40
Third World Conflict working group, 267
34th Infantry Division, 62–63
Tho, Le Duc, 226
390th Engineer General Services Regiment, 36, 36–37
Three Wise Men, 103, 104
"Toward a More Effective Defense"(CSIS), 264
Townsend Harris (ship), 46
Toynbee, Arnold, 89
training problems, 171
Treloar, Sergeant, 56
Tripartite Declaration, 136
Truman, Harry, 76, 79, 98, 107, 275
tunnel networks, 45
Turkey, 226
tutoring, 22
235th Engineer Combat Battalions, 38
II Corps, 62

U-2 surveillance flights, 135–136, 141, 152, 153, 154
U-boats, 41–42
UK. *See* United Kingdom
The Uncertain Trumpet (Taylor), 177
United Arab Republic, 146
United Kingdom (UK), 40
United Nations, 79, 90, 220; General Assembly of, 125, 147; Security Council at, 140; support from, 139
United States, 136, 144–145, 239; Arab-Israeli War role of, 223; atomic attacks on, 124; Pakistan relations with, 179; satellite program of, 143; spreading ideas of, 126; tensions with Cuba of, 155

United States Army Court of Military Review, 244

United States commander in chief, European Command. *See* USCINCEUR

unit pride, 172

Universal Military Training and Service Act, 97

An Unsung Soldier: The Life of Gen. Andrew J. Goodpaster (Jordan), x

uranium, 92

USCINCEUR (United States commander in chief, European Command), 216

"U.S. Helps Train an Anti-Castro Force at Secret Guatemala Base." (New York Times), 156

USS Arkansas, 23

U.S.S. Edmund B. Alexander, 40

USS New York (BB-34), 23

USS Pueblo, 202

Van Allen radiation belt, 144

Van Campen, Captain, 48, 53

VC. *See* Viet Cong

VCI. *See* Viet Cong infrastructure

Vessey, John, 260

VI Corps, Fifth Army, 45

Viet Cong (VC), 179, 186, 188, 207, 226

Viet Cong infrastructure (VCI), 208

Vietinghoff, Heinrich von, 42

Vietminh, 128

Vietnam, xv, 129, 182, 186, 192, 194, 209, 212, 241; alternative approach to, 194; American embassy in, 210; antiwar sentiment on, 208; communist aggression in, 179; creation of, 128; deputy commander in, 205; forces increased in, 193; McNamara on, 191; negotiation possibilities for, 193. *See also* North Vietnam; South Vietnam

Vietnamization, 210–211

Vietnam War, xiii, 95, 121, 288; Case-Church Amendment ending, 238; fallout from, xv, 209, 211, 226

Virginia Military Institute (VMI), 275

VMI. *See* Virginia Military Institute

Volturno River, 46

Walter Reed Army Hospital, 196, 213, 277

Walters, Vernon, 99, 216

war, ix, 80, 124, 192

War Department, 69, 71

War Department's Plans Division (WPD), 70

war games, 183–185

"War of the Worlds" (Wells), 35

Warsaw Pact, 102, 217; forces of, 217, 220; Hungary withdrawal from, 137

Watergate scandal, 223, 227

weapons-grade nuclear material, 125

weapons of mass destruction, 269

wedding, 31

Wedemeyer, Albert C., 70

Weinberger, Casper, 267

Weisbrode, Ken, ix

Wells, Orson, 35

West, Bland, 244

West, Mae, 41

Westmoreland, William, 172, 205; command by, 182–183, 186; replacement of, 209; troops requested by, 191

West Point, 21, 244, 246, 248, 252, 259; academics at, 20, 26, 248–249; advantages in, 15–16; approach at, 247–248; Army Corps of Engineers officers from, 9; athletics at, 20–21, 253–254; Cadet Leader Development System at, 253; cheating scandal at, 243; competition for appointment to, 11–12; counterculture at, 253; curriculum at, 16, 249–250; Department of Economics, Government and History at, 24; disadvantages in, 16; drugs at, 258–259; ethics at, 254–257; football at, 254; General Order of Merit at, 252; graduation from, 28; honor at, 18, 254; Honor Code at, 246, 256; institutional failure at, 246; leadership of, xv, 245, 255; MacArthur at, 253; military training at, 251–253; plebe at, 2.10 –18, 246, 252; policy board at, 247–248; priorities at, 257; reflecting on, 27–28; reforms at, 248, 256; retirement from, 260; return to, 23–24; transformation at, 15, 260; women at, 258

West Point Academic Board, 248, 249, 250

West Point Study Group, 245, 250

Wheeler, General, 191
White, Paul Dudley, 147
White House Fellows Program, 280
Whitman, Ann, 117, 160
Wilson, Secretary of Defense, 119, 120
Winslow, Colonel, 36
women, 258
Women's Army Corps, 37
Wood, Robert, 93
Woodrow Wilson International Center for Scholars, 237
Woodward, Bob, ix
Worden, Robert, 98
World War I, 2, 11, 18, 23
World War II, xiii, xv, 2, 80; Battle of the Bulge in, 181; fiftieth anniversary of, 276; United States interventions after, 239
World War II Veterans Committee, 276
wounds, 59, 63
WPD. *See* War Department's Plans Division
Wright, Jack, 170
Wright, Quincy, 77
Wurzburg, West Germany, 168

Yugoslavia, 148

Zero Defects, 168
Zhou Enlai, 131
Zhukov, Georgy, 127
Zimmerman, Don, 82
Zuckerman, Sol, 225
Zumwalt, Elmo ("Bud"), 210

About the Author

C. Richard Nelson worked for General Goodpaster at the Atlantic Council after retiring from the Army and the CIA. In the Army, Nelson was an airborne, ranger, artillery officer serving in Laos and Vietnam as well as on the Army Staff and with the director of net assessment, Office of the Secretary of Defense, where he was responsible for analyses of the military balance in East Asia. At the CIA, he served in the National Intelligence Council where he authored many National Intelligence Estimates and other analyses for the highest levels of government. He was also the assistant national intelligence officer for science and technology. As director of the International Security Program at the Atlantic Council under Goodpaster, he organized working groups of experts and produced several international security policy studies. Nelson also taught national security affairs at the Army's Command and General Staff College, the National Defense University, and George Mason University. He has a BS from West Point, an MA from the University of Michigan, and a PhD from the University of Kansas.

DATE DUE 9.17

11.21.17		